SOCIALIST REGISTER 2 0 0 7

COMING TO TERMS WITH NATURE

Edited by LEO PANITCH and COLIN LEYS
with Barbara Harriss-White, Elmar Altvater and Greg Albo

THE MERLIN PRESS, LONDON
MONTHLY REVIEW PRESS, NEW YORK
FERNWOOD PUBLISHING, HALIFAX

First published in 2006
by The Merlin Press Ltd.
96 Monnow Street
Monmouth
NP25 3EQ

www.merlinpress.co.uk

British Library Cataloguing in Publication Data is available from the British
Library

Library and Archives Canada Cataloguing in Publication
Socialist register 2007 : coming to terms with nature / edited by Leo
Panitch ... [et al.].
Includes bibliographical references.
ISBN-10: 1-55266-195-4 (pbk.)
ISBN-13: 978-1-55266-195-6 (pbk.)
1. Capitalism--Environmental aspects. 2. Environmental protection.
3. Socialism. I. Panitch, Leo, 1945-
HC79.E5S567 2006   333.7   C2006-903937-2

ISSN. 0081-0606

Published in the UK by The Merlin Press
ISBN-10. 0850365783 Paperback
ISBN-13. 9780850365788
ISBN-10. 0850365775 Hardback
ISBN-13. 9780850365771

Published in the USA by Monthly Review Press
ISBN-10. 1583671528 Paperback
ISBN-13. 9781583671528

Published in Canada by Fernwood Publishing
ISBN-10. 1552661954 Paperback
ISBN-13. 9781552661956

Printed in the UK by MPG Books Ltd., Bodmin, Cornwall

CONTENTS

CONTRIBUTORS

Greg Albo teaches in the Department of Political Science at York University, Toronto.

Elmar Altvater is at the Otto Suhr Institute for Political Science, Free University, Berlin.

Henry Bernstein is professor of Development Studies at the School of Oriental and African Studies, London.

Achim Brunnengräber is at the Otto Suhr Institute for Political Science, Free University, Berlin.

Daniel Buck teaches at the School of Geography and the Institute for Chinese Studies at Oxford University, and is a Fellow of St. Cross College, Oxford University.

Elinor Harriss is a graduate student in Social Policy and Social Work, Oxford University.

Barbara Harriss-White is professor of Development Studies at Queen Elizabeth House and Fellow of Wolfson College, Oxford University.

Minqi Li is at the Department of Economics, University of Utah.

Brenda Longfellow is an award-winning filmmaker and an Associate Professor in the Department of Film at York University, Toronto.

Michael Löwy is Research Director in Sociology at the National Centre for Scientific Research (CNRS) in Paris.

Joan Martinez-Alier is at the Department of Economics and Economic History, Universitat Autonoma de Barcelona.

Philip McMichael is professor of Rural and Development Sociology, Cornell University.

Costas Panayotakis teaches Sociology at the New York City College of Technology of the City University of New York.

Jamie Peck is at the Department of Geography, University of Wisconsin–Madison.

Heather Rogers is a writer, journalist and filmmaker living in New York and author of the 2005 book, *Gone Tomorrow: The Hidden Life of Garbage*.

Neil Smith is professor of Anthropology and Geography and the Director of the Center for Place, Culture and Politics at the Graduate Center, City University of New York.

Erik Swyngedouw is professor of Geography at Oxford University and Fellow of St. Peter's College, Oxford University.

Dale Wen is a fellow at the International Forum on Globalization (IFG), San Francisco.

Frieder Otto Wolf was a Member of European Parliament for the German Green Party and currently teaches political philosophy at the Free University of Berlin.

Philip Woodhouse teaches at the Institute for Development Policy and Management, University of Manchester.

PREFACE

This, the 43rd volume of the *Socialist Register*, has been one of the most challenging to put together, even though – or because – it deals with what may well prove to be the most important issue facing socialists in our life-time. This is not just a matter of the complex science and technology involved in understanding the looming environmental crisis, or the variety of problems involved. Over the past dozen or so years the *Register* has published some twenty essays pertaining to the environment, several of which have been widely cited. But when we decided to devote a whole volume exclusively to 'coming to terms with nature' the greatest challenge we faced was that the absence of a strong eco-socialist left is reflected in a corresponding lack of coherence in eco-socialist theory. We see this volume as contributing to the development of a better eco-socialist understanding of contemporary capitalism, and the kind of politics that could lead to an ecologically sustainable as well as a democratic socialism.

Marx and Engels, and some of their socialist contemporaries and successors, paid some attention to the damage done by capitalism to the environment, and Marx in particular was far ahead of his time in understanding the mutually constitutive relationship between society and nature. But until very recently these issues have not been a main focus of socialist thought, or practice; productivism often trumped other concerns – and by no means only on the part of Soviet or Chinese managers. Socialist theory and analysis have been primarily concerned with understanding the logic of capitalism and its successive forms of existence, the relations of class power which are indispensable to it, and ways of resisting and replacing it with something better. The idea that environmental problems might be so severe as to potentially threaten the continuation of anything that might be considered tolerable human life has been entertained, but usually only as a fairly remote, if frightening, possibility. It has rarely been treated as something potentially imminent, needing to be considered as a matter of urgency, nor has a legacy of irreversible ecological damage bequeathed to future generations been seriously 'factored in' to our thinking about the problems that any future socialist society will have to cope with.

But the speed of development of globalized capitalism, epitomised by the dramatic acceleration of climate change, makes it imperative for socialists to deal seriously with these issues now. It is true that scientists differ over the rate at which carbon dioxide emissions are leading to global warming. Some think that a 'tipping point' has already been passed at which a vicious circle of effects will from now on speed up climate change beyond anything that even drastic measures to reduce carbon emissions can ameliorate. Others think that the rate of change will be slower, although still faster than any measures like the Kyoto Protocol, or any technological breakthrough yet envisaged, can significantly affect. But even this more optimistic view implies potentially devastating consequences for hundreds of millions of people due to rising sea levels, changes in deepwater ocean flows, the loss of melt-waters from high mountain ranges, and droughts and floods affecting food production throughout much of the world. And while climate change is the most general environmental effect of capitalist growth, it is far from the only one: the world is scarred by increasingly severe regional disasters due to the overuse of water, trees and soil; epidemics caused by fast-mutating viruses and antibiotic-resistant bacteria, resulting especially from factory-farming; the concentration of toxins in the food chain – the list is endless. The effects of all this are multiplied by the relentless urban concentration of the world's population, more and more of it into desperately impoverished and danger-ous slums. Our opening essay presents vivid images that capture a broad sample of all this from Haiti to China to the Arctic.

The search for technological breakthroughs, primarily driven by con-cerns about 'peak oil' in relation to capitalism's dependence on fossil fuels – a dependence which Elmar Altvater argues here is in any case inescapable – encounters the problem of the further consumption of non-renewable resources. Hydrogen as a fuel takes non-hydrogen energy to produce – and so does equipment to trap solar energy and convert it to electricity. The same applies to technological fixes such as the scheme recently proposed by the Livermore Laboratory in California to reduce global warming by deflecting sunlight from the earth – 55,000 mirrors in space, each bigger than Manhat-tan – which would consume vast amounts of non-renewable energy and ma-terials, and would undoubtedly also have vast unintended consequences. As it is, current rates of growth on a world scale and the ecological degradation this causes are generating new levels of conflict over access to fuel, water and other resources, including wars which are already having appalling human consequences.

Nonetheless, it is important to try to avoid an anxiety-driven ecological catastrophism, parallel to the kind of crisis-driven economic catastrophism that announces the inevitable demise of capitalism. A more complex understanding of the role and nature of crises and contradictions is required. OPEC's Sheik Yamani had a point when he said 'the Stone Age didn't end because we ran out of stones'. Without at all sharing such complacency, we need to recognize the dynamism and innovativeness generated by capitalist competition and accumulation – 'value in motion' – that could yet allow capitalism to 'prevail' (as one of our essays puts it). Indeed capital is already feeding on 'the environmental crisis', from carbon trading under Kyoto, to the garbage industry's 'green commerce', to the way corporate agriculture privileges biotechnological solutions over existing food cultures or land reform. All this is dissected in essays in this volume, as is the commodification of more and more areas of nature and social life – everything from water to our own DNA, and even the process of policy making itself. This means that if capitalism 'prevails' it will be more and more authoritarian, because people will resist the kind of inequality that will be generated, threatening as it will their access to the basic requirements of life.

Capitalists and politicians everywhere now rhetorically endorse calls for global cooperation to reduce the threat to the biosphere. But the best general measure of capitalist behaviour is how financial markets fall when slower – let alone reduced – growth rates are contemplated. And the best general predictor of government action is the interests of capital, both national and global, and the way electoral politics are grounded in growth-based consumerism. In the foreseeable future there will not be a genuine global policy to halt global warming; and as more and more states are tending to be reconstructed on the American neoliberal model they are progressively losing their capacity to plan effectively for a rational policy even at the national level, as our essay by Barbara Harriss-White and Elinor Harriss on renewable energy in the UK makes painfully clear.

The protection of society at large has only ever been secured by pressure from popular mass movements operating on nation states. The contemporary environmental movement, impressive as it is, lacks many of the sources of strength that class movements previously had, which were key to the achievement of many environmental advances in the past, especially in the provision of municipal hygiene and infrastructure. There has always been a working class and socialist environmentalism, long predating the current environmental justice movement. Part of the ecological task today is, as it was in the past, to secure clean water, transportation, sanitation and housing, although the task is now compounded by a formidable new range of issues – climate change, fossil fuels, new pollutants. But these too have distributional and class aspects, for the most part blithely ignored by the current turn of much of the ecological movement, especially in the North, to 'market ecology'.

The challenge to be overcome in this respect was one of our concerns in planning this volume. It was put very clearly by one of our corresponding editors, Hidayat (Gerard) Greenfield, writing from the frontlines of the environmentalists' and workers' struggles in Indonesia:

> We often seem to be caught between a 'corporate control/greed' paradigm on the part of mainstream NGOs and social movement and community organisations, and 'nothing new' on much of the radical Left. The first sees ecological destruction as the consequence of the irresponsible behaviour of big, greedy corporations. There is often little systemic understanding of this corporate behaviour, and solutions tend to rely on specific kinds of regulation, accountability, corporate social responsibility, etc., ignoring the compulsion of the market and the powerful force of commodification. Nonetheless, these approaches have generated very important campaigns against major corporations (e.g. Union Carbide/Bhopal, Monsanto/GMOs, Freeport/mining destruction, Dow Chemical/Agent Orange, etc.) and often involve sustained community mobilisation and action. The 'nothing new' approach treats ecological destruction as integral to capitalism – but saying 'it's capitalism; it's the system' not only fails to mobilise people, but may in fact discourage them – leaving them feeling overwhelmed, confronting the entire system: everything. When we try to fight everything, we end up fighting nothing. There also seems to be a smugness, an arrogance, about an answer that says: it's capitalism, stupid! The response – in terms of organised class struggle – is left unexplored, or is lost in slogans. And the flipside of this is to describe every environmental protest as an expression of anti-capitalist (now anti-globalization or anti-imperialist) resistance – with everyone laying claim to these local protests against ecological destruction as if they were part of their own movement. And here again we are left to wonder what precisely is the contribution of the socialist Left.

Our hope is that this volume will contribute to overcoming this problem, at least by insisting that the preservation of the ecosphere must become an integral part of the socialist project, by treating the issues involved in sufficient depth to challenge readers to decide what they think about them, and incorporate them into their analysis of contemporary events. The left, fighting for the improvement of the standard of living of the world's masses and for emancipation, must also fight for a new relation of humankind to nature, developing in the process a new democratic and participatory environmental politics, in sharp contrast to those contemporary environmentalists who have embraced 'market 'solutions'. Without pretending to do anything as ambitious as outlining an alternative agenda, we have tried to present different socialist perspectives that reflect contested and even opposing positions. And we want to point to the need to deal with immediate questions of practice posed by the vast range of environmental conflicts around the world today.

Which of these conflicts should socialists take up as strategic priorities? With what currents within the environmental justice movement should socialists be allied? Can such alliances avoid the kind of eco-populism that, as our essay on Africa shows, fails to recognize that under the pressures of capitalist competition petty commodity production can be as environmentally degrading as large-scale production? And should it not also be recognized that just as the traditional socialist commitment to industrialization and growth can now be seen to have been problematic, so is the eco-populist nostalgia for imagined pre-capitalist forms? And more specific questions arise. What alternatives are there for energy production and/or conservation that make social sense even within capitalism? Should we adopt an uncritical approach to the current dramatic trajectory of economic growth in China, despite what one of the essays in this volume demonstrates to be its devastating ecological effects? If not, how do we propose that living standards should be raised in lower-income countries? Should socialists not only call for a massive redistribution of the world's wealth but also make clear that this must entail a reduction of consumption in the North? What vision do we have of alternative ways of living for working-class people, beyond pointing to their alienation and frustration within the vicious circle of 'producing more, selling more, consuming more'?

Answers to these questions need to speak to the near future, and will only come through developing the new environmental politics we have called for, as taken up by the three concluding essays in the volume. Not the least important point they make is that answers to these questions will also have to be compatible with a socialist strategy for a post-capitalist world. This must include the indispensability of planning for any ecologically viable socialist society. It is time to reclaim planning from the failed practices of authoritarian communism, as well from the giant corporations (and state financial agencies) that in fact rely on extensive planning to manage neoliberal capitalism. It is also time, as Greg Albo's critical survey of current conceptions of eco-localism shows, to think hard about the kinds of local, national and global institutions – and the kinds of linkages among them – that will be required to make democratic planning possible, and to grapple with the many difficulties that democratic planning will always involve.

The question remains, how to get there. The 'red-green' alliances that were so widely discussed and proffered as a new opening for the left in the 1980s were largely still-born, despite this being a political moment when the conceptual project of eco-socialism was gaining ground. Some of the reasons for this may be found in the failure, in both democratic and eco-socialist terms, of the most important of the Green parties, the German Greens, which affords some crucial lessons in eco-socialist movement and party-building, as argued here by a former Green Party member of the European Parliament. The anti-globalization movement has seemed, in recent years, to provide the space to re-ignite an eco-socialist vision. But here all the difficulties of creating effective and democratic agencies of political mobilization, education and transformation are still to be solved.

We are very grateful to Barbara Harriss-White, Elmar Altvater and Greg Albo for their assistance in planning and editing this volume, and especially to Barbara Harriss-White who first pressed upon us the importance of the *Register* coming to terms with nature, and who organized a workshop at Oxford in February 2006 which allowed many of the contributors to this volume to meet and discuss their draft essays and the issues involved. This exemplifies the important role that our contributing and corresponding editors play in the production of the *Register*, and we are happy that one of our authors in this volume, Henry Bernstein, has agreed to join their number. We are grateful to all our authors for the effort they have put into writing their essays for this volume, while noting as usual that neither they nor we necessarily agree with everything in it. We want to thank Alan Zuege for his continuing role as the *Register's* outstanding editorial assistant; and we also owe thanks, as usual, to Adrian Howe and Tony Zurbrugg at the Merlin Press. Finally, we want especially to thank Frederick Peters for overseeing the launching of our new website, http://www.socialistregister.com, including the archive of *Register* essays it contains, going all the way back to 1964.

In producing a volume devoted to coming to terms with nature we have continued to be astonished that so many mainstream environmentalists manage to separate the treatment of ecology from the analysis of the current political field of social forces, as if markets and technocracy can solve ecological problems without reference to politics and democracy. On the contrary, in grappling with ecological dilemmas, we have tried to relate them to the themes that have preoccupied the *Register* in recent years, above all neoliberalism and imperialism. No one around the world who shares these preoccupations can fail to want to honour a debt of gratitude to the work of Harry Magdoff, who passed away at the beginning of 2006. Harry, whose first contribution to the *Register* appeared in its second volume in 1965, sustained a close and important relationship between it and the *Monthly Review* over the ensuing four decades, and played a leading part in fostering environmentalism, as one of MR's central concerns. We will miss him greatly.

LP
CL
June 2006

WEATHER REPORT:
IMAGES FROM THE CLIMATE CRISIS

BRENDA LONGFELLOW

In the summer of 2004 I began filming scenes for what I thought was going to be a lyrical and quirky look at weather stories and weather lore across Canada. Climate change, or a section I called 'The Politics of Weather', was obviously going to be included but at that moment I thought it would be confined to one section, interspersed with weather proverbs or amusing *bon mots* from amateur weather observers. Like most people, I had a vague idea of carbon cycles and a dim appreciation of the complexities of Kyoto and emissions reductions. I was wary of apocalyptic scenarios but susceptible to low-level dread at the steadfast accumulation of international weather disasters, not to mention the increasing summer temperatures and smog days in my own city of Toronto. I left lights on, I used my dryer, I drove to work (I love my car). But the climate crisis is an issue that gets under your skin; ask any climate activist. That's because its dimensions are so all-encompassing and the task of addressing the issue is so urgent. It's a geopolitical issue as much as it is a local issue. It connects to the immediate materiality of our individual bodies, as much as it implicates energy regimes, models of development, how we organize cities, suburbs and transportation systems, public utilities and private corporations. It crosses issues of social justice in the global south and the crisis of democracy just about everywhere, and it puts the future on the agenda for all of us, in a way, as Andrew Ross suggests, that has not been seen since the mass socialist movements of the 1930s.[1]

Unlike the 1930s, however, the future, as it is imagined from the cusp of the twenty-first century, seems fairly dystopic, and socialist utopias, archaic and nostalgic residues of a far-gone past. But as much as the climate crisis conjures up images of a catastrophic eco-future, I believe it also bears the potential to imagine alternative futures that could contrast starkly with the ascendancy of the market and the relentless processes of economic globalization, de-regulation and marketization that have now extended to all corners of the globe, including former 'communist' countries like China with enormous ecological and geo-political implications.

But how on earth to follow all of those interconnections in a single film without grossly oversimplifying, or overwhelming the filmmakers (and any audience the film might have) with a barrage of mind-boggling detail? Over the two years my filmmaking partners[2] and I spent raising money and shifting the focus of the film, our animating idea was to explore the social and political impacts of the climate crisis at a local level. The climate crisis may have global dimensions but its effects and the manner in which it is experienced depends on complex and particular social, political, economic and interpretive mediations of class and race, economic power and coded social vulnerabilities, as became so blindingly obvious in the aftermath of Katrina and the razing of New Orleans. We decided to try to think about the climate crisis as Bruno Latour's 'hybrid object' par excellence[3], and look for stories that revealed surprising connections, like the increase in prostitution in Kenya and the persistent drought in the Horn of Africa, or the unprecedented monsoon flood in Mumbai last summer and rampant real estate development or, as the Inuit leader, Sheila Watt-Cloutier likes to point out, Inuit hunters falling through the ice and the prevalence of SUVs in southern cities.

After watching nearly every film on climate change that had been made, we were equally determined to try to dislodge the predominant liberal discourse that had so frequently framed the climate crisis in the mainstream media as a problem caused by 'humankind' ('Christianized', Andrew Ross argues, 'by the language of retribution and penitence').[4] Blaming the 'human species' conveniently eclipsed the fact that only a tiny sector of the species actually bears a disproportionate historic responsibility for the dumping of greenhouse gases in the atmospheric commons. The moral harangue of species blame may salve the guilty conscience of Christians, but it stalls any real confrontation with existing political systems, the hierarchized distribution of wealth, and the enormous power of the international oil cartel and associated extractive industries to influence the energy policies of comprador governments. Suggesting links between the recent windfall profits of the oil cartel or the massive financial investments in the tar sands and the absence of real government action in shifting energy platforms to renewables, seemed one way, at least, of confronting the complexity of the real politics involved in the issue.

Most climate activists seem to have a very deadpan sense of humour and a dark ironic appreciation of the fact that given this *real politik*, a doomsday scenario is not out of the picture. There is now a clear scientific consensus that the world has ten to fifteen years to turn the crisis around in order to avoid 'dangerous' climate change, (and that means massive reductions of CO_2 emissions, in the order of 70–80 per cent, far beyond the paltry 5.2 per cent target legislated by Kyoto). The stark material reality, however, is that only a few countries will meet their Kyoto targets. A report on 'Key GHG (Greenhouse Gas) Data' released just before the last Conference of the Parties to the United Nations Framework Convention on Climate Change in Montreal in December 2005,[5] cheerily notes that Annex 1 (developed country signatories) emissions have decreased by 5.9 per cent. But that success story pales when one examines the data from individual countries which reveal that the reduction is almost entirely attributable to the tanking economies of Eastern Europe (Lithuana is a shining example, having achieved greenhouse gas reductions of -77 per cent). The U.K. made what has to certainly be considered a significant reduction (-13 per cent) but many attribute that to Thatcher's decision to destroy the coal miners' union, and to the discovery of vast reserves of 'clean' gas in the North Sea – and to the closure of several major polluting companies, especially in the steel industry – than to any profound commitment to decarbonize the economy.[6] The United States, which emits 24 per cent of the global total of CO_2 emissions, has seen its emissions increase by 20 per cent from 1990 to the present; and in the same period, Canada achieved the dubious distinction of having the highest percentage increase of emissions, an astonishing 57 per cent, a growth directly attributable to the development of the Alberta tar sands, slated to become the world's number one single emitter of greenhouse gases.

Turning to Kyoto's 'Annex 11' countries (developing country signatories like India and China, which are not obliged to reduce emissions, at least in the first period of the Kyoto mandate to 2012), the idea that they would voluntarily subscribe to deep emissions reductions of the order that seems to be demanded is delusionary. According the World Bank's 'Green Data Book', between 1990 and 2001, India's carbon emissions increased by 57 per cent, while China's increased by 33 per cent.[7] Officials from both countries have clearly stated that poverty eradication is the greater immediate imperative than global warming and from their perspective that means increased fossil fuel development. On some profound level, who can blame them? 35 per cent of India's population live on less than a dollar a day, in China 70 million peasants live in abject poverty, while India and China's per capita carbon emissions are less than one-quarter of the world average, and 22 times less than the United States; it's all a question of scale. Given the rapid pace of urbanization and industrialization, increased vehicular usage and the continued use of older and more inefficient coal-fired plants, if all predictions are correct, China will soon surpass the United States as the single largest emitter of greenhouse gases.

Even if we stopped all carbon emissions tomorrow, the system is still locked into an irrevocable amount of warming. This may seem a welcome thing for Canadian winters, but it has already precipitated a range of unprecedented weather events and disasters and it is clear that the impacts will be felt by the most vulnerable and by those who have benefited the least from the wealth and kind of development linked to fossil fuel capitalism.

HAITI. OCTOBER 2004

One can never know the mysterious workings of God's way. I believe he sent the hurricane to test our faith. And our faith remains strong, we are waiting for a miracle.

Louis St. Cille, local pastor, Gonaives, Haiti

In September of 2004, a series of unprecedented hurricanes – Frances, Charley, Ivan and Jeanne – battered the Gulf coast of the US, Mexico and Haiti. Gonaives, Haiti, one of the poorest cities in a country where 80 per cent of the population live in abject poverty, was particularly hard hit: three thousand people drowned in the deluge, whole neighbourhoods were swept away and the ramshackle huts which had housed thousands in the outlying regions were demolished. Two weeks later, Chris Romeike (my cameraperson) and Marco Fania (a sound recordist) and I flew down. When our SUV died as we drove through the flood with water up to our windows, we managed to borrow an alternative from CARE and immediately set out to explore the city.

While most of the bodies had been cleared the city was still inundated, and we witnessed a raucous mass of humanity, wading, motorcycling and biking through the water, many in their bare feet. Jouet Joseph was in charge of the CARE relief operations in the city and he took us to one of the mobile food relief centres where hundreds of women and children pressed into line, to wait for the dispensation of meagre UN rations: a can of oil, a bag of rice and beans.

For decades, Haiti has been plagued by poverty, corruption, dictatorships, military *coups de état* and foreign military intervention. There is literally no social infrastructure. Many of the people we had spoken with had heard no warning of the hurricane. Largely illiterate and dispersed in villages with no access to radio or television, they were caught completely unaware when the hurricane arrived in the dead of night, spilling 25 centimetres of torrential rain in a half hour and sparking a devastating flood and mudslide as the drains clogged and a torrent of mud and debris raged through the city. Those who could, clung to the few surviving trees, raced to the tops of buildings or ran to the hills; those who couldn't, succumbed, including a disproportionate number of children.

Gonaives brought home what extreme vulnerability to weather disasters actually means. In Cuba, a poor country but one with an elaborate and community-based disaster preparedness network, Fidel Castro went on national television in a five-hour marathon to warn Cubans of the oncoming hurricane, and there were no fatalities. In Florida, where there was 18 billion dollars of damage over the course of the hurricane season, a figure exacerbated by the extensive property development along the coasts, there was only a handful of fatalities. But in Haiti the population was left vulnerable to a kind of genocide by natural disaster.

Of course there is nothing natural about 'natural' disasters. As any social ecologist will tell you, disasters represent the complex outcome of a collision between the sedimented reality of class and social inequities and an ecological event. Introduce a Category Four hurricane to a country where the brutal immiseration of the population has led to massive deforestation (what other energy source do the poor have access to but the trees they cut to make charcoal?) and it's a recipe for catastrophe. With 98 per cent of the landmass deforested in Haiti, there were no natural barriers and the water could not percolate into the ground.

Inside the town's largest public school Jean Eders, a slight and stoic man in his late thirties, methodically scrapes the mud from the walls with his bare hands. He lost his six year old child in the flood and it's all he can do to keep busy, scraping buckets of mud out of his house, and helping restore the school for the children who have survived. On the outskirts of town the local pastor, Louis St. Cille, stands in front of the remains of his church. A skeletal rig of steel bars arches over a huge mound of branches, mud and refuse. During the night of the flood a dozen parishioners had sought refuge in the church. All perished. Despite this, the pastor remains optimistic: who can say what God will do or why, he asks. 'We are waiting for a miracle'. At the other end of town, religious fatalism is easily eclipsed by the palpable anger of the Gonaives Citizen's Committee. The Chair of the Committee, Ego Pasteur, stands by their small meeting room as the heat of the day wanes and giant bulldozers dig into the mountains of mud that have buried his town. He wants to demand a UN investigation. It's culpable homicide, he insists, he wants to enumerate the name of every person that drowned in the flood. It matters, he says, to know each name.

CHINA. APRIL 2005

There is one advantage to the autocratic command and control structure of power in China. If they wanted to impose a forced transition to a post-carbon world, they could do it by fiat, overnight, but that is just not likely to happen.

Wen Bo, environmental activist, Global Greengrants, Beijing

It's spring and we're flying into Lanzhou in Gansu province, hoping to capture some of the phenomenal dust storms that have been increasingly engulfing the region over the last twenty years, spreading the sands of the Gobi desert across once fertile grassland. From the air, it's clear it's a semi-arid region, there's not a trace of green. But it doesn't hit you fully until you are driving into town from the airport past a Mad Max landscape of monotone beige, broken only by the methodically etched terraces on the mountains pocked by row after row after row of tens – no, hundreds – of thousands of newly-planted shrubs. We'll see dozens of these tree-planting efforts all over this part of China, it's the main line of defence in the war against the ravages of desertification and it's a bit of a national mania. By law, every citizen is obligated to plant three trees a year. Then there are the national tree-planting days, and local tree-planting celebrations. On our first shooting day in Gansu we meet an exuberant bunch of school kids from Jiudong Middle School, in the town of Jiudong, Liangzhong District, who have been let out of school for the afternoon to take turns digging holes for the spindly popular saplings that their teacher tells us mainly die due to lack of water and irrigation. We're taken later to a model tree-planting farm to meet Mr. Shi Shuzhu, an 80 year-old model worker/tree-planter, whose face adorns the giant billboards along the road exhorting the population to take arboreal action.

China's Environmental Protection Agency reports that the Gobi Desert expanded by 52,400 square kilometres (20,240 square miles) from 1994 to 1999. Five years later, desertification is reaching crisis levels. As in Haiti, it's a confluence of factors that is producing the disaster. Overgrazing and limited stewardship of the land, combined with rising global temperatures, are conspiring to create a dust-bowl of truly historic dimensions. Slowly but surely, arable land in this region is being eroded, casting thousands of farmers as environmental refugees who are forced to leave the land to look for wage employment in the big cities in the east. At the Centre for Desertification located in the oasis town of Wuwei we meet the scientists who are eager to show us the great strides the Chinese state has made in addressing desertification. Straw meshes are placed on the sand to keep it from blowing, and there are dozens of varieties of drought resistant shrubs and trees, although as we walk through the well-kept tree nursery one of the cadre confides, off-camera, that while they may have won the battle for the oasis, they are losing the war against the desert.

The traffic is fierce in downtown Beijing and the noise is deafening as fleets of taxis, buses, new cars, and the few remaining bikes compete for road space. A gray pall of smog shrouds the sleek futuristic office buildings and impenetrable banks of chrome and steel. Wen Bo, a young activist who works with Global Greengrants dispersing grants from the West to environmental groups in China, is sanguine about the rampant development. The paradox is that China could go one way or the other, he suggests.

Later that day, we link up with Mr Lu Tonjing, an ebullient retired man who is a dead ringer for a young (and considerably slimmer) Mao. Mr. Lu was a coal miner during the 1960s Cultural Revolution but participated in the Communist Party as an official photographer of party events and documenter of heroic worker scenes. These days he takes photographs of environmental devastation in the countryside.

A short flight to Inner Mongolia and we meet up with a friend of Mr. Lu's and his ancient van which will take us into the heart of the area that is experiencing the worst desertification. Half-way there, past the small grim industrial towns and dried-up river beds, we see the sky turn ominously dark, as a fierce wind begins whipping up particles of sand and dust. Chris, my cameraman, grabs his goggles and the sand cover for the camera and sets up on the side of the road. Suddenly we are in the thick of the sandstorm. We watch as a peasant farmer and his wife labour up hill with their cart against the onslaught, whipping out goggles and scarves to cover their faces. These storms can last for days, and are often visible from space, but this one subsides after an hour.

Although he has not been in the region for a couple of years and there are no road signs, Mr Lu uncannily leads us down a single lane dirt road into a village of the damned. Twenty years ago the village was surrounded by lush grassland, now there are forty foot dunes of sand in everyone's back yard. A small grove of trees, which in times past had offered shade and succour to the village's sheep herd, is now buried save for the tips of the trees which poke out of the dunes, a weird blackened and stunted forest. The Yellow River used to run through the village, or so our parents say, a man tells us as he stops to answer his cell phone. The chief of the village and his brother in law have a fatalistic attitude toward the encroaching desert. They've reduced the number of sheep they herd but they have no plans for the future if the sands take over the small bits of grassland they are able to preserve. We can only live day to day, they admit. Mr. Lu is enraged at the colossal injustice of the scene before him. Where will these people go, he declaims – into the Yellow River? Are they to be left here to be buried like the trees?

It's very fashionable these days to demonize China and to raise implicit Malthusian phobias about the Asiatic hordes. With 1.5 billion people the environmental footprint of China is huge, and it is extraordinary to think that at the rate they are exploiting water and land resources the economy could continue to accelerate at 9 per cent every year. But with huge and increasingly resented disparities in income between urban and rural residents, there's a very hard nugget of political reality that fuels the behemoth of economic development.

DALLAS. MAY 2005

> The energy industries now constitute the largest single enterprise known to mankind. Moreover, they are indivisible from automobile, farming, shipping, air freight, and banking interests, as well as from the governments dependent on oil revenues for their very existence. With annual sales in excess of one trillion dollars and daily sales of more than two billion dollars, the oil industry alone supports the economies of the Middle East and large segments of the economies of Russia, Mexico, Venezuela, Nigeria, Indonesia, Norway, and Great Britain.[8]
>
> Ross Gelbspan, author of *Boiling Point* and *The Heat Is On*[9]

Driving through downtown Dallas, the radio announces an unseasonable temperature of 75 degrees Fahrenheit. The Reverend Michael Crosby is talking on his cell phone as he walks down the street to the Exxon Mobil annual general meeting. He and Sister Patricia Daly are the leading forces in Campaign Exxon Mobil, a shareholder activist group that has links with some of the largest pension funds and investor groups in the US, such as Christian Brother Investments, CERES, or the Interfaith Center on Corporate Responsibility (ICCR), whose combined investment portfolio is worth hundreds of billions of dollars. They've crafted three shareholder resolutions on climate change which demand that Exxon clarify its stand on the science, investigate its obligations under Kyoto and appoint members to the Board of Directors who at least have some environmental expertise. It's a long shot and they know it.

In the cavernous foyer of the Meyer Centre, festooned with booths and displays of Exxon's corporate prowess, the shareholders filter in. The Vice President, a nervous woman in a suit and braces, tells us that it's not true

that Exxon is a 'climate change denier', they are now absolutely committed to moving forward on the issue. They've even given a grant to Stanford
University to initiate research on renewables. (Given Exxon's record profits
the amount actually represents .009 of their surplus. More, in fact, was spent
on their new corporate image than on diversification of energy sources).
We're not allowed into the auditorium to film the actual meeting so we
sneak in without our cameras. There are two microphones on the floor: 'Yea'
and 'Nay'. On the 'Yea' side are the NGO crowd, the environmentalists, the
activists, a bit pinched in the ties and corporate suits they've worn for the occasion. On the other are the stalwart shareholders, the retirees and company
boosters. In the middle is the booming figure of Lee Raymond, Exxon's
CEO, the grand master, cutting off the microphones when the 'Yea' side goes
on too long, accepting his part in the play with ironic noblesse oblige; this is
not, after all, where the real decisions get made.

Outside the Meyer Centre, a small group of protestors from Chalmette,
Louisiana hold aloft a large banner. Anne Rolfes, a young lawyer tells us the
cancer rates in the region are off the chart and it's all because of Exxon's
refineries. Reverend Crosby emerges and tells us they are thrilled: 28 per
cent of shareholders voted for his resolution that Exxon investigate its legal
responsibility under Kyoto. It seems a small step, but we'll celebrate victories
where we can.

On December 15th, the *Globe and Mail* reported that oil and gas have
moved into the top spot as Canada's most valuable exports, 9.2 billion dollars
worth, all of it destined for the US market. Exxon, like other members of the
non-OPEC energy cartel, is aggressively exploring new sources of gas and
oil, in offshore Nigeria, in the Alaskan North Slope and the Caspian basin,
and shows no signs of diminishing its commitment to the extraction and
selling of fossil fuels.

In 2005, world oil production and profits rose to an all-time high. Conoco
Phillips, the third-largest US oil company, reported a rise in quarterly profits of 89 per cent; BP's profits increased by 34 per cent, and Exxon's by 75
per cent, the highest amount in US corporate history. While the poor and
abandoned of New Orleans were finally being bussed out of the sweltering
superdome in Houston, oil peaked at nearly 70 dollars a barrel.

MONTREAL. DECEMBER 2005

You would never know it's a climate convention, the place is over-run with men in suits, business types. Even the NGOS are talking this business jargon because the ideology that has now won out at the international level is that markets are the way to solve the problem that markets created in the first place.

Daphne Wysham, Co-Director,
Sustainable Energy and Economy Network

The earth might be warming but it was a chilly -15C in downtown Montreal December 3rd, as we walked with tens of thousands of other protestors stamping our toes to keep warm in time with the exuberant band of young drummers who led the procession down Rue St. Catherine. The demo, like 32 other demonstrations world-wide, was timed to coincide with the mid-point of the climate negotiations going on inside the Palais du Congrés where 12,000 delegates from around the world were congregating at the Conference of the Parties (COP) to the United Nations Framework Convention on Climate Change to fine tune the Kyoto Accord and open discussions on a post Kyoto agenda. As activists unfurled banners reading 'The World is Watching', 'Time is Running Out', the contrast between the folks on the street and the suits and negotiators – the senior bureaucrats and carbon traders inside – was striking.

We were there to follow Sheila Watt-Cloutier, the Chair of the Inuit Circumpolar Conference, who was vigorously lobbying to have special provisions included in the Kyoto agreement to recognize the particular circumstances of climate change in the Arctic. The Arctic Climate Assessment Report had come out the previous year and its findings were startling: the Arctic climate is changing at a rate almost twice as fast as that experienced in lower latitudes, and by 2050 the permanent ice pack will have entirely melted in the summer. This was not news to the Inuit, who for decades have been reporting changes in the climate and environment that are happening at severely accelerated rates.

Watt-Cloutier was also to deliver a petition at the Montreal COP conference to the Inter American Human Rights Commission, charging the United States government with violation of Inuit human rights by its refusal to sign on to Kyoto. It was a brilliant political strategy to shift the paradigm of the climate crisis into a human rights framework, and her lawyers were confident that litigation would be the next frontier of climate activism. In a side bar off the main event Sheila gave a wonderfully moving and impassioned speech, calling the world to look to the Arctic for political leadership on fighting and adapting to climate change. It was high political theatre and we had to battle for elbow room with four other camera crews.

Meanwhile the real buzz at the convention was happening around carbon trading, the chief market mechanism of the Kyoto Protocol that allows rich nations to purchase carbon credits from the developing world in order to meet their legislated targets. Carbon trading is a source of some controversy in the climate change movement, with most mainstream environmental groups supporting it as an imperfect, but none the less necessary first step, while others denounce it as a transparent corporate grab that allows the developed world to continue pumping CO_2 into the atmosphere without any guarantee that the credits purchased will actually go toward sustainable development in places like China or Chad. December 5, 2005 was 'Carbon Day' at the COP conference and we interviewed Mr. Andrei Marcu, the Head of the International Emissions Trading Association, who told us that Europe could be a 30 billion dollar carbon market in a few years and that he was satisfied that carbon trading finally allowed us to place a value on nature, and that was the only way it would ever be preserved.

At the end of the week, the Americans and their Saudi allies had managed to stall and halt any serious discussion on a post 2010 mandatory regime of deep emission reductions. The Americans were luring the Chinese and Indians into their Asia Pacific Initiative with its avowed commitment to avoid all targets and commitments that were not voluntary.

THE ARCTIC. APRIL 2005

> There's an up side to global warming. With the opening of the North West Passage and expansion of shipping, the Arctic could become the economic mecca of Canada in the 21st century. We have 30 percent of Canada's known gas reserves in Nunavut, there's a massive iron ore deposit at Mary River north of Iqaluit, there's diamond mining, uranium. With a deep sea port, Iqaluit could be a boomtown.
>
> Honourable Edward Picco, Minister of Energy and Education,
> Government of Nunavut

In April, we flew into Pangnirtung, a small hamlet of 1600, an hour's plane ride from Iqaluit. With the weather increasingly unpredictable in these parts, locals insist that any plan has to be continuously amended with the tag-line 'weather permitting'. Temperatures were seasonable, although earlier in the year, at the end of February, a sudden warm spell had jacked the temperature up to 6 degrees centigrade; at that time 'Pang' was one of the warmest places in Canada. The ice started melting on Cumberland Sound, the streets were filled with puddles, and the caribou and seal meat stored in sheds under peoples' houses began to rot.

Jamesie Mike, a diminutive and amazingly fit 77 year-old, with a mischievous sense of humour, donned polar bear pants and kamiks (seal skin boots) and escorted us to his backyard overlooking the fjord to analyze cloud formations. He is 'Mr. Weather' in these parts, a gifted reader of weather signs, equipped with binoculars and a Citizens' Band (CB) radio, he keeps in touch with hunters out on the land, warning them when increasingly volatile weather systems move in. Lately, he says, weather is more and more unpredictable and it is getting harder and harder to read the signs, nothing is stable anymore.

The big event of our stay in 'Pang' is a trip to the floe edge of Cumberland Sound with a group of hunters and three Inuit Rangers. It's a beautiful sunny day, an hour and a half snowmobile ride from the hamlet, to get to the open water. Sheila had always talked about melting of the ice as a mobility issue, but I didn't quite get it until that trip. The ice is a crucial extension of the land mass in winter that allows hunters to travel hundreds of kilometres in search of seal, caribou, whale and walrus. Without that access the whole food supply is interrupted.

Fifteen years ago the floe edge used to be 70 kilometres away, now it's about 15, that's how fast the ice is melting. The hunters test the ice constantly with their self-fashioned 'harpoons', a bowie knife on the end of a hockey stick. Joanassie Maniapik, an extraordinary elder, is the first to get a seal, a bob of a black head a mile out, one shot from his rifle and it's a direct and painless hit. When he was young you could walk across Cumberland Sound in July. Now it rains in the winter, he says, and we have thunder, we have never seen that. He believes his elders predicted massive changes in the weather, a prediction that goes back deep into time, a prophecy that is just coming true.

Back in Iqaluit just in time for the closing days of Toonik Tyme, the city's annual celebration of spring, we meet Ed Picco, Minister of Energy and Education for the Nunavut Government (or NG as its known up here). He avows that while climate change is having a dramatic impact on traditional hunting culture, economic interests are amassing there which see the melting of the permanent ice pack ice and opening of the North West Passage as a positive spin-off of climate change. It's ironic but it is going to be the third big wave that will hit the Inuit, after colonialism and climate change. The week before we arrived with Transport Canada, the Arctic Council and the Canadian Marine Conservancy Council were meeting in Iqaluit to discuss the prospects for shipping if the North West Passage opens over the summer.

OUR LAST LEGS

We have two more major locations to visit: India just in time for monsoon season, and Kenya, which up to two weeks ago has been suffering through a devastating six-year drought. For years the monsoon arrived faithfully in Mumbai on June 10, rituals and celebrations were planned around the date. Now the patterns are shifting dramatically and it's anyone's guess what will happen. Last year on July 26 the monsoon dropped 37 inches of water on Mumbai in a 24-hour period. One thousand people, mainly slum-dwellers, drowned or were electrocuted by downed wires, and the city was without transportation and electricity for weeks. City officials blamed the floods on plastic bags clogging the city's ancient storm sewers and have initiated a nuisance squad that raids unsuspecting merchants caught using the contraband material. A Citizen's Commission organized their own hearings, heard thousands of depositions by slum-dwellers, and concluded that unregulated rampant development was the chief culprit as it paved over the Mithi River's flood plain and diverted the course of the river to accommodate airport runways.

We are also trying to imagine what the last chapter will be, and that's certainly been the hardest one to get our heads around. In the two years that we have been working on this film we have witnessed a genuine growing political momentum around the issue. There is a multitude of initiatives from the very local (like the Stop the Gas Power Plant coalition in my own neighbourhood) to all the continuing international negotiations. My email 'Inbox' is full of notices of conferences, trade meetings, publications and job postings, all related to the business and struggle of climate change. Perhaps the most telling of all, the issue has begun to be picked up by popular culture. A documentary feature, *An Inconvenient Truth*, is making the rounds, with Al Gore delivering an informative lecture on the topic with an impressive high tech display of statistics and graphs. In the last six months *Rolling Stone*, *Vanity Fair* and *WIRED* have all had cover articles on the climate crisis. *WIRED* featured the piercing blue eyes of Gore on its cover (with an emblazoned by line: 'The Pro-Growth, Pro-Tech Fight To Stop Global Warming') and editorialized that green capitalism, and a new generation of 'neo-green' entrepreneurial activists who are starting hemp clothing lines or trendy e-businesses represent an exciting political advance that will finally solve the problem. Green, concludes *Vanity Fair*, is definitely the new black.

Clearly we can't just end with the bad news, that the triumph of market-oriented solutions to the crisis is not going to result in the kind of deep changes needed to get to the 'soft landing' that scientists talk about, a result achievable only by cutting CO_2 emissions by 60-80 per cent in the next ten to fifteen years. We'd only depress people if we pointed to the massive failure of national governments to act responsibly, a failure never more clear than in Canada where our newly-elected Conservative government is doing its best to scuttle our Kyoto commitments.

If we have to end with a good news beat, it might be that there is still time to turn things around, even though the effort to do that will involve a massive mobilization of political will on a number of different fronts in order to de-carbonize and rewire transportation and energy systems on an international level. As Keith Stewart, a climate campaigner for the World Wildlife Federation told us, we don't even need to wait for the development of new technologies like clean coal, carbon sequestration or hydrogen, the favourite techno-fixes of the Bush regime. Wind, solar, and geo-thermal power and, most importantly, massive conservation and efficiency, can get us to a soft spot, but we need to act, and we need to act now. Catch-phrases like 'sustainable development' have been picked up by the World Bank and international credit agencies to rationalize the continuing processes of resource extraction and the trickle-down effect (which never does), but there are other models of community-led and -controlled development that are animating mobilization in the global South, based on principles of local democracy and equity.

At the 2005 Montreal COP convention Tom Athanasiou, a climate activist and writer, told us that one of the most interesting features of new computer modeling programmes was the way they have begun to take social values into account. You can plot climate change, taking into account the exponential factors of albedo, cloud formations, water vapour and positive feedback loops, but the most crucial factor in determining outcomes was the potential shift in societal priorities and values. Will material acquisition and consumption continue as the arbiter of value, or will issues of social justice, equity and community triumph? That is what will determine our climate futures. And there is nothing predictable about that.

NOTES

1   Andrew Ross, *Strange Weather*, New York: Verso, 1991, p. 170.
2   Julia Sereny and Jennifer Kawaja, producers; Glen Richards, editor and Chris Romeike cameraperson.
3   Bruno Latour, *We Have Never Been Modern*, translated by Catherine Porter, Cambridge: Harvard University Press, 1993.

4   Ross, *Strange Weather*, p. 198.
5   Available at http://unfccc.int.
6   Paul Brown, 'Corus Woes Help CO_2 Goals', *Guardian*, 8 April 2003.
7   http://web.worldbank.org.
8   http://dieoff.org/page82.htm.
9   *Boiling Point*, New York: Basic Books, 2004; *The Heat Is On*, Updated Edition, Reading: Perseus Books, 1998.

NATURE AS ACCUMULATION STRATEGY

NEIL SMITH

A commodity, according to the classical political economists, comprises and combines a use value and an exchange value. Value, they recognized, was the product of human labour; for Marx it was measured by socially necessary labour time. Capital, he argued, was 'value in motion', and capital accumulation was the process by which capitalist societies multiplied social value through the exploitation of labour. Capitalism has always employed labour power to invest value in use values harvested from nature, and so what could it mean to suggest, as the title of this paper does, that nature has become an accumulation strategy? It is increasingly evident, I want to argue that in the past three decades a new dimension of the capitalist production of nature has considerably transformed the social relationship with the natural world.

'On or about December, 1910', Virginia Woolf once famously commented, 'human nature changed'. At about the same time James Joyce thought he perceived the shattering of space, an insight recycled more than half a century later by Henri Lefebvre who highlighted the birth of cubism (which he dated to Picasso's 1908 painting of Les Demoiselles d'Avignon) as the moment of a new 'production of space'.[1] It is now commonplace to think of this period prior to World War I as the crucible of new conceptions of space (and time), embodied not only in artistic and cultural modernism but in such scientific innovations as relativity theory and quantum mechanics, in unison with shifts in the historical geography of capitalism. Far less common, at least in political discourse, is serious reflection on Woolf's observation which, after all, had to do with human nature rather than space or time. Her claim is traditionally treated as enigmatic, metaphorical, a literary more than a literal claim, which emanated from intense discussions within London's Bloomsbury circle. What after all could it mean to say that human nature – the paragon of seeming unchangeability – had changed? And yet Woolf was onto something, anticipating however fancifully a very real shift in the social relation with nature – except that it would not really materialize for another half century. The central proposition explored here is that we are currently living through a period in which the core socio-economic relationship with nature is being dramatically transformed.

CAPITALIZED NATURE – NATURE BANKING

Beginning in the 1980s and 1990s, an extraordinary range of new 'ecological commodities' came on line. Ironically, they owe their existence, first and foremost, to the success of the environmental movement in the 1960s and 1970s. Subsequent environmental legislation and regulation, developing quite unevenly across different local and national contexts, sought to limit environmental despoliation at the hands of capital, and in the process – sometimes deliberately, sometimes not – created a certain scarcity of what can be called 'allowable natural destruction'. This in turn led to the development of entirely new markets in ecological 'goods' and (especially) 'bads'. Whereas the traditional commodification of nature generally involved harvesting use values as raw materials for capitalist production – wood for tables, oil for energy, iron ore for steel, various corns for bread – this new generation of ecological commodities is different. Whether they do or do not become the raw material for future production is incidental to their production. Instead, these commodities are simultaneously excavated (in exchange-value terms) from pre-existing socio-natural relations and as part of their production they are reinserted or remain embedded in socialized nature – the more 'natural' the better. Green capitalism may be touted as a means of softening the environmental impacts of the capitalist exploitation of nature, or criticized as simply environmental veneer for sustained exploitation, yet whatever the truth of these propositions the significance of 'green capitalism' is far more profound. It has become nothing less than a major strategy for ecological commodification, marketization and financialization which radically intensifies and deepens the penetration of nature by capital.

Consider the example of wetlands. In recognition of the beneficent socio-ecological worth and work of wetland habitats, and the danger of their disappearance in the face of urban, suburban, resource and agricultural development, the state at various scales has implemented laws intended to mitigate the loss of such environments. In the United States in the late 1980s, for example, George W.H. Bush, seeking to differentiate himself from a predecessor whose disdain for environmentalism was legendary ('when you've seen one redwood', California's Ronald Reagan famously said, 'you've seen them all'), and intent on becoming 'the environmental president', insisted that there would be 'no net loss of wetlands'. As new environmental legislation increasingly required and embodied the conservation of wetlands, a market in 'wetland credits' quickly emerged. This process was defined in federal law as follows:

> Wetland restoration, creation, enhancement, and in exceptional cases preservation undertaken expressly for the purposes of compensating for unavoidable wetland losses in advance of development actions when such compensation cannot be achieved at the development site....[2]

At its simplest, a developer who intends to develop an area of wetland can live up to conservation requirements by purchasing credits either from landowners who agree to sequester commensurate amounts of wetland from any future development, or from companies that make it their business to reconstruct or expand previously degraded wetlands. In the 1990s this inspired a burgeoning 'wetland mitigation banking' industry in the US to facilitate, coordinate and manage the creation, exchange and banking of wetland credits.[3]

In this case the commodity produced is, in the most immediate sense, the restored or conserved wetland, and its worth rests precisely in the fact that it cannot be productively consumed. In Marxist terms, the entire process produces a new economic scarcity, namely of mitigable wetlands, where none existed previously. Surplus value is harvested either from the dead labour dormant in the prior destruction of the site – dead labour that now suddenly finds a new exchange value to which it can attach – or from the work of restoration. More than anything, however, the resulting wetland credits represent a draw on ground rent produced by the new or conserved amenity, a credit with only a momentary symbolic connection to the specific work that gave rise to it. Whatever its physical or ecological characteristics, therefore, the central use value of the restored wetlands is precisely their ability to garner exchange value under the new conditions of created scarcity.

The case of wetlands credits and banking is far from anomalous. If anything it is something of a latecomer in the ecological commodities industry. The idea of pollution credits first surfaced in the 1970s, but only in the 1980s did an early model for these burgeoning ecological commodity markets emerge in the form of 'debt-for-nature' swaps. These involved various combinations of NGOs, debt-holding banks and governments, and international agencies such as the IMF and World Bank, as well as debtor governments. Some portion of national debt would be forgiven if debtor nations – almost all from the global south – agreed to preserve various tracts of 'natural' land. These were soon superseded in scope and complexity and the model proliferated.

In the US the Clean Air Act of 1990, a revision of the 1972 Act, was a watershed regulatory moment in the capitalization of nature.

Today the best-known ecological commodities are probably those produced by carbon sequestration programmes. In a declared effort to slow down or minimize global warming, these work in a similar way to wetland credits: to absorb carbon dioxide from the atmosphere, landowners possessing tracts of forest land (generally in poorer tropical countries) are paid not to cut their forests, while major polluters in more industrial parts of the world can purchase these credits as a means to allow them to continue to pollute. Alternatively, corporations which cut their emissions – not just carbon but sulphur dioxide, nitrous oxide, and many other pollutants – by more than the levels prescribed by local, national or international regulations (for example the Kyoto accords) earn credits that can be sold on the market to producers who fail to reach their required emission reductions. In the spring of 2006 carbon credits in Europe were selling on the open market for about 30 euros per ton, although the price volatility of this new commodity quickly took its toll.[4] Other markets for nature credits have emerged for many ecological commodities: biodiversity credits, fishery credits, air and water pollution credits, rare bird credits, and so forth. In Georgia, International Paper is breeding the endangered red-cockaded woodpecker on land it owns; woodpecker credits have already traded at $100,000 and International Paper hopes in the future to earn as much as $250,000 per credit for these.[5] Nature is increasingly transformed into a biodiversity bank; as Cindi Katz has observed, nature's comprehensive 'conversion to a resource in some global accounting ledger has fundamentally altered its status and temporality'.[6]

Whereas the marketization of nature in this way has been championed as a market-friendly amelioration of environmental destruction, it is also widely understood that its effects are not wholly positive. In so far as the site of mitigation may be kilometres or continents away from the site that benefits, this marketization is more likely to deepen uneven development and intensify poverty. The Costa Rican peasant farmer who gets carbon sequestration credits for not cutting the forest may experience a one-time windfall but no permanent enhancement of the family's standard of living, whereas the US corporate polluter buying credits contributes not only to continued pollution but to an intensified accumulation of capital. A parallel, intensified unevenness occurs when protected reserves are turned over for ecotourism, insofar as the world's rich, whose wealth is premised on 'development', are able to consume supposedly pristine nature so long as that nature remains pristine, undeveloped. Nor is it clear that such credits even work in ecological terms. Biodiversity credits may leave various Amazonian habitats intact, for example (or they may not), but the intensified poverty of local inhabitants often leads to significant if not accelerated environmental degradation anyway. By the same token, while wetland restoration in North America is regulated, there is no guarantee concerning the quality or even the medium-term result of that restoration, and there is certainly no evidence of overall reduction in wetland loss. If one takes a wider geographical perspective on wetland mitigation, it is tempting to paraphrase Engels's assessment of 'the housing question': the bourgeoisie has no solution to the environmental problem, they simply move it around.[7]

The development of markets in ecological commodities is neither ac-cidental nor simply an unintended consequence of otherwise well-meaning environmental legislation. As Morgan M. Robertson has put it, the marketi-zation and banking of such commodities is crucial 'in creating and stabilizing new areas for capitalist activity...'.[8] Marketizing nature is precisely the point. A US National Academy of Sciences committee estimates that between 1993 and 2000, more than $1 billion was invested in US mitigation permits cover-ing perhaps 24,000 acres.[9] The industry established its own umbrella associa-tion in 1998, the National Mitigation Banking Association, which seeks to 'promote federal legislation and regulatory policy'. Their 2006 conference, which attracted conservation developers (no contradiction), environmental management corporations, environmental 'service' providers, state and fed-eral regulators, venture capitalists and representatives of the US Army Corps of Engineers, among others, was entitled 'Environmental Banking: Cultivat-ing This Green Frontier'.[10]

For these and other environmental capitalists nature has indeed become a new frontier, and not unlike earlier 'frontiers', that frontier became almost instantaneously financial. An 'environmental derivatives' market very quickly sprang up whereby ecological credits are bundled together and sold in bulk to speculative financiers banking on the increased price of already established credits. The World Bank opened its BioCarbon Fund in 2004, capitalized with an initial $30 million and aiming for $100 million, which allows inves-tors (minimum investment US$2.5 million) to contribute to carbon seques-tration in return for an income generated by the sale of credits. Since 2005, in line with Kyoto targets, the European Union has begun trading in and regulating carbon credits. While the Environmental Protection Agency runs an emission trading system in the US it is purely voluntary, as is the Chicago Climate Exchange, recently established by green capitalists and NGOs.

This intensified commodification, marketization and financialization of nature is of course an integral element of a much larger project of neoliberal-ism.[11] Neoliberalism's substitution of private market economic measurement for social calculation, and its insistence that anything of social worth must be tradable in the global market, applies precisely to the emergence of new markets in ecological commodities, mitigation banking and environmental derivatives. The power of this bundling of nature into tradable bits of capital should not be underestimated, but nor should it be exaggerated. The neo-liberalization of nature is far from complete, not without its obstacles, and anything but a smooth process.[12] That said, while the financialization of nature may only be in its infancy, its scope and trajectory are already becoming clear.

Financialized credits for wetlands and carbon, industrial emissions and wildlife are part of a larger process by which the production of nature is being dramatically intensified and its dimensions multiplied. The colonization of terrestrial biology is very much a part of this process. Biotechnology allows science to bore into and transform the core of specific life forms, and this has myriad results. On the one hand, new commodities are produced, such as genetically modified (GM) seeds, crops and other organisms, themselves involving commodification on a completely new scale: subatomic commodities such as laboratory-manufactured genes. This in turn has set off a frantic episode of bio-prospecting in which corporate pirates scour the natural world for patentable genetic material. This may involve sending doctoral scientific adventurers to the Amazon to collect samples – raiders of a future nature? – but it might just as well involve the laboratory manufacture of genetically transformed mammals. Donna Haraway has explored the implications of this regarding one of the first such genetically modified mammals, OncoMouse™, produced by Harvard University and now owned and trademarked by Dow Chemical.[13] The surgical and medicinal applications of myriad new genetic commodities, she has suggested, raise the prospect of a cyborg world that dissolves sharp boundaries between human and non-human nature.

THE PRODUCTION OF NATURE,
ALL THE WAY DOWN

Capitalist nature has always been commodified in the sense that naturally-provided use values, whether iron ore or labour power or services such as the ability to transport, are plucked for productive consumption and in turn alter the form of nature: the earth is gouged, soil is colonized, workers are transformed by work (physically and mentally, for better or worse), and transport technology shortens the temporal distance between spatially separate places. The social provision of sustenance has always involved a certain 'production of nature'.[14] In capitalist societies, however, the production of nature mutates from an incidental and fragmented reality to a systemic condition of social existence, from a local oddity to a global ambition. The notion of the production of nature – quite literally the alteration of the form of received nature (whether or not that nature has been previously transformed by human work) – may sound quite quixotic insofar as nature seems to be the epitome of that which neither is nor can be socially produced. Yet the universal production of nature was written into the DNA of capitalist ambition from the start; neoliberal globalization is only its latest incarnation.

The production of nature under capitalism generates its own distinct ideologies. On the one hand the radical objectification of nature in the process of industrial production both generates and reaffirms the positing of nature as an external reality vis-à-vis society, humanity, the social. Nature is broadly conceived as a repository of biological, chemical, physical and other processes that are outside the realm of human causation or creation, and the repository too of identifiable objects – subatomic and molecular, specific organisms and species, terrestrial 'bodies', and so forth. Modern science serves up such objects conceptually as discrete targets of instrumental social labour and simultaneously ratifies this purview of an external, exploitable natural world. But western societies, among others, generally also consider human beings as themselves subjects of nature, integral parts of the natural world. However instinctive the externalist conception of nature may be today, as recently as the eighteenth century in Europe it was far from general. Apart from anything else, theological and absolutist ideologies of nature were utterly antagonistic to conceptions of an external nature. On the face of it, of course, a nature wholly beyond and different from society is an untenable idea, quite literally absurd, and the externalist conception fostered its own alter ego: nature may indeed be external to society, but it is simultaneously universal. That is, the entire world – human and non-human – is subject to natural events and processes. The contradiction between these externalist and universalist conceptions has grown into a hallmark of capitalist ideologies of nature.[15]

In a remarkable section in *The German Ideology*, Marx and Engels captured the power of this capitalist production of nature. Responding critically to Feuerbach's idealism, they observed that science, trade and industry are provided with their raw material by the 'sensuous activity' of human beings:

> So much is this activity, this unceasing sensuous labour and creation, this production, the basis of the whole sensuous world as it now exists, that, were it interrupted only for a year, Feuerbach would not only find an enormous change in the natural world, but

would very soon find that the whole world of men and his own perceptive faculty, nay his own existence, were missing.

'In all this', they continued, ' the priority of external nature remains unassailed':

> nature, the nature that preceded human history, is not by any means the nature in which Feuerbach lives, it is nature which today no longer exists anywhere (except perhaps on a few Australian coral-islands of recent origin) and which, therefore, does not exist for Feuerbach.[16]

Although Marx never developed this critique in any comprehensive way, its implications are clear. Insofar as the unresolved contradiction between an external and a universal world marks capitalist ideologies of nature, the critical response is not simply a denial of either or both components of this ideology; as ever, this ideology is not simply wrong but rather presents a distorted and inverted vision of the world, with its origins in a very specific class perspective. The externality and universality of nature are real enough, but these are not to be taken as ontological givens. The ideology of external-cum-universal nature harks back to a supposedly edenic, pre-human or supra-human world, systematically erasing the very *processes* of externalization which make such an ideology sensible. (By corollary, of course, this external conception of nature becomes a powerful ideological tool for justifying racial, gender, class, sexual and other forms of social difference and inequality as 'natural' rather than social in their genesis.) Crucial here is the eclipse of the capitalist labour process through which nature is commodified and thereby externalized. By contrast, Marx and Engels make social labour central to nature, so much so that the production of nature becomes 'the basis of the whole sensuous world as it now exists'.

If we live now amidst 'social nature',[17] none of this in any way denies the power or existence of 'natural' processes. Gravity, biological process, chemical and geological change cannot be summarily suspended, and in no way owe their origins or continued operation to social labour, however much their effects may in various, limited ways be countermanded, altered, re-routed, or differently engineered: flying in a plane is a powerful way to countermand gravity − as long as the fuel lasts − but the work involved in making the plane, and making it fly, just as powerfully affirms the so-called laws of nature. It goes without saying that 'natural' science has done an unprecedented job of deciphering how nature works, but this world-historical achievement comes at a cost. The processes of externalization and objectification have facilitated inordinate efforts at the *mastery* of nature, but the resulting lack of self-reflexivity – the refusal to incorporate an understanding of how human labour, much of it science-driven, has itself transformed the 'natural' world – has been highly destructive. On one side, the apparently infinite regress of physicists' and cosmologists' discoveries of smaller and smaller sub-atomic particles, registered only as electronic blips or images on a computer screen, or as abstract mathematical results, increasingly seems to reflect the operative scientific logic more than what may or may not be happening 'in nature'. On the other, the lack of such reflexivity has not only facilitated a massive industrial transformation of nature but also fostered a broad-based societal blindness about the destructive results of this process, from air and water pollution to nuclear weaponry and global warming. The theoretical power of Donna Haraway's work has been precisely the integration of this insight concerning the centrality of labour into her revisioning of biotechnological nature.

Two clarifications are important here. First, many Marxists and critics alike have argued that human societies generally, and capitalism in particular, attempt a certain 'domination of nature'. For the Frankfurt School, on one side of the political spectrum, this was always conceived as an inevitable condition of the human metabolism with nature.[18] On the other hand deep ecologists, Gaia hypothesists and other ecological essentialists recognize a parallel attempt at domination, but they see it not as inevitable but as a destructive social choice. There is no question that the broad intent of science in a capitalist society is explicitly aimed at the domination of nature, but that project embodies an aggressive externalization of nature, as we have seen, and in different ways this externalization of nature is also embodied, whatever the degree of lamentation, in the domination-of-nature thesis. The *production*-of-nature thesis, by contrast, not only assumes no such comprehensive domination but leaves radically open the ways in which social production can create accidental, unintended and even counter-effective results vis-à-vis nature. In political terms, the domination-of-nature thesis is a cul-de-sac: if such domination is an inevitable aspect of social life, the only political alternatives are an anti-social (literally) politics of nature or else resignation to a kinder, gentler domination. The German Greens split along exactly this fissure in the 1980s with one wing veering toward eco-anarchism while the other joined the Bundestag.

The second clarification is related to the first. The production of nature thesis makes no pretence to the *control* of nature. At best, we may want to think about a Gramscian hegemony over nature but even that formulation may be too extreme. Just as capitalists never entirely control the production process, its results, or the global capitalism it generates, so capitalist society does not entirely control nature. Global warming and genetically modified organisms are certainly socially produced but they are by no means entirely controlled. Nor should future societies entertain any fantasy of controlling nature.

By the same token, it should also be emphasized that the production of nature is in no way synonymous with a social constructionist vision of nature.[19] While the best constructionist accounts emphasize the combined material and discursive construction of nature,[20] and often invite a discussion of race, gender, sexuality and other forms of social difference in relation to nature, the connection between materiality and discourse often remains vague, the social origins of discourses are underspecified, and the source of change in given social constructions of nature is obscure: nature 'is seen' (passive voice) as one thing or another in such constructions, but the social processes by which it might come to be 'seen' differently are rarely broached. At best, discourse itself is often seen to steer social change, and discursive constructionism comes to substitute for, instead of augment, any sustained focus on social production or the political-cum-social economy of nature. The production-of-nature thesis, by contrast, expresses the historical generation of ideological discourse within shifts in social productive practices – 'external' nature, for example, as an expression of the commodification of nature.

The explosion of ecological commodification and capitalization has significantly deepened the production of nature. It became a mantra of 1990s constructionism that 'nature is discursive all the way down', but the dramatic transformation of 'socionature'[21] today signals, if anything, that it is the *regulation and production* of nature that threatens to penetrate 'all the way down'. Currency rates and interest rates, credit markets and stock markets have always somewhat affected the regulation of raw material extraction, but the deepening of the production of nature today adds a wholly new dimension. Although this process is certainly in its infancy, it is intensifying rapidly, and financial markets are now increasingly in a position to influence if not orchestrate a range of environmental policies: which forms of pollution are produced and which are eradicated, how much environmental degradation is acceptable, where should it go and where should it not go, who pays. The capitalization of nature explicitly regulates such *social* decisions according to financial markets. When the price of ecological credits changes, investment priorities do too; when the weather changes, the price of pollution credits changes as traders anticipate greater or lesser generation of electricity; when interest and currency rates change, environmental policies are directly affected by capital moving in or out. Exactly this logic led Lawrence Summers, chief economist at the World Bank before taking the presidency of Harvard, to argue that Africa was 'underpolluted': the environmentally-induced loss of life in more developed countries was more expensive to the world economy compared with the cheapness of life (lost wages) in Africa.

The fundamental victory of late-twentieth century environmental politics was precisely to highlight and isolate environmental destruction as the integral result of capitalist patterns of production and consumption. If still incompletely, the market has now retaken and recolonized environmental practices. Bitter mutual antagonism is replaced by financial partnership: 'what's kind to nature' is also 'kind to profits'.[22] This represents a sweeping political co-optation and victory for capital and a defeat for environmental -cum-socialist politics. For capital, most crucially, it represents not just an ideological victory but an extraordinary economic opportunity insofar as it opens up an entirely new domain for capital accumulation. Any choice over what kinds of environments and landscapes are to be produced, and for what purposes, increasingly passes from any semblance of broad social discussion into narrow class control orchestrated through the market.

If the commodification and financialization of nature 'all the way down' marks the new phase of the production of nature, a parallel shift is also under way. The fantasy guiding the biotechnological conquest of nature involves nothing less than an effort to bypass the very externality of nature that capitalism itself promulgated. Dependence on the availability of external nature for every cycle of production represents a considerable obstacle and source of insecurity for capital. Insofar as organisms can be harvested and engineered to reproduce themselves continuously, the need for continued plunder of external nature for raw materials is attenuated. The social reproduction of nature in the laboratory – whether in a university science park or a corporate farmer's field, a hospital operating room or a test subject's daily regime of pharmaceuticals – obviously does not entirely supplant the power or necessity of external nature. Rather, it absorbs nature more fully and completely within the circuits of capital. For all that capitalism is more voracious than ever in vacuuming a supposedly external nature in search of commodifiable use values, we can also glimpse the start of a new capitalist regime whereby the task of producing a usable nature begins to pass from so-called external to social nature.

The increasingly social reproduction of nature incrementally infiltrates any remnant of a recognizably external nature. 'Second nature', in Hegel's or Marx's terms, is today less and less produced out of and in opposition to first nature; rather first nature comes to be produced from within and as a part of this second nature itself.[23] Such a self-reproduction of value – reproducing

OncoMouse™ biologically in the lab, or GM seed in a corporate field or factory – is the wet dream of capital, increasingly within reach in some sectors of production. Nature is not only thereby 'improved', but this improved nature also reproduces itself with very little additional work. Should this nature escape, however – a free OncoMouse™ daring to reproduce in the walls of its Harvard lab or GM seed blown free to reproduce in neighbouring Saskatchewan fields – it must be hunted down, re-commodified, privatized, certainly brought to court to determine the ownership of that nature, and, should its ownership be found unsanctioned, killed.[24]

FROM THE FORMAL TO THE REAL SUBSUMPTION OF NATURE

So how do these developments transform our theoretical and political understanding of the social relationship with nature? Many Marxists and critics alike assume that Marx's conception of nature can be equated with the realm of use values, seeing exchange value as the social contribution to the commodity form. While parts of volume one of *Capital* might be read this way, the same work produces a much more nuanced argument that avoids such a simple externalization of nature. Marx is quite eloquent about the ways in which the development of capitalism intensifies and transforms not just Feuerbach's nature, but *human* nature generally, *as labour*. Manufacturing crushes the worker under what he calls the 'Juggernaut' of capital. Buried within his discussion of the fate of labour at the hands of capital is an argument that now applies to the fate of nature.

In simple manufacturing, Marx says, 'the organisation of the social-labour process is purely subjective': insofar as individual workers are either hired or are not, they agree to sell their labour power for a wage or they do not, and they still retain considerable control over the immediate production process. The accumulation of capital is also still organized largely through the expansion of absolute surplus value; that is, larger and larger numbers of workers are employed in more and more extensive places of production using more and more raw material. Modern industry, which takes over from simple manufacturing, not only intensifies the dependence of the worker on the system of production but, Marx says, reverses the polarity of power. Modern industry constitutes 'a productive organism that is purely objective, in which the labourer becomes a mere appendage to an already existing material condition of production'. Capital accumulation here is increasingly accomplished in the form of relative surplus value, garnered through the intensification of production via technological innovation and other forms of labour control. The labourer is increasingly stripped of his or her control and individuality, replaced by the 'collective labourer'. Elaborate systems of industrial machinery operate 'only by means of associated labour' in which 'the co-operative character of the labour-process is... a technical necessity dictated by the instrument of labour' rather than by the labourer.[25]

Both historically and logically, this shift plays a major part in Marx's critique of capitalism and its evolution. He codified it in terms of a distinction between the formal and the real subsumption of labour to capital. The formal subsumption of labour took place when workers entered a wage relationship with capital but still maintained some immediate, creative control over the daily labour process. The real subsumption of labour to capital occurred when workers became cogs in the machinery of modern industry, hence the reversed valence of power. Not only were they subsumed as a result of the direct wage relation; they were now subsumed within the multidimensional web of capitalist technology and social organization. If Marx was theorizing in a world that barely yet knew the modern assembly line, nor the interventionist state, this insight can nonetheless be generalized beyond the narrow confines of the industrial factory. Whether working in the office or in transporting materials to and from market, whether in raw material extraction or in the global factory, modern-day workers are even more intensely integrated into what the Autonomia Marxists usefully came to call the 'social factory'.

Marx conceived the shift from the formal to the real subsumption of labour in simultaneously historical and analytical terms, and the same twinning of historical and analytical intent applies to the conceptual framework necessary to understand the current production of *nature*. With the formal subsumption of nature, capital accumulation is facilitated predominantly by a continual expansion in the conversion of extracted material into objects of production. More and more oil and wood, cotton and coal are extracted for production. Colonialism functioned as a primary strategy for, among other things, this formal subsumption of nature. By either by economic or military means (or more usually both), ruling classes in the centres of capitalist production scouted the earth in search of appropriate use values, engaging or transporting labour as part of this process. The struggles to end formal colonialism in Africa, Asia and the Caribbean, which began to succeed following World War I and intensified after World War II, may have abolished direct foreign control of many colonial governments, but did much less to circumscribe the power of European and increasingly North American corporate control over resource extraction.

The transformation to *real* subsumption is marked not simply by an intensification of this dependence of capital accumulation on nature. Rather, a two-sided shift takes place. First, while capital has always circulated through nature, whether in agricultural production or in land 'improvement' of myriad kinds, the real subsumption of nature not only intensifies this circulation but transforms it from an incidental effect of capital accumulation to an intended strategy: what were once unintended consequences become strategic goals. The production of nature becomes capitalized 'all the way down'. Second, the reverse process, namely the circulation of nature through capital, is similarly transformed from an incidental to a strategic process. This occurs in two ways. In terms of biotechnology, produced natures – whether in the body of OncoMouse™, in the offspring of a cloned Scottish sheep, in the genetic profile of seeds or other organic products (vegetable or animal) – circulate as commodities in everything from research objects to donatable body fluids and organs, meat and bread, pharmaceuticals and milk. This technological deepening raises to a new level the appropriation of relative rather than absolute surplus value.

But at the same time these produced natures circulate financially in the garb of commodity futures, ecological credits, corporate stocks, environmental derivatives, and so forth. The residue of nature in these financial 'instruments' may not be immediately visible, but that is hardly the point; financialized commodities would not exist without the earlier attachment of exchange value to some aspect of (produced) nature. Just as the commodity price of a swath of wetland or a residential plot is equally invisible until a social negotiation settles it, nature's contribution to a mitigation credit or an environmental derivative remains hidden until an investor is required to justify or determine what the underlying social commodity actually looks like. At that moment, when speculators find that the sinking price of their credits and derivatives does not even entitle them to a claim over part of a Florida swamp, but rather resides in carbon long dissipated into the atmosphere or never produced in the first place, both the power and the vulnerability of the financialization of nature become starkly evident. Much as the real subsumption of labour strips the labourer of individuality, the real subsumption of nature, through its capitalization and financialization, strips nature of its specificity: a $40 ton of unproduced Costa Rican carbon is entirely equatable – the commodity equivalent – with a $40 ton of produced carbon from the Houston oil industry. Through its financialization, the real commodity – carbon produced and unproduced – is now integral to the multidimensional web of capitalist technology and social organization, in short the social factory. And whether carbon is or is not released into the atmosphere becomes, literally, a matter of capitalist equivocation.

This distinction between the formal and real subsumption of nature has been explored by William Boyd, Scott Prudham and Rachel Schurman.[26]

They make a trenchant argument that different forms of nature translate into different modes of organization of industrial production; the structure of the diamond industry is quite unlike that of cattle farming, for example, due in part to the different nature-given conditions of raw material availability, transmutability and marketability. The real subsumption of nature, they suggest, takes place when certain 'biological systems – in marked contrast to extractive sectors – are industrialized and may be made to operate as productive forces in and of themselves'.[27] Their subsequent analysis makes a series of distinctions, for example between nature-based and non-nature-based industries, but the crucial connection aligns the formal and real subsumption of labour with the division between biological and non-biological industries. 'The key to understanding the difference between formal and real subsumption of nature', they contend, 'lies in the difference between biological and non-biological systems and the unique capacity to manipulate biological productivity'.[28] For them, under the formal subsumption of nature, capitalists 'confront nature as an exogenous set of material properties', whereas under the real subsumption of nature, capitalists are able 'to take hold of and transform natural production'.[29]

Powerful as the focus on biotechnological change is, this analysis too quickly reduces the distinction between real and formal subsumption to that between biological and non-biological industries. At a very simple level, agriculture and fishing have always cultivated or confronted nature – soil, animals (domesticated or otherwise), climate – as productive forces.[30] By corollary, nature was never simply 'exogenous' for Marx, even when only formally subsumed by capital. Boyd, Prudham and Schurman note that for Marx, 'the distinction between the formal and real subsumption of labour turned on the distinction between absolute and relative surplus value'. But that is only part of the story. What is missing here is a recognition of the crucial role played by *cooperation* which for Marx was a product of the nature of human beings in the deepest sense.[31] Without cooperative human labour – the innate power to work together and the larger creative ability of cooperative compared with individualized workers – the historical hegemony of relative over absolute surplus value would have been impossible. It was precisely the power of technological and social organization to harness this nature-given power of human cooperation that made the real subsumption of labour (and the institutionalization of relative surplus value) possible.

Underlying and in part explaining this lacuna concerning labour and nature is an explicit adherence by these authors to an external conception of nature: indeed they define nature as 'the nonhuman, biogeophysical world', leaving little room for any 'nature' in labour, as Marx theorized, or for labour as fulcrum of the production of nature.[32] Most important, the conflation of biological versus non-biological nature with real versus formal subsumption of nature not only elides the biology of *human* nature but also locates the real subsumption of nature too narrowly in the biological world. Even the formal subsumption of nature always deployed biological systems as forces of production, as with industrial agriculture, and today's real subsumption of nature, while crucially biological, is not entirely so. The real subsumption of nature is also orchestrated through the explosion of intellectual property rights, for example, which, on the back of capital, have bored into nature via the core of scientific discovery and invention (biological and otherwise), buttressing evolving claims concerning artistic and cultural commodity production. Just as important, ecological credits, mitigation markets and environmental derivatives – all examples of what Marx called 'fictitious capital'[33] – also play a central role. In the same way that mortgages and pensions became part of the daily life of many workers during the twentieth century, playing a crucial role in socializing the real subsumption of labour beyond the workplace (narrowly defined), the fictitious capital of ecological credits and environmental derivative markets is integral to socializing the real subsumption of nature.

Regulation theorist Michel Aglietta has argued that around the beginning of the twentieth century – precisely the period in which Woolf announced the transformation of human nature, and Lefebvre claimed that space had changed – a radical shift took place in the conditions of the reproduction of capital.[34] Looking specifically at the United States, Aglietta argued that the 'predominantly extensive regime of accumulation' extended itself horizontally through the geographical sway of capital and the search for surplus value, and extended itself vertically by building up 'successive layers' of industrial innovation. By contrast, the 'intensive regime of accumulation', which takes over historically, reverses this priority. It creates a 'new mode of life', integrating new norms of social consumption and new forms of state regulation with transformed forces of production.[35] The resulting Fordism was premised on the historical shift from the formal to the real subsumption of labour, or, as Aglietta puts it, 'the creation of collective means of production', rooted as they are in cooperative labour.[36] That transition is now being replicated a century later as regards the real subsumption of nature. The extensive production of nature that has characterized capitalism since its infancy has, since the 1970s, been challenged and increasingly superseded by an intensive production of nature.

CONCLUSION: NATURE AS
ACCUMULATION STRATEGY

On the basis of her research on genetically transformed organisms, including OncoMouse™, Donna Haraway concluded in the late 1990s that the body now represented an accumulation strategy for capital: 'Life itself is a capital-accumulation strategy'. Cindi Katz has broadened this into a suggestion that nature *per se* may now represent an accumulation strategy for capital.[37] As the parallel with Aglietta's analysis would indicate, the emergence of nature as an accumulation strategy applies not simply to changes in the production of nature but to changes in its consumption too. The natural foods industry which sprang from 1960s hippie environmentalism, quickly became a multi-billion capitalist enterprise. Oil companies, among the world's greatest polluters, routinely advertise their decimation of nature as environmentally friendly, not least by celebrating their purchase of carbon credits. Recycling, once a quack demand by marginal environmentalists, is now (whatever its other merits) a major industrial sector that not only enjoys significant state subsidy and is run in some US states by the mafia, but has forcibly enlisted the work of consumers – sorting, storing and even delivering recyclables – in a very real subsumption of daily life to capital.[38] In 2006 WalMart, the world's largest retail chain and emblem of capitalist consumptionism, announced that it was 'going green' with organic methods, sources and products. Little wonder that establishment environmentalists could belatedly come to the obvious realization that liberal environmentalism is dead.[39] Actually, it is only dead as an anti-capitalist movement; it is very much alive, thriving and profiting as a multi-billion dollar enterprise in the board rooms of the same capitalist powers that it once challenged.

Remnant conservative opposition to environmentalism should not be taken as contrary to this argument. As regards wetlands, for example, the US Supreme Court seems to be squeamish about its support for existing wetlands legislation, without which the wetlands mitigation market may not expand as quickly as it otherwise would. On Kyoto, the US refusal to accept the protocols agreed on by most of the world is widely seen as a narrowly conservative and rather pugilist rejection of environmentalism. But in both cases these challenges to environmental legislation represent not so much a rejection of any and all environmental politics – George W. Bush is the son of the 'environmental president' – as a protection of some capitalist prerogatives over others. Concerning wetlands, the struggle is very much about the sanctity of private property, enlisting individual property owners against big government. The US rejection of the Kyoto accords represents an internal ruling class jostle between more environmentally 'friendly' energy capitalists – think BP advertising – and more aggressive cowboy capitalists who, while quite happy to invest in the environmental market, see their immediate profits in terms of direct energy production for an expanding market. US rejection of Kyoto betokens a squabble within the global ruling class about the details of how to profit from the new environmental consciousness and who gets to profit how from the new capitalization of nature. At one level, the so-called conservatives simply have not yet caught up to the opportunities of environmental capitalism and will go down in history as such. On the other hand, they are on the side of an energy industry which is making record profits while presenting itself as environmentalist.

As with the subsumption of labour, there is no sharp historical distinction between the formal and real subsumption of nature. Just as sweatshop labour proliferates in many industries in Asia, Latin America and Africa, the extensive expansion of capital into nature remains a powerful frontier of capital accumulation, whether with bio-prospecting in the Amazon or oil drilling in the US Arctic; the outer edge of this extensive expansion today is transplanetary, the coming colonization, scientific exploration, and exploitation of what we still call 'outer space'. What is new today is not that this horizontal integration of nature into capital has ceased, even if in some arenas it is significantly circumscribed as many raw materials become scarcer, harder to locate, and more expensive to extract. Rather, partly in response to these increasing constraints, a new frontier in the production of nature has rapidly opened up, namely a *vertical integration of nature* into capital. This involves not just the production of nature 'all the way down', but its simultaneous financialization 'all the way up'. Capital is no longer content simply to plunder an available nature but rather increasingly moves to produce an inherently social nature as the basis of new sectors of production and accumulation. Nature is increasingly if selectively replicated as its own marketplace.

Writing in the mid-1970s, Aglietta detected a 'crisis in the regime of intensive accumulation', a crisis which in retrospect we now recognize as the harbinger of a new phase of accumulation and a restructured capitalism dominated by neoliberalism and so-called globalization.[40] In the 1980s the increasing appropriation of nature as an accumulation strategy contributed to the resolution of this regime crisis; today it promises to provide the nervous system of a new phase of capitalist accumulation. None of this happens without contradiction, of course, not least of which is that the new vertical capitalization of nature makes the fate of capitalism more dependent on nature, not less. In the past, economic recessions and depressions have traditionally provoked a slowdown in the appropriation of nature, an ironic environmental benefit amidst economic hardship. With the intensification of nature as an accumulation strategy, however, the destruction of value embedded in ecological commodities and credits both reaches further into the core of capital and threatens heightened environmental destruction. The same credit system that supposedly protects a wetland or forest can lead to its destruction when the credit system itself collapses.

Yet this does not happen without political opposition. Insofar as nature is more intensely integrated into capital as an accumulation strategy, the comprehensiveness of this social production of nature under capitalism becomes more and more apparent, and the necessity of a broad political response ever more urgent. It is important to fight GM crops, for example, on the grounds that they can contaminate and forever alter other organisms, including human beings, but if the analysis here has any meaning it also suggests that such a narrow focus on the use value of nature is not only limiting but skewed, and unlikely to generate a successful political challenge to the strategic production of nature per se. As the global capitalist class arrogates to itself comprehensive power over the production of nature, a power camouflaged in the language of markets, private property and free trade, an adequate response must be just as ambitious. In short, while struggles over GM organisms, biotechnology, working and health conditions, and other means of the capitalization of nature are of central importance, and have to be fought and won, it is just as vital to have a longer-term eye on the constitutive social relations. Put bluntly, if the production of nature is a historical reality, what would a truly democratic production of nature look like? The chance is there to take Virginia Woolf at her word, looking forward rather than backward, and to think how nature ought to change. And to think what kind of social power it will take to democratize that production of nature.

NOTES

I am very grateful to Deborah Cowen and Scott Prudham for their insightful arguments and suggestions which have immeasurably helped in the preparation of this essay.

1   Virginia Woolf, 'Mr. Bennett and Mrs. Brown', in *The Captain's Bed and Other Essays*, New York: Harcourt Brace, 1956, p. 25; Stephen Kern, *The Culture of Time and Space, 1880-1918*, Cambridge: Harvard University Press, 1983; Henri Lefebvre, *The Production of Space*, Oxford: Basil Blackwell, 1991, p. 96.

2   Federal Register. Federal Guidance for the Establishment, Use and Operation of Mitigation Banks, 60(28), 28 November 1995, pp. 58605-58614.

3   Morgan M. Robertson, 'No Net Loss: Wetland Restoration and the Incomplete Capitalization of Nature', *Antipode*, 32(4), 2000; Morgan M. Robertson,

'The Neoliberalization of Ecosystem Services: Wetland Mitigation Banking and Problems in Environmental Governance', *Geoforum*, 35(3), 2004.

4   See the essay by Brunnengräber in this volume.

5   R. Bayon, 'Making Money in Environmental Derivatives', *The Milken Institute Review*, March, 2002; Kevin St. Martin, 'Making Space for Community Resource Management in Fisheries', *Annals of the Association of American Geographers*, 91, 2001.

6   Cindi Katz, 'Whose Nature, Whose Culture? Private Productions of Space and the Preservation of Nature', in B. Braun and N. Castree, eds., *Remaking Reality: Nature at the Millenium*, New York: Routledge, 1998.

7   Friedrich Engels, *The Condition of the Working Class in England*, Moscow: Progress Publishers, 1973.

8   Robertson, 'The Neoliberalization', p. 362.

9   Bayon, 'Making Money'.

10   http://www.mitigationbankingconference.com

11   Randy Martin, *The Financialization of Everyday Life*, Philadelphia: Temple University Press, 2002.

12   Scott Prudham, 'Commodifying GMOs in Canada: Some Recent (Mis)adventures', *Antipode*, forthcoming; Noel Castree, 'Commodifying What Nature?', *Progress in Human Geography*, 27(3), 2003; Robertson, 'The Neoliberalization of Ecosystem Services'.

13   Donna J. Haraway, *Modest_Witness@Second_Millennium.Female©_Meets_Onco-Mouse™*, New York: Routledge, 1997.

14   Neil Smith, *Uneven Development: Nature, Capital and the Production of Space*, Oxford: Basil Blackwell, 1984, chapter 2; Neil Smith, 'The Production of Nature', in George Robertson and Melinda Mash, eds., *FutureNatural*, London: Routledge, 1996; Margaret FitzSimmons, 'The Matter of Nature', *Antipode*, 21(2), 1989; Noel Castree, 'The Nature of Produced Nature: Materiality and Knowledge Construction in Marxism', *Antipode*, 27(1), 1995.

15   Smith, *Uneven Development*, chapter 1.

16   Karl Marx and Friederich Engels, *The German Ideology*, New York: International Publishers, 1970.

17   Bruce Braun and Noel Castree, eds., *Social Nature*, London: Routledge, 2001.

18   Alfred Schmidt, *The Concept of Nature in Marx*, London: New Left Books, 1971; William Leiss, *The Domination of Nature*, Boston: Beacon Press, 1974.

19   See for example, William Boyd, W. Scott Prudham and Rachel A. Schurman, 'Industrial Dynamics and the Problem of Nature', *Society and Natural Resources*, 14, 2001, p. 557.

20   See for example, Braun and Castree, *Social Nature*.

21   Erik Swyngedouw, 'Modernity and Hybridity: Nature, *Regeneracionismo*, and the Production of Spanish Waterscapes', *Annals of the Association of American Geographers*, 89, 1999.

22   Matthew Wald, 'What's Kind to Nature Can be Kind to Profits', *The New York Times*, 17 May, 2006.

23   Smith, *Uneven Development*.

24   Prudham, 'Commodifying GMOs in Canada'.

25   Karl Marx, *Capital*, Volume I, New York: International Publishers, 1967, p. 386.
26   Boyd et al., 'Industrial Dynamics'.
27   Ibid., p. 555.
28   Ibid., p. 564.
29   Ibid., p. 557.
30   Cf. 'It seems paradoxical to assert that uncaught fish, for instance, are a means of production in the fishing industry. But hitherto no one has discovered the art of catching fish in waters that contain none': Marx, *Capital* I, p. 181.
31   Ibid., chapter 13.
32   Boyd et al., 'Industrial Dynamics', p. 568. For a revised, more sophisticated recognition of the critique of external ideologies of nature, see Prudham, 'Commodifying GMOs in Canada'.
33   Karl Marx, *Capital*, Volume III, New York: International Publishers, 1967, chapters 25 and 29.
34   Michel Aglietta, *A Theory of Capitalist Regulation*, London: New Left Books, 1979.
35   Ibid., pp. 71-2.
36   Ibid. p. 79.
37   Haraway, *Modest_Witness*, p. 65; see also David Harvey, 'The Body as Accumulation Strategy', *Society and Space*, 40, 1998, pp. 401-21; Cindi Katz, 'Whose Nature'.
38   See the essay by Heather Rogers in this volume.
39   Michael Schellenberger and Ted Nordhaus, 'The Death of Environmentalism. The Politics of Global Warming in a Post-environmental World', 2004, available at http://www.thebreakthrough.org.
40   Aglietta, *A Theory of Capitalist Regulation*, p. 99.

THE SOCIAL AND NATURAL ENVIRONMENT OF FOSSIL CAPITALISM

ELMAR ALTVATER

The 'westernization' of the world has led to a pattern of production and consumption which builds intensively on the nearly limitless availability of matter and energy, sophisticated technology, and the existence of natural 'sinks' in which solids, liquids and gas-emissions can be dumped. The effects on the local, national and global natural environment are mostly negative. Global transportation is responsible for the consumption of large quantities of fossil energy and thus for an increase of CO_2-emissions, thus aggravating the climate crisis. Labour-intensive production processes are located where labour is cheap, and environmentally harmful processes where environmental laws and regulations are least exacting, and so least expensive.

At first glance it seems as if services and finance do not exert negative effects on the environment. However, the idea that we now live in a 'virtual economy' of bits and bytes, and that economic growth is being decoupled from energy consumption, is nothing but 'a myth' (or as Harry Frankfurt says, 'bullshit').[1] Financial markets exert pressure on the real economy, enforcing the payment by borrowers of the financial claims of creditors (banks and funds) – payments that are only affordable if real growth rates remain high. This pressure has been seen as an efficient lever for securing increasing competitiveness, just as the absence of this pressure in formerly socialist countries has been seen as one of the main causes of their economic failure. Therefore finance indirectly enforces growth and, concomitantly, a rising consumption of energy as well as of material resources (although increasing efficiency in the use of matter and energy may partially offset this pressure). The financial instabilities and crises of recent decades have also jeopardized social stability, pushing large strata of the populations in the worse affected countries into precarious life conditions and poverty. Even the World Bank admits that these effects are responsible for ecological degradation in large parts of the world.

The reason for capitalism's high economic impact on the environment is to be found in its double character. It has a value dimension (the monetary value of the gross national product, of world trade, of FDI, of financial flows, etc.) but is also a system of material and energy flows in production and consumption, transportation and distribution. Economic decisions concerning production first consider values and prices, profit margins and monetary returns, on capital invested. In this sphere the ruling principle is only the economic rationality of profit-maximizing decision-makers. But the decisions they take have important impacts on nature, due to the material and energy dimension of economic processes.

Under capitalist conditions the environment is more and more transformed into a contested object of human greed. The exploitation of natural resources, and their degradation by a growing quantity of pollutants, results in a man-made scarcity, leading to conflicts over access to them. Access to nature (to resources and sinks) is uneven and unequal and the societal relation of man to nature therefore is conflict-prone. The 'ecological footprints' of people in different countries and regions of the world are of very different sizes, reflecting severe inequalities of incomes and wealth.[2] Ecological injustices therefore can only usefully be discussed if social class contradictions and the production of inequality in the course of capital accumulation are taken into account.

The environment includes the energy system, climate, biodiversity, soils, water, woods, deserts, ice sheets, etc. – i.e. the different spheres of the planet Earth and their historical evolution. The complexity of nature, and the positive and negative feed-back mechanisms between the different dimensions of the environment in space and time, are only partly known. Therefore environmental policy has to be made in the shadow of a high degree of uncertainty. This is why one of the basic principles of environmental policy is that of *precaution*.[3] The effects of human activities, particularly economic activities, on natural processes, and the feed-back mechanisms within the totality of the social, political and economic systems, constitute the so-called societal relation of man to nature. Only a *holistic* attempt to integrate environmental aspects into discourses of political economy, political science, sociology, cultural studies etc. can make possible a coherent understanding of environmental problems and yield adequate political responses to the challenges of the ongoing ecological crisis.

NATURAL RICHES AND THE ECONOMIC
WEALTH OF NATIONS

At the centre of the analysis of capitalism's relation to nature is its inherent and unavoidable dependence on fossil fuels, and particularly on oil.[4] To understand this properly we must first briefly consider the advantages of fossil fuels for capitalist accumulation. In general terms petroleum's Energy Return on Energy Input (EROEI) is very high. Only a small amount of energy needs to be invested in order to harvest much greater amounts of energy, because the entropy of petroleum is very low and its energy concentration is very high, yielding a high energy surplus. Compared with the flows of solar energy, fossil energy is a 'thick' energy source, to the point where fossil energy can easily come to seem responsible for the surplus value produced in a capitalist system. However this is not the case. A physical surplus and an economic surplus value are as different as use values and exchange values, or as the physical barrel of oil ('wet oil') and the futures price of that barrel on the Chicago stock exchange ('paper oil'). Again, we encounter the decisive importance of the double character of capitalist exchange relations.

An important *caveat* has to be introduced here. Solar energy of course has the highest EROEI, because solar energy flows, which power all processes of life on earth (plants, animals and human beings), come in the form of solar radiation (light and heat) without the need for any energy input by living beings on earth. However, energy inputs *are* required for the transformation of solar radiation into useful energy for humankind. The role of agriculture is a telling example. Energy – i.e. the efforts of the farmer and his family and workers, the energy of animals, etc. – is invested to obtain a higher return from the energy contained in plants and livestock (this is why the EROEI in a pre-fossil economy and society is never infinite).

In a fossil energy regime the EROEI is high in recently developed oil-fields, and then decreases because in most cases the energy input grows and the energy output decreases, until further exploitation becomes irrational, in terms of both energy and later also economics. Then the energy source is transformed into an energy sink, 'and the oil will simply remain in the ground. It is for these reasons that the world will never technically run out of oil; rather, it will ultimately become simply too energy-intensive to extract low-quality or geographically inaccessible oil'.[5] What has been said about a single oilfield can be said about oil-extraction in general. The EROEI decreases in step with the exhaustion of global oil reserves. The implications of this are obvious. Oil production not only reaches a peak and then declines (the so-called 'Hubbert-curve');[6] equally important is the fact that the amount of energy that has to be invested in the extraction of a declining output must grow. Although irrational in terms of energy, it may still seem economically rational because of the calculation in value terms. The energy invested (e.g. water power) may be cheaper than the energy return (e.g. in the form of non-conventional oil), although calculated in calories the reverse is true.

By confusing physical and value processes some ecologists accuse Marx of systematically underestimating the 'value of nature' in the process of value-production.[7] But the rebuke is only relevant insofar as the labour process is concerned. Of course, nature is as important as labour in converting matter and energy into use. Nature is remarkably productive – the evolution of species in the history of the planet, and their tremendous diversity and variety, prove it – but it is not *value-productive*, because it produces no commodities to be sold on the market. There is no market in nature. The market and commodities are social and economic constructs, not a natural heritage, even if neoliberal economists assume otherwise. It is labour which turns nature into commodities. This is why resource-rich countries very often remain poor, and why resource-poor countries very often become wealthy, because they have the capacity to transform natural riches into economic wealth by dominating the process of capitalist valorization.

From the viewpoint of energy analysis the production process may look very different from the way it looks from the viewpoint of commodity- and value-analysis. Juan Martinez-Alier says in this regard: 'The productivity of agriculture has not increased, but decreased, from the point of view of energy analysis';[8] but in terms of commodity-production in agriculture, and in terms of return on invested capital, its productivity has increased. Therefore it is possible for Dutch agricultural producers to compete with Mexican producers of horticultural products such as eggplants on the North-American market. They simply do not take the full inputs of fossil energy into account, so that productivity in value-terms seems to be high, while productivity in energy-terms is low or even negative.

The transition to industrial systems and to the predominant use of fossil energies was much more dramatic than that which transformed societies of hunters and gatherers into a social order of sedentary agricultural systems. It was a revolutionary break in the history of the societal relation of human beings to nature because it was no longer the *flow* of solar radiation which served as the main energy supply for the system of production and the satisfaction of human needs, but the use of the mineralised *stocks* of energy contained in the crust of the earth.

The greatest expansion of human demand for natural resources followed the Industrial Revolution in the latter half of the eighteenth century, and the first half of the nineteenth. One of the main advantages of fossil energy for capitalist accumulation is the *congruence* of its physical properties with the socioeconomic and political logics of capitalist development.[9] In comparison with other energy sources fossil energy fulfils almost perfectly the requirements of the capitalist process of accumulation. It fits into capitalism's societal relation to nature.

First, fossil energy allows the transformation of pre-capitalist patterns of space and place into capitalist ones. The local availability of energy resources is no longer the main reason for the location of manufacturing or other industries. It is simple to transport energy resources anywhere in the world, giving rise to logistical networks which today cover the globe. Energy supply therefore becomes only one factor among many others in decisions about where production is to take place. The availability of local sources of energy has only a minor impact on the competition for the location of investment in global space.

Second, in contrast to solar radiation, which changes its intensity between day and night and with the rhythms of the seasons, fossil energy can be used 24 hours a day and 365 days a year with constant intensity, allowing the organization of production processes independently of social time schedules, biological and other natural rhythms. Fossil energies can be stored and then consumed without reference to natural time patterns, in accordance only with the time regime of modernity and a timetable that optimizes profits. Benjamin Franklin's famous statement 'time is money' could therefore seem not crazy but as an appropriate norm of human behaviour in 'modern times'. Moreover, fossil energy allows for the extreme *acceleration* of processes, the '*compression* of time and space'.[10] In other words, it allows for an increase in productivity, reducing the time needed for the production of a given amount of products.

Third, fossil energy can be used very flexibly in production, consumption and transportation, and in the use of time and space. The development of electricity networks and the electric motor, the illumination of whole cities at night and the invention of the internal combustion engine, were decisive steps in an increasingly flexible use of energy-inputs, in the mobilization and acceleration of economic processes and in a degree of individualization of social life never before experienced in human history. Now, managerial decisions could follow the logic of profitability without needing to take energy restrictions or spatial and temporal constraints into account. Accumulation and economic growth, i.e. the 'wealth of nations', became increasingly independent of natural conditions and their limitations. These advantages of fossil energy for the capitalist system make it unique and indispensable. The congruence of capitalism, fossil energy, rationalism and industrialism is perfect.

An ensemble of four forces has subsequently driven the whole set of dynamic developments: (1) the 'European rationality of world domination' and its translation into technical devices and organizational expertise;[11] (2) the 'great transformation' to a disembedded market-economy – the theme of Karl Polanyi;[12] (3) the dynamics of money in the social form of capital, which Marx analyzed in *Capital*;[13] and (4) the use of fossil energy. Together these forces have produced what Georgescu-Roegen called a 'Promethean revolution',[14] comparable to the Neolithic revolution of several thousand years ago, when humankind discovered how to transform solar energy systematically into crops and animal products, by establishing sedentary agricultural systems.

This *ensemble* of dimensions of the fossil energy regime gives an impression of the ingredients of its dynamics and the range of social scientific approaches which must be applied in order to understand the mechanisms involved in the transformation of natural riches into economic wealth. Without the continuous supply and massive use of fossil energy modern capitalism would be locked into the boundaries of biotic energy (wind, water, bio-mass, muscle-power, etc.). Although something like capitalist social forms occasionally could be found in ancient societies (in Latin America and Asia as well as in Europe), they could not grow and flourish without fossil energy. The entropy of the available energy sources was too high, and the EROEI too low, to allow significant surplus production. Therefore growth was limited, and in fact the average annual growth rate was close to zero before the industrial revolution of late eighteenth century.

But in the course of the industrial revolution economic growth rates jumped from 0.2 per cent to more than 2 per cent a year until the end of the twentieth century; world population also increased faster than ever before.[15] In pre-capitalist and pre-industrial times economic growth was dependent on population growth which, in turn, depended – this was the rationale behind Malthus' theory – on the supply of goods and services for subsistence and reproduction. But after the industrial revolution economic growth became independent of population growth, due to an enormous increase in productivity and a concomitant increase in the production of relative surplus value. Therefore, contrary to Malthus' predictions, but in accordance with the optimistic message of Adam Smith and David Ricardo, per capita incomes also increased, with the widening and deepening of the division of labour by means of expanding markets and the establishment of free trade. It is interesting to note that in the first millennium the income divergences between Western Europe, Japan, Latin America, Eastern Europe, Africa and Asia were very small. In the course of the fossil-industrial revolution, however, things changed completely. The gap between rich and poor nations widened and inequality became the name of the game. From the second half of the eighteenth century average growth rates increased remarkably, but this failed to reduce the inequalities between peoples and regions in a globalizing world; on the contrary, inequalities increased.[16]

ENTROPY AND LIFE CONDITIONS

In view of these numbers the question arises: is growth possible for ever? Is growth 'triumphant'?[17] The answer has to be 'no', because nothing on earth grows eternally without any limits, and this also applies to the capitalist economy. The time will come when 'the party's over'.[18] The limits of growth are among the conditions of life and the laws of evolution on planet Earth, and are a direct consequence of the limits of the resources – and especially fossil resources – which fuel growth. Although the accumulation of capital and growth are almost wholly powered by fossil energy (and thus dependent on an *isolated* system, with finite resources), human and natural life in general is almost entirely dependent on solar radiation (i.e. on the influx of solar energy into an open system). Daylight, the warming of the atmosphere, of the waters and the soils, the growth and evolution of living beings, the provision of food, are the result of solar radiation and only to a minor extent of the use of fossil energy. The satisfaction of primary human needs is only possible by using energy in the form of organic foods (containing proteins, fats, carbohydrates, vitamins and minerals, water), and other organic materials transformed into clothing and shelter – not to mention our dependence on oxygen.

Nicholas Georgescu-Roegen points out that humanity in principle only disposes on 'two resources of wealth':

> first the finite stock of mineral resources in the earth's crust which within certain limits we can decumulate into a flow almost at will, and second, a flow of solar radiation the rate of which is not subject to our control. In terms of low entropy, the stock of mineral resources is only a very small fraction of the solar energy received by the globe within a single year. More precisely, the highest estimate of terrestrial energy resources does not exceed the amount of free energy received from the sun during *four days*! In addition, the flow of the sun's radiation will continue with the same intensity (practically) for a long time to come. For these reasons and because

the low entropy received from the sun cannot be converted into matter in bulk, it is not the sun's finite stock of energy that sets a limit to how long the human species may survive. Instead, it is the meager stock of the earth's resources that constitutes the crucial scarcity....[19]

The consumption of fossil energy has repercussions on the man-nature-relation. History consists of the increase of entropy and the associated irreversibility of all processes, whereas capital operates on a logic of reversibility and circularity. Capital has to appropriate the surplus and invest it again in the production process, to secure the appropriation of a growing surplus – a surplus which must be produced, since the production process has been financed with credits, and debt must be serviced. The performance indicators of capital very clearly exhibit the circularity and reversibility of the flow of capital. Capital outlays 'return', and the returns must be greater than the investment. Profitability, the marginal efficiency of capital, the return on capital, shareholder value and other terms clearly demonstrate that the Weberian instrumental rationality, based on a comparison of means (i.e. investment) and objectives (i.e. profit), animates capitalism. In contrast, natural processes of transformation of matter and energy are characterized by irreversibility, as well as the natural growth process of living beings like plants and animals; all living beings are aging. This follows ultimately from the law of entropy.

Every production process also has two aspects: producing not only the desired outputs, but also (mostly negative) side effects. It is a natural law that it is impossible to transform 100 per cent of energy- and matter-input into products designed for the satisfaction of human needs. In the interpretation of Ilya Prigogine an increase of entropy is the inevitable expression of a transformation of matter and energy in the process of natural – and we may add – social evolution, i.e. there is no evolution without increased entropy.[20] In 'enjoying our lives' we simultaneously increase entropy and worsen life conditions on earth.[21] Marx was fully aware of this double-sidedness of the satisfaction of human needs and of the destruction of the natural environment:

> All progress increasing the fertility of the soil for a given time is a progress towards ruining the more long-lasting sources of that fertility. The more a country proceeds from large-scale industry as a background of its development..., the more rapid is this process of destruction. Capitalist production, therefore, only develops the techniques and the degree of combination of the social process of

production by simultaneously undermining the original sources of all wealth – the soil and the worker.[22]

The degree of entropy depends decisively on the energy regime. The Neolithic revolution raised it by developing devices to capture solar energy and transform it into concentrated energy, useful for humans. This was the revolutionary achievement of agriculture. The development of agriculture resulted in an increase in food production, and greater reliability of food supplies. The surplus produced by farmers – whom the physiocrats of the eighteenth century saw as the sole 'productive class' – made it possible to feed 'unproductive classes' of artisans, clerks and rulers. But the agricultural system based on capturing solar energy flows disappeared almost completely as a result of the industrial and fossil revolutions. Eric Hobsbawm in his *Age of Extremes* suggested that the second half of the twentieth century was the first time in human history when the number of people living on the countryside and working as farmers in agriculture (as 'harvesters of solar energy') was lower than the number working in urban manufactures and services.[23]

In the transition from an agricultural to an industrial society the congruence of capitalism, rationalism, industrialism and fossil energy becomes central. But the key role of fossil energy in this congruence makes it an obstacle to further development. First, it will eventually run out; and second, its combustion produces so much harmful emission that living conditions on earth are deteriorating. In terms of thermodynamic economics, the transition to a capitalist industrial system means that the planet is treated as a *closed* and even *isolated* system. For solar radiation from outside (and likewise the irradiation of heat into the outer space) is replaced by fossil energy sources taken from inside the crust of the Earth. But life on Earth remains dependent on the sun's radiation. Between life conditions (*open system*) and economic conditions (*isolated system*) on earth a 'firewall' has been socially and politically constructed. Today, and possibly for ever, it is impossible to power the machine of capitalist accumulation and growth with 'thin' solar radiation-energy. It simply lacks the advantages mentioned above, i.e. the potential of time and space compression, which 'thick' fossil energy offers. And meanwhile the fossil energy regime of the capitalist economy has an extremely destructive effect on all the forms of life on earth which are 'powered' almost completely by solar radiation. The degradation of nature – i.e. the greenhouse effect, ozone layer depletion, loss of biodiversity, desertification, the disappearance of tropical rain forests etc. – is unquestionable. The price of the advantages of the fossil energy regime is ecological destruction and the necessity of finding a solution to the limits of fossil energy's availability.

PEAK OIL AND CLIMATE CHANGE

Of all the forms of fossil energy oil is the one which has above all been key to capitalist development over the last hundred years. The peak, and thus the limits, of oil production have a major effect on the capitalist accumulation process, because the above-mentioned congruence is over. The 'external limits' of resources aggravate 'normal' capitalist crises – and oil production will peak soon, as the geologist Marion King Hubbert already predicted in the 1950s, when everybody believed in an abundance of oil. He foresaw that US oil production would peak at the beginning of the 1970s, which is exactly what happened. After that the USA switched from being an oil-exporting to an oil-importing country.

Until the beginning of the 1980s global oil discoveries were larger than oil consumption. Since then, however, consumption has exceeded discoveries, so that oil reserves are shrinking. The stocks of oil are limited, and supplies will likely run out in four decades.[24] Oil production is peaking. Some geologists say that it already happened.[25] Others are more cautious and predict the peaking of oil production in the course of the next decade. Then the first half of the global reserves will have been used up. Down to 2004 the accumulated global consumption of oil was about 944 billion barrels. For the consumption of the second half less time will be needed, because the demand for oil will increase in spite of attempts to save energy, to increase the efficiency of its use, to improve the energy mix and to make more use of renewable resources.[26]

This is for two interconnected reasons. First, the crucial role of global financial markets, with their high real interest rates and claims on rates of return, enforce high real growth rates of GNP. Under the prevailing patterns of technology deployment, such high growth rates only can be achieved by an intensive use of fossil energy. Thus the operation of global financial markets has an impact on the oil market.[27] The second reason stems from the globalization of Western production and consumption patterns, which are extremely energy-intensive. Newly-industrializing countries crowd into markets and add to the already insatiable demand of the OECD countries, above all of the USA, which consume nearly one fourth of global oil production (20 million barrels per day out of a total of about 80 million barrels in 2006).

However, peak oil is not the whole story. The exploitation of known reserves becomes more expensive over time because pressure, viscosity and other physical and chemical properties of oil fields deteriorate in the course of extraction. Water must be pumped in, in order to sustain the pressure necessary for bringing oil to the surface. Drilling is becoming increasingly complicated, especially in off-shore areas and unconventional oil-fields, but also in 'old' oilfields. Moreover, peak oil is only partly an objective fact.[28] It is dependent on extraction-technologies and knowledge about, and the evaluation of, oil reserves. The first factor is emphasized by neoclassical economists: investment in the exploration of oil fields and oil logistics and refinement can help to increase the supply of oil in pace with growing demand. This is also the line of argument of the International Energy Agency, which says that about US$3 trillion must be invested in exploration, drilling, pipelines and refineries in order to increase oil production from about 80 to 120 million barrels per day. The second factor influencing the reserve calculations is the exploration of non-conventional oil and gas, such as heavy oils, deepwater oil and gas, polar oil and gas, etc., and the costs of extraction in relation to the market price of crude oil.[29]

A third factor is the evaluation of known and presumable reserves. This is highly dependent on the interests of all the parties involved in oil markets – producers, consumers, brokers and dealers. Therefore the estimates of world reserves vary substantially, ranging from 1,149 billion barrels (BP's 2003 estimate) to 750 billion barrels (estimate of the Association for the Study of Peak Oil, or ASPO). The data published by the International Energy Agency are based on information provided by private oil companies. These data are biased by the strategies deployed by the companies concerned. Shell in 2004 is an exemplary, though extreme, case. The company was obliged to reduce its highly overvalued published reserve figure by 3.9 billion barrels, i.e. by more than 20 per cent, to meet the requirements of the stock market supervisors. A major reason for this 'error' and its correction was 'creative book-keeping'. The company had exaggerated the reserves for its annual report, in order to boost its market value (and with it, the salaries of its top managers).

OPEC countries for their part are interested in high reserve figures for two reasons: First, they increase their estimate of reserves in order to get a higher OPEC production quota. Typically, during the late 1980s 'six of the 11 OPEC nations increased their reserve figures by colossal amounts, ranging from 42 to 197 per cent, simply to boost their export quotas'.[30] Iraq reported in 1983 (during the war against Iran) an increase of reserves of 11 billion barrels, although there was no verifiable discovery of new fields. In 1985 Kuwait notified an increase of 50 per cent in its reserves, without any proof, and did so again in 2006. The second reason for reports of high reserves is to influence oil consumers. High reserves in oil-producing countries signal that in the future there will be no shortage of oil, and that therefore the search for alternatives (i.e. for renewable energy) is an unnecessary expense. On the other hand the reserves may be *under*estimated in order to increase the hidden reserves of an oil company, or to push up the oil-price in order to make it profitable to explore non-conventional oil (deep sea-oil; oil-sand; polar oil, heavy oil) and to invest in costly new infrastructure (pipelines, tankers, refineries, etc.).

Uncertainty about the real amount of reserves is therefore remarkably high, as the difference cited above between the figures given by BP and ASPO clearly shows. But what is absolutely certain is that the reserves are declining, even though at an industry conference in Johannesburg in September 2005 the Saudi oil minister Ali al-Naimi informed the world that his country would soon almost double its 'proven' reserve base and add 200 billion barrels to its current reserves estimate of 264 billion barrels. Sceptics suggest, in contrast, that Saudi Arabia already is running out of oil because the country is approaching the peak or has already passed it. Moreover, the costs of extraction are increasing, even in the largest Saudi Arabian Ghawar oil-field.[31] The Saudi estimate is very likely flawed, simply because the higher the reserves, the higher the market power of the oil producer.[32]

The effects of the emissions of greenhouse gases in the course of oil consumption are also highly contested. In capitalist calculations the ecological limits of production and accumulation are recognized only as an increase in the costs of production and distribution, and as a pressure on the rate of return. Calculations by the German Institute for Economic Research (DIW) suggest that the annual costs of climate change will be about $2,000 billion from the middle of the century onwards.[33] The hurricanes of autumn 2005 already caused damage valued at about US$200 billion, not counting the human cost or their destructive effects on the social fabric.[34] The effects of production and consumption on society and nature are irrelevant for capitalist decision-making, so long as they remain 'external' to the calculations of single firms. But this is the case only so long as the 'carrying capacity' and the recuperative capacity of nature and social systems are sufficient to withstand the pollution caused. Otherwise these effects become part of the 'general conditions of production', increase the costs of production, and have a negative effect on profitability and accumulation, until a crisis finally breaks out.[35]

Attempts to internalize these costs, e.g. by emissions trading, do not offer a real solution. Emissions certificates, or the 'clean development mechanism', are designed as financial instruments which serve the financial industry, not the environment.[36] It is possible to substitute artificial paper money for natural gold,[37] but it is not possible to substitute certificates and bonds, traded on a special stock exchange, for an increase of CO_2 particles in the atmosphere, or for a rise in average temperatures. Here again the two forms of oil as a commodity are evident: as a use value, with the natural characteristics of sat-isfying human needs and violating the natural environment, and as exchange value, with a monetary form. The first form of oil ('wet oil') is the object of geopolitical calculations, mostly undertaken by neo-conservative think tanks and politicians. The second form ('paper oil') is left to regulation by the mar-ket mechanism, cheered on by neo-liberal think tanks and politicians. As we approach the end of the fossil energy regime conflicts are becoming sharper, both on the input side, over access to oil resources, as well as on the output side, over the environmental consequences of petrol-combustion.

Climate change is evidently occurring much faster than had been as-sumed, so that pressure for immediate action, i.e. for a considerable reduc-tion of greenhouse-gas emissions, is increasing. One of the worst scenarios of climate change has been presented, paradoxically, in a study commissioned by the Pentagon and carried out by Peter Schwartz and Doug Randall of the Global Business Network.[38] Different regions of the world will experience different patterns of climate change. Some may well be hit in the near future by colder periods, because of the changing pattern of global air and water circulation. The study adopts the view taken by the International Panel of Climate Change (IPCC) that average global temperature is likely to increase by up to 5.8^0 C by 2100. Since this increase in temperature will melt the Greenland ice sheet, the Gulf Stream may change its direction due to lower density and salination in the waters of the North Atlantic. This process is ex-pected to be very rapid, 'disrupting the temperate climate of Europe…Ocean circulation patterns change, bringing less warm water north and causing an immediate shift in the weather in Northern Europe and eastern North America…'.[39] Over time, Europe would be severely affected as 'conflicts over land and water use are likely to become more severe – and more violent. As states become increasingly desperate, the pressure for action will grow'.[40]

Even if climate change is less dramatic than this analysis suggests, and does not occur as suddenly as assumed in the Pentagon scenario, and even if new technologies are developed for improving energy efficiency, for capturing and storing carbon gas in the deep oceans or in the underground of dry oil fields, and even if there is 'abiogenetic' oil in the soil.[41] This does not gainsay how conflict-prone the use of fossil energies will very likely remain – both on the 'input side' of energy provision at the beginning of the energy-chain, and on the 'output side' of greenhouse gas emissions at the end of it.

OLIGARCHIC ENERGY RESOURCE DISTRIBUTION AND PETRO-IMPERIALISM

Every nation, constrained by the logics of industrial and post-industrial capitalism, needs to have access to the common good of fossil fuel reserves.[42] But the transformation of natural riches (matter and energy) into the wealth of nations is not possible for all peoples. The 'wealth of nations' is a 'positional', an 'oligarchic' or 'club' good for the minority who belong to the club of global oligarchs.[43] The 'others' are more or less excluded from access to it.

How does the social process of exclusion work? When the distribution of the positional good, of oil under conditions of shortage, is left to market forces and the processes of price formation, some oil consumers cannot afford to pay for it. This is the market economy form of dispossession. It is fully compatible with the institutional order and the belief system of a 'free market society'. Another mode of distributing oil resources is the exercise of political power and military violence to achieve dispossession by force. Most likely a mixture of these two modes will rule the 'Great Game', the battle for the control of scarce oil resources in the twenty-first century. These are the forces at play in the new 'petro-strategy', the emerging oil- and greenhouse-imperialism, in which geo-economics and geopolitics are combined. It is not very likely that fossil resources will be distributed through a democratic, solidaristic rationing of oil reserves.[44]

As we have seen, the dynamics of modern capitalism are due to productivity increases, powered by fossil fuel. The production of relative surplus value is the key to increased profits, positive interest rates and − in the peaks of the business cycle − even rising wages. Under conditions of energy shortage and increasing energy prices the accumulation of capital falls back on absolute surplus value production; accumulation increasingly takes the form of processes of dispossession of the less powerful by more powerful private corporations and national states.[45] The 'oil security' of countries and alliances is competitive and conflict-prone, and leads to a decline in human security. Less powerful peoples and classes are excluded from crucial decisions about the development of the world, and are hit by a growing proportion of the negative external effects of growth. Their living conditions deteriorate as the natural environment undergoes a progressive deterioration.

The highly developed countries, particularly the United States, rely on both market power and military power in conflicts over oil-resources, and for the defence of the country in the conflicts which can be anticipated to arise from climate change. The neo-liberal glorification of a free market in a global 'geo-economy' and the 'geo-political' recourse to national military power are central axiom of the ideologies of American neo-conservatives. In the cynical words of Thomas Friedman, the invisible hand of the market must be supported by the visible fist of the American army. This, however, only reflects a long tradition of US 'oil–empire' strategy: American wealth, power and supremacy have been founded on 'cheap and abundant oil flows', and on the Rockefeller–Baku-connection, from the nineteenth century to the present.[46]

'Oil security' is one of the priorities of the US and other powerful oil-consuming countries or blocs, such as the EU.[47] It represents nothing else than a political attempt to ensure that the previously mentioned congruence between social form, economic dynamics, rationality and energy provision, on which the capitalist system depends, is maintained. 'Oil security' has several dimensions: first, the strategic control of oil territories; second, the strategic control of oil logistics (pipe lines, the routes of oil tankers, refineries and storage facilities); third, influencing the price of oil by controlling supply and demand on markets; and fourth, determining the currency in which the price of oil is invoiced. When we consider the many strands in a complex strategy of oil security or 'oil imperialism' the formula of 'blood for oil' seems much too simple. Yet it is essentially correct.

Strategic control over oil regions can be secured either by means of diplomacy, and the establishment of friendly inter-state relations, as in the Gulf region; or by means of subversion, as in some Latin American and African countries; or by using massive military power, as in Iraq, and to a lesser extent also in Central Asia – and perhaps in the future against Iran and Venezuela. The tradition is long. Adam Smith already distinguished between having diplomatic relations with 'civilized' nations and the use of military power against 'barbaric' nations (today the latter are apt to be called an 'axis of the evil').[48] The strategic objective of military interventions by 'civilized' against 'non-civilized' nations today is represented as a civilizing mission, as in the former Yugoslavia, in Afghanistan and Iraq, and elsewhere. The war waged on Iraq seems to be an irrational undertaking, because a military occupation imposed on a country against the resistance of a hostile population is extremely expensive and, in ways which are difficult to estimate, may well involve a serious weakening of the hegemony of the global superpower.[49] Nevertheless, since 2001 the USA has been well prepared to control the oil regions; it disposes of more than 700 military bases in all parts of the world, many of them aimed at controlling the Caucasus, Central Asia, the Gulf and parts of Africa.[50]

The strategic control of oil logistics is also expensive, but less so. It requires the collaboration of many governments in countries traversed by pipelines, and of countries with coasts which oil tankers pass close by. Central Asia has been labelled '*Pipelineistan*'; that is, the group of states in the region through which the Caspian oil passes. Based as it is on authoritarian and corrupt regimes, US dominance over these states is, however, precarious, and faces challenges not only by 'terrorists' but also by considerable sections of the populations concerned. The crucial role of pipelines became evident in the course of the conflict between Russia and the Ukraine in 2005/06 over the transport of gas from Siberia to Western Europe, and in connection with the planned construction of a pipeline from Russia to Germany that would go through the Baltic Sea without crossing any of the neighbouring Baltic countries or Poland (the North European Gas Pipeline). In Latin America the governments of Venezuela, Brazil, Argentina and Bolivia are trying to establish a continental pipeline system with the aim of intensifying Latin American integration by providing a common infrastructure, rather than creating an open market from Alaska to Tierra del Fuego as the USA, especially, intended with the Free Trade Area of the Americas. Networks of gas and oil pipelines are gaining in importance as the fossil energy regime becomes globalized and oil and, to a lesser extent, gas grow scarcer.

Influence over the supply of oil can only be exercised effectively by influencing OPEC. In the near future the great bulk of oil will come from the OPEC countries of the Middle East, because the oil fields of other, non-OPEC oil producing-countries are expected to deplete sooner. ASPO estimates that by 2010 more than 50 per cent of the world's oil production will come from OPEC countries in the Middle East. Putting diplomatic pressure on individual oil producers, such as the pressure put on Saudi Arabia by the USA, and pushing ahead with oil exploration in parts of the world which have not yet been fully incorporated into the US-dominated global oil-empire, may help to increase the oil supply. The occupation of Iraq, and the establishment of a US-dependent and therefore only formally sovereign Iraqi government, allows the USA to exert some influence on OPEC decisions, since Iraq is a member country and can be used as a vehicle for US oil interests. It is, however, doubtful whether these measures can have a long-lasting impact, simply because Middle-Eastern oil production is also approaching its peak.

A further significant dimension in the struggle for oil is that of finance. The collapse of the Bretton Woods system of fixed exchange rates in the early 1970s reflected the way the US dollar was weakened vis á vis other currencies both by the loss of the competitive advantage the US had enjoyed for some two decades after the Second World War and by the cost of the war against the Vietnamese people. Faced with this situation, the oil-exporting countries had only one chance to compensate for the losses they incurred due to the decline of the US dollar as the currency in which oil contracts were denominated: they seized the opportunity of the Israeli–Arab Yom Kippur war of October 1973 to increase the oil price. The jump from less than $2 to more than $11 per barrel was experienced in oil-importing countries as a severe 'shock'. At that time an option that was not available to oil producers was invoicing their oil in a currency other than the US dollar. More than thirty years later, however, the situation has fundamentally changed. One of the reasons is the 'financialization' of oil trading on future markets, and the concentration of oil quotations on the Chicago and London stock exchanges. The role of 'paper oil' in the formation of oil prices is increasing, since financial innovations on globalized and liberalized financial markets allow it. The price of oil is now determined not only by 'wet oil' but also by 'paper oil'. It is in this context that the Iranian threat to establish an Iranian oil exchange, trading in alternative currencies, especially in the Euro, putting the 'petro-euro' in competition with the 'petro-dollar', may be especially significant.[51]

So long as the big export surplus countries continue keeping their reserves in US dollars it is unimportant whether oil is priced in US dollars or euros or any other currency. However, at the end of the day the issued dollars return to the USA, presented by external creditors. Their claims must be met in real terms (by exports of US goods and services) or by the sale to them of real assets in the USA, or there will be an exchange of foreign claims into other currencies or gold. The USA, which since the 1970s has become a structurally importing country, would then have to reduce its imports and stimulate exports. This is only possible by means of an increase in the domestic savings rate and a decrease in domestic consumption, military expenditures included. A switch of other countries' reserves out of US dollars into other currencies would thus be a blow to the seignorage position of the imperial power.

The days of the congruence of capitalism and the energy regime perfectly based on the use of oil, gas and coal are, or soon will be, over. It is unlikely that new discoveries of oil reserves can keep pace with growing demand. The oil price is going up and is already becoming an obstacle to growth for many oil-consuming countries.[52] On the other hand, for oil-producing countries, their natural riches frequently become a curse because of the thirst for oil of powerful oil-importing countries, leading to geopolitical tensions and vulnerability. 'Global resource warfare' is not just the consequence of oil-shortage and climate effects but is mainly caused by attempts to secure the prerequisites for the systemic congruence between growth and accumulation of capital.[53]

A 'SOLAR REVOLUTION': THE TRANSITION TO
A RENEWABLE ENERGY REGIME

There seems in fact to be only one realistic alternative to oil imperialism – a shift from dependence on oil to a dependence on renewable energy sources, on the radiation energy released by the sun (and its derivatives such as photovoltaic, eolic, water, wave and biotic energy, etc.), or on volcanic and geothermal energy. The Neolithic revolution shows that it is possible to bring about a remarkable increase in the productivity of labour and resources on the basis of solar energy, and a similar increase in productivity after the transition from the fossil regime to a 'solar society' cannot be excluded. Technical and social progress will not end with the fossil energy regime, but it will have to be directed into new non-fossil, and non-capitalist, trajectories.

At present any shift to non-fossil renewable energy is a response to energy scarcity and therefore a temporary and sometimes an emergency solution. The Brazilian experience after the first oil price shock of 1973 is an example: the military government of the time initiated a 'pro-alcool' programme for the production of ethanol from sugar cane. About 35 years later Brazil's democratic president Lula da Silva has offered technological expertise in the production of ethanol to other governments in Latin America, in order to help face the recent energy crisis. In the volcanic regions of Central America and the Andes it also is possible to tap volcanic and geothermal energy. But these alternative energies build upon the technology of fossil capitalism and on capitalism's social form, its temporal and spatial structures, and thus only impart a very limited impulse to human development.

The transition to renewable energy requires appropriate technologies, but requires even more appropriate social institutions and economic forms. A system based on renewable energy also needs a certain congruence of social form, technology, economic regulation and the energy used, which in this case can be understood as involving a *solar revolution*. Such a revolution must involve a radical transformation of the patterns of production and consumption, life and work, gender relations and the spatial and temporal organization of social life. Capitalist crises are not restricted to the energy crisis, and social movements with comprehensive perspectives and projects are emerging aimed at realizing new social forms such as a 'solidary economy' and reviving old cooperative forms of a 'moral economy'. The social basis of a society based on renewable energies is spreading. It must be more radical than anything aspired to, let alone achieved, by the socialist revolutions of the twentieth century – a holistic endeavour, which can only be carried out over an extended period of time. The reason is obvious. Capitalism was the most dynamic social system in the history of mankind because of the congruence of social forms and mechanisms, rationality and energy provision. A society based on renewable instead of fossil energy sources must develop adequate technologies and above all social forms beyond capitalism. The relation of society to nature cannot remain the same when the fuel driving capitalist dynamics is running out.

NOTES

I am grateful for useful comments on earlier versions of the text by Birgit Mahnkopf, Achim Brunnengräber, Ursula Huws and others, and for linguistic corrections by Patricia Margerison.

1   Andrew McKillop, 'The Myth of Decoupling', in Andrew McKillop with Sheila Newman, ed., *The Final Energy Crisis*, Copenhagen, London: Pluto Press, 2005, pp. 197-216; Harry G. Frankfurt, *On Bullshit*, Princeton: Princeton University Press, 2005.

2   J.B. Opschoor, *Environment, Economics and Sustainable Development*, Groningen: Wolters Noordhoff Publishers, 1992; Wuppertal Institut für Klima, Umwelt, Energie, *Zukunftsfähiges Deutschland. Ein Beitrag zu einer global nachhaltigen Entwicklung*, Basel: Birkhäuser, 1995.

3   For a discussion of the many aspects of the precautionary principle see Poul Harremoës, David Gee and Malcolm MacGarvin, *Late Lessons from Early Warnings: The Precautionary Principle 1896-2000,* Environmental Issue Report Number 22, Copenhagen: European Environment Agency, 2002.

4   In a more elaborated paper it would be necessary to differentiate between coal, oil and gas. Their role in the history of capital accumulation is quite different. In this article fossil fuel mostly refers to petroleum, and the analysis of coal and gas is excluded.

5   William R. Clark, *Petrodollar Warfare. Oil, Iraq and the Future of the Dollar,* Gabriola Island: New Society Publishers, 2005, p. 79.

6   Kenneth S. Deffeyes, *Beyond Oil. The View from Hubbert's Peak*, New York: Hill and Wang, 2005; Colin J. Campbell, 'The Assessment and Importance of Oil Depletion', in McKillop, *The Final Energy Crisis*, pp. 29-55.

7   E.g. Stehen Bunker, *Underdeveloping the Amazon*, Chicago: University of Illinois Press, 1985; see also the interesting debate on the 'value of nature' in Hans Immler/Wolfdietrich Schmied-Kowarzik, *Marx und die Naturfrage – Ein Wissenschaftsstreit*, Hamburg:VSA, 1994.

8   Joan Martinez-Alier, *Ecological Economics. Energy, Environment and Society*, Oxford: Basil Blackwell, 1987, p. 3.

9   I do not deal with nuclear energy because of space limitations. But nuclear energy is no alternative to fossil energy. First, it is also running out (in about four decades) and second, the negative external effects (from nuclear accidents like that of Chernobyl to the disposal of nuclear waste) are so significant that its use is ecologically irrational and ethically unjustifiable.

10   David Harvey, *Justice, Nature & the Geography of Difference*, Oxford: Blackwell, 1996; Elmar Altvater and Birgit Mahnkopf, *Grenzen der Globalisierung. Politik, Ökonomie und Ökologie in der Weltgesellschaft*, Fourth Edition, Münster: West-fälisches Dampfboot, 2004. Since time and space are the coordinates of nature in which we live, however, their compression involves breaking with the natural conditions of work and life, of the 'external' environment as well as of the 'internal' environment – i.e. of human health.

11   Max Weber, *Wirtschaft und Gesellschaft,* Studienausgabe, Tübingen: J.C.B. Mohr Paul Siebeck, (1921) 1976, p. 534.

12   Karl Polanyi, *The Great Transformation: The Political and Economic Origins of Our Time*, New York: Viking Press (1944) 1957.

13   Karl Marx, *Das Kapital*, 3 Bände, in *Marx-Engels-Werke*, Bände 23-25, Berlin: Dietz Verlag, 1970.

14   Nicholas Georgescu-Roegen, *The Entropy Law and the Economic Process*, Cambridge: Harvard University Press, 1971.

15   Angus Maddison, *The World Economy. A Millenial Perspective*, Paris: OECD Development Centre Studies, 2001. Maddison showed that in the first millennium after Christ, from 0 to 1000 AD, world population grew at an average annual rate of 0.02 per cent from 230.8 million to 268.3 million. Between 1000 to 1820 the number increased to 1041.1 million. GDP per capita followed a similar trend: in the first millennium there was a slight decrease, from an average of $444 to $435 a year per capita (in 1990 dollars). Between 1000 and 1820 AD there was an increase to $667 per capita.

16   Ibid., p. 28.

17   Richard A. Easterlin, *Growth Triumphant. The Twenty-first Century in Historical Perspective*, Ann Arbor: Michigan University Press, 1998.

18   Richard Heinberg, *The Party's Over*, Gabriola Island: New Society Publishers, 2003.

19   Georgescu-Roegen, *The Entropy Law*, p. 303.

20   Ilya Prigogine and Isabelle Stenger, *Dialog mit der Natur*, München: Piper, 1986.

21   See Georgescu-Roegen, *The Entropy Law*, p. 288.

22   Karl Marx, *Capital*, Volume 1, Penguin Books: Harmondsworth, 1976, p. 638-9.

23   Eric Hobsbawm, *Age of Extremes. The Short Twentieth Century 1914-1991*, London: Michael Joseph, 1994, chapter 10.

24   There is no consensus among analysts about oil availability and the extent of reserves. The oil industry (BP) estimates that there are still 1150 bn barrels of secure reserves in the ground whereas the Association for the Study of Peak Oil only calculates ca 750 bn barrels. But even on the basis of the former estimate, and without taking into account increasing demand, BP itself estimates that the (static) reserves will only last another 41 years, or not quite the time of two generations. See BP Statistical Review of World Energy, June 2005; and for overviews, Deffeyes, *Beyond Oil*, Seppo Korpela, *Oil Depletion in the United States and the World*, A working paper for a talk to Ohio Petroleum Marketers Association at their annual meeting in Columbus, Ohio, 1 May 2002, available

at http://www.peakoil.com and Korpela, 'Prediction of World Peak Oil Production', in McKillop, *The Final Energy Crisis*, pp. 11-28.

25   See Deffeyes, *Beyond Oil* and his updated prediction based on new data that the peak of global oil production was passed on 16 December 2005: http://www.princeton.edu/hubbert/current-events-06-02.html.

26   In a two-paged advertisement in the *Financial Times*, 26 July 2005, Chevron writes: 'It took us 125 years to use the first trillion barrels of oil. We'll use the next trillion in 30'.

27   It only can be mentioned here that there are also two other pressures exerted by the financial system on quantities and prices of supply on world oil markets. One arises from speculation on future markets; much of the increase in oil prices in the years since 2004 is due to financial speculation. The other is due to the fact that rich oil producers of the Gulf region have heavily invested their 'petro-dollars' into financial assets so that their income in the meanwhile is as dependent on returns on invested capitals and interest flows as on oil rents.

28   Off-shore drilling has the disadvantage of high extraction costs but it has the 'advantage' of insulating oil-drilling from the peoples concerned about it and thus of avoiding conflicts. On the Nigerian case see David Hallowes and Mark Butler, *Whose Energy Future? Big Oil Against People in Africa. groundWork Report 2005*, Pietermaritzburg: groundWork, 2005.

29   Colin Campbell and Jean H. Laherrère, 'The End of Cheap Oil', *Scientific American*, March, 1998, pp. 44.

30   Ibid.

31   André Salem, 'Wundersame Ölvermehrung', *Internationale Politik*, February, 2006, pp. 44-49.

32   Colin Campbell, 'The Assessment and Importance of Oil Depletion', in McKillop, *The Final Energy Crisis*, pp. 38; see also: http://www.energybulletin.net/9314.html.

33   Claudia Kemfert, 'Die ökonomischen Kosten des Klimawandels', *DIW-Wochenbericht*, 42, 2004.

34   In the cases of the Tsunamis around Christmas 2004 and the devastating hurricane in New Orleans the rescue work of help organizations, of governments and international organizations was in some ways even more destructive than the natural disaster, as Naomi Klein convincingly has pointed out: 'The Rise of Disaster Capitalism', *The Nation*, 2 May 2005.

35   This is the theme of James O'Connor, *Natural Causes. Essays in Ecological Marxism*, London: Guilford Press, 1998.

36   For a good discussion of the implications of the clean development mechanism in Africa, see Megan Lindow, 'A New Source of African Finance', in Patrick Bond and Rehana Dada, eds., *Trouble in the Air. Global Warming and the Privatised Atmosphere*, Durban: TNI/Centre for Civil Society, 2005, pp. 54-63.

37   Gold is a telling example of the abstraction of economics from natural boundaries. Gold is, by its very nature, a limited resource, although socially and economically it functions as money. Since capitalist accumulation ignores natural boundaries and money is a social construct, the function of money has been de-coupled from the natural form of gold and ascribed to paper-money or

electronic bits and bytes. Money in a nature-form has nearly completely disappeared. Attempts to revive gold as the natural form of money, as Jaques Rueff tried to do under de Gaulle in the 1960s, are a ridiculous and anachronistic undertaking.

38   Peter Schwarz and Doug Randall, *An Abrupt Climate Change Scenario and Its Implications for United States Security*, Washington: Pentagon, 2003, available at http://www.ems.org.

39   Ibid., p. 9.

40   Ibid., p. 16.

41   There are arguments against the peak oil thesis based on the hypothesis of an abiogenic, volcanic origin of oil. If there are massive oil reserves deep in the crust and mantle of the earth then the world's oil supply may extend far into the future. The hypothesis is rather old; it can be traced back to the writings of Alexander von Humboldt in the early 19th century. It was developed during the cold war in the former Soviet Union and is coming up again towards the end of the (biogenic) fossil energy regime. However, the hypothesis is not proved by geo-science and is heavily criticized for fostering complacency about the existing fossil energy regime. Even if there are abiogenic oil reserves it has to be calculated whether the EROEI is positive in the case of oil drilling at depths of 5000 meters and more (for a good overview on the controversy on the biogenic or abiogenic origin of oil see the Wikipedia entry, 'Abiogenic Petroleum Origin', http://en.wikipedia.org).

42   Comparable to other natural resources, oil can be understood as a global public good because it came into being over hundreds of million years by natural processes and not with the help of human activities. Today the global commons, the natural riches, are transformed into private wealth by means of the assignment of property rights, the transformation of resources and goods into commodities which are sold against money on global markets. The private appropriation of commons is the other side of an expropriation or dispossession of peoples. This double sided process of valorization ('Inwertsetzung'), of transforming commons into private goods in history is only possible by the exercise of political power and therefore in history this process has always been pushed by the state. In most cases it also has triggered resistance.

43   Roy Harrod, 'The Possibility of Economic Satiety – Use of Economic Growth for Improving the Quality of Education and Leisure', in Committee for Economic Development, *Problems of United States Economic Development*, Volume 1, New York: Committee for Economic Development, 1958, pp. 207-13; Fred Hirsch, *Die sozialen Grenzen des Wachstums*, Reinbek: Rowohlt, 1978.

44   A fourth form is that of charity, which President Chavez practised in winter 2005/2006. He seized the opportunity of energy shortages in the USA by offering cheap and subsidised Venezuelan oil for US citizens in need of otherwise unaffordable energy supply. Poor people who cannot afford to pay the oil-bill, to fill the gas-tank or to pay for electricity also are forced to switch to other heating energies, from wood by cutting the remaining forests or from industrial waste collected from nearby factories. Many poor people have no alternative

except to look for non-fossil energy provision or to 'steal' energy by tapping electricity lines.

45   David Harvey, 'The "New" Imperialism: Accumulation by Dispossession', in *Socialist Register 2004*; David Harvey, *The New Imperialism*, Oxford: Oxford University Press, 2003; Massimo de Angelis, 'Separating the Doing and the Deed: Capital and the Continuous Character of Enclosures', *Historical Materialism*, 12(2), 2004.

46   Michael Klare, *Blood and Oil. The Dangers and Consequences of America's Growing Dependency on Imported Petroleum*, New York: Metropolitan Books, 2004. For the Friedman quip, and others in this vein, see the opening paragraph of Leo Panitch and Sam Gindin's essay, 'Global Capitalism and American Empire' in the *Socialist Register 2004*.

47   Ibid.; Cheney-Report: National Energy Policy Development Group, *National Energy Policy – Reliable, Affordable, and Environmentally Sound Energy for America's Future*, Washington: US Government Printing Office, 2001. For an overview on Europe, see Frank Umbach, 'Europas nächster Kalter Krieg', *Internationale Politik*, February, 2006.

48   Adam Smith, *An Inquiry into the Nature and Causes of the Wealth of Nations*, edited by E. Cannan, Ann Arbor: The University of Chicago Press, 1976, fifth book.

49   It is not possible to calculate rationally and exactly the costs of a war. It only is possible to estimate the dimensions of costs in monetary terms. Joseph Stiglitz and Linda Bilmes come to the conclusion that the costs of the Iraq war and the occupation, assuming it lasts no longer than 2010, will reach up to 2200 billion US$ (*Süddeutsche Zeitung*, 5 April 2006).

50   Chalmers Johnston, *Der Selbstmord der amerikanischen Demokratie*, München: Goldmann, 2004.

51   See William R. Clark, *Petrodollar Warfare: Oil, Iraq and the Future of the Dollar*, Gabriola Island: New Society Publishers, 2005.

52   Andrew Simms quoted in Hallowes and Butler, *Whose Energy Future?*, p. 44.

53   See Clark, *Petrodollar Warfare*, p. 93; Andy Stern begins his book *Who Won the Oil Wars?* with the sentence: 'Since the birth of the modern oil industry in the middle of the 19th century, the pursuit of oil has brought out three characteristics in mankind: greed, corruption and belligerence'. Stern, *Who Won the Oil Wars? Why Governments Wage Wars for Oil Rights*, London: Collins & Brown, 2005, p. 7.

THE ECOLOGICAL QUESTION: CAN CAPITALISM PREVAIL?

DANIEL BUCK

There are signs everywhere that the natural resources that provide the inputs for our material commodity economy are being used up faster than they are being replaced by the physical, biochemical and ecological processes that produced them in the first instance (the most salient example is oil, but why stop there?). Amid cries that we may have already reached 'peak oil', accelerating conversion of the world's tropical rain forests and all they imply to 'use values' in the present, rapid depletion of the world's fisheries, rising prices for metals and minerals, and a growing consensus among the scientific community that human–induced global warming is not only a fact, but that we may be approaching catastrophic 'tipping points', it is easy, logical, and even sane to arrive at the conclusion that this, surely, must be the crisis that finally will destroy the wild juggernaut of capitalism.

This is the 'ecological question'.[1] But these apocalyptic visions of resource exhaustion forcing capitalism's final crisis rest upon overly narrow understandings of what, exactly, constitute natural resources. Natural resources are posited to be out there, natural things that can be picked up, cut down, mined or otherwise gathered, processed, and used. They are finite, and once used up will be gone. There is some hedging of this position, of course: forests can be re-planted, tin cans and bottles can be recycled. But this view takes resources to be strictly natural, rather than just as much social. That is, it overlooks how things found in the natural world only become useful to human societies in the context of particular socio-technical frameworks. It thus fails to adequately grasp technology and especially the dynamism of technological innovation and change under capitalism. Furthermore, these visions of final crisis tend to confuse particular manifestations of capitalism – that is, particular historical social formations – with capitalism itself, thus underestimating the flexibility of the beast. This short essay will unpack both of these assertions to argue that capitalism very likely will survive the 'ecological challenge', though this need not imply that the future will be rosy, utopian, or even based upon some kind of post-resource (as in post-industrial) political economy. Finally, the almost exclusive focus of the debate on the ways that capitalism must be regulated by the state into adopting solutions, should be shifted to take better account of the ways that capitalism could very well accumulate its own way to solutions – at whatever cost to humanity.

MARKET- OR PRICE-DRIVEN TECHNOLOGICAL CHANGE

The simplest and most intuitive, though as we shall see fully inadequate, reason that capitalism will not fail due to resource exhaustion is that when something becomes relatively scarce, its price will tend to rise. This engenders a host of possible reactions, ranging from reduced consumption of a resource through simple economizing, to increased extraction from sources previously too marginal, difficult, dangerous, or for whatever other reasons too expensive. Timber will be cut further from roads or on steeper slopes, mines shafts will be dug deeper or following less productive veins, and so on. Higher prices also create new incentives to develop more efficient and cost-effective ways to extract and process resources, and encourage shifts to existing but hitherto more costly substitute resources or technologies. For example, recent rapid increases in oil prices have driven chemical companies to start looking at coal again, as a substitute for oil.[2] Or, solar and wind power technologies, far too costly when oil is selling for $9 a barrel (in 1998), start looking economically feasible when oil reaches $70.

These kinds of shifts, reactions to exogenous price shocks, are real and will play an important role in ameliorating the economic impact of increasing resource scarcity. But as oil becomes scarce and climbs above $100, even $400 or $500 a barrel, it will threaten the kind of radical time-space de-compression suggested by Elmar Altvater,[3] and with it the collapse of the vast systems weaving together industry, agriculture, and our cities and modern societies. Surely, then, such incremental adaptations and improvements on existing techniques will not be enough? At this point we are usually reminded of stories such as predictions in the late nineteenth century that the impending exhaustion of coal reserves would lead to the collapse of the industrial world – predictions made just before the discovery of petroleum. Can this civilization-saving discovery be replicated, or was that just a one-off? What miraculous new discovery will save us this time?[4]

The usual answer to these questions is that new scientific breakthroughs and technological advancements will save us. But the very story of the discovery of oil poses a prior question – why was it not discovered before? Since oil had been there all along, usually thought of as a sticky smelly nuisance, what was it about that particular time and place that produced its discovery? And for that matter, this notion about shifting to other technologies and resources in response to shifting price parameters, does it not also assume that those technologies are already out there, ready to be picked up and used? That those resources are already resources, that is, already 'discovered'? Is part of the problem our use of the word 'discovery'? Looked at this way, it should be apparent that the term natural resource is to an important extent an oxymoron, that something in the natural world only becomes useful to humans in the context of a particular socio-technical framework that can make use of it. And this puts the question of technology change back at the center of analysis.

ACCUMULATION-DRIVEN TECHNOLOGICAL CHANGE

While the dynamics described above are real and an important driver of change, they are 'weak' versions of technology change that misunderstand the centrality of technology to the capitalist mode of production. Part of the problem is that technology change is assumed to be external, exogenous, rather than an intrinsic part of the internal dynamism of capitalism itself. At the very heart of Marx's analysis of capitalism is labour, which is 'first of all, a process between man [sic] and nature, a process by which man, through his own actions, mediates, regulates, and controls the metabolism between himself and nature'.[5] We are thus reminded that all societies, in all places and times, have in common the performance of labour (which is always social labour in one form or another) on nature in order to convert it into the use values that people consume in order to survive,[6] at whatever socially and historically determined level of consumption.[7] All labour is thus social and ultimately related – no matter how distantly – to the conversion of nature to use values. At first glance it appears that Marx posited nature as out there, resources which human labour can 'appropriate' and convert to use values. But this human labour is not innocent or 'natural'. Several chapters later in *Capital* we read that 'technology reveals the active relation of man to nature, the direct process of the production of his life, and thereby it also lays bare the process of production of the social relations of his life, and of the mental conceptions that flow from those relations'.[8] So even though people 'confront the materials of nature as a force of nature', this confrontation or activity is not only social, it is always already mediated, performed through, and indeed constituted by technology.[9] Further, this passage highlights how technology lies at the center of a web of dialectically-related components of a social formation (the components, in the most expansive sense, being technology, relations of man to nature, the forces and relations of production, and mental conceptions).

Social formations are always historical, and this leads us to an additional and even stronger sense in which technological dynamism is at the heart of capitalism. Capitalists must compete, and as Marx demonstrates in *Capital*, and more poetically in the *Communist Manifesto*, relentless competition forces them to constantly innovate just to avoid being thrown into the ranks of the proletariat. The bourgeoisie simply 'cannot exist without constantly revolutionizing the means of production'.[10] In this larger context, the limited notions of change depicted in the previous section appear as relics of the kind of narrow thinking produced by mainstream economic theories of perfect competition, where capitalists react rationally to shifting price signals in the market.[11] They manoeuvre to keep up or stay ahead of one another within a given framework of competition, generally by looking for ways to cut costs and develop cheaper ways to do the same thing – in short, more efficient ways to allocate existing resources. Change in this mode is reactive and thus strangely passive. It is incremental, and rarely changes the framework of competition, resulting instead in a falling rate of profit, to which capitalists react by again reducing costs. One problem with this is that it implicitly assumes that capitalists like to compete on a level playing field, that they actually believe their own hype about free market competition. But what any capitalist really wants is a monopoly, a solid and unassailable market position vis-à-vis the competition. One of the most assured ways to achieve that (short of friends in high places) is not by beating one's competitors incrementally within a given framework, but by transforming the framework, by breaking through to a whole new framework and gaining an absolute rather than relative advantage (if only temporarily, until the others catch up). The huge profits that can accrue to the agents of such transformations push capitalists to actively seek out new forms of absolute advantage by creating something new, whether new products, whole new ways of doing things (new forms of organization), new production processes or machinery... new materials...new resources....

So the real action in the game is not about the most efficient allocation of existing resources, but the creation of new ones. Relentless competition drives innovation in the strongest sense, which in turn spills over to transform other aspects of modern life: 'constant revolutionizing of production, uninterrupted disturbance of all social relations, everlasting uncertainty and agitation, distinguish the bourgeois epoch from all earlier times. All fixed, fast-frozen relationships, with their train of venerable ideas and opinions, are swept away, all new-formed ones become obsolete before they can ossify. All that is solid melts into air…'.[12] Social formations, those webs of relationships constituting a kind of whole or totality, are thus always not only historical but also constantly in motion, hurtled along by the incessant waves of creative destruction unleashed by bourgeoisie innovation. And at the heart of any social formation is technology, or to be more precise, since a formation is always historical, a particular and particularly historical technological framework or set of scientific and technological knowledges and practices.

FRAMES OF LONG-WAVE DEVELOPMENT

Capital has at its core a logic of continuous self-expansion, and when the different components of a social formation work together in a synergistic enough fashion the formation expands.[13] This growth and expansion take the material and social form of long waves of industrialization of specific territories. In *The Capitalist Imperative*, Michael Storper and Richard Walker argue that at the heart of each long wave are one or more 'base technologies' that comprise a technological framework. Contrary to popular understandings, and myths of eccentric inventors and professors tinkering in their labs, innovations often occur in industry ahead of scientific understanding (the scientists then figure out why it works). Shifts occur when capitalists, driven by strong and unrelenting competition, make or deploy a series of greater and lesser inventions to break through into a new technological framework, creating whole new industries and opening up new possibilities in existing ones. Capitalists race to take advantage of the new opportunities, but these spread through industries unevenly. For each long wave of development over the last few centuries we can identify clusters of leading industries which are 'propelled by the unfolding possibilities of one or more base technologies' that define whole epochs of economic history.[14]

The history is complex and overlapping, but to give just a few overly simple examples: spinning, weaving, and iron smelting and casting helped usher in the Industrial Revolution; advances in machine-making transformed industrial technology in the second half of the nineteenth century; electricity, chemistry, and the internal combustion engine reworked everything again around the turn of the twentieth century; only to be transformed again by advances in electronics, petrochemicals, and aerospace and a handful of other areas in the post-war era. One of the most important leading edges of capitalist development in the last few decades has been the silicon/digital revolution, and we are still watching it continue to expand and play out as even the most mundane things are reworked around the new possibilities and capabilities of the new framework.[15] Soon we will all have toasters made with metal parts embodying machine-tool principles developed in the late nineteenth century, plastic components derived from the petrochemical revolution of the post-war period, and guided by programmed chips developed in the late twentieth century.

This view of capitalism as existing in the shape of particular, historical social formations that are in motion, constantly upset and driven forward as fierce and relentless competition forces capitalists to make breakthrough innovations that revolutionize production and unsettle social relations in waves of creative destruction, fits well with spatio-material histories of capitalism. Technological breakthroughs drive rounds of territorial expansion as the growth of leading sector industries literally produce regional economies, usually leapfrogging over regions produced in previous long waves to produce new ones.[16] Of course, a long wave of producing and competing within a given framework is desirable for capitals for a while, as they must put down the fixed capital and make large investments to viably produce and compete. But eventually the new possibilities inherent in a technological framework reach diminishing returns or are exhausted, and the tendency to equalization and falling rate of profit sets in. Once it does, the only real money to be made is by breaking through the current frameworks (this is not to imply that capitalists wait until a framework is exhausted to begin trying to develop breakthroughs), and the process repeats itself, usually developing along a whole new spatial trajectory. This often takes the form of industrializing new regions, though it can also take the form of re-industrializing and transforming previously industrialized ones.

THE SURVIVAL OF CAPITALISM

So, will capitalism survive? We will answer in three registers. First, what do we mean by the survival of capitalism? Even the quick sketch in the previous section should illustrate that capitalism is not defined by or dependent upon any particular technological milieu or framework, or any particular source of motive power. It is, ultimately, about social relations. For Marx, machines making machines represented the epitome of capitalism, but not the essence. The essence of capitalism is commodities making commodities. The social division of labour and social relations featuring the separation of the proletariat from the means of production are thus analytically prior to machinery, and thus also to any particular source of energy fuelling mechanized production. Capital, as value in motion, does not care about what it makes, the machinery used, or the motive source. It cares only about its own self-expansion and valorization. Even if the post-oil economy fulfils the dystopian post-apocalyptic visions of a return to simple animal, human, and perhaps water and wind power as motive forces, we will still have capitalism as long as we have an industrial reserve army unencumbered by ownership or control of the means of production, as long as the production of commodities by commodities prevails. We must be careful not to confuse particular historical formations of capitalism with capitalism itself.

Second, apocalyptic visions of the final crisis implicitly assume that capitalism will end everywhere. But capitalism has never existed everywhere: its history can be divided between histories of its development in the core and its expansion into and incorporation of places once peripheral. Even in the core its conquest is not and never will be total. The first line of *Capital* begins 'The wealth of those societies in which the capitalist mode of production *prevails...*' (emphasis added), implying that even in the developed core it only prevails, not that it is total. While there may be an internal tendency for capitalism to colonize and commodify all aspects of modern life,[17] even a cursory glance at the ways the line of commodification shifts with each reconstitution of the modern household,[18] and at how capitalism creates non-capitalist spheres outside and even inside itself on which to feed,[19] serve to illustrate that the capitalist mode of production, like Gramsci's hegemony, will never be total and complete. So, how deep and total a capitalism do we need to say it is still capitalism? Even in the event of a radical round of time-space de-compression, who is to say that large pockets of human activity will not continue to exist in which the capitalist mode of production *prevails*? Just because there is an expansionary logic intrinsic in the commodity form does not mean that capitalism cannot contract. And once it contracts, it will have larger areas outside itself in which to expand. But even the metaphors of expansion and contraction are ultimately too clumsy, belying the more complex ways that trajectories of uneven capitalist development territorialize, re-territorialize, and even de-territorialize places in an unconstant geography.

Finally, we come to the ways that capitalism may well accumulate itself out of, or through, an ecological crisis. The survival of capitalism need not be anywhere as stark as surviving pockets of people using antiquated sources of motive power to produce a limited range of inferior commodities for limited distribution. Capitalism is relentlessly in motion, constantly propelling itself forward into new technological frameworks and across space. New frameworks bring new long waves of development, and technological shifts have a way of creating their own demand. Creative destruction sweeps through the installed base of commodities, and everyone must update everything – it is still easy for us to remember the almost silent and only slightly annoying compulsion to switch from VCR to DVD machines, and to sense the coming switch from cathode-ray tube televisions to digital ones. It is just as easy to imagine how breakthroughs in fields such as nanotechnology, biotechnology, and genetic engineering will lead to not just new fuels and more energy-efficient products and industrial processes, but whole new realms of products made of materials and by processes we cannot yet imagine. And these new products and processes will create their own demand, will create new industries that will pull along whole ensembles of supporting services and businesses, and in the process will produce whole new regions (or re-produce existing ones).[20]

Already we hear people saying that the current, highly dispersed spatial pattern of settlement in the West is so completely predicated upon cheap energy that it will be unsustainable and have to be reworked with peak oil.[21] This sounds like a crisis, but from the standpoint of capital actually represents an opportunity – construction and new spatialization is a huge source and part of economic growth under capitalism.[22] All of that building will constitute new demand, and it will be built from new materials using new technologies, giving rise to new sets of industries that supply them, and new kinds of services that supply them in turn. New spatial forms create whole new markets for new kinds of goods – just witness the way suburbanization in post-war America went hand in hand with the elaboration of many of that generation's propulsive industries – automobiles, household appliances, food industries…[23]

Some will argue at this point that shifts to new technological trajectories will entail the devaluation and write-off of massive amounts of capital already fixed in the physical landscape, in the form of our housing and building stock, freeways and transportation networks, and so on, and that the capitalist system could not withstand such a financial shock. But it is important to remember that economic landscapes are frequently swept away in periodic rounds of creative destruction, and that this process is internal to the dynamism of capitalism itself. Fixed capitals only matter in terms of the rate of depreciation. Capital as value-in-motion does not care what fleeting forms it assumes, as long as it valorizes and expands itself within (socially-determined) specified time horizons.[24]

CONCLUSION

Although we have become accustomed to a paucity of R & D investment in alternative energies, that will very likely soon change. Where will the investment come from to fund the research and experimentation for all of this technological change? Rising energy costs will open spaces for new investment in research and development. But more importantly and fundamentally it will come from capital itself, which, even in the form of the huge pools of accumulated value that the multinational oil conglomerates represent, ultimately does not care about oil, or any particular product line, place, or industry. It cares only about its own expanded reproduction.

This is not to put the whole burden on the individual capitalist. Another source of investment, and potential coordination of innovation, is the state. Polanyi argued that society can fight back against the ravages of undue marketization. We usually think of members of the bourgeoisie acting individually in competition with one another, but we must not forget, as Marx himself shows, how they must act collectively at times in order to be able to continue to reproduce themselves as a class (enacting labour laws, education). Whatever one's theory of the state and its relation to the economy, society, and the bourgeoisie, even oil capitals are beginning to make noise about the need to develop alternatives (e.g. the Chevron ad: 'we used the first billion barrels in 125 years, the next billion will take only 35 years…and then it's gone'; or BP's rebranding of itself as Beyond Petroleum). The race for alternative energy sources – some of which may be cleaner, some may not – and the concomitant spillover technologies, has already begun.[25]

There is a strong case to be made that capitalism will survive. But the main point here is that analysis of the ecological question must begin with a more nuanced understanding of resources and technology, must move beyond the simple poles of techno-optimism (science, technology and human ingenuity will save us) and environmental pessimism (resources are running out).[26] And while capitalism may survive, this is not to say that we can safely embrace rosy visions of utopian futures and abandon apocalyptic dystopian ones. We can wonder at the marvellous inventions to come without forgetting the dark sides of new technologies: new technologies of control, surveillance, and exclusion; new contradictions, externalities, and pollutions that we cannot yet imagine (or that are imagined in only the most dystopian science fictions). Nor is this to envision a rosy democratic future, in which radical new technologies will make energy and food and water cheap and plentiful and available to all without effort. Technological breakthroughs create whole new areas of activity and possibility, new sites or commons, as technological developments that are internal to capitalism succeed in creating new terrains that are outside the circuits of capital, only to internalize them again through rounds of privatization, enclosure, primitive accumulation, and monopolization. The classic story of enclosures concerns the removal of the English peasantry from the commons, but we have seen many examples in recent history: the commodification of seeds,[27] water,[28] the Internet, engineered mice,[29] and the human genome. In the current construction of markets for carbon offsets and futures we may be seeing the incipient commodification of the very air we breathe, air which may be increasingly noxious for all those that cannot afford to purchase commodified and distributed clean air.[30]

NOTES

I would like to thank Chris Benner, Gordon Clark, Barbara Harriss-White and Erik Swyngedouw for helpful comments on the first draft of this essay.

1   The 'ecological question' resonates with a long line of 'questions' or problematics within the Marxian tradition: Marx's 'The Jewish Question', Karl Kautsky's 'The Agrarian Question', and Manuel Castells' 'The Urban Question'.
2   *New York Times*, 18 April 2006.
3   Elmar Altvater, this volume. The concept of time-space compression was originally developed by David Harvey (*The Condition of Postmodernity: An Enquiry into the Origins of Cultural Change*, Cambridge: Blackwell, 1989), building on Marx's depiction of the compulsion of capital to 'annihilate space by time'. As very astutely deployed by Altvater in this volume, time-space *de*-compression refers to the unravelling of the ways distance and time have been reduced ɛnd woven together by new and highly complex systems of transportation that rɛly primarily on cheap fossil fuel.
4   It would do well to keep in mind that while there must, indeed, be some finite end to oil, there is also a strong argument to be made that 'peak oil' is in important senses a myth. See Retort (Iain Boal, T.J. Clark, Joseph Matthews, Michael Watts), *Afflicted Powers: Capital and Spectacle in a New Age of War*, London: Verso, 2005, pp. 38-78.
5   Karl Marx, *Capital: A Critique of Political Economy,* Volume 1, Translated by Ben Fowkes, London: Penguin Books, 1976, p. 283.
6   Ibid., p. 290.
7   Ibid., p. 275.
8   Ibid., p. 493.
9   Ibid., p. 283.
10   Karl Marx and Friedrich Engels, *Manifesto of the Communist Party*, cited from *The Marx-Engels Reader*, Second Edition, edited by Robert C. Tucker, New York: Norton, 1978, p. 476.
11   This part of the essay draws heavily from Michael Storper and Richard Walker, *The Capitalist Imperative: Territory, Technology, and Industrial Growth*, Cambridge: Blackwell Publishers, 1989.
12   Marx and Engels, *Manifesto*, p. 476.
13   Harvey, *Condition of Postmodernity*; Storper and Walker, *Capitalist Imperative*, pp. 202-03; Robert Boyer, *The Regulation School: A Critical Introduction*, New York: Columbia University Press, 1990.
14   Storper and Walker, *Capitalist Imperative*, p. 199.
15   Ibid., pp. 199-202. See also Peter Dicken, *Global Shift: Industrial Change in a Turbulent World*, Third Edition, New York: Guilford Press, 1998, p. 148.
16   Storper and Walker, *Capitalist Imperative*; Annalee Saxenian, *Regional Advantage: Culture and Competition in Silicon Valley and Route 128*, Cambridge: Harvard University Press, 1994.

17   Guy Debord, *Society of the Spectacle*, Detroit: Black and Red Books, 1977. See also Henri Lefebvre, *The Production of Space*, Translated by Donald Nicholson-Smith, Oxford: Blackwell, 1991.

18   David Goodman and Michael Redclift, *Refashioning Nature: Food, Ecology, and Culture*, London: Routledge, 1991.

19   David Harvey, *The New Imperialism*, Oxford: Oxford University Press, 2003.

20   Even our portrayal of technological change in this regard is not strong enough. We refer the reader to Neil Smith's explication of 'the production of nature' in this volume, for an even stronger version of the increasingly intense ways capitalism incorporates nature's own processes into production circuits.

21   China is increasingly emulating this spatial pattern with the rapid construction of highways, upscale suburbs and suburban shopping centers, all articulated with its propulsive 'pillar' automobile and household appliance industries.

22   Carol Heim argues persuasively that 'city-building' was a very significant driver of economic growth in twentieth century America. My argument about strong technological change echoes what she terms 'hypermarket forces': 'speculation and the search for large capital gains from property development and increasing land values. Such gains, rather than marginally higher rates of return from reallocation of capital and labor in production, are the incentive behind much city-building, suburbanization, and redevelopment or gentrification'. Carol E. Heim, 'Structural Changes, Regional and Urban', in Stanley L. Engerman and Robert E. Gallman, eds., *The Cambridge Economic History of the United States, Volume 3 The Twentieth Century*, Cambridge: Cambridge University Press, 2000.

23   Goodman and Redclift, *Refashioning Nature*.

24   David Harvey, *The Limits to Capital*, Oxford: Basil Blackwell, 1982.

25   Of course, in the present capitalist formation, innovation and technological change have become highly organized, institutionalized, and even industrialized in ways that go far beyond this simple schematization of single capitalists and the state. Institutions ranging from venture capital to university-industry partnerships and regional or even national initiatives actively strive to push the envelope. Academics and planners now pay considerable attention to the spatiality of innovation, that is, to the innovative potential of actors embedded in urban and regional networks that transcend individual firms. But heavy institutional and financial intermediation does not change the basic argument here, that the logic of capital accumulation is the single most important driver of technology change. For a just sample of what is now a very large literature, see Annalee Saxenian, *Regional Advantage: Culture and Competition in Silicon Valley and Route 128,* Cambridge: Harvard University Press, 1994; Lewis M. Branscomb, Fumio Kodama, and Richard Florida, eds., *Industrializing Knowledge: University-Industry Linkages in Japan and the United States*, Cambridge: MIT Press, 1999; Storper and Walker, *Capitalist Imperative*; Michael Best, *The New Competition: Institutions of Industrial Restructuring*, Cambridge: Harvard University Press, 1990; Martin Kenney, *Biotechnology: The University Industrial Complex*, New Haven: Yale University Press, 1988; Manuel Castells and Peter Hall, *Technopoles of the World: The Making of 21st Century Industrial Complexes*, London: Routledge, 1994; William Baumol, *The Free-Market Innovation Machine: Analyzing the Growth Miracle of*

Capitalism, Princeton: Princeton University Press, 2002; and Richard Florida, *The Rise of the Creative Class: And How It's Transforming Work, Leisure, Community and Everyday Life*, New York: Basic Books, 2003.

26 Our argument should not be construed as a cavalier dismissal of efforts to conserve resources or put a halt to global warming. Rather, it is a critique of certain strains of thinking about capitalism and its relationship to nature and sustainability.

27 Jack Ralph Kloppenburg, Jr., *First the Seed: The Political Economy of Plant Biotechnology, 1492-2000*, New York: Cambridge University Press, 1988.

28 Erik Swyngedouw, this volume.

29 Donna J. Haraway, *Modest_Witness@Second_Millennium. FemaleMan©_Meets_OncoMouse™: Feminism and Technoscience*, New York: Routledge, 1997.

30 For just a glimpse at the kinds of politics and struggles that might accompany such a commodification, see Swyngedouw's account of the privatization of water in this volume.

UNSUSTAINABLE CAPITALISM: THE POLITICS OF RENEWABLE ENERGY IN THE UK

BARBARA HARRISS-WHITE
AND ELINOR HARRISS

All living organisms and social arrangements are physical systems; capitalism is no exception and we have ignored this at our peril.[1] The physical engine of capital relentlessly destroys carbon and methane sinks, releasing greenhouse gases. It wreaks havoc with ecosystems, biodiversity and human wellbeing. By early 2006, some expert climate change modellers had estimated that the global CO_2 concentration level above which dangerous climate change is unstoppable had already been reached. While the building of an ecological capitalism is being imagined,[2] the creation of any kind of 're-humanized nature' under capitalism cannot be achieved without an increase in physical waste and increased entropy, as defined by Elmar Altvater in his essay in this volume.

In the final chapter of his influential book, *The Future of the Market*, Altvater seeks the genesis of a new kind of socialist project in a 're-moralization of resource allocation' which he thinks neither markets, nor the 'thin' democracy permitted by markets, allow.[3] He concludes: '(t)oday the further evolution of society is possible only if the economic rationality of market procedures is firmly embedded in a complex system of social, non-market regulation of money and nature'.[4] Energy must be central to such a project, but the systems properties of its fixed physical infrastructure exemplify the formidable obstacles it faces. For many good reasons nuclear energy is an unacceptable option;[5] and if energy conservation (or so-called 'energy efficiency') is recognized as insufficient, we are left with renewable energy generation.[6] It is from renewable energy that Altvater's alternative of a low-impact, 'entropy-minimizing', democratically-regulated social infrastructure might be developed.

Any alternative must start from where we are now. This essay describes how the market-driven politics of energy in the UK (whose economy is now

powered by coal, oil, gas and nuclear energy[7]) are blocking the development
of renewable energy, which has physical and technological properties consistent with new, lower-waste forms of capitalism and also with a sustainable
socialist economy.

RENEWABLE ENERGY: THE ISSUES

Renewable energy is energy in which the energy transfers in production
are too small to deplete the resource.[8] It started to develop in the 1970s, due
much less to Rachel Carson, Barbara Ward or the Club of Rome than to the
first oil crisis and the need to ensure energy security. By far the most quan-
titatively important 'green' source, accounting for 95 per cent of renewable
energy, is hydro-electric power. This was developed long before the politics
of renewables emerged, and not with a view to economizing on CO_2. (It isn't
all that green either – the flooded organic matter in dammed lakes produces
huge quantities of methane as it rots.) Next in importance is gas from landfill,
sewage and waste. This is a secondary revenue stream for companies which
commodify waste. For the most part it is the product of sealed municipal
rubbish dumps. British waste, not being much recycled, contains organic
matter whose decomposition generates methane and CO_2 which can drive
small turbines. Of course, the process generates 'additional combustion products' – more waste, pollution and hazards. But landfill itself is estimated to
contribute nearly half of the UK's methane emissions, so that its conversion
into energy is now regarded as 'green', and as such is eligible to receive state
incentives and a guaranteed market.[9]

It was not until 2000 that the Utilities Act officially identified a set of
renewable sources of energy in Britain (the full range of which is outlined
in the Appendix to this essay). Alongside hydro-electric power and energy
from waste[10] the list includes, first, wind turbines, the production of which,
apart from small specialized firms, is under oligopoly control and consists of
by-product lines from other industries. Then there is solar energy from photovoltaic panels, a decentralized field of accumulation with a small number
of significant installation firms and an expanding base of small builders. Agricultural and forest residue and biofuels (in the UK mainly from varieties
of willow and poplar) is a very small sector at present, and wave power is
completely undeveloped – although a Scottish firm is to build a commercial
wave power station in Portugal. Geothermal energy is also undeveloped.

None of these sources is at the cutting edge of research; most are at the
infant industry/development stage, and some are already established as fields
of accumulation.[11] Moreover, what counts as 'renewable' has been continually and opportunistically re-defined. In July 2005, in a Washington agree-

ment among states on the Pacific rim, 'cleaner' coal, one of the world's most polluting industries, was even relabelled a green technology.[12] Meanwhile 'sustainability', which has never been given a testable definition, is used interchangeably with 'renewables'; it has been watered down to 'resources sustainably available in the environment', and even leached into mere 'growth'.[13]

Two powerful arguments have been made for renewable energy as a socially and politically transformative technology. One stresses the potential of its optimal small scale to service 'sustainable communities' and to decentralize and democratize energy control.[14] This argument is mainly beamed at 'late-developing' countries where energy grids are defective, transmission losses are profligate, decentralized energy generation is necessary and 'rural communities' which could manage it are believed to exist. Another argument, which stresses the social value of 'self reliance', can be used at any social scale. Self-reliance is a very far cry from socialism, but insofar as supply security would be one of the basic socialist securities, then renewable energy does not impose any obstacles to it, as so much existing capitalist technology does.[15]

The economic efficiency of renewable energy has, however, come under relentless attack, on three main grounds. One is that the operating costs of renewable energy are, and always will be, essentially higher than those of fossil energy. A second concerns the lack of security and the unreliability of renewable energy, either for base or peak load generation. A third highlights the technical difficulties and costs of making decentralized generators compatible with the electricity network.[16]

Against the first criticism, concerning cost, it needs to be said that all energy technologies have required protection until scale economies and learning effects have been realized. The subsidies provided for research and development in renewable energy are only a minute fraction of those provided historically for fossil and nuclear technology.[17] 'Capital costs' also change over time for other reasons: green technology is currently being created in the OECD, transferred to developing countries, reverse-engineered there and re-exported to its countries of origin.[18] The debate over cost will not be resolved until the total costs over the lifetimes of all types of generating source have been computed on reasonable assumptions about optimal scale.[19] But, not least because of the secrecy in which nuclear energy is shrouded, this research has apparently never been carried out.

The second objection is that renewable energy can only play a walk-on part in any energy scenario due to the physical impossibility (let alone prohibitive capital cost) of providing the excess capacity needed to cover fluctuations in both demand and supply, and of providing cover for maintenance and repair. Against this it can be argued that optimal mixes of renewable energy can meet fluctuations in predictable ways, particularly once the technical problem of storage batteries has passed from the research to the development stage. It can also be argued that the physical potential of renewable energy has been deliberately underestimated. This potential is huge: for instance, a 'combination of offshore and onshore wind could provide up to 35 per cent of the UK's electricity'.[20]

The third misgiving, about the engineering infrastructure, needs to be taken quite seriously. Capital in the UK has from the beginning cherry-picked energy sectors and developed them as monopolies. An electricity grid was subsequently created, into which energy from generators throughout the country could be supplied and distributed in accordance with demand and supply movements, and subsidised as a 'natural-monopoly' public service. Half a century old, and impossible to either replicate or dismantle, the British grid is not designed to enable the easy connection of decentralized micro-generators or to protect the operation of the grid under conditions of decentralized maintenance and repair. It cannot be denied that cost-effective technology will have to be developed if the number of small-scale renewable energy sources is to be vastly expanded and linked to the grid.

The case for renewable energy can also be based, of course, on conceptions of social justice. This seems to be better understood on the periphery than in the heart of the capitalist system. To quote the Indian National Forum of Forest People and Forest Workers: 'the major impact of the temperature increase foreseen for this century will be increased climatic turbulence and a rise in sea level; the impact is expected to be disproportionately visited on the poorest workers in the most deprived physical ecology', while '(t)he major responsibility for avoiding social, environmental and planetary crisis should fall on industrialized countries' which have caused this destruction.[21] The global climate change negotiations have been unequal and unjust both in the process and in their outcomes; people alive today are actively reducing the capacity of the earth's atmosphere and biosphere to sustain not only current generations living at the ecological and social margins, but also future generations everywhere.[22] Polluters have an obligation in natural justice drastically to reduce, at whatever economic cost, their emissions of damaging greenhouse gases, both to mitigate climate change and to enable adaptation to it. But how far do people see and acknowledge this obligation? One of the last public remarks the former Labour Foreign Minister Robin Cook made before his death in 2005 was to express perplexity about the contrast between the mobilization of public sentiment on behalf of Africa, but not about climate change, that 'will swamp progress made on debt... [and] cause Africa to suffer more'.[23]

Finally, there is a self-interested geopolitical argument focused on the collective threat of the greenhouse gases expected to be produced by the coal-based industrialization of populous countries such as India and China. In a 'soft' version of this argument, industrializing countries will be subsidised by the heavily-polluting old industrial countries (or by companies headquartered in them), to protect carbon sinks and develop renewable energy.[24] A harder version of the development argument stresses the need for a demonstration effect – the extreme improbability that newly-polluting countries will follow any unorthodox models, especially ones requiring substantial state direction and subsidy, unless the OECD or G8 countries do so first. In the absence of evidence that long-established, massive polluters are meeting their obligation to develop renewable energy, many people in developing countries feel they too have a 'right to pollute'.[25]

Renewable energy means less destructive entropy, and is urgently needed to stabilize climate change in five decades' time; it has been successfully demonstrated in small-scale applications and yet is also not resistant to scale economies, and has already been proved to be consistent with a range of forms of ownership from corporate capital to experiments in common ownership; it has also been developed on a much larger scale elsewhere – notably in Scandinavia and Germany; and the use of renewable energy by industrialized countries is a *sine qua non* for a demonstration effect on China and India, whose additions to global warming are about to become catastrophic.[26]

This brings us to the main focus of this essay, the lamentable record of the UK in relation to the development of renewable energy. What are the conditions retarding the development of renewable energy sources in the UK? These conditions are mainly political. In the first of the two sections which follow, the focus is on the state and its politics; in the second on the politics of markets and civil society. Markets, moreover, are inter-connected. We must look at the politics of all the significant markets which might be threatened by the emergence of renewable energy, and at the interests (including those of labour) which might resist its development. We have to deal not simply with the market-driven politics of commodification,[27] and not only with the politics of 'new' technologies and energy sources, but also with the politics of 'path dependence'. What may look like a simple question about the slow development of renewable energy has the widest possible ramifications.[28]

UK ENERGY POLITICS I:
STATE PARTICIPATION AND REGULATION[29]

Under capitalism, the state is compelled to participate in energy production in order to contain the many sources of risk, to manage the network of networks by means of which electricity is produced and distributed, to manage the R and D phase of desirable new technology, to mediate trade-offs, moderate social interests and cater to the needs of key constituencies ('fuel-poor' pensioners, for example), as well as raise resources for all this. It has to regulate and coordinate energy markets within the broader framework of state-market relations. Most modern states are up-front about these complex obligations, but the British state, even though it is not completely gripped by neoliberal ideology, has been shedding them. Over the last two decades the British state has swung from active participation to a politics of discursive aspiration. In opposition, the Labour Party was ambivalent about leaving electricity in the hands of private capital; in power, it has presided over the creation of so much excess private energy capacity that by 2000 it was undermining not only nuclear energy but also renewable energy not to mention energy conservation or energy efficiency.

New Labour has been officially committed to evidence-based policy-making, with clear emissions reduction goals and with a leader who repeatedly claims that climate change is 'our top priority'.[30] But the UK's CO_2 emissions have *risen* at least 5.5 per cent above 1997 outputs, when Labour came to power, and rose by 2.5 per cent over 1997 levels in the first six months of 2005 alone. With just 1 per cent of the world's population the UK produces 2.2 per cent of the world's greenhouse gases. Only 2.7 per cent of UK electricity generation is from renewable energy – a 'lamentable record' compared with Spain (16 per cent), Denmark (20 per cent), Finland (26 per cent), and Sweden (47 per cent).[31] Stuck for years at the 'infant industry' stage, renewable energy in the UK has been described by the leading authority on energy policy, Dieter Helm, as 'not much more than a political lobby'.[32] In 2000, the House of Commons Audit Committee described UK climate change strategy as 'seriously off course'.[33] In 2004 the House of Lords' Science and Technology Committee deplored 'the minimal amount that the Government have committed to renewable energy-related R and D'.[34] And in 2006 the Environmental Audit Select Committee accused the Treasury of 'mystifying institutional inertia on green policies'.[35]

Yet New Labour's *rhetorical* commitment to environmental protection has remained heavy and consistent.[36] Why then has its development in the UK been so slow, and why has this fact not attracted more attention?

The architecture of bureaucratic politics

Responsibility for vital sectors of the economy is often spread across more than one department of government, just as responsibility for defence is not restricted to the Ministry of Defence. On the one hand this reflects the importance of such sectors, and might even be interpreted as rational – a case of 'policy mainstreaming' across the state (of the kind that is today advocated, among other things, for gender!). But then strong co-ordination is required to prevent conflicting departmental/ministerial objectives from creating incoherence, and that is most notably absent.

In the case of UK energy policy, responsibility is spread across the Department for Environment Food and Rural Affairs (DEFRA) whose responsibilities include targets, regulation, globally sustainable development, and emergencies; the Department of Trade and Industry (DTI) with responsibilities for energy generation, utilities regulation, and a low carbon economy; the Department of Communities and Local Government, responsible for urban planning, on-site renewable energy, and energy efficiency; the Department for Transport, concerned with marine and land-based environmental risks, fuel and transport infrastructure, and sustainable travel; the Office of the Deputy Prime Minister, responsible for what are known as 'residual neighbourhood renewal functions'; the Treasury, where the economic instruments to compensate for the impact of climate change are centred; and, last but not least, the Department for International Development (DFID), responsible for overseas aid related to renewable and non-renewable energy. Also involved in energy policy-making are the Prime Minister's Office, two formal sectoral agents (the Chief Scientific Adviser and the regulator, known as Ofgem), the Head of the Economic Service (who straddles the Treasury and the Cabinet, and chairs the review of the economics of climate change), the Environment Agency (the major 'quango', as semi-independent 'quasi non-governmental' organizations are known in the UK), and many advisory bodies with state funding (such as the 'Carbon Trust', advising on renewable energy with authority from the energy industry).

Far from being coordinated, some of these departments and agents are known to be at loggerheads. For example, the publication of the 'plan of action' review on climate change targets, inaugurated in 1997, was delayed by a year from the summer of 2005 due to differences between DEFRA (optimistic) and the DTI (pessimistic) on the likelihood that the targets could be met.[37] Departments have been reorganized and relabelled and their remits altered,[38] and internal departmental inconsistencies have seriously affected the public interest. The DFID, for instance, is rhetorically committed to renewable energy, yet has funded only £3.6 million in research on renewable energy over the entire decade ending in 2004, a sum completely swamped by its investments in oil infrastructure and other fossil fuel projects.[39] Yet DFID might have been expected to spearhead the whole British response to climate change, given its responsibility for development in the Third World, if only because this is where mitigation and adaptation, seen from a global perspective, would be cheapest. In addition, conflicts of economic interest have long been politically institutionalized.[40] Industry groups openly devise government policy (the Emissions Trading Group, for instance, makes official policy for carbon trading) and individual government advisers, supposedly giving disinterested advice to the government, personally embody conflicts of interest (one was discovered in October 2005 to be simultaneously advising the government, the nuclear lobby and green energy clients),[41] while the periods in office of 'environmental trustee-politicians' and civil servants are often inappropriately short.

The maze-like structure of energy policy-making is a recipe for policy failure – and also one that may be easier for business to infiltrate than the structure of a unified, dedicated department. Not that there is much evidence that infiltration is resisted. Quite the reverse.

From hard production technology to dematerialized markets[42]

New energy markets require significant and stable public subsidies. In the case of renewable energy this is not merely a problem of providing subsidies for capital and running costs; it also involves the public costs of managing the integration of renewable energy into the ageing electricity network. State economic support for renewable energy is generously estimated as having been the equivalent of 2.5 per cent of the subsidy for the nuclear industry's processing costs alone.

In the light of what has just been said it is not surprising that the British state has a history of incompletely informed and highly politicized decisions on energy technology. In the name of theories of market efficiency, it has shed both public ownership and its risk-bearing role. Irreversible decisions on energy have been taken on assumptions of cheap and abundant supplies, consumer sovereignty, and market competition. The problem of climate change has been treated sector by sector and policy tweak by policy tweak. Yet at the same time policies are being promoted based on the need for the state to compensate for market *failure*, the need to stabilize market shares and the necessity for stable finance for implementation.[43] Indeed, such policies as it has for renewable energy – subsidising renewable energy use and taxing energy to subsidise the development of renewable energy, as well as setting (shifting) targets for the market share of renewable energy – can be seen as state compensation for the failure of the very market mechanisms it otherwise promotes and extols. Furthermore, the state has been left bearing the cost of the long-term liabilities for the coal and nuclear industries (pollution, waste disposal and land rehabilitation). Labelled 'residual', they are anything but.

The British state has shrunk from practising an explicit policy of 'picking winning technologies', 'creating champions', or even bearing the vital long-term costs and risks of infrastructure provision, leaving such decisions to 'market forces'. But simultaneously it veers in the opposite direction. It has finally managed to define the renewable energy sector both broadly and arbitrarily in order to meet its own pollution reduction targets at least cost – for example by labelling energy from waste as 'renewable'. But it has remained unwilling to correct non-environmental market failures (in R and D and finance) which handicap the very same set of renewable energy sources. It actively discouraged tidal energy technology at the development stage, by aborting the controversial Severn and Mersey barrages for capturing tidal energy. (The very recent revival of the Severn barrage by a consortium backed by the Secretary for Wales has met with a hostile reception from environmental lobbies.[44]) It suddenly gave landfill gas expanded scope for meeting renewable energy targets, and equally suddenly halted subsidies to solar energy in such a way as to jeopardize its development phase.[45]

Apparently unwilling to bear the risks of its own policies, and adamant that British industry's competitiveness must not be threatened, the government has shifted the development costs of renewable energy onto consumers. And not only the costs: the government is now invoking moral duty and placing responsibility for reducing carbon emissions on the purchasing behaviour of private individuals.[46]

Stealth has been required to protect the coal industry, so instead of a tax on the production of carbon, which might have concentrated business minds wonderfully, energy has been taxed instead – with negligible effects on the carbon content of supply. Misleadingly labelled the Climate Change Levy, this energy tax was introduced in 2000, festooned with politicized exemptions and 'negotiated agreements' (but not exempting the then out-of-favour nuclear energy sector).[47]

Even the 'Non-Fossil Fuel Obligation', which had required a set proportion of electricity produced by renewable energy to be purchased by the regional electricity companies at a premium price, and which was justified as a cross-subsidy to renewable energy, was grossly under-fulfilled – and the DTI has never explained why. Of some 3,000 MW of renewable energy contracted for, only 907 MW materialized. This under-performance has been challenged by the European Commission but the issue remains unresolved.[48] At its maximum in 1995-6, 8 per cent of the tax which the special price represents was actually used to support renewable energy, and that money was distributed through competitive contract auctions. The bulk of the receipts have actually been used to help bail out *nuclear* energy, and not through competitive bidding. Similarly, a 'Renewables Obligation', according to which non-renewable private electricity suppliers were required to slowly ratchet up their proportions of renewable energy, is clearly being resisted and under-fulfilled. Yet in 2005 the Labour government scuppered an all-party Climate Change Bill that would have increased the state's modest powers of enforcement.[49]

Instead, advised by expert groups from industry (the Energy Task Force led by Lord Marshall of British Airways and the Confederation of British Industry; and the Emissions Trading Group which rejects renewable energy), the British government has played its contracted part in operationalizing the Kyoto Protocol (the many problems with which are analyzed by Achim Brunnengräber in this volume). Even though the regulation of emissions is less efficient than a carbon tax as a way of mitigating climate change, the government supported the creation of property rights in the form of certificates for carbon markets. These were so-called 'carbon credits' (though the carbon-charged, coal-fired generators were exempted). Industries which default on their CO_2 emission targets in relation to a 'guestimated' 1990 baseline can continue to pollute provided that they purchase 'rights' to preserve existing carbon dumps, or buy stakes in projects purporting to economize on energy, to an amount equivalent to their 'excess' pollution. If they pollute less than their limit they may sell their unused 'rights' or credits to other polluting firms.[50] A new sector of carbon brokers and consultancies is rapidly emerging which prospects for carbon dumps to privatize in the third world, and which negotiates the price of excess carbon emissions. Currently the price is too low to act as a disincentive to the use of fossil energy. Emissions trading is defended on the unambitious grounds that the institutional pre-conditions are now being established for real carbon-compensating markets to develop. But the price of carbon would have to be very much higher than it is at present for carbon sequestration technology to be made profitable, let alone materially effective.

The Labour government appears to have capitulated, then, to political forces which we will revisit later in this essay. Advised by a task force (composed of energy industry representatives and 'independent' regulators, with no representatives at all from the state) charged with devising the regulative framework for renewable energy, it has settled on a set of unsystematic and relatively poorly-funded incentives for renewables (see Appendix). These have favoured wind power, a technology originally favoured in the early 1980s by the old Department of Energy on the recommendation of – typically, again – an advisory unit at the British Atomic Energy Authority.[51] Far from picking winners, more than two decades had to pass before a plan for £6bn of investment in offshore wind power was announced by the government. And this is not public, or even state-subsidised, investment; it is a mere target set by the government for private capital to achieve.[52]

State regulation: the politics of necessity, and the politics of 'aspirational discourse'

Market enthusiasts argue that a universal supply of a basic necessity such as electricity can be assured through private rather than public ownership provided independent regulators have adequate enforcement capacity.[53] But this condition is practically *never* met. Worldwide, so-called independent regulators are all too often found to be 'captured' by governments or bureaucrats who prevent them from acting in accordance with their remit. British regulatory culture is characterized by flexibility and discretion. The capture of Ofgem, the gas and electricity markets regulator, by the New Labour government was seen when it was required in 1998 to support coal and to delay combined-cycle gas turbines. During the 1990s state control over the regulator had already grown massively – along with the costs of regulation – culminating in the vast number of rules and regulations in the Utilities Act of 2000.

But the state in turn was captured by capital and, as the next section shows, abandoned its responsibility for the reduction and stabilization of CO_2 emissions. The scope of the Utilities Act was drastically pruned by 'industry revolts'. The changing roles of coal, oil and gas in electricity generation illustrate this further. Britain's energy sector is increasingly dominated by gas turbines and imported private oil and gas. Price shocks for gas, in 1999-2000 and 2005-2006, factored in relative scarcities, risks and market turbulence due to the replacement of longer term contracts by spot purchases. Private imports of coal have surged, compensating for high gas prices with scant regard either for climate change or for the development of renewable energy which in 2000 Ofgem had been ordered to support. The sorry result was that in late 2005, under 'intense industry pressure', the UK government made a legal appeal to the EU to increase its carbon credits.[54]

Here is where the politics of aspirational discourse comes in. 'Our first priority is climate change', said Lord Whitty, the environment minister, in 2004. 'Low carbon dioxide emissions are at the heart of our way of life', declared the Labour Party Manifesto in 2005. 'No country has done more than

Labour (sic) to advance the cause of action on climate change', announced the minister for environment, food and rural affairs, Margaret Beckett, in January 2006.[55] Such is the disconnect between the Labour government's claims about its achievements and the facts on the ground (such as they are) that something else is at stake. The paramountcy of utterance – often completely un-technical utterance – has a political role and real material consequences.

First, aspirational utterance – the 'priority', the urgent political cause – dominates the public presentation of climate change politics and renewable energy. Since 1990, the government's targets on the reduction of carbon dioxide emissions have been unstable. By and large they have become increasingly ambitious, moving from a 1992 target of getting emissions back to the 1990 level, to – from 2000 onwards – a target of emissions 60 per cent below that level. The velocity of production of statements about targets has also accelerated, while the target dates have receded farther and farther into the future – from 5 to 10 years at the start, to 45 to 99 years at present. The technological means and policy instruments by which these targets are to be reached have never been well specified; the public is deluged with arbitrary slogans and binary choices (first the dash for gas versus imported coal; then nuclear power versus gas; now cleaner coal or nuclear power versus renewable energy). The weighting of announced means and instruments also changes with a speed unrelated to the investment time spans required. They remain strategically vague. The targets and target dates for renewable energy are comparatively modest, yet even these are currently far from being on track.

Energy policy is climate-change policy, and it is hard to see what it is doing other than serving as a mass tranquillizer. David Cameron's 'New Tory' party has also discovered the allure of aspirational climate-change policy, putting 'the environment at the heart of the repositioning of the party' and 'urging the government to re-state its absolute commitment'.[56] As of mid-2006, the government was still delaying by many months the publication of research evaluating the dangers of climate change.[57] Sir Nick Stern, the government's chief economist, was not due to report on the economics of climate change until the autumn of 2006 and any hope of cross-party consensus on climate change policy had been abandoned. The material consequence is that while the political system is tranquillized, to judge by trends in aggregate CO_2 emissions it is very much business as usual for polluting production, distribution and consumption.

The second point is that aspirational discourse may allow a given policy to serve changing and multiple objectives over time. Under the complicated, contradictory and unstable regulative regime that prevails for UK energy, wind and solar energy generation and energy efficiency have all suffered from the 'multiple objectives' syndrome. Relabelled as social policy (help for the 'fuel-poor', investment in housing, rural development, changes in consumer behaviour, social inclusion, improvements in the quality of life) and hardly ever incentivized, renewable energy and energy efficiency policy is offloaded onto a further set of departments and agencies, each with their distinctive politics, and devolved to regions of the state where all hope of coordination is lost.

Of 300 local councils surveyed in 2005 by the Local Government Association, over 90 per cent reported no progress on renewable energy. Two-thirds attributed this to 'lack of leadership' by the government or to active political undermining by Whitehall. At the local level, renewable energy is under-funded and under-staffed. A third of the officers of the non-performing councils also blame resistance by voters and councillors.[58] The permutation of multiple objectives and decentralized responsibility clearly works to prevent the renewable energy sector from developing – and energy efficiency from improving.

Dieter Helm concludes cautiously that while there was a UK energy policy in the past, there is now, despite the regular publication of White Papers, no energy policy addressing 'the new problems of the environment'.[59] The British government has either actively destroyed – or has passively agreed to lose – the in-house technical knowledge base necessary for devising systematic, stable policy, even in the increasingly discursive and un-grounded way in which policy is now framed. This knowledge-base and every component of the policy process is being systematically commodified. It has also lost the in-house capacity to devise regulatory infrastructure or 'management technology'. Without strategic authority, the British state is itself undermined and fragmented. It is politically disabled.[60]

Given all this, can it really be said that renewable energy's halting progress is due to its being inefficient? Sweden's and Denmark's progress at least suggests that renewable energy can be efficient. The truth is that renewable energy has not been seriously promoted. On the contrary, the political marginalization of renewable energy has prevented it being seen as a serious energy option. Already three years before the muzzled public debate of 2006, renewable energy was being de-prioritized even at the level of discourse because of the British Prime Minister's apparent personal wish to rehabilitate nuclear energy.[61] The politics of renewable energy reveal a weakened state at the mercy of industrial interests, and it is to these we now turn.

UK ENERGY POLITICS II: MARKETS AND CIVIL SOCIETY[62]

The struggle for market shares generates a politics as important as that initiated by the state. The practice of treating energy policy by sectors masks the political struggle between companies and between individual companies and the state. Even though it is also labelled as a sector, renewable energy exists in two extreme forms of capitalist organization. One is what one commentator called a 'fashion statement' by diverse corporate capitals, while the other is a much larger set of small specialist firms. There is little connection between the two. Despite green rhetoric, corporate capital may have used its influence deliberately to slow down the renewable energy it controls, while small-scale, specialized renewable energy capital is divided between competing renewable energy sources and subjected to inconsistent and intermittent state support which has without doubt constrained its development.

Through their collective organizations, moreover, very powerful disunited industrial interests scramble over a wide range of concessions, subsidies, brokerage activities and infrastructural provisions, all of which are preconditions for their competing, inside and outside the energy sector. Through their funding of, and influence over, knowledge-based services and quangos, they are vitally implicated in the creation of policy about policy on climate change. At the same time the collective organization of renewable energy currently consists of a multiplicity of special lobbies, while the politics of collective action by civil society is entangled around energy at all levels from informal geopolitical activity at the highest scale of strategic importance, down to the NIMBY politics of rural Wales (where the terrain is most attractive to wind-power energy companies). The politics of renewable energy includes not only combative collective action on the part of all these interests but also the inputs of intellectual interests – epistemic communities which have reason on their side, but little else.

The politics of market structure

One of the ways in which analysts depoliticize policy is by considering the structure of energy sector by sector. They are consumed by the drama of privatization and its environmental tensions (not the least of which is the maximization of sales and the minimization of pollution).[63] In the operations of energy companies, however, the various energy sources and markets are mixed up together. And not just energy companies, but industrial capital as a whole. Companies combine energy sources in a great variety of permutations and coordinate their energy investments better than the state coordinates energy policy. What is the impact of the fact that the main political actors are companies, not sectors?

The energy sector used to be structured as a monopoly at each stage. Now it is shaped like an hour glass. Generation is by a range of firms but dominated by a powerful oligopoly; the grid is a monopoly – a heavily regulated quango – while street-level distribution, billing and retailing is done by many firms. Individual companies shape the structure of UK energy and wield huge political clout. The crises and the scandals which attract public attention are a distraction from the deeply contradictory roles they play.[64] Shell's Lord Oxburgh, for example, is a high profile advocate for the urgency of the problem of climate change.[65] Yet according to Henderson Global Investors (a 'socially responsible' investment fund manager), Shell and BP alone are responsible for 40 per cent of the CO_2 emissions of the leading 100 companies on the Financial Times' Stock Exchange listing and have a large appetite for electricity. BP is also at the heart of carbon trading policy formation. As early as 2001 BP had succeeded in reducing CO_2 emissions from its UK facilities to below 1990 levels. Yet it compensates for under 10 per cent of the 82 million tonnes of CO_2 generated by its operations by carbon-offset, 'sustainable efficiency' projects. BP's products remain massive polluters, generating 5 per cent of the entire world's fossil fuel emissions.[66]

Just as General Electric proclaims that 'climate change is a critical driver of new business opportunities',[67] Shell re-markets itself as an 'energy company' and says it cannot 'make sufficient solar panels to satisfy demand', while BP has ostentatiously re-branded itself as 'Beyond Petroleum' and adopted a sunflower logo to boot. Yet renewable energy accounts for just 1 per cent of the $8bn that BP spends annually on fuel exploration and production, which is even less than 'the very small proportion of capital expenditure' devoted to renewables by Shell. BP has also lobbied to block legislation to introduce curbs on greenhouse gas emissions in the USA.[68] Big business thus not only benefits from the government's obsession with aspirational policy discourse, but also uses a distinctive complementary discourse involving the selective use of evidence. For the oil majors, renewable energy is currently little more than a public relations exercise for those fooled by – or with interests in – the politics of utterance.

The politics of collective organization and collective action

While individual firms must continually seek to exercise political leverage, the energy sector is also collectively organized. The collective organizations of capital with an interest in energy policy occupy such a crowded, active, complex and secretive field that its internal politics cannot be described, let alone analyzed, in this essay. We can, however, describe its architecture and make inferences about politics from its outcomes. The big players include the

Confederation of British Industry, the Institute of Directors, the Engineering Employers' Federation, aggressive transport and fuel lobbies, investment fund managers and insurance companies. Smaller players include the energy market regulators, lobbies concerned with subsidies for the energy consumption of vulnerable households, and even groups of officials with turfs to defend. With few exceptions (such as unions with a vested interest in nuclear energy), trade unions are conspicuous by their absence from this kind of politics.

The nuclear lobby's successful campaign has been a good example of the blurring of boundaries between the state and the nuclear industry. The British media relations of the major French atomic energy company EDF, which is already operating in Britain, are directed by the brother of the Chancellor of the Exchequer, Gordon Brown. The head of corporate affairs for British Nuclear Fuels Limited is chairman of the Nuclear Industries Association, and the NIA's chief executive in turn came from the UK Department for Trade and Industry. Other lobbyists have come from the Labour Party, and their energetic involvement has been a key factor in breaking the former cross-party consensus against nuclear power.[69]

Although capital's collective action on energy is anything but unified, and whether or not any of these groups act *deliberately* to thwart the development of a specialized renewable energy sector, it is notable that special pleading has been deployed by corporate lobbies in order to resist CO_2 emission targets under the Kyoto Treaty, to broker agreements giving exemptions from the Climate Change Levy, the requirement to use green energy under the Renewables Obligation, and to secure selective and lavish subsidies for 'transition periods'. Helping to support the very industries which are most energy-intensive they have 'turn(ed) climate change policy on its head', Helm concludes.[70] Construction industry lobbies have routinely resisted the implementation of energy efficiency requirements because they would raise the price of new houses – although if the government had a comprehensive fiscal policy aimed at improving energy efficiency, and properly implemented inspection and enforcement, their opposition could surely be neutralized.

Meanwhile, replete with contradiction, there is even a renewable energy equivalent of collective corporate social responsibility, with the Ashden Awards for renewable energy funded by British Airways, Sainsbury's, and trusts and foundations which are in turn funded by other major fossil energy-consuming corporations.[71] Even more significantly, a letter sent to the British Prime Minister in June 2005 by one lobby, the Corporate Leaders' Group of the Prince of Wales' Business and the Environment Programme (and signed by the CEOs of 14 UK-based MNCs, including Shell and BP) is instructive: it criticized the government for having failed to create a 'transparent, long term framework to help underpin the scale of investments that are now necessary'.[72] So much for New Labour's embrace of the notion that 'market forces will solve the problem' – which was the government's reply to a similar request a year earlier from the House of Lords' Committee on Science and Technology.[73] Meanwhile, city investors like pension funds and re-insurers press blue chip MNCs to lobby the state for clear ground-rules for investment in the context of climate change. Insurers have a keen interest in climate change because they wish to factor climate-change-related disasters out of their liabilities. And in June 2006, the cream of the cream of British industry was moved to repeat their demand to Blair for 'eco-efficient' regulation.[74]

Not only is the renewable energy sector marginalized in this kind of politics, its own collective organizations have proliferated and its interests are fractured. No need to divide and rule; renewable energy is naturally divided. Lobbies with clear material interests at stake include the Renewable Power Association, the Micro Power Council, the Renewable Generators Consortium and the British Wind Energy Association,[75] while the Chartered Institute of Wastes Management is the landfill gas sector's advocate (two Department of Trade and Industry forums were held in 2005 to enable private capital to network with 'developers and contractors' in this sector).[76]

The material interests of others are less apparent. The Green Alliance and the Forum for the Future exemplify organizations that receive funds from various major polluting industries, departments of government, environmental utilities and quangos, private environmental consultants, banks and charities; with governing boards that reflect the interests of funders, and with overlapping and complicitous missions involving policy formation and information on renewable energy and energy efficiency. The Aldergate Group, another such hybrid, argues for 'smart regulation' to corner innovation rents from 'eco-efficiency'.[77] Climate Change Capital is a bank that advises large energy-intensive companies and their financial backers on climate change regulations, negotiating EU carbon allowances, brokering emissions reduction projects (elsewhere), and investing residually in renewable energy.[78] The Carbon Trust is a think-tank funded by the state with a range of experts from the corporate sector provoked into action by the Climate Change Levy. Energy Watch, also funded by the state, presents itself as 'independent of industry and regulator' and is dedicated to media campaigns and the provision of useful market information for consumers and producers. The Renewable Energy Foundation, on the other hand, is a consortium of nearly 100 local groups opposed to on-shore wind farms and backed by wealthy individuals.[79]

Sorting out the wolves in sheeps' clothing in the field of renewable energy is not easy.

The politics of civil society and of social embeddedness

Energy politics are socially embedded at all levels: from the Washington military and political security networks, which are enmeshed with big energy security networks and their associated think tanks and (global) bulletins, to increasingly powerful local NIMBY ('Not In My Back Yard') political organizations. The movement against on-shore wind generation, for example, is increasingly professionalized and science-based, able to put prices on environmental externalities – and supported by Prince Charles.[80] It seeks to preserve one moment in the history of the landscape and represents a significant obstacle to the development of wind power.

In embedding energy politics, the so-called 'quality' press plays a deeply contradictory role. Theirs is a polluting industry, implicated in what they criticize; and their vital role as major sources of evaluative information conflicts with their parallel agenda promoting the high-consumption lifestyle (including private cars and airline travel) required by their sources of advertising revenue. 'I think it's pretty obvious that a media company does not have a carbon issue' declared a spokesman for News Corporation, clearly in denial about the polluting impact of the production of newsprint (let alone journalists' air miles).[81]

Despite being a champion of climate change science, and despite a general scientific consensus on the nature and urgency of man-made climate change, British science is divided about the social response to it. The 2000 Royal Commission on Environmental Pollution expressed the general position of the science elite of the Royal Society, which has played a major role in what public consciousness there is about climate change. The Royal Society favours a rapid and radical shift to a low-carbon economy. It was part of the unprecedented coalition of G8 Science Academies (together with those of China, India and Brazil) whose statement in 2005 stripped any residual credibility from those who stress the uncertainty attached to climate science forecasts.[82] In practice, however, scientists are divided between enthusiasts for high-tech carbon sequestration, advocates of nuclear energy and research on fusion, supporters – rarer – for the low-tech and known technologies of renewable energy, and in a few cases, those who associate themselves with the desire for the simplification of lifestyles and a lowering of consumption levels.

Scientists in general should not be presumed to have expert knowledge of either the politics or the economics of climate change, or to be proof against the private temptation to behave in ways which deny the scale and urgency of the problem. The criteria for high ratings in the state's Research Assessment Exercise embed and incentivize polluting behaviour – e.g. flights to academic conferences – throughout the academic sector. Even so, organizations of concerned scientists proliferate – along with their reports.[83] One such report, however, published under the imprimatur of the Royal Institute of International Affairs in December 2005, is significant both for its content and for its financial patronage. Reasoning strongly against both deliberative democracy and expert science in decisions on nuclear energy, it concluded in favour of firmness in 'unpopular' decisions – by strong implication to 'go for nuclear'. The work was funded, among others, by British Nuclear Fuels Ltd and Electricité de France.[84]

The organizations of lobbies that speak for environmentalists also proliferate, of course. The most prominent of the mass-membership, knowledge-based, campaigning NGOs in the UK include the World Wildlife Fund, Greenpeace, Friends of the Earth, Carbon Trade Watch, the UK Stop Climate Change Campaign, and Stop Climate Chaos (a poor relation of the 'Make Poverty History' campaign). They work by disseminating environmental information, giving advice on energy-efficient private consumption choices, mass events, the postal persuasion of MPs and CEOs (the 'Big Ask'), boycotts, cyber-activism and sometimes direct action.[85] Their material bases, however, are hard to track, and not all such organizations have uncompromised funding.[86] The political fault lines among them are not so much varying degrees of support for renewable energy as their positions on the international interests involved in carbon markets, and on the conversion of carbon sinks into carbon dumps as 'solutions' to climate change.[87] Only implicitly anti-capitalist, for most of them the word capitalism (let alone the word socialism) is taboo. The jury is out over the question whether the proliferation of organizations with intellectual but non-material clout can generate a kind of 'political correctness' which has a real impact on state behaviour, or whether it merely adds to the colourful marketplace of ideas and procrastinating 'policy policy'.

CONCLUSIONS: CLEAN ENERGY AND DANGEROUS POLITICS

There is no coherent policy for the development of renewable energy in the UK, or indeed for the energy sector as a whole. The politics of renewable energy is enmeshed in the interests of capital, and for the most part these interests are defined in terms of their investments in energy technologies for which renewables would be substitutes.

The British government has moved from intervening in technologies, quantities and prices, and from fiscal mechanisms and marginal transfers to renewable energy, towards a politics of repeated utterances and increasingly utopian targets in relation to them. Is the government in collective denial? Is it a weak prisoner of capital? The government purports to be consulting the public in the 2006 consultation for a new energy white paper, but it presents the issue as a mere choice between imported gas and expanding domestic nuclear power. Consultation has been crudely pre-empted by the Prime Minister's announcement that 'nuclear energy is back on the agenda with a vengeance'.[88] The 'debate' that then ensues does not acknowledge the relevance of renewable energy to the 60 per cent emissions reduction target to which the UK is committed let alone to the UK's energy footprint in the rest of the world.

The state's withdrawal from the production and distribution of energy, and its fractured energy policy architecture, enable its penetration by interests undermining renewable energy. Yet these interests shoot themselves in the foot because current bureaucratic political arrangements also prevent the formation and implementation of a coherent energy policy. State regulative autonomy is doubly compromised – by the 'independent' regulators' vulnerability to state capture, and by the state's capture by capital. In turn capital sheds activity that is low-profit and high-risk, and renewable energy is regulated so as to be both. The result is not serving capital well, but meanwhile renewable energy is marginalized.

The discourse of both state and business needs taking seriously – not only in its cynicism but also in its indifference, bordering on contempt for the chief victims, present and prospective. Undemocratic modern politics cannot be understood without the opiate role of discourse. The destruction of energy policy and the timid entry of renewable energy into politics is happening as the modes of policy formulation and implementation are themselves being transformed in very troubling and undemocratic ways.[89] Climate change policy serves to hide increasing *total* energy emissions, relentlessly polluting energy use and increasing waste. This discourse co-exists with the devaluation and abusive dismissal of discussion based on non-economic values. It has long protected the privatization of control over the energy economy, and is now being employed in a new phase of commodification of all aspects of policy: the agenda, the making of regulative law, resourcing, and the mechanics of access. The state thus cedes to a diffuse set of private interests the capacity to steer public debate, and the privatization of the 'public good' of policy is naturalized and uncontested.

The British state is now almost completely saturated by the ideology of the market, a soft prey to capital. In the energy field, a mix of market-driven politics and state capitulation has undermined the framework of systematic regulation and stripped the state of its capacity to make the long-term plans necessary for capital to invest, let alone provide stable conditions for capital realization in a sector populated by firms with a tendency to crisis. It is unable even to satisfy reasonable needs for long-term policy or to provide the infrastructural and regulative security required by capital for its energy investments. The state also abdicates its minimalist role as co-ordinator of last resort, mediator between interests, and linker of policy between sectors, subcontracting these roles to capital – roles which capital cannot perform coherently. It has been stripped of any capacity to define the general interest or the public good. In this situation, the 'energy sector', indispensable as it is to every aspect of society, is much more dangerously vulnerable than the public is led to imagine. While retail energy prices are currently rising, by themselves neither price nor information is making mass social behaviour and the energy economy move towards renewable energy at the pace necessary to stabilize climate change in 50 years' time – or perhaps ever.

Capitalism is not fixing the environment. It is not able to, either in theory or in historical practice.[90] Not in theory because of the logic and thermodynamics of capitalist growth; not in practice because of its path dependence, and because of the contradiction between the pace of physical system dynamics and that of the global economy. Market-driven politics have ensured that renewable energy remains far from starting to form any kind of technological base, either for an alternative model of capitalist development – in the UK or in an engagement with large developing countries which are about to enter a highly polluting phase of industrialization. Sustainable capitalism is a fiction, and the politics of renewable energy are merely a reflection of the fiction.

And, sad to say, at least in the field of energy there is no sign of any politics capable of generating a new kind of social, non-market regulation of money and nature. Workers themselves are unable to resolve the problems of the destructive nature of capitalism. On the shop floor they have been carefully manoeuvred into impotence. Rising disposable incomes have made workers complicit in the existing policy drift, a complicity reinforced by the psychological need for security and by the various social mechanisms which serve to avoid or deny reality. Furthermore it appears rational for labour not to mobilize, at least in the traditional fashion, since mass mobilizations (over Iraq, or Making Poverty History, for example) have been met with indifference on the part of the political establishment.

To be sure, in a global context workers' perspectives can look very different. The Indian National Forum of Forest People and Forest Workers asks and answers two important questions. Who has the strongest interest in halting the flow of fossil carbon into the atmosphere? Who has a material interest in equalizing and limiting the use of above-ground carbon dumps? They say that those with the strongest interest are the victims of climate change-related disaster; people fighting immediate destruction due to the exploitation of fossil fuels, pipelines, logging and the commodification of forests in the name of the Clean Development Mechanism (the 'third world' component of the carbon trade regime). They themselves form and give support to groups for environmental justice, and energy efficiency, and to those monitoring the use of fossil energy and its impact.[90] All this said, the development of renewable energy is included neither in their questions nor their answers, their power is very limited and their links with anti-climate change movements in the UK are exiguous. Still, they will no doubt be strengthened when the devastation related to climate change comes closer to home.

APPENDIX
RENEWABLE ENERGY SOURCES AND THEIR INCENTIVE MECHANISMS

Source	Target (1)	RO (2)	CCL exemption (3)	Capital grants
Landfill gas	Δ	Δ	Δ	
Sewage gas	Δ	Δ	Δ	
Energy from waste	Δ		Δ	
Hydro >10 MW installed capacity	Δ			
Hydro <10 MW, installed capacity	Δ	Δ	Δ	
Onshore wind	Δ	Δ	Δ	
Offshore wind	Δ	Δ	Δ	Δ
Agricultural and forestry residues	Δ	Δ	Δ	
Energy Crops	Δ	Δ	Δ	Δ
Wave power	Δ	Δ	Δ	
Photovoltaics	Δ	Δ	Δ	

Source: 'New and Renewable Energy: Prospects for the 21st Century – The Renewables Obligation Preliminary Consultation', Department of Trade and Industry, London: TSO, October, 2000. In Dieter Helm, *Energy, the State and the Market: British Energy Policy since 1979*, Oxford, OUP, 2004, p. 363.

Notes:

(1) eligible for promotion under the 10 per cent target for renewable energy generation required to be met by power companies

(2) covered under the Renewables Obligation

(3) exempt from the Climate Change Levy

NOTES

This is the short version of a paper with the title 'Undermining Sustainable Capitalism: The Market-driven Politics of Renewable Energy' that will be posted on the website of the Socialist Register http://socialistregister.com. A draft of this paper was presented at the Workshop on the Ecological Challenge and its Political Economy, February 2006, funded by British Academy, the Lipman-Miliband Foundation, Queen Elizabeth House and Wolfson College and organized through QEH, Oxford University. We are grateful to the workshop participants for their responses, especially to Pritam Singh; to Rebecca Clark, Jo Hamilton, Alan Hunt, George Monbiot and Robin Oakley for information (some of which is confidential), and to Dieter Helm for his useful engagement. Thanks also to Oxford graduate students Ben Champion, Chris Hansen, James Keirstead and Thomas Simchak who brainstormed with BH-W in March 2005. We are grateful to Elmar Altvater whose book triggered this project and to Queen Elizabeth House for a grant to support the review of literature carried out by EH. BH-W bears sole responsibility for errors of fact or interpretation and for the conclusions.

1   John Bellamy Foster, 'The Scale of our Ecological Crisis', *Monthly Review*, 49(11), 1998; Tim Dyson 'On Development, Demography and Climate Change: The End of the World as We Know It', *Population and Environment*, 27(2), 2005.

2   Most energetically in texts on environmental economics and on development in which capitalism is euphemized as 'the market', 'the economy', 'the private sector' or 'growth', and the environment is stylized as a costable externality.

3   Elmar Altvater, *The Future of the Market*, London: Verso, 1993, especially chapter 5, 'Towards an Ecological Critique of Market Economy', pp. 181-235. This quote is from p. 202, see also p. 213.

4   Ibid., p. 260.

5   Nuclear energy would not be central to such a project on grounds of the carbon dioxide generated by mining increasingly poor grades of uranium; the costs and logistics of managing radioactive tailings and of extracting fissile uranium isotopes; the CO_2 generated in the construction, maintenance and decommissioning of plants and the removal of spent fuel; the creation, disposal and protection of waste without precedent in its toxicity and cost – which awaits technology which might redefine it as a raw material; the technology's physical form as a target for terrorist attack; its history of vulnerability to catastrophic leaks and accidents (*not reduced* with advanced gas reactor technology); the risk of nuclear weapons proliferation (currently thought to be low); its history of un-viably high costs and externalities which have always been met by public subsidies and (implicit) public insurance. M. Schneider's attempt to cost the carbon dioxide generated by France's nuclear industry puts it at 10 per cent of

France's total. M. Schneider, 'Oui, le nucléaire produit des gaz à effet de serre', *L'Ecologiste*, 1(2), 2000. Developed on the back of fossil energy, it is not a low entropy solution. Even so, environmental scholar-activists such as James Lovelock and George Monbiot have concluded that nuclear technology is inevitable, should political arrangements fail to change, energy efficiency continue to decline globally and consumption levels continue to rise. Should this happen, there would be a non-trivial skills shortage. Furthermore a thousand nuclear reactors worldwide would deplete all known uranium sources. So it is not a long term generalizable solution either. A. Simms, P. Kjell and D. Woodward, *Mirage and Oasis: Energy Choices in an Age of Global Warming*, London: New Economics Foundation, 2005, pp. 31-2, 37, 42; D.M. Donaldson and G.E. Betteridge, 'Carbon Dioxide. Emissions from Nuclear Power Stations – A Critical Analysis of FOEY', *Atom*, 400, 1990, pp. 18-22; *New Scientist*, 26 March 2005. In 2003 DTI Secretary Patricia Hewitt discounted the idea that nuclear energy would be other than phased out in the UK. In 2004, BH-W was advised by Michael Meacher (the former Labour environment minister who resigned on account of the Iraq War) not to waste time with this essay because 'Tony Blair favours nuclear'; a view subsequently reiterated in *New Scientist*, 17 July 2004, p. 6. In 2006, as this essay was drafted, the British public was being psycho-politically prepared for a revival of nuclear energy.

6   For the energy needs of the ever-growing transport sector and for carbon sequestration see Dieter Helm, *Energy, the State and the Market: British Energy Policy since 1979*, Oxford: Oxford University Press, 2004, pp. 346-52; see W. Keepin and G. Kats, 'Greenhouse Warming: A Comparative Analysis of Nuclear and Efficiency Abatement', *Energy Policy*, 15(6), 1988, pp. S38-S61 on the dramatic contrast between the case for the immediate benefits from energy efficiency (up to 40 per cent savings; B. Boardman, *Prospects for Achieving the 40 per cent House*, Oxford: Environmental Change Institute, Oxford University, 2005); and on the one hand, the ready existence of technologies, and on the other, the ad hoc and poorly-funded projects for energy conservation in the UK and the US and the active sabotage of attempts to lift energy efficiency up the political agenda on the other hand (Simm et al., *Mirage and Oasis*, pp. 4-5). The UK is unusual in that transport accounts for a greater proportion of its CO_2 generation than does electricity, according to *The Times*, 24 October 2004. According to the government's chief scientific adviser, David King, carbon sequestration, the de-contamination and burying of CO_2 pollutants is a 'technological fix' unavailable in the time span required to stabilize climate change (*Observer*, 26 July 2005; *Observer*, 11 June 2006). Its immense cost and unlikely geological feasibility speak more to the allure of hi-tech solutions to science than they do to seriousness of purpose.

7   As of 2004, the main fuels used by final consumers in the UK were: petroleum products 47 per cent, natural gas 34 per cent, and electricity 17 per cent. The fuels used to generate electricity were: gas 38 per cent, coal 35 per cent, nuclear 22 per cent, other fuels 3 per cent, oil 1 per cent, and hydro-electric power 1 per cent. Transport accounts for 33 per cent of all energy use in the UK as compared with the domestic sector's 28 per cent, the industrial sector's 21 per

cent, and the commercial sector's 6 per cent. *Digest of UK Energy Statistics*, 2004: http://www.dti.gov.uk/energy/inform/dukes/dukes2004/index.shtml.

8   Helm, *Energy*, p. 348.

9   Helm, *Energy*, p. 348. http://www.chemsoc.org/exemplarchem/entries/2004/ plymouth_Whittleton/index.html quoting source in *Europa* 2004 and http:// www.gsce.com/energy/landfill_gas_methane.htm.

10   There is practically no literature to help us understand the hidden politics of the eleven sectors officially recognized as sources of renewable energy. The high media exposure of wind and solar energy obscures the far greater current sig- nificance of hydro-electric power and landfill gas. Perhaps because landfill gas helps to tackle the pollution caused by landfill, rather than because it is seen as a solution to the greenhouse gas problem, it does not even receive a mention in the New Economics Foundation's 2005 report on renewable energy vs. nuclear energy. Yet there are 174 landfill gas projects in the UK with guaranteed mar- kets under the Non-Fossil Fuels Obligation and with considerable expansion possibilities. It is a normal field of private accumulation, supplying electricity to 700,000 homes and raising returns to the management of rubbish dumps.

11   Global investment in renewable energy is minute compared with that in fossil energy. A. Simms, J. Oram and P. Kjell, *The Price of Power: Poverty, Climate Change, the Coming Energy Crisis and the Renewable Revolution*, London: New Econom- ics Foundation, 1988, p. 9. Worldwide the trend is in the opposite direction; the proportion of electricity generated from renewable energy globally has dropped from 24 per cent in 1970 to 13 per cent now – remaining high even so because of wood-burning (Andrew Simms, 'It's Time to Plug into Renew- able Power', *New Scientist*, 3 July 2004); Jenny Hogan and Philip Cohen, 'Is the Green Dream Doomed to Fail?', *New Scientist*, 17 July 2004. The government of Sweden is exemplary, even planning to be practically oil-free by 2020 and intending to work with Saab and Volvo to develop bio-fuels. John Vidal, 'Swe- den Plans to be World's First Oil-Free Economy', *Guardian*, 8 February 2006.

12   On the pollution of coal see Helm, *Energy*, p. 180-1; on relabelling coal as green see *Guardian*, 25 August 2005.

13   Helm, *Energy*, pp. 303, 361.

14   'Community Renewable Energy Co-op planned for Oxfordshire', Energy4All web site 'Latest News' posting, 30 June 2006, http://www.energy4all.co.uk; 'Renewable Energy Crucial for Sustainable Communities says Minister', 10 August 2004, PublicTechnology.net, http://publictechnology.net; 'The Need for Co-operative Solutions', Co-operatives^{UK}, http://www.cooperatives- uk.coop/live/cme996.htm.

15   By which is understood conditions of unalienated production for the long term common good. However it is sobering to acknowledge that the lifetime of a wind turbine is a mere 25 years.

16   Helm, *Energy*, pp. 360, 349, 360-1; 'Britons "In Favour of Wind Farms"', BBC News online, 19 Sept 2004, http://news.bbc.co.uk; Marcus Rand, 'Why We Need Wind Power', *Guardian*, Letters, 10 May 2004.

17   R. Duke and D. Kammen, 'The Economics of Energy Market. Transformation Programs', *The Energy Journal*, 20(4), 1999; 'The Untimely Death of Salter's

Duck', *Green Left Weekly*, 64, 1992; BBC Weather Centre: postings about Alternative Fuels, http://www.bbc.co.uk/climate/adaptation/renewable_energy. shtml; Ben Crystall, 'The Big Clean-Up', *New Scientist*, 3 September 2005; Simms, 'It's Time to Plug'.

18   Vestas and Sulzan have branches in India and export wind turbines to the EU.

19   On operating costs see UKERC, 'UK Energy Research Centre Dispels Myths Surrounding Intermittent Renewable Energy', 5 April 2006,   http://www. ukerc.ac.uk; Greenpeace, *Submission to the Stern Review on the Economic Aspects of Climate Change*, London: Greenpeace, 2006; 'Untimely Death of Salter's Duck'; Helm, *Energy*, pp. 362-5; Hogan and Cohen, 'Is the Green Dream'.

20   Simms et al., *Mirage and Oasis*, pp. 3-5. Simms et al. argue that the theoretical potential for solar, wind, geothermal, hydro, biomass and energy from oceans is about 2.3 million times greater than current human use. See also Thomas B. Johansson et al., 'The Potentials of Renewable Energy', Thematic Background Paper for the 'International Conference for Renewable Energies', Bonn, Germany, 1 to 4 June 2004; See Paul McGarr, 'Capitalism and Climate Change', *International Socialism*, 107, 2005 on the predictability of wave and tide power. See also Greenpeace, *Submission to the Stern Review*.

21   Soumitra Ghosh, *Climate Change and the Market Politics of Environment*, Nagpur: National Forum of Forest People and Forest Workers, 2004, pp. 4-6, where the impact of erosion, flooding, drought and temperature changes on disease ecologies, agriculture, forest, water resources and soil structure is summarized. See also A. Simms and J. Walter, *The End of Development? Global Warming, Disasters and the Great Reversal of Human Progress*, London and Dhaka: New Economics Foundation and Bangladesh Centre for Advanced Studies, 2002, pp. 3, 5.

22   Kari Norgaard, 'Denial, Privilege and Global Environmental Justice', *Working Paper 2003.2*, Oslo: Centre for Environment and Development, University of Oslo, 2003, p. 1.

23   *Guardian*, 10 June 2005.

24   550 coal-fired power stations are to be built in China between 2005 and 2030 according to Jonathan Porritt, Chair of the government's Sustainable Development Commission (*Observer*, 26 July 2005). 10 terrawatts is needed to industrialize while the Clean Development Mechanism created under the Kyoto Protocol involves perhaps at best a 10-15 per cent subsidy to energy from polluting signatories.

25   Simms et al., *Mirage and Oasis*, p. 30.

26   See the essay by Minqi Li and Dale Wen in this volume. Despite plans for China to invest in nuclear energy and renewable energy, this is a coal-based industrialization and local environmental damage in China itself is accelerating, as is the damage due to global warming. See Chinese Academy of Social Sciences, *China Modernisation Report*, Beijing, 2006; versus Greenpeace China, 'The Story of Yellow River', Beijing, 2005.

27   Colin Leys, *Market-Driven Politics*, London: Verso, 2001; Beatrice Hibou, ed., *Privatising the State*, London: Hurst, 2004; George Monbiot, *Captive State*, London: Macmillan, 2000.

28   Sources of information to answer it are also extremely diverse and many are fast-moving. To make them tractable, our main guide to state politics is Dieter Helm's *Energy, the State and the Market: British Energy Policy since* 1979, which is based on a close reading of all UK energy policy documents, and is ordered sector by sector. The section on the politics of markets and civil society is less comprehensively covered by Helm and draws on a wider range of sources.

29   This section uses Helm., pp. 2-13, 295, 350-65, and 481.

30   Prime Minister's speech on climate change, 14 September 2004, http://www.number10.gov.uk/output/Page6333.asp.

31   Friends of the Earth press release, 'Emissions Breach Kyoto Target', 5 September 2005, http://www.foe.co.uk; Conal Walsh, *Guardian*, 27 June 2005. Of that 95 per cent is hydro-electric power and biofuels. Simms et al., *Mirage and Oasis*, p. 8; and The Environmental Agency, 'Renewable Energy: Key Issues', at http://www.environment-agency.gov.uk; Helm, *Energy*, p. 351. Bryony Wellington, 'Cash Point', *Earthmatters*, Spring, 2005.

32   Helm, *Energy*, p. 350.

33   Reported in http://www.transport2000.org.uk.

34   £12.2 m in 2002-3 compared with $250m in the US. Quoted in Simms et al., *Mirage and Oasis*, p. 42. The House of Lords' recent report on the 'Economics of Climate Change' criticized the IPCC for their 'high emissions scenarios' and argued that 'there are some positive aspects to global warming', that 'far more attention should be paid to adaptation' and that 'current nuclear power capacity... should be retained'. House of Lords, *The Economics of Climate Change*, House of Lords, Select Committee on Economic Affairs, 2nd Report of Session 2005-06, 6 July 2005.

35   Patrick Wintour, *Guardian*, 28 March 2006.

36   Larry Elliott, *Guardian*, 12 June 2006.

37   Wintour, *Guardian*, 28 March 2006.

38   See, for recognition and relief, A. Oxman, D. Sackett, I. Chalmers and T. Prescott, 'A Surrealistic Mega-Analysis of Redisorganisation Theories', *Journal of the Royal Society of Medicine*, 98, 2005, pp. 563-8.

39   DFID has made gentle criticisms of the World Bank in its press release, 'United Kingdom position on the World Bank response to the Extractive Industries Review (EIR)', available at http://www.dfid.gov.uk. For the World Bank's actual investments see Simms et al., *The Price*, p. 14. The WB has 22 times more fossil energy projects than renewable ones according to Larry Lohmann of the Corner House, in Ghosh, *Climate Change*, p. 16; Simms et al., *The Price*, p. 14.

40   Monbiot *Captive State*.

41   A revelation resulting from the green energy company being exposed as run by serial fraudsters. The Insight Team, 'Green Adviser Takes Cash for Access to Ministers' and 'The Conmen and the Green Professor', *Sunday Times*, 2 October 2005.

42   This section uses Helm, *Energy*, pp. 2-12, 42, 179-92, 303, 345-80 and 404-5.

43   For instance, the state compensates for market failure by subsidising renewable energy; it has (shifting) targets for the market share of renewable energy and it

taxes energy through the 'Climate Change Levy' in order to subsidise the development of renewable energy.

44 Steve Morris, 'Estuary Energy Plan Makes Waves', *Guardian*, 26 April 2006; see Helm, *Energy*, p. 349 on the tidal estuary projects.

45 Paula Kirk, 'Gulf between Blair's Pledges and Action leaves Solar Power in the Lurch', SFL Project, Sustainable Energy Action Limited, London, 2005; McGarr, 'Capitalism and Climate Change'; Simms et al., *Mirage and Oasis*, p. 11; 'Scrapping the Clear Skies and Solar PVA Grand Funding Mechanisms', *Renew*, 155, 2005; R. McKie, *The Observer*, 11 June 2006.

46 Margaret Beckett, quoted by Patrick Wintour, *Guardian*, 28 March 2006; Gordon Brown, *BBC News*, 22 April 2006.

47 For the tax rates see Helm, *Energy*, p. 357.

48 http://www.dti.gov.uk/energy/nuclear/technology/history.shtml – see also Simms et al., *Mirage and Oasis*, p. 26.

49 Friends of the Earth press releases, 'Scottish M.P.'s Climate Change Bill "Needs Backing" says FoE', 3 February 2005, http://www.foe-scotland.org.uk and 'UK Needs New Climate Change Law, Says Coalition', 13 July 2005, http://www.foe.co.uk.

50 See Marco Verweij, 'Curbing Global Warming the Easy Way: An Alternative to the Kyoto Protocol', *Government and Opposition*, 38(4), 2003.

51 'The Untimely Death of Salter's Duck' (see note 17); Rand, 'Why We Need Wind Power' (see note 16).

52 McGarr, 'Capitalism and Climate Change'.

53 The 'politics of necessity' is a component of a major ESRC funded multidisciplinary project, 'cultures of consumption': http://www.consume.bbk.ac.uk. See http://seis.bris.ac.uk/~lwbmm/necessity-politics-details.html for the project led by Bronwen Morgan on what used to be called the utilities and their regulation. This section uses Helm, *Energy*, pp. 42, 303, 362-8 and 380.

54 Helm, *Energy*, p. 380. On the Utilities Act see pp. 362-3, 368; on the EU pollution permits, see Friends of the Earth press release, 'Government Legal Challenge to Allow UK to Pollute more under EU Climate Scheme', 18 October 2005, http://www.foe.co.uk. The construction industry is also lamentably poorly regulated, has every incentive not to comply with energy efficiency laws and to act politically to preserve its current production conditions (George Monbiot, *Guardian*, 30 May 2006).

55 See respectively, Labour Party Manifesto 2005, http://www.labour.org.uk/manifesto; http://www.greenparty.org.uk/files/reports/2004.

56 Patrick Wintour, 'Carbon Emission Targets Delayed by Government Row', *Guardian*, 31 January 2006; see also http://www.sternreview.org.

57 Wintour, 'Carbon Emissions'.

58 P. Hetherington, *Guardian*, 8 February 2006.

59 Helm, *Energy*, pp. 362, 425.

60 The phrase is Cindy Katz's in 'Under the Falling Sky: Apocalyptic Environmentalism and the Production of Nature', in A. Callari, C. Biewener and S. Cullenberg, eds., *Marxism in the Postmodern Age*, London: Guilford, 1994, p. 277. See also Helm, *Energy*, pp. 351, 353.

61   Michael Meacher M.P., 2004, personal communication.

62   This section uses Helm, *Energy*, chapter 19, pp. 345-71.

63   Ibid., p. 356-7, 366.

64   Energy companies have had a tendency to be delinquent: see the cases of Enron, British Energy, NEUSA in California, Powergen, Centrica (Helm, *Energy*, p. 30); G. Monbiot, *Guardian*, 13 June 2006.

65   Lord Oxburgh, *Guardian*, 15 June 2005.

66   Robin McKie, interview with David King, who declared that failure to cut carbon emissions 'is not an option'. *Observer*, 27 June 2005;'What BP is Doing', report filed under 'Environment and Society' at http://www.bp.com.

67   Jonathan Porritt, *Observer*, 23 June 2005.

68   K. Griffiths, *Independent on Sunday*, 12 June 2005; T. Macalister, 'Shell wants London to be Windy City', *Guardian*, 19 December 2003; Corporate Europe Observatory, 'Greenhouse Market Mania-UN Climate Talks Corrupted by Corporate Pseudo-Solutions', November, 2000, briefing available at http://www.corporateeurope.org; N. Mathieson, *Observer*, Special Report on Energy, 11 June 2006, p. 3.

69   One pro-nuclear former Labour MP represents a client of BNFL; another has abandoned party politics to do PR for a US decommissioning firm; while a third runs the Transatlantic Nuclear Forum. See T. Macalister, *Guardian*, 11 July 2006, p. 22.

70   Helm, *Energy*, pp. 353-7.

71   http://www.ashdenawards.org.

72   Richard Wachman, *Observer*, 26 June 2005, p. 15.

73   *New Scientist*, 17 July 2004 p. 6.

74   See Jonathan Porritt, the Chair of the Government's Sustainable Development Commission, *Observer*, 26 July 2005; and Larry Elliott, *Guardian*, 12 June 2006: 'Executives from Vodafone, Unilever, BAA, John Lewis Partnership, Tesco, Shell and eight other companies demanded urgent action from the prime minister'.

75   Helm, *Energy*, p. 350; P. Brown, *Guardian*, 24 June 2005. The BWEA has a membership of 300 companies and has recently expanded its concept of wind to cover wave and tidal energy.

76   http://www.dti.gov.uk/news/newsarticle020106b.html.

77   Elliott, *Guardian*, 12 June 2006.

78   http://www.climatechangecapital.com.

79   'The Wind Debate. New Anti-Wind Lobby', *Renew On Line*, 52(Nov-Dec), 2004, available from http://eeru.open.ac.uk/natta/rol.html.

80   A. Alderson, 'Prince Charles: Wind Farms are Horrendous', *Telegraph*, 8 August 2004; D. Ward, *Guardian*, 3 March 2006.

81   The context for this statement was the dismal performance of US corporations in a Carbon Disclosure Project in 2005: D. Adam, *Guardian*, 15 September 2005.

82   'Joint Academies G8 Statement on Climate Change', http://www.royalsoc.ac.uk/landing.asp?id=1278.

83 In the US climate change science is alleged to be under surveillance and harassment by the Republican Party backed by its oil interests. P. Brown, *Guardian*, 30 August 2005.

84 M. Grimston, *The Importance of Politics to Nuclear Rebuild*, London: Chatham House, 2005. The case *for* deliberative democracy may be found in Thomas Dietz, Elinor Ostrom and Paul Stern, 'The Struggle to Govern the Commons', *Science*, 302(5652), 2003, pp. 1907–12. The case *for* expert science in policy making is made by the Chief Scientific Officer to the Government, David King in 'Governing Technology and Growth', in Calestous Juma, ed., *Science and Innovation in Africa*, London: Smith Institute, 2005.

85 See http://www.foe.co.uk/campaigns/climate/press_for_change/ and http://www.greenpeace.org/international/campaigns/climate_change/take_action.

86 The funding of environmental NGOs from DEFRA and the FCO blurs the boundary between the state and civil society organizations, just as DFID's funding qualifies the independence of development NGOs.

87 According to Larry Lohmann (http://www.thecornerhouse.org.uk), the WWF supports Third World carbon dumps, subject to (unattainable) quality standards of maintenance.

88 'Blair Backs Nuclear Power Plans', BBC News online, 16 May 2004, http://news.bbc.co.uk.

89 See Colin Leys, 'The Cynical State', in *Socialist Register 2006*.

90 S. Ghosh, *Climate Change*. The question how renewable energy consumer demand is created and imagined, constructed, represented, organized and resisted is so big that it is outside the scope of this essay.

NEOLIBERAL HURRICANE:
WHO FRAMED NEW ORLEANS?

JAMIE PECK

Tropical Depression 12 formed over the Bahamas on August 23, 2005, triggering a sequence of events that would result in a most unnatural urban crisis. When Hurricane Katrina made landfall in Louisiana, some six days later, the city of New Orleans was bracing itself for what Mayor Ray Nagin had called the 'storm most of us have long feared'.[1] The Mayor had ordered the city's first mandatory evacuation, but it was known that many of New Orleans' poorest and sickest residents had been unable to evacuate. Although the eye of the storm narrowly missed the city itself, a series of catastrophic breaches of the levee system on August 29 inundated four-fifths of the urban area with several feet of toxic floodwater. If the level of preparedness for this long-anticipated disaster was lamentable, the management of the subsequent emergency was tragic. A lethally tardy and poorly coordinated response from the Federal Emergency Management Agency (FEMA) compounded the problems faced by state and local agencies, whose limited organizational capacities were quickly overwhelmed. The abject failure of the evacuation effort was captured in searing media images of tens of thousands of displaced New Orleanians crowded, in unsanitary and dangerous conditions, into the city's Convention Center and Superdome. Lacking adequate food, water, and medical supplies, these 'refuges of last resort' were not themselves fully evacuated until September 3 and 6, respectively. But yet more shocking, for many commentators, was that in the days after the storm, the city's social order apparently ruptured: the police lost control of the streets, looting and violence ensued, all of which was broadcast, in occasionally hysterical form, by the global media. A social disaster, compounded by political indifference and governmental failure, added up to what the *Economist* would call 'The shaming of America':

> Since Hurricane Katrina, the world's view of America has changed. The disaster has exposed some shocking truths about the place: the bitterness of its sharp racial divide, the abandonment of the dispossessed, the weakness of the critical infrastructure. But the most astonishing and most shaming revelation has been of its government's failure to bring succour to its people at their time of greatest need.[2]

The scale of the human, environmental, and social catastrophe wrought by Katrina may, quite literally, never be known. The official death toll currently stands at over 1,800, with as many people still unaccounted for. One-and-a-half million people were displaced by the storm, one third of whom may never return to the Gulf Coast. Damage estimates, quickly politicized, range from $40 to $120 billion, while the bill for reconstruction effort could be as high as $250 billion. The 'recovery' of New Orleans, a city now slowly repopulating, is expected to take years.

Much of the commentary on Katrina and its aftermath has focused, quite understandably, on the Bush Administration's manifest ineptitude and apparent indifference. But there is another story about post-Katrina New Orleans, less talked about, but no less important. It concerns the 'management' of the fiscal and policy fallout of the disaster by conservative and free-market think tanks, like the Heritage Foundation, the Manhattan Institute, Cato, and the American Enterprise Institute. Here, the response has been considerably more sure-footed, and the consequences profound. As the Bush Administration floundered, both institutionally and politically, in the days following the flood, the conservative think tanks did not hesitate to wade in. The initial reactions of these ideological first-responders were occasionally off key, but before long they were acting in concert, 'framing' the disaster in a manner designed not only to contain its political and financial costs, but more than this, to enable a brazen extension of the neoliberal project.

While think tanks often take pride in their intrepid exploration of the 'unthinkable' reaches of policy,[3] in the immediate aftermath of Katrina this extended into saying the unsayable. As mainstream politicians quickly learned that contemplating anything less than a complete reconstruction of New Orleans was practically unacceptable,[4] think tank scholars pondered much more freely the possibly 'doomed' fate of New Orleans, the city's long-standing cultural association with death, its possible loss 'to the forces of nature'; indeed, the very 'improbability' of the place, which – like Venice – 'was created in defiance of the forces of nature'.[5] There was also some rather intemperate reaction to 'distorted' reporting on the Katrina tragedy in Europe and elsewhere, where the politically motivated were seen to be too ready 'to blame President Bush for the actions of Mother Nature', while being tragically unaware that 'a Hobbesian world waits explosively, just below [the] skin – here in America, just as in any place'.[6] The suggestion that Katrina's might could have been related to global climate change was also rebuffed, as 'disgusting exploitation' by 'environmental extremists' like Sir David King, the British Government's chief scientific adviser.[7] And, just as predictably, there was a visceral reaction to the offer of aid from Cuba and Venezuela: the United States, Heritage sputtered, does not accept charity from 'self-serving autocrats'.[8]

But the role of conservative think tanks extends far beyond the cut and thrust of daily political exchange. On the longer horizon, their function is to help lend a measure of form and coherence to governmental policy respons-es, in light of the right's programmatic agenda, and to cajole and guide the (often wayward) political class.[9] They do this by working on the 'inside', with government officials and elected politicians, and on the 'outside', through the conventional media and, increasingly, the blogosphere. And while they may share, in broad terms, a common ideological orientation, there is also something of a division of labour amongst the think tanks. For example, the Manhattan Institute tends to favour 'long-range' interventions, seeking to shape the principles and premises of policy debates in fields like welfare and policing, while the Heritage Foundation is located within walking distance of Congress, for good reason – it is closely attuned to the challenges of short-term policy management. If the Manhattan Institute strives to 'turn intellect into influence', to borrow its tag line, Heritage endeavours to transform influence into action.[10]

Working off a series of well-established scripts, the conservative think tanks were within days constructing a 'principled response' to Katrina, predi-cated upon fiscal restraint and 'offsetting' budget cuts in Washington, DC, but extending into what amounts to an audacious neoliberal reconstruc-tion agenda for the Crescent City. This includes an enlarged role for private enterprise in market-led development, governmental outsourcing, and city governance; selective institutional roll-backs, focused on the social state; re-doubled crime control, making the city safe for tourists and gentrifiers; and an interventionist program of 'moral reconstruction', aimed at those stranded in the storm's wake. Yet if this is to be the fate of New Orleans, it was never a pre-ordained one. Katrina presented an urgent and challenging problem for the conservative think tanks, and they committed significant resources to the response. Recognizing the significance of the events on the Gulf, key play-ers in the think tanks were back at their desks immediately after the storm, even while Bush Administration officials completed their vacations. While the conservative think tanks may have been relatively successful in 'reframing' Katrina, and supplying a package of workable policy rationales and ruses to the Bush Administration, their strenuous efforts also reveal the politically constructed – if not jerrybuilt – nature of this 'free-market' response. The character and content of their response, my focus in this essay, also speaks to fissures and fault lines within the neocon/neoliberal project itself. But, for now, let's see how the conservative intelligentsia told the story.[11]

UNTHINKING KATRINA

'No American city has ever gone through what New Orleans must go through', wrote Manhattan Institute analyst Nicole Gelinas in the midst of the deadly flooding, since notwithstanding the immediate crisis, no city had had to contend with 'flight of its most affluent and capable citizens, followed by social breakdown among those left behind, after which must come the total reconstruction of economic and physical infrastructure by a devastated populace'. Herself one of the city's former residents, and a graduate of Tulane University, Gelinas confessed in a *New York Sun* editorial that, '[t]he truth is that even on a normal day, New Orleans is a sad city'.

> New Orleans can't take care of itself even when it is not 80 percent underwater; what is it going to do now, as waters continue to cripple it, and thousands of looters systematically destroy what Katrina left unscathed? ...The city's government has long suffered from incompetence and corruption.... On television this week, the mayor has shown no clear inclination to take charge and direct post-Katrina rescue and recovery efforts for his population, as Mayor Giuliani did in New York on and after 9/11... New Orleans teems with crime, and the NOPD can't keep order on a good day... Socially, New Orleans is one of America's last helpless cities.[12]

The underlying explanation for New Orleans' 'helplessness' here is the city's subjection to a hypertrophied form of the American urban condition, as it has been characterized by conservatives: the breakdown of social control triggers a middles-class exodus, leaving behind a welfare-dependent underclass whose proclivity to cultural dysfunction and economic disconnection then goes unchecked; a complicit and corrupt municipal administration is unable – by definition, since it is part of the problem – either to read the causes or manage the consequences. Having travelled further than most down this spiral of self-fulfilling decline, Gelinas counselled, New Orleans may now lack the capacity even to save itself: '[s]ure, the feds must provide cash and resources for relief and recovery – but it's up to New Orleans, not the feds, to dig deep within itself to rebuild its economic and social infrastructure'. Yet her sense was that this would take nothing less than '*a miracle*. New Orleans has experienced a steady brain drain and fiscal drain for decades, as affluent corporations and individuals have fled, leaving behind a large population of people dependent on the government'. In order to avert a still greater urban crisis the only hope, Gelinas felt at the time, lay with an injection of Giuliani-style leadership. New Orleans Mayor Nagin, visibly reeling in the face of his city's destruction, would have to *manage* first himself, then the crisis: '[h]e must not waver, or a priceless city will be borne by the waters into Newark, 1967'.[13]

The following day, as media portrayals of the city's descent into chaos began to focus on reports of violence and looting, Gelinas' analysis turned yet more pessimistic. In what had become a 'perfect storm of lawlessness', the New Orleans 'criminal class [had] taken over the stricken city'.

> Katrina didn't turn innocent citizens into desperate criminals. This week's looters... are the same depraved individuals who have pushed New Orleans' murder rate to several multiples above the national average in normal times.... Today may not be the best day to get into New Orleans' intractable crime problem, but it's necessary, since it explains how this week's communications and policing vacuum so quickly created a perfect storm for the vicious lawlessness that has broken out.... On a normal day, those who make up New Orleans' dangerous criminal class – yes, likely the same African-Americans we see looting now – terrorize their own communities.... Failure to put violent criminals behind bars in peacetime has led to chaos in disaster.... Now, no civil authorities can re-assert order in New Orleans. The city must be forcefully demilitarized, even as innocent victims literally starve.[14]

If American think tanks are often criticized for their tendency to rush to prefabricated policy prescriptions,[15] a somewhat different dynamic seems to have been at work here. Perhaps reflecting the Manhattan Institute's role as a supplier of basic ideational resources for neoconservative/neoliberal policy-makers – as opposed to the kind of quick-fire policy formation in which Heritage and its ilk specialize – Gelinas was (re)presenting her own form of causal interpretation. Recirculating staples of underclass analysis, she confidently drew distinctions between the behaviour and motivations of the 'core criminal class' and the hapless group of benign dependants ('impoverished women, children, and elderly folks') who had trudged *en masse* to Superdome and Convention Center 'expecting their government to take care of them'.[16] These segments of the underclass were seen to be behaving rationally, if dysfunctionally, within a governmentally-engineered universe of perverse incentives.[17] This was the Manhattan Institute's standard diagnosis of New York City's problems in the 1970s, along with the 'broken-windows thesis', which saw even minor untended lawlessness as intrinsically degenerative, spawning an hypertrophied culture of urban crime.[18] While the 'new urban right' has developed responses to these entrenched problems – reform the poor with systemic welfare reform and zero-tolerance policing; bring back the middle classes with tax breaks and reformed schools – these are not, re-alistically speaking, short-term policies.[19] Hence the undercurrent of weary fatalism in these initial dispatches from the Manhattan Institute. Reflecting this sentiment, Theodore Dalrymple expounded on the 'thin line' separating civilization from 'barbarism and mob rule', while David Brooks thought he detected not a 'tipping' but a 'bursting point', from which New Orleans had emerged as an 'anti-9/11 [in which] nobody took control'.[20]

The post-Katrina policy vacuum sucked in prefabricated conservative di-agnoses of the American urban condition – the usual cocktail of race, crime, and dependency – but even professional opinion-shapers seemed initially at a loss how to construct much more than a rhetorical response. It was as if, in a period in which the governmental system itself temporarily lost traction, the most persistent critics of the misinterventionist state momentarily lost their bearings. And nowhere was the vacuum more profound than at the federal level, where the White House appeared paralyzed, successively, by indifference, incomprehension, and indecision.[21] Returning from vacation in Texas, President Bush had taken an aerial detour over the flood zone to assess the damage for himself. Acknowledging that New Orleans' recovery would be a 'difficult road', the President reaffirmed his confidence in the ill-fated Michael Brown, then head of FEMA, as the Administration's point man in the stricken region, praised the 'armies of compassion' for their charitable responses, and appealed lamely for better coordination of the emerging re-lief program. While his Administration contemplated a 'comprehensive relief effort', Bush symbolically underlined the absence of federal control of the situation by standing in the Rose Garden and reading out the Red Cross emergency number, 1-800-HELPNOW.[22] One of the Administration's few decisive acts of the day was to open up the Strategic Petroleum Reserve, in order to relieve pressure on the nation's gas prices.

Initially at least, the response of the Washington think tanks was almost as flat-footed. Even the Heritage Foundation, the most closely attuned to the daily rhythms of the political cycle, had its attention focused elsewhere at the beginning of the crisis. With harrowing images of corpses floating in New Orleans floodwaters dominating the national media, Heritage's opening salvo in the post-Katrina policy debate was to warn of the perils of price controls, including a meditation on the 'disaster' of governmental intervention in the oil market during the 1970s.[23] This rather discordant tone continued the next day, when Heritage researchers alternately pressed for both Arctic drilling and the deregulation of emission controls as means of easing post-Katrina gas prices; offered reassurances that, fortunately, the economy was in good shape – aided by the continuing 'disintegration' of the AFL-CIO and the 'bravery' of Congress for refusing to raise the minimum wage for a seventh straight year; and indulged in some uncharacteristically inconclusive hand-wringing about the scale of the catastrophe in the Gulf.[24] Not until veteran fiscal hawk Ronald Utt joined the fray did a more rounded, apposite, and self-assured Heritage response begin to take shape. Having praised private and charitable responses to the disaster, Utt rhetorically asked if members of Congress would also be prepared to make a 'sacrifice' – recognizing this 'higher purpose' by renouncing 'frivolous pork barrel spending' in the recently enacted highway bill. Impishly, Utt proposed that the funds earmarked for the now-infamous 'bridge to nowhere' in Alaska could be reallocated to the Gulf Region, perhaps for a bridge reconstruction project gifted by 'the People of Alaska'.[25]

The metaphor of the politically indefensible bridge to nowhere would become a staple for fiscal conservatives in the following days and weeks. Codifying a theme that reverberated across the conservative blogs and letters-to-the-editor pages, Heritage posted a set of 'instructions for writing an op-ed' on the members' section of its web site, echoing the message that essential spending for Katrina recovery efforts should be clawed back from the 'fiscally reckless' highway bill.[26] This line of attack was amply echoed by other free-market think tanks, most notably by Cato and the American Enterprise Institute (AEI), themselves still smarting over the passage of the $244 billion highway bill in early August, 2005 – which infamously contained some 6,373 'earmarks', a bloated package of congressional members' local projects with a total value of nearly $25 billion.[27] By now, the think tanks had recovered their footing, and were concertedly moving ahead of the public debate.

Less than two weeks after Katrina's strike, by September 12, Heritage was ready to announce a full package of 'principled solutions' to the rebuilding challenge. Presenting a tightly-framed small-government strategy, the team of senior Heritage researchers outlined the following guidelines:

- The federal government should provide support and assistance *only in those situations that are beyond the capabilities of state and local governments* and the private sector. State and local governments must retain their primary role as first responders to disasters....
- Federal financial aid, when necessary, should be provided in a manner that promotes accountability, flexibility, and creativity. In general, tools such as tax credits and voucher programs, which *allow individuals and families to direct funds*, should be utilized to encourage private-sector innovation and sensitivity to individual needs and preferences.
- Consistent with genuine health and safety needs, *red tape should be reduced or eliminated* to speed up private-sector investment and initiative in the rebuilding of facilities and the restoration of businesses. Regulations that are barriers to putting people back to work should be suspended or, at a minimum, streamlined.
- Congress should reorder its spending priorities, not just add new money while other money is being wasted. *Now is the time to shift resources to their most important uses and away from lower-priority uses...* It is critical that America focus on building capabilities for responding to a catastrophic disaster, not on catering to the wish lists of cities, parishes or counties, states, and stakeholders.
- *Private entrepreneurial activity and vision, not bureaucratic government, must be the engine to rebuild.* New approaches... such as enhanced choice in public school education should be the norm, not the exception.... The critical need now is to encourage investors and entrepreneurs to seek new opportunities within these cities. Bureaucrats cannot do that. The key is to encourage private-sector creativity – for example, by declaring New Orleans and other severely damaged areas 'Opportunity Zones' in which capital gains tax on investments is eliminated and regulations [are] eliminated or simplified.[28]

The comprehensive plan developed by Heritage deployed what would become a keyword in the subsequent reconstruction debate – *offsets*. Any new federal spending commitments, the Heritage team argued, must be 'offset by reductions in other spending', since under no circumstances must there be 'mission creep' into uncompensated spending, new programs, or worse still, 'any entitlement expectations for disaster relief'. The Bush Administration was applauded for showing the 'courage' to suspend the Davis-Bacon Act, which requires that contractors working on federally funded construction projects should be paid the prevailing wage, on the grounds, ostensibly, that this would both hold down costs and stimulate job creation.[29] And along with this came a potpourri of staple conservative demands – rolling back the Clean Air Act and restrictions on oil drilling; removing tariffs; accelerating tax cuts within the 'Opportunity Zone', including voucher schemes for healthcare, education, and job training; incentives for private providers and faith-based organizations across these and other policy fields; expansion and retasking of the National Guard; capping Medicaid entitlements; streamlining FEMA while rolling out a network of regional offices for homeland security, managed by political appointees; and the repeal of the Estate (or 'death') tax. Pressing a broad package of conservative proposals, the Vice President of Heritage editorialized in the *Los Angeles Times* against 'reflexively pouring money into the Gulf' through Congressional displays of 'checkbook compassion'.[30]

On the other hand, 'unexpected' events, like hurricanes, must not, under any circumstances, disrupt the defining programmatic element of the conservative agenda: tax cuts. In an unsubtly entitled intervention, 'New Orleans vs. New York?' – just two weeks after the storm – the Manhattan Institute's Steven Malanga pointed out that New Yorkers had 'already done their share to lend aid' to the victims of Katrina in the form of short-term charitable giving. His more serious concern was that a 'post-Katrina mindset in Washington' might lead to a postponement of the scheduled extension to dividend and capital-gains tax cuts, badly needed for Wall Street's continued recovery.[31] Never one to flinch in the face of potential controversy, Grover Norquist of Americans for Tax Reform had struck while the Superdome tragedy was still unfolding, arguing that those politicians that were arguing for a delay in the rolling programme of tax cuts were 'exploiting this tragedy'; instead, the long-awaited repeal of the Estate Tax should proceed immediately, on the grounds that it would stimulate economic growth.[32] Norquist has been described as the 'V.I. Lenin of the anti-tax movement', pressing for deep tax cuts on principle, irrespective of the immediate political-economic climate – a measure of the long-term horizons of the conservative movement, where there is 'no interest in politics on the margin or in managing the next recession or the one after that'.[33]

By mid-September, with President Bush about to give a major speech in New Orleans on the reconstruction effort, the drumbeat message on offset spending had intensified to the point that real pressure was being exerted on the Republican leadership. Former House Leader Tom DeLay's remark that 'there is simply no fat left to cut in the federal budget' had caused consternation amongst fiscal conservatives in the think tank community.[34] Heritage and AEI got into something of an 'offset' race to identify the longest and most inflammatory list of 'dispensable' federal programmes. In addition to the fiscally conservative 'gimmie' of highway pork, the AEI proposed terminating the USAID program for malaria prevention and the National Endowments for the Arts and for the Humanities, while privatizing air traffic control, NASA, the US Postal Service, and Amtrak; meanwhile, Heritage took aim at just at some of the 'easy places to start cutting', like Americorps, the Corporation for Public Broadcasting, community development block grants, 130 programs serving the disabled, 90 early childhood development projects, 342 economic development initiatives, and farm subsidies – especially for celebrity 'hobby farmers' like David Rockefeller and Ted Turner.[35]

But these were mere diversions relative to the main task to which the free-market think tanks were dedicated in the run-up to Bush's New Orleans speech – to influence the principles, and if possible, the price-tag of what would clearly be a massive rebuilding effort. In this latter respect, there was a high degree of consonance in the positions of the free-market think tanks. Like Heritage, AEI was pressing for emergency assistance tied more to people than places, and based on short-term loans, vouchers, and temporary provisions. Yes, there should be a concerted effort to repair the damaged infrastructure, but ultimately 'it's important to let markets decide how fast New Orleans springs back'.[36] An AEI colleague, James Glassman, likewise insisted that the 'revival should be as spontaneous as possible'. But since New Orleans was never a city that 'worked' in the first place – 'the world got a taste of that dysfunctionality… during the storm… [C]orruption, squalor and stupidity do not equal charm' – a radically new approach would be called for:

> The inevitable commission that will oversee the rebuilding must realize that the world's best designers, developers and innovators will be drawn to the city only if they are relatively unrestricted. New Orleans could become a laboratory for ideas like tax-free commercial zones and school reform. This is the ultimate libertarian city and the last thing it needs is top-down planning…. I'm optimistic. New Orleans has a unique chance to make a fresh start and, in fact, become more like cities that do work (Chicago and Phoenix come to mind) while retaining its spirit of mystery, absurdity, beauty and decadence.[37]

At least some of this conservative optimism was well founded. When President Bush addressed the nation from New Orleans' Jackson Square two days later, he promised that an entrepreneurial city would rise from the floodwaters, assisted by a package of tax-breaks, short-term loans and guarantees for small businesses branded the 'Gulf Opportunity Zone' (GO Zone); there would be temporary jobs and short-term extensions to unemployment benefits, and evacuees would not 'have to travel great distances or navigate bureaucracies to get the benefits that are there for them'; there would be an Urban Homesteading Act, to encourage home ownership, and Worker Recovery Accounts, to help individuals reenter the workforce; the federal government would join forces with the 'armies of compassion – charities and houses of worship, and idealistic men and women' in the rebuilding effort; the flood protection system would be rebuilt 'stronger than it has ever been'; and there would be a 'team of inspectors general reviewing all expenditures' in order to ensure that the taxpayers' money was being spent honestly.[38]

DOING WHAT IT TAKES

If the free-market think tanks were quietly satisfied with many aspects of the Administration's proposals – indeed they were uncredited originators of several of them – there was considerable unease with what would become the headline-generating line from Bush's speech – 'we will do what it takes, we will stay as long as it takes'. Fearing an open-ended spending commitment, Cato reflexively warned of an impending 'budget disaster'.[39] For their part, Heritage scholars were somewhat more circumspect, working feverishly through less public channels, but also highlighting 'dangers' with aspects of the Administration's plan. While welcoming the announcement of the GO Zone – practically a Heritage creation – they reiterated their demand for offsets (a word Bush did not use once in his speech), citing the apparent reluctance of Congress to make tough choices,[40] and forecasting that 'local officials [will] see this as an opportunity to put forward an extensive wish list'.[41] Obliviously extending its own wish list, Heritage also called for Education Smart Cards, more support for charter schools, and – fearing a 'cost explosion' – a cap on emergency healthcare provisions, together with the appointment of an Emergency Regulatory Relief Board in order to minimize bureaucratic creep. AEI also identified a need for a 'red tape tsar', and would have preferred more emphasis on vouchers and private-sector financing: '[o]nce responsible intervention to restore order and infrastructure has occurred, individual desires and market forces should continue to shape the design of cities, not a federally financed return to the status quo ante'.[42]

While at the same time presenting intricate plans for the re-regulation of housing, education, labour market, health, national security, and transport policy, the free-market think tanks are nevertheless perpetually fearful of a particular kind of governmental bloat – involving the proliferation of 'paper plans', the growth of command-and-control decision-making through 'vast bureaucracies', and 'out-of-control' spending. While the nightmare scenario of Senator Edward Kennedy's New Deal-style Gulf Coast Regional Re-development Authority never represented a serious threat, it was one that the conservative think tanks liked to ventilate frequently, at least for effect.[43] More serious, in just about every way, was the very real and imminent menace of 'Big Government Conservatism', Bush-style. As Heritage president Ed Feulner editorialized, just after the Administration's plans for the Gulf region had been announced:

> At some point, a hurricane is downgraded from a crisis to a problem.... But as lawmakers scramble to throw money at the problem, it's worth remembering that no level of government has distinguished itself in the last several weeks.... [We] shouldn't respond to government failures by making the government larger and still more unwieldy. The best way to rebuild New Orleans will be for the government to get out of the way. Congress and state governments can do this by eliminating or reducing regulations and allowing communities to decide for themselves how best to rebuild.... Let's make sure that in responding to the temporary problems of Katrina, we don't simply create the permanent problem of ever more – and ever more expensive – bureaucracy.[44]

Similar concerns were generously amplified by the *Wall Street Journal*'s editorial page, which for some time has had a symbiotic relationship with the free-market think tanks. Under the headline 'Hurricane Bush' the *Journal* opined bombastically that, '[t]he people who couldn't flee the storm were not ignored by "small government conservatism"', as if that still exists outside Hong Kong. The city's poor have been smothered by decades of corrupt, paternal government – local, state and federal', concluding that, '[i]t was certainly a collapse of government, but more accurately of bureaucracy and the welfare state'.[45] A week earlier, the *Journal*'s deputy Washington editor, David Wessel, had gloomily proclaimed that, '[t]he era of small government is over. Sept. 11 challenged it. Katrina killed it' – a statement that reverberated widely around the think-tank community.[46] Illustrating the tight nexus between the financial press, the free-market think tanks, and fiscal conservatives in Washington, the Republican Study Committee (RSC)[47] had been meeting at the Heritage Foundation to hatch their own version of the rebuilding plans, producing a 'sea of conservative ideas' that were subsequently published by the *Journal*. Parroting Heritage's reconstruction blueprint, the RSC's chair, Representative Mike Pence, declared that, '[w]e want to turn the Gulf Coast into a magnet for free enterprise. The last thing we want is a federal city where New Orleans once was. [We want] a flat-tax free-enterprise zone'.[48]

One week later, the RSC launched 'Operation Offset' – proposing more than $71 billion in cuts from the 2006 federal budget in order to cover the costs of Gulf Coast reconstruction, while pressing for a much wider and deeper programme of 'savings' (totalling more than $500 billion) over the ensuing decade.[49] Not surprisingly, Heritage warmly welcomed the package, much of which had been hatched in its own offices, while at the same time presenting the initiative as an outcome of 'grassroots energy'.[50] The *Wall Street Journal* also voiced its support, declaring the White House's position on Katrina spending to be 'irresponsible and even insidious', having previously accused members of Congress of getting 'in the way of this natural economic recovery by exploiting Katrina to spend like they're back on Bourbon Street'.[51] A parallel effort was also beginning to gain ground in the Senate, led by spending hawks John McCain and Tom Coburn, who called on the President to present his own package of offsets and rescissions.[52] This initiative was conspicuously welcomed on the conservative/libertarian blog, *Porkbusters*, which was established on September 18, 2005 to fight the cause of offset spending cuts, post-Katrina.[53]

During this time, the think tanks were stepping up their attacks on the spendthrift ways of the Republican leadership, mischievously praising House Democratic Leader Nancy Pelosi's audacious pledge to return $70 million in 'highway pork' from her own district to assist the recovery effort, indeed taking the calculated taunting to the national press.[54] Perhaps the mood in Washington was already beginning to shift, then, prior to the presentation of the Louisiana delegation's $250 billion reconstruction package in early October – the 'extensive wish list' that Heritage had predicted on the day of Bush's Jackson Square speech. The President immediately called a press conference to declare a subtle, but critical, shift in policy: 'The heart of America is big enough to be generous and responsible at the same time... As the federal government meets its responsibilities, the people of the Gulf Coast must also recognize its limitations'. Bush emphasized that the recovery effort would be private-sector led, going on to promise to 'work with members of Congress to identify offsets, to free up money for the reconstruction efforts'.[55] The chair of the RSC, Representative Mike Pence, immediately issued an obsequious press release, calling attention to the President's new-found commitment to the principle of offsets.[56] And the fiscally conservative think tanks dutifully reiterated the same line, also crediting the Administration's far-sighted embrace of offset budgeting.

The PELICAN (Protecting Essential Louisiana Infrastructure, Citizens, and Nature) Plan was immediately besieged. Heritage characterized it as a 'breathtaking display of parochial self-interest', favourably citing the criticisms of RSC stalwart, Representative Jeff Flake, in the *Wall Street Journal*, that 'we risk setting... an unsustainable precedent that it is the responsibility of the federal government to ensure that the victims of natural disasters are made whole'.[57] PELICAN was similarly dismissed by the AEI as 'pork gumbo', resident scholar Newt Gingrich stepping into the fray to portray the funding request as deficit-busting audacity from a cabal of local lawmakers historically prone to corruption:

> While we all feel for Louisiana's residents, there are limits to what American taxpayers can – and should – be asked to contribute on top of their already large tax bill. More worrisome, too much federal largesse can have negative consequences on behavior. What are the odds, for instance, of more responsible behavior by state and local officials when the federal government picks up all costs? And will private individuals and businesses make sound decisions – purchasing insurance to cover risks, for example – when Uncle Sam bails out poor choices?[58]

Compassion fatigue, it seemed, was now extending beyond the tight network of fiscally conservative activists. But more importantly, a conservative position on New Orleans had now stabilized, with the aid of insistent incantation from the think tanks via briefings, blogs, editorials, and daily policy memos. The dominant motif, or policy 'frame', was now *responsibility*: fiscal responsibility in Washington; personal and local (government) responsibility in New Orleans. Conveniently, this new-found policy fix served both ideological ends (federal overreach is checked in favour of local bootstrapping) and partisan objectives (since both the state and local administrations in question were controlled by the Democrats).

As Heritage noted, the House Leadership was finally succumbing to a combination of orchestrated pressure and relentless reason, while acknowledging that it would take 'political courage' to respond to what they could now describe as the *President's* call for a fiscally responsible offset package.[59] Unless a line was drawn in the sand, federal spending would balloon to the point that taxes would have to rise by 50 per cent – and then 'France will look good by comparison', Ed Feulner wryly observed.[60] Reviewing national press coverage, Heritage also declared that the now-fabled 'bridge to nowhere' had become a potent emblem of fiscal irresponsibility, in fact a 'national embarrassment'.[61] To borrow a metaphor often used in think-tank circles, a tipping point had apparently been reached: the Washington version of 'behaving responsibly', it now seemed, was defined by sending less, not more, money to the Gulf Coast. The 'rainbow in the aftermath of Katrina', as Feulner put it, was that the 'tipping point' had arrived '[n]ow excessive spending is on everyone's mind'.[62]

More than this, the twin cases of Katrina spending and the Alaskan bridge provided an object lesson in the determination of legitimate federal responsibility and spending. The spontaneously choreographed challenge, to which all the free-market think tanks would rise, was to intensify the recurrent demand for offset spending, to brand all nonessential forms of spending as 'pork', and as the AEI put it, 'to get the federal government out of the disaster-relief business [in order] to promote responsible behaviour on the part of individuals and businesses'.[63] The provision of flood insurance, or for that matter no-strings-attached welfare payments, would only encourage what AEI's Véronique de Rugy described as 'dangerous' and irresponsible behaviour, inducing 'people to constantly make the same mistake'. The small print in the PELICAN Plan that suspended work requirements and welfare time limits in New Orleans had also irked the conservative intelligentsia, a Heritage analyst concluding that this meant that 'welfare recipients would not be expected to play a constructive role in the recovery'.[64] Meanwhile others at Heritage saw an opportunity to roll back federal labour policies, including Unemployment Insurance coverage in the affected area, fearing that the Administration's proposed $5,000 Worker Recovery Accounts might reinduce an entitlement mindset, encouraging cooks, taxi drivers and bartenders to invest in training that they patently did not need.[65]

REBUILDING NEW ORLEANS' MORAL LEVEES

When Senator John Kerry observed, quite plausibly, that the Republicans' plans for the Gulf Region would transform it 'into a vast laboratory for right-wing ideological experiments… recycling all [the conservatives'] failed policies and shipping them to Louisiana', Heritage immediately countered that the root cause of the problems facing the region were those Great Society programs in the fields of welfare, housing, education, and job training, which had in effect left the poor defenceless.[66] Since it was the welfare state that placed the poor in the path of the storm, so the argument went, it would be no less than perverse to pour money into programmes that destroy work ethics and encourage illegitimacy: '[t]he poor of New Orleans have been victims twice', Cato's Michael Tanner had pointed out in the immediate aftermath of the disaster, so 'let's not victimize them a third time'.[67] The Hoover Institution's Thomas Sowell likewise presented the main challenge as one of 'rebuild[ing] New Orleans' moral levees'.[68] Less compassionately, George Neumayr, Executive Editor of *The American Spectator* and a recent media fellow at Hoover, railed against those New Orleans residents who he alleged had 'no intention of leaving', since the criminally inclined foresaw a 'target-rich environment', while the passive majority were 'just waiting for their welfare checks at the beginning of September', stayed put, and drowned. Had 'chronically craven and indolent' local officials had the wit to announce that the next round of welfare checks would be issued in Baton Rouge, Neumayr concluded, then no doubt 'people would have somehow found a way to get out'.[69]

There had been more than a little unease, in free-market think tank circles, with the President's Jackson-Square acknowledgement of 'deep, persistent poverty [with] roots in a history of racial discrimination', and with what he characterized as a 'legacy of inequality'.[70] The Bush Administration's achievements in the area of welfare reform were also regarded as modest, if not tokenistic – more funding for a compassionate conservative programme of 'marriage incentives', but little else. The Heritage Foundation's welfare guru Robert Rector, amongst others, thought that the time had now come to 'experiment boldly'. Lecturing the dependent residents of New Orleans 'how not to be poor', Rector contended that the root cause of the city's poverty was neither racial discrimination nor an absence of job opportunities, but the collapse of the nuclear family, coupled with low levels of parental work – both trends that have disproportionately affected the black community. The falling marriage rate was fuelling welfare dependency amongst blacks, while propagating the dysfunctional 'culture of the underclass: drug abuse, promiscuity, and violence'; and the appropriate response should be 'moral renewal':

> The post-Katrina debate [has focused] on jobs and construction, joined with occasional proposals about relocating dysfunctional families or voucherizing services. But it is families, not houses, that really need rebuilding. If the proposals continue to ignore the social causes of poverty, they will merely reproduce the original slums of New Orleans in fresh concrete. Twenty years from now, another hurricane will swamp the city and pundits will wonder again where all the poor folks have come from.[71]

Striking his trademark tone, Charles Murray, now W. H. Brady Scholar at AEI, informed the readers of the *Wall Street Journal* that the conventional repertoire of policy responses simply does not work for the underclass, whose defining characteristic is 'behaving destructively'. The underclass, he cautioned, should not be confused with the responsible poor, who work and get married; rather, they are the 'looters and thugs' and 'inert women' for whom conventional policies simply fail:

> We already know that the programs are mismatched with the characteristics of the underclass. Job training? Unemployment in the underclass is not caused by lack of jobs or of job skills, but by the inability to get up every morning and go to work. A homesteading act? The lack of home ownership is not caused by the inability to save money from meager earnings, but because the concept of thrift is alien. You name it, we've tried it. It doesn't work with the underclass.[72]

It was this brand of argumentation, of course, that first made Murray's name, more than a quarter century ago, at the Manhattan Institute. And it has been one that his followers have pursued with gusto. 'For a while it looked like Hurricane Katrina would accomplish what the NAACP [National Association for the Advancement of Colored People] never could', *City Journal* contributing editor Kay Hymowitz reflected, 'reviving civil rights liberalism as a major force in American politics'.[73] *Newsweek*'s post-Katrina cover story, 'The Other America' had vividly recalled Michael Harrington's formative contribution to the War on Poverty, just as Senator Edward Kennedy's Gulf reconstruction proposals explicitly begged comparisons with the achievements of the Tennessee Valley Authority.[74] But, as Hymowitz blustered, this moment of retro-liberalism had 'only lasted about five minutes'; now it was down to conservatives to respond to the real problem – the breakdown of the nuclear family, together with its racially and socially uneven consequences. Hymowitz's colleague Nicole Gelinas likewise dismissed as 'amorphous talk' the President's evocation of racism, poverty, and inequality in the aftermath of the hurricane. What New Orleans really needed, she contended, was improved levee protection, since 'civil engineering actually works, unlike the social engineering that Bush has invited with his lament about urban Southern poverty'. With the physical infrastructure appropriately fixed, then it might be possible to deal with New Orleans' 'immutable civic shame, before and after Katrina', the city's 'culture of murder'.[75]

After documenting in gruesome detail the city's pre-and post-Katrina 'murder rampage' – together with images of black men caught in the commission of ostensibly illegal acts, in one case in the gunsights of a white police offer – Gelinas argued that the problem is a supply-side one, since 'New Orleans' legions of weak, female-headed, underclass black families supply generation after generation of … "lightly parented" young men to fuel the carnage'. In the short term, there will be no revival of New Orleans until public safety can be assured, she argued, which in turn calls for the importation of both Rockefeller-style drug laws and NYPD-style policing.

> Day in and day out, Katrina or no Katrina, New Orleans is America's most dangerous city.… But New Orleans's long history of street carnage is not a topic for polite discussion in Katrina's aftermath. Polls and pundits have a million solutions for the city, from building more affordable housing to ensuring better schools to creating an incubator for the nation's 'creative class' to offering tax credits for resettlement. But none addresses the city's most obvious, and intractable, problem, the one that has kept New Orleans from thriving for years.… Evacuees – and businesses – know that even Cat-5 levees can't protect them from the day-to-day mortal fear of living in New Orleans.… Only when New Orleans can assure safety can it begin to make up some of the losses it has sustained over a generation of mismanagement. Only then can it build a real private economy and robust public institutions that will attract a thriving middle-class population.[76]

Pointedly drawing attention to Houston's late-2005 crime spike, Gelinas subsequently argued that this is no longer only a problem for the Crescent City itself, since 'Katrina's floods dispersed throughout the unprepared South the uniquely vicious New Orleans underclass culture of drugs, guns, and violent death'.[77]

Writing in the AEI's monthly magazine, *The American Enterprise,* Joel Kotkin moved to cement this solidifying conservative orthodoxy, detailing his vision of post-Katrina urban policy. Announcing that the storm had torn 'the lid off a virtual Superdome of liberal illusions', Kotkin launched a scathing attack on 'rotten administration' at the state and local level, and the 'collapse of responsibility and discipline' that in his mind was a function of New Orleans-style urban welfarism:

By becoming mass dispensers of welfare for the unskilled, play-pens for the well-heeled and fashionable, easy marks for special interests, and bunglers at maintaining public safety and dispens-ing efficient services to residents and businesses, many cities have become useless to the middle class, and toxic for the disorganized poor. Today's liberal urban leadership across America needs to see the New Orleans storm not as just a tragedy, but also as a dispeller of illusions, a revealer of awful truths, and a potential harbinger of things to come in their own backyards. Look beyond the tour-ist districts. Few contemporary cities are actually healthy in terms of job growth or middle-class amenities. Most are in the grips of moral and economic crisis. If we are lucky, the flood waters of Katrina will wash away some of the '60s-era illusions that fed to-day's dysfunction. Honest observers will recognize that this natural disaster, which hit the nation so hard, was set up by the man-made disaster of a counterproductive welfare state.[78]

Fundamentally, the agenda of the new urban right is about setting the 'ground rules' for appropriate behaviour in cities, largely modeled on mid-dle-class norms; establishing the preconditions for economic growth, largely through the kinds of minimalist supply-side interventions metaphorically represented, in this case, by the cat-5 levee; and maintaining social order through ruthless application of the force of law, facilitated by zero-tolerance policing. This, clearly, is anything but a noninterventionist programme, but its interventions are profoundly selective. It represents a form of revanchist neoliberalism, practised at the urban scale.[79] The neoliberal face of this pro-gramme caters explicitly to business, taxpayers, and the middle classes, for whom the restructured city must be made profitable, safe, and welcoming. Meanwhile, the programme's revanchist face justifies a new round of socially invasive interventions on a criminalized, feckless, and morally bankrupt class of the urban poor, from whom preferred citizens must be shielded at all costs. This is a form of urban policy not so much *for* cities, or even in the interest of cities, as one that is applied *to* them – restoring bourgeois urbanism by way of a kind of post-welfare policy corrective.

Before Katrina dramatically raised the stakes, New Orleans was perceived by US conservatives as one of urban America's lost causes, an outpost of dis-figured welfare statism, rotting from the inside. As George Neumayr saw it:

New Orleans did not fall from without; it fell from within. The chaos after Hurricane Katrina did not cause a civilizational collapse;

it simply exposed and magnified one that had already occurred... A strange admixture of upper-class decadence and underclass pathology, New Orleans has long been a stew of disorder and dysfunction, convincing many New Orleans residents, years before Hurricane Katrina, to evacuate what they regarded as an increasingly unlivable city... The squalor and crime in the Superdome represented nothing more than the squalor and crime transferred from New Orleans' legendarily hellish housing complexes [and the] countless images of stranded women, children, and elderly were explained far more by the absence of fathers than by the tardiness of FEMA.[80]

From this perspective, 'the city's fall was inevitable', a predestined outcome of the orgy of welfare dependency, crime, family breakdown, and corruption that preceded the storm, conditions that rendered the city socially, economically, and morally defenseless – before both 'nature and human nature ran amok'.[81] The fall of New Orleans was for the conservative intelligentsia a governmental-assisted cultural implosion, merely brought on by the hurricane. When they looked at the devastation of New Orleans, what they saw was a 'hurricane of entitlements'.[82]

WHO FRAMED NEW ORLEANS?

If conservatives were initially placed on the defensive by Katrina – having manifestly failed to provide basic security and protection, having publicly demonstrated both ineptness and indifference – they responded, as Lakoff and Halpin have argued, by 'filling the framing gap so quickly and so effectively that... they may be able to parlay this disaster into an even greater power grab than they made out of September 11'.[83] The outpouring of conservative commentary, editorializing, and detailed policy advocacy, particularly from the think tanks, does indeed seem to have been decisive in substantially reframing the issue of New Orleans' fall and reconstruction. Their influence can be read in the changing posture of the Bush Administration, from defensiveness and disorientation in early September, 2005, through cautious and ultimately confident containment of the 'Katrina problem' by the year's end. By the time of the 2006 State of the Union address, New Orleans barely rated a mention. No longer was the rhetoric about 'doing what it takes', by the new year Bush was snippily retorting at a press conference, 'I want to remind the people in that part of the world, $85 billion is a lot'.[84] Meanwhile, evidence of the Administration's evasion and unfulfilled promises in the Gulf reconstruction programme continued to grow.[85]

What began as a 'decidedly unnatural disaster', in Neil Smith's words, has been ruthlessly transformed into a malformed reconstruction programme that blames, and morally reregulates, the most vulnerable victims, while setting in train '[w]holesale gentrification on a scale unseen in the United States'.[86] This is about as far from a 'people's reconstruction' as one could imagine[87] – a programme of contracted-out urban structural adjustment, designed in Washington and New York. An urban catastrophe that disproportionately impacted the poor, the infirm, and the elderly perversely resulted in the paring of programmes designated for precisely these groups. According to the neoliberal script, it was not a lack of resources, private transportation, or out-of-town support systems that placed some of the most-needy New Orleans residents in the storm's path; it was the long-run consequences of urban welfarism – and its racialized cast of supported characters, including the workless, the feckless, and the lawless, absentee fathers, inert mothers, and criminalized youths.

There is a tragic truth in the ways in which Katrina 'laid bare' the operating model of American neoliberalism, its inequities and limitations.[88] But by the same token, the relentless political management of the hurricane's protracted aftermath exposes the continuing grip of this project, manifest in what has been a forceful display of orchestrated ideological recoil. The only partly hidden hands of think tank protagonists were feverishly at work in fashioning this 'free market' response. These new cadres of organic intellectuals are more than mere 'orators': they also *construct*, *organize*, and give direction to state projects.[89] As such, their strenuous and concerted actions in the wake of Katrina again reveal the essential truth that in as far as the neoliberal project demonstrates unity, this is very much a *constructed* unity. It is also a contradictory unity. Beneath the veneer of common purpose, there are sharp – and potentially fatal – differences in the means and ends of small-government fiscal conservatives and big-government social conservatives.

Even though the new urban right was ready with a prefabricated crisis narrative when Katrina struck, the subsequent performance of the free-market think tanks reveals not only the potency, but also some of the incipient limits, of this post-welfare *doxa*. The bourgeois urban vision of the Manhattan Institute, just like the truncated, small-government federalism of the Heritage Foundation, did not emerge through a simple process of historical succession, as a singular and ready-formed alternative to Keynesian-welfarist urbanism. Rather, it has been formed incrementally, albeit in the context of a radical and overarching vision, as a tendentially consonant hybrid of a range of conservative, libertarian, pro-business, anti-statist, neoliberal and 'post-liberal' ideological arguments, claims, propositions, and 'second-hand ideas'. What might be characterized in retrospect as a (formidable) neoliberal project, or even a hegemonic 'market order', was of course a socially constructed one, the product of several decades of ideological investment and intellectual entrepreneurship, all facilitated by a favourable political–economic climate.

While the speed and force with which neoliberal nostrums filled the post-Katrina void can be read as a sombre commentary on America's contemporary *realpolitik*, and the circuits of power and persuasion that sustain it, at the same time, the tensions and differences that were exposed along the way represent manifestations of the *problematically* hybrid character of the market revolution. For example, the post-Katrina debate reveals that fiscal constraint is evidently easier to preach than to practice; that the morally interventionist impulses of compassionate conservatives routinely try the patience of libertarians, just as they alarm budget hawks; that wholesale contracting-out risks compromising fiscal accountability; that small-government conservatives find it increasingly difficult to trust big-government conservatives; and so on. In principle, the exhaustion of the neoliberal project might just as easily result, therefore, from *internal* ideological fractures – or for that matter from various forms of social, political, and fiscal overreach – as from 'external' contestation. For now, if the fast-policy relays between New York City, Washington, and New Orleans tell us anything, it is a story of continuing neoliberal hegemony, for all the project's shaky foundations and flawed realization. Only for a relatively brief moment did the manifest urban tragedy of New Orleans – the like of which has never been seen before in the contemporary United States – disrupt business-as-usual neoliberalism. Within the space of a few months, if not weeks, it had become clear that the longer-run outcomes of Katrina would not be a reversal, or even a midcourse adjustment of the process of neoliberalization, but in fact an *acceleration* of its extant programs of social regression and market governance. When the *long* history of neoliberalism is eventually written,[90] where will New Orleans be placed?

NOTES

An expanded version of this paper appears in *Urban Geography*. It is used here with permission of Victor Winston and Sons and Bellwether Publishing, Ltd.

1   *New York Post*, 29 August 2005, p. 2.
2   'The Shaming of America', *Economist*, 10 September 2005, p. 11.
3   Richard Cockett, *Thinking the Unthinkable*, London: Harper Collins, 1994; Lee Edwards, *The Power of Ideas: The Heritage Foundation at 25 Years*, Ottawa, IL: Jameson Books, 1997.
4   When Republican Speaker of the House, Dennis Hastert, candidly mused that the rebuilding of New Orleans might not 'make sense', he was forced, within

hours, to retract the statement, quoted in *Washington Times*, 2 September 2005, p. A1.

5   Michael Ledeen, 'The Doomed Cities', *National Review Online*, 1 September 2005, http://www.nationalreview.com; Helle Dale, 'Preventing Future Catasrophies: Answers Needed on Katrina Response', *Washington Times*, 8 September 2005, A21.

6   Michael Novak, 'Hurricane Hysterics: A Message to Europe about Katrina', *National Review Online*, 14 September 2005, http://www.nationalreview.com. Helle Dale, 'Post-Katrina Frenzy', *Washington Times*, 14 September 2005, A19.

7   James K. Glassman, 'Katrina and Disgusting Exploitation', *Tech Central Station*, 31 August 2005, http://www.tcsdaily.com; Steven F. Hayward, 'Katrina and the Environment', *Environmental Policy Outlook*, American Enterprise Institute, Washington, DC, September/October, 2005. The prevailing view in the meteorological science community is that global warming is a plausible cause of a significant increase in the intensity of hurricanes (of Category 4 and 5 strength), though this does not necessarily equate with an increase in incidence. See B. Henson and D. Hosansky, 'Busy Times in the Tropics', *UCAR Quarterly*, Fall, http://www.ucar.edu, and P.J. Webster et al., 'Changes in Tropical Cyclone Number, Duration, and Intensity in a Warming Environment', *Science*, 16 September 2005, pp. 1844-46. This question of meteorological science has been developing political dynamics of its own in the months since Katrina: see Donald Kennedy, 'The New Gag Rules', *Science*, 17 February 2006, p. 917, and Valerie Bauerlein, 'Cold Front: Hurricane Debate Shatters Civility of Weather Science; Worsened by Global Warming?' Wall Street Journal, 2 February 2006, p. A1.

8   Stephen Johnson, 'Thanks, but No Thanks for Aid from Self-Serving Autocrats', *Web Memo*, No. 834, Heritage Foundation, Washington, DC, 2005.

9   See Jamie Peck and Adam Tickell, 'Conceptualizing Neoliberalism, Thinking Thatcherism', in H. Leitner, J. Peck and E.S. Sheppard, eds., *Contesting Neoliberalism: Urban Frontiers*, New York: Guilford, 2006.

10   See Jamie Peck, 'Liberating the City: Between New York and New Orleans', *Urban Geography*, forthcoming.

11   Methodological note: the attributed contributions of 'neoliberal' (i.e. [neo]conservative, libertarian, and/or free-market) think tank scholars represent the primary source in this paper. The Manhattan Institute, the Heritage Foundation, the American Enterprise Institute, and Cato represent the focus of the analysis. In general, the most 'public' forms of output are utilized – e.g. a *City Journal* online posting or Heritage *Web Memo* subsequently published as a newspaper editorial will be credited as the latter, though in practically every case these can also be found, verbatim, on the think tanks' voluminous web sites. The interpretation here has been aided by a programme of interviews with think tank scholars and activists, part of a larger project on think tanks that the author is conducting with Adam Tickell.

12   Nicole Gelinas, 'Will New Orleans Recover?', *New York Sun*, 1 September 2005, p. 9.

13   Ibid.

14   Nicole Gelinas, 'A Perfect Storm of Lawlessness', *City Journal* online, 1 September 2005, http://www.city-journal.org.

15   James G. McGann, *Scholars, Dollars and Policy Advice*, Philadelphia: Foreign Policy Research Institute, 2004.

16   Gelinas, 'A Perfect Storm of Lawlessness', p. 1.

17   Like the imaginary inner-city New York couple of the 1970s, Harold and Phyllis, created by Charles Murray in his *Losing Ground: American Social Policy 1950-1980*, New York: Basic Books, 1984.

18   George L. Kelling and Catherine M. Coles, *Fixing Broken Windows: Restoring Order and Reducing Crime in Our Communities*, New York: Free Press, 1996.

19   For a broader analysis of the new urban right, see Peck, 'Liberating the City'.

20   Theodore Dalrymple, 'The Veneer of Civilization', *National Review*, 26 September 2005, pp. 24-26; David Brooks, 'The Bursting Point', *New York Times*, 4 September 2005, p. 11.

21   Amongst the torrent of (largely scathing) media commentary on the federal government response to Katrina, see Angie C. Marek, 'A Crisis Agency in Crisis', *U.S. News & World Report*, 19 September 2005, pp. 36-38; Anna Mulrine, 'Lots of Blame', *U.S. News & World Report*, 19 September 2005, pp. 26-35. Compare Michael Parenti, 'How the Free Market Killed New Orleans', *ZNet Commentary*, 3 September 2005, http://www.zmag.org.

22   'President Outlines Hurricane Katrina Relief Efforts', Office of the Press Secretary, White House, Washington, DC, 31 August 2005.

23   Ben Lieberman, 'A Bad Response to Post-Katrina Gas Prices', *Web Memo*, No. 827, Heritage Foundation, Washington, DC, 2005. This was by no means a fluke. The American Enterprise Institute was initially preoccupied with just the same issues, issuing levelheaded reminders of the laws of supply and demand, indeed celebrating the 'positive side of price-gouging and greed' (John R. Lott, *A Look at the Positive Side of Price-Gouging and Greed*. Washington, DC: American Enterprise Institute, 2005).

24   Ben Lieberman, 'No Easy Answers for Post-Katrina Gas Prices', *Web Memo*, No. 831, Heritage Foundation, Washington, DC, 2005; Tim Kane, 'Labor Day Review: In Katrina's Wake', *Web Memo*, No. 827, Heritage Foundation, Washington, DC, 2005; James J. Carafano, 'Responding to Katrina: The Realities of a Catastrophic Disaster', *Web Memo*, No. 830, Heritage Foundation, Washington, DC, 2005.

25   Ronald D. Utt, 'The Katrina Relief Effort: Congress Should Redirect Highway Earmark Funding to a Higher Purpose', *Web Memo*, No. 832, Heritage Foundation, Washington, DC, 2005. On the origins of the 'bridge to nowhere' story, see Rebecca Clarren, 'A Bridge to Nowhere', *Salon.com*, 9 August 2005.

26   'Congress should Redirect Highway Pork to the Katrina Relief Effort', 9 September 2005, http://www.heritage.org.

27   See Véronique de Rugy, 'Fools Rush In', *Tech Central Station*, 7 September 2005, http://www.tcsdaily.com; Chris Edwards, *Both Parties Find Trough to Their Liking*, Washington, DC: Cato Institute, 2005.

28   Edwin Meese, Stuart M. Butler and Kim R. Holmes, *From Tragedy to Triumph: Principled Solutions for Rebuilding Lives and Communities*, Special Report, No. 05,

Washington, DC: Heritage Foundation, 2005, emphasis added.

29   Ronald D. Utt, 'President's Bold Action on Davis-Bacon will Aid the Relief Effort', *Web Memo*, No. 836, Heritage Foundation, Washington, DC, 2005. Davis-Bacon was restored two months later, following Congressional pressure, a decision widely bemoaned by the conservative think tanks (see Tim Kane and David B. Muhlhausen, 'Should Federal Labor Policy be any Different after the 2005 Hurricane Season?', *Backgrounder*, No. 1893, Heritage Foundation, Washington, DC, 2005).

30   Stuart M. Butler, 'Lose the Rules', *Los Angeles Times*, 13 September 2005, p. B13.

31   Steven Malanga, 'New Orleans vs. New York?', *City Journal* online, 15 September 2005, http://www.city-journal.org.

32   'Death Tax Repeal/Katrina', Memorandum to Members of the United States Senate, 2 September 2005, http://www.atr.org.

33   Michael J. Graetz and Ian Shapiro, *Death by a Thousand Cuts,* Princeton: Princeton University Press, 2005, pp. 28-29.

34   Véronique de Rugy, 'Hurricane Relief Spending: How will we Pay for It?', *Tech Central Station*, 12 September 2005, http://www.tcsdaily.com; Brian M. Riedl, 'A "Victory" Over Wasteful Spending? Hardly', *Web Memo*, No. 839, Heritage Foundation, Washington, DC, 2005; Ronald D. Utt, 'Congress Faces Pressure to Surrender Pork for Flood Relief', *Web Memo*, No. 841, Heritage Foundation, Washington, DC, 2005.

35   Riedl, 'A "Victory" Over Wasteful Spending?'.

36   Kevin A. Hassett, 'Let's Tie Katrina Aid to People, Not just Places', *Bloomberg.com*, 12 September 2005.

37   James K. Glassman, 'How to Rebuild a Great City', *Scripps Howard News Service*, 12 September 2005, http://www.shns.com, p. 2.

38   'President Discusses Hurricane Relief in Address to Nation', Jackson Square, New Orleans, Office of the Press Secretary, White House, Washington, DC, 15 September 2005.

39   Jonathan Weisman and Jim VandeHei, 'Bush to Request More Aid Funding; Analysts Warn of Spending's Impact', *Washington Post*, 15 September 2005, p. A1.

40   A few days earlier the House majority leader Tom DeLay had told reporters, 'Bring me the offsets, I'll be glad to do it. But nobody has been able to come up with any yet' (quoted in *Washington Post*, 15 September 2005, p. A1).

41   Stuart M. Butler, James J. Carafano, Alison A. Fraser, Dan Lips, Robert E. Moffit and Ronald D. Utt, 'How to Turn the President's Gulf Coast Pledge into Reality', *Web Memo*, No. 848, Heritage Foundation, Washington, DC, 2005, p. 3.

42   R. Glen Hubbard, 'A Post-Hurricane Action Plan Should Focus on People', *Financial Times*, 19 September 2005, p. 19.

43   Michael Franc, 'Legislative Lowdown – Week of September 19th', *Human Events*, 19 September 2005, http://www.humaneventsonline.com.

44   Ed J. Feulner, 'Don't Bind New Orleans in Red Tape', *San Francisco Chronicle*, 19 September 2005, p. B5.

45   *Wall Street Journal*, 15 September 2005, p. A20.

46   David Wessel, 'Small Government Rhetoric gets Filed Away', *Wall Street Journal*, 8 September 2005, p. A2. See the echoes in 'Did Big Government Return with Katrina?', *Cato Policy Report*, Vol. XXVII, 2005, pp. 4–5; Michael Franc, 'Hurricane of Entitlements', *National Review Online*, 20 September 2005, http://www.nationalreview.com; William A. Niskanen, 'The End of Small Government?', *American Spectator*, 20 September 2005, http://www.spectator.org.

47   The Republican Study Committee is dominated by fiscal conservatives on the right of the Republican Party, inheritors of the Contract with America project.

48   Quoted in *Wall Street Journal*, 15 September 2005, p. B1. See also Michael Franc, 'Legislative Lowdown – Week of September 26th', *Human Events*, 26 September 2005, http://www.humaneventsonline.com; Robin Toner, 'Thumbing Nervously through the Conservative Rulebook', *New York Times*, 11 September 2005, Section 4, p. 1; John R. Wilke and Brody Mullins, 'After Katrina, Republicans Back a Sea of Conservative Ideas', *Wall Street Journal*, 15 September 2005, p. B1. For the Heritage plan, see Meese et al., *From Tragedy to Triumph*.

49   RSC [Republican Study Committee], *Operation Offset: RSC Budget Options 2005*, Washington, DC: Republican Study Committee, 2005.

50   Franc, 'Legislative Lowdown – Week of September 26th'; Alison A. Acosta Fraser and Michelle Muccio, 'The Growing Disconnect: Federal Spending and Congressional Leadership', *Web Memo*, No. 865, Heritage Foundation, Washington, DC, 2005. Reflecting the increased importance of blogs amongst conservative activists, Heritage recommended tasking teams of 'citizen journalists' to pore over the plans for Gulf Coast reconstruction in search of examples of dubious spending, calling on the President to extend the Freedom of Information Act to all documents relating to the reconstruction effort (Mark Tapscott, *Using FOIA to Keep Katrina Recovery Honest*, Washington, DC: Heritage Foundation, 2005). Mark Tapscott, in fact, is one of Heritage's own hyperactive bloggers. Director of the Foundation's Center for Media and Public Policy, his online bio cryptically describes his 'location' as Washington, DC – 'Follower of Christ, devoted husband of Claudia, doting father of Marcus and Ginny, conservative lover of liberty, journalist, Formula Ford racer, Okie by birth/Texan by blood/proud of both, resident of Maryland'. Some 157 of the top 250 political blogs reflect right-wing views. The Manhattan Institute credits the blogosphere not only with the removal of both Dan Rather from CBS and Howell Raines from the *New York Times*, but even with Bush's victory over Kerry in 2004. See Brian C. Anderson, 'The Plot to Shush Rush and O'Reilly', *City Journal*, 16, 2005, pp. 16–28.

51   *Wall Street Journal*, 21 September 2005, p. A26 and 8 September 2005, p. A18.

52   The Senate's self-styled Fiscal Watch Team called for a 'package of offsets' totalling $130 billion, including a 5% reduction in spending on all federal programmes except those which impact national security, a pay freeze for federal employees, a two-year delay in implementation of the Medicare prescription drug benefit; cuts in the recently passed highway bill. See http://www.coburn.senate.gov.

53   *Porkbusters* is at http://www.truthlaidbear.com/porkbusters, featuring advocacy

of the Pork Barrel Reduction Act (S.2265) and a Pork Hall of Fame (#1 being, not surprisingly, Senator Ted Stevens of Alaska, of 'bridge to nowhere' fame). *Porkbusters* is an offshoot of *Instapundit*, sometimes known as a 'warblog', due to its hawkish stance on the Iraq war, and one of the most widely read blogs in the world.

54   Andrew M. Grossman and Ronald D. Utt, 'Pelosi Leads the Way on Highway Bill Give-Back', *Web Memo*, No. 852, Heritage Foundation, Washington, DC, 2005; Ronald D. Utt, 'Give up your Bike Path, Bridge for Hurricane Relief', *USA Today*, 28 September 2005, A11. Frustration with the Republican leadership, however, had been building for some time amongst fiscal conservatives, particularly since the passage of the Medicare bill in 2003. See Véronique de Rugy and Nick Gillespie, 'Bush the Budget Buster', *Reason*, 19 October 2005, http://www.reason.com; Stephen Slivinski, *The Grand Old Spending Party: How Republicans Became Big Spenders,* Policy Analysis No. 543, Washington, DC: Cato Institute, 2005.

55   'President Holds Press Conference', Office of the Press Secretary, White House, Washington, DC, 4 October 2005. The President also made the case that post-Katrina realities called for an extension of the Patriot Act and increased oil-refining capacity ('The storms that hit our Gulf Coast also touched every American, with higher prices at the gas pump').

56   RSC, *Pence Praises President's Call for Budget Cuts,* Washington, DC: Republican Study Committee, 2005.

57   Michael Franc, 'Legislative Lowdown – Week of October 4th', *Human Events*, 4 October 2005, http://www.humaneventsonline.com.

58   Newt Gingrich and Véronique de Rugy, 'Pork, Pelicans, and Louisiana', *Washington Times*, 18 October 2005, A19; Véronique de Rugy, 'Pork Gumbo', *Tech Central Station*, 7 October 2005, http://www.tcsdaily.com.

59   Ed J. Feulner, *Getting Serious about Spending,* Washington, DC: Heritage Foundation, 2005; Michelle Muccio and Alison A. Fraser, 'House Leadership Reacts to Calls for Fiscal Responsibility', *Web Memo*, No. 879, Heritage Foundation, Washington, DC, 2005.

60   Ed J. Feulner, *A Line in the Sand on Spending,* Washington, DC: Heritage Foundation, 2005.

61   Ronald D. Utt, 'The Bridge to Nowhere: A National Embarrassment', *Web Memo*, No. 889, Heritage Foundation, Washington, DC, 2005; Press Room, *Newspapers Across the Nation Agree: Congress Must Address Spending,* Washington, DC: Heritage Foundation, 2005.

62   Ed J. Feulner, 'A Rainbow in the Aftermath of Katrina: Realization that Overspending Must Stop', *Investor's Business Daily*, 31 October 2005, p. A21.

63   Véronique de Rugy, 'Taming the Spending Beast', *Press-Enterprise*, 20 November 2005, p. D1. See also David C. John, 'Providing Flood Insurance after the Disaster is a Mistake', *Web Memo*, No. 888, Heritage Foundation, Washington, DC, 2005.

64   Franc, 'Legislative Lowdown – Week of October 4th', p. 1.

65   Kane and Muhlhausen, 'Should Federal Labor Policy be any Different'.

66   Franc, 'Legislative Lowdown – Week of September 26th'.

67   Quoted in *Washington Times*, 9 September 2005, p. A23

68   Thomas Sowell, 'Who will Rebuild New Orleans' Moral Levees?', *Investor's Business Daily*, 7 September 2005, p. A14.

69   George Neumayr, 'The Desolate City', *American Spectator*, November, 2005, p. 50.

70   'President Discusses Hurricane Relief in Address to Nation'.

71   Robert Rector, 'How not to be Poor', *National Review*, 24 October 2005, p. 28.

72   Charles Murray, 'The Hallmark of the Underclass', *Wall Street Journal*, 29 September 2005, p. A18.

73   Kay S. Hymowitz, 'Marriage and Caste', *City Journal*, 16, 2005, pp. 29-37.

74   Michael Harrington, *The Other America*, New York: Macmillan, 1962.

75   Nicole Gelinas, 'Who's Killing New Orleans?', *City Journal*, 15, 2005, p. 16.

76   Ibid., pp. 16, 21, 24-25.

77   Nicole Gelinas, 'Katrina Refugees Shoot up Houston', *City Journal* online, 4 January 2006, http://www.city-journal.org.

78   Joel Kotkin, 'Ideological Hurricane', *The American Enterprise*, January/February, 2006, p. 29.

79   Neil Smith, 'Giuliani Time: The Revanchist 1990s', *Social Text*, 16, 1998; Jamie Peck and Adam Tickell, 'Neoliberalizing Space', *Antipode*, 34, 2002; Neil Brenner and Nik Theodore, eds., *Spaces of Neoliberalism*, Oxford: Blackwell, 2002.

80   Neumayr, 'The Desolate City', pp. 48, 50.

81   Ibid., p. 50.

82   Franc, 'Hurricane of Entitlements'.

83   George Lakaff and John Halpin, 'Framing Katrina', *The American Prospect*, 7 October 2005, http://www.prospect.org.

84   'Press Conference of the President', White House, Office of the Press Secretary, White House, Washington, DC, 26 January 2006.

85   Spencer S. Hsu, 'Post-Katrina Promises Unfulfilled', *Washington Post*, 28 January 2006, p. A1

86   Neil Smith, 'There is no Such Thing as a Natural Disaster', in Social Science Research Council, *Understanding Katrina: Perspectives from the Social Sciences*, 2005, http://www.understandingkatrina.ssrc.org.

87   Naomi Klein, 'Needed: A People's Reconstruction', *The Nation*, 26 September 2005, p. 12. On progressive responses to Katrina, see Eric Mann, *Letter in Support of the Movement in New Orleans and the Gulf Coast*, Los Angeles: Frontlines Press, 2005.

88   Mike Davis, 'Capitalisme de catastrophe', *Le Monde Diplomatique*, October, 2005, pp. 1, 4; Bruce Braun and James McCarthy, 'Hurricane Katrina and Abandoned Being', *Society and Space*, 23, 2005; Karen Bakker, 'Katrina: The Public Transcript of "Disaster"', *Society and Space*, 23, 2005.

89   Antonio Gramsci, *Selections from the Prison Notebooks*, New York: International Publishers, 1971, p. 10.

90   David Harvey, *A Brief History of Neoliberalism*, Oxford: Oxford University Press, 2005.

CHINA: HYPER-DEVELOPMENT AND ENVIRONMENTAL CRISIS

DALE WEN AND MINQI LI

China's spectacular economic growth has been one of the most dramatic developments in the global economy over the past quarter century. Between 1978 and 2004 the Chinese economy expanded at an annual rate of 9.4 per cent. No other large economy has ever grown so rapidly for so long in the economic history of the world. As a result, measured by purchasing power parity, China now accounts for about 15 per cent of the world output, and about one-third of the world economic growth that has taken place since 2000.

However, China's economic growth has taken place at an enormous social and environmental price. A rapid increase in social and economic inequality, environmental degradation, mounting rural crisis, growing urban unemployment and poverty, pervasive government corruption, deteriorating public services (especially in basic education and health care), as well as escalating social unrest, have grown to dangerous levels and could potentially lead to an explosive situation.[1]

We focus in this essay on the environmental impact of accumulation and profit-oriented development in China. Given its enormous population and its growing importance in the global economy, the implications of China's environmental crisis go far beyond China itself. It has become an important and growing element in the developing global environmental crisis.

It is unlikely that either the Chinese environmental crisis, or the global crisis, can be effectively addressed within the existing institutional framework. To build an environmentally sustainable society the economic system has to be fundamentally transformed so that production and consumption activities are oriented towards meeting the basic needs of the general population rather than the pursuit of profit and wealth accumulation.

1. FROM STATE SOCIALISM TO CAPITALIST DEVELOPMENT

Between the 1950s and the 1970s, China developed on a state socialist or Maoist model. Maoist China was by no means an ideal society. Even apart from the errors and excesses of Mao's rule, economic inequalities and bureaucratic privileges continued to exist. The economy suffered from inefficiencies and imbalances. The issues of environmental sustainability were poorly understood. The focus on heavy industrial development led to a number of environmental blunders. However, these problems need to be set in their historical context. Pre-revolutionary China was an oppressed, peripheral state with a tiny industrial platform. The new state was confronted with the hostility of powerful foreign states and forced to respond to the pressures of capital accumulation and military competition imposed by the world system. These circumstances greatly limited the choices available to the state. Yet despite these historical limitations, the experience of Maoist China demonstrated that the quality of life of the working masses could be greatly improved in a socio-economic system based on egalitarian principles.

In the cities and industrial enterprises, the means of production were mostly owned by 'all the people', i.e. the state. The phrase 'iron rice bowl' was used to describe the industrial employment system and its associated benefits. Wages were quite low. But workers enjoyed lifetime employment, guaranteed pension benefits, health care, housing and education for dependants, paid maternity leave, and other benefits that created a high level of social equity and security. In the rural areas, land and other means of production were owned by collectives or communes. Despite various economic problems and low levels of material consumption, the commune system provided a wide range of social benefits, including basic public health care and education – the 'five guarantees' (food, clothes, fuel, education for the young, and decent burial upon death) for villagers who were unable to work and had no family support. So the majority of the rural population could live with security and dignity.

Possibly the greatest achievement of Maoist China was its success in meeting the basic needs of the great majority of the population at very low levels of per capita income and consumption. Between 1960 and 1980, the average life expectancy at birth of the Chinese population rose from 36 to 67 years, an increase of 31 over twenty years. By comparison, over the same period, the average life expectancy of all low-income countries increased from 44 to 53 years, an increase of only 9. Between 1970 and 1980, the rate of illiteracy in China fell from 47 per cent to 33 per cent, a 29 per cent decline. Over the same period, the average illiteracy rate of all low-income countries fell from 61 per cent to 53 per cent, down only 13 per cent. Towards the end of the Maoist period, China's performance in basic health and education indicators generally matched or were better than the average performance of middle-income countries, despite China's very low levels of per capita income. By comparison, in the period of market-oriented reform, China has fallen behind other low and middle income countries in the improvement of basic health and education indicators, despite China's spectacular economic growth.[2]

China's market-oriented reform started officially in 1979. During its first ten to fifteen years salient features of the reform included: breaking up rural communes, designating Special Economic Zones for foreign investment and free market experiments, and introducing 'market mechanisms' into state owned enterprises. As a result, worker benefits were reduced and the social safety net was steadily eroded.

In the 1990s, the Chinese leadership further embraced economic globalization and liberalization. Towards the end of the 1990s, most of the small and medium-sized state owned enterprises and nearly all of the collectively owned enterprises were privatized. Foreign and domestic capital is now encouraged to take a stake in the remaining large state-owned enterprises. The number of Special Economic Zones has exploded and foreign enterprises have further flourished, taking advantage of China's huge cheap labour force, regulatory loopholes and generous tax breaks. Hundreds of millions of Chinese workers now work under sweatshop conditions.

In 2001, China joined the World Trade Organization. Under the WTO accession terms China is obligated to eliminate all import quotas and significantly scale down its tariff protection on industrial imports. Foreign firms and investors have their rights greatly expanded.

While the Chinese leadership continues to claim that the goal of the reform is to build a 'socialist market economy', as far as the actual economic and social conditions are concerned, China has become a global corporate haven of low social and environmental standards. China is now capitalist in all but name.[3]

2. CAPITAL ACCUMULATION, PROFIT SEEKING AND THE ENVIRONMENT

The current economic globalization system rests upon production for profit. The pursuit of profit and constant, intense pressure from market competition force individual entrepreneurs and corporations as well as states to pursue capital accumulation on an ever larger scale. The endless pursuit of growth is not only a necessary outcome of economic globalization, but is indispensable for the survival of the Chinese model. Despite the promise of 'trickle down' income effects, neoliberal globalization has caused ever-rising inequality in income and wealth distribution within and between states in the last thirty years. If not alleviated by some economic growth, the tendency towards rising inequality could soon translate into absolute declines in living standards for the great majority of the world's population, producing a socially unsustainable situation. In the case of China, despite a 9.4% annual growth in the last twenty-plus years, relative poverty and even absolute poverty is growing – for example more and more people cannot afford basic services like primary health care and education, causing growing social unrest. More and more people are disillusioned by the empty promise that 'the rising tide will lift all boats'.

Economic growth means a growing consumption of material resources. Moreover, production and consumption processes generate material wastes that pollute the environment. Unlimited economic growth therefore tends to deplete natural resources and cause environmental degradation. Potentially, the consequences could be so extreme that the very survival of human civilization could be at stake. Theoretically, if technological progress can bring about an ever-lower environmental impact per dollar, in principle population and affluence can grow indefinitely. In practice, unless certain basic laws of physics and ecology can be violated, no production or consumption activities can take place without using some resources and having some impact on the environment. There are physical limits to the reduction of the environmental impact of human activities. To the extent that environmental technological progress suffers from diminishing returns to scale (that is, more and more dollars of expenditure may be required to accomplish a given reduction of environmental impact), there are economic limits as well.[4]

Admittedly, in the Maoist era industrial development was mainly focused on creating a system of social equity. The links between natural resources and social well-being were poorly understood in many aspects. As bad as some industrial practices were then, at the aggregate level, the extent of resource depletion and environmental degradation were limited by the very low levels of material consumption that prevailed.

As China shifts towards a market system and tries to integrate with the global economy and culture, and as the Chinese economy expands at breathtaking pace, resource depletion and environmental degradation are all now occurring on a gigantic and growing scale. As China becomes the global centre of manufacturing exports it has simultaneously become the centre of resource depletion and the generation of industrial wastes. China has become not only the world's workshop but also the world's dumping ground. Its natural environment is rapidly being pushed to the brink of collapse.

In a candid interview with the German magazine *Der Spiegel*, Pan Yue, China's deputy minister of Environmental Protection Administration, addressed the environmental crises: 'Our raw materials are scarce, we don't have enough land, and our population is constantly growing. …Cities are growing, but desert areas are expanding at the same time; habitable and usable land has been halved over the past 50 years. …[China's GDP miracle] will end soon because the environment can no longer keep pace'.[5]

The situation is dire, and not only for China. Climate change, water pollution and shortages, acid rain, wildlife extinction, and many other environmental factors affect the sustainability of the entire planet.

3. AGRICULTURAL PRIVATIZATION AND ENVIRONMENTAL DEGRADATION

Agriculture is the economic sector that arguably has the most intimate relations with the environment. Before 1979, most Chinese farmers were organized into collective communes. China's market-oriented reform began with *de facto* privatization of agricultural production. The first step was the implementation of the family contract system. This system broke up the communes and gave contracts of land to individual families. Initially, agricultural output and rural incomes increased significantly. But economic growth in the rural areas slowed down considerably in the mid 1980s. By the late 1980s and early 1990s, most rural areas entered a state of stagnation or even degeneration. Today, China's rural areas face an unprecedented social and environmental crisis.

Since 1979, Chinese agriculture has been transformed through the massive use of chemical fertilizers, pesticides, and hybrid seeds, made possible by the industrial and technological build-up in the pre-reform era. Initially, chemical-based agriculture worked wonders, helped by the water works and irrigation systems built in the commune era. Fertilizer usage more than doubled between 1978 and 1984, helping farmers to achieve record harvests.

Another factor that contributed to the short-term increase in household income was the exploitation of communal assets. For example, immediately following the implementation of the family contract system, there was no control over the rampant cutting of trees, which had been planted by the communes over the previous 30 years as roadside windbreaks to prevent erosion. Between 1985 and 1989, there was a 48 per cent decline in the area covered by windbreaks nationwide.[6]

The official media attribute the rural boom in the early reform years (1978-1984) to the de-collectivization process. In fact, more than two-thirds of the gains in that period were achieved before 1982, when the large-scale de-collectivization started. Other factors, such as rising grain prices and the use of chemical fertilizers, contributed much more to the short-lived success. The same technical factors contributed to the stagnation which followed. After the state price control on agricultural inputs was lifted in the mid-1980s, prices skyrocketed. Within two years, fertilizer prices rose 43 per cent and pesticide prices rose 82.3 per cent, and these prices continued to rise by more than 10 per cent annually throughout the 1990s. But by now, farmers were trapped in a vicious circle, compelled to pump more chemicals onto the fields to keep up yields as the organic matter in the soil declined.

The *de facto* privatization of agriculture has had profound long-term environmental and economic effects. Given the high population density, Chinese family farms are often less than one hectare, or even half a hectare. This rules out any possibility of economies of scale. Many technological inputs like tractors or grain-thrashing machines are too expensive for individual families. As a result many villages experienced de-mechanization in the initial years of privatization. As farmers put more labour into tasks previously done by machines, they have to cut back on other types of work, including good environmental practices like the application of organic and green manure.

Compared to the communes, family farms are much more vulnerable to natural disasters and market fluctuations, which put pressure on farmers to overtax the environment. The small size of the farms makes integrated environmental management difficult. As one farmer observed: 'When I apply pesticide, the pests simply migrate to my neighbour's field; the next day when he applies pesticide, all the pests come back to my plot. We end up wasting lots of chemicals while achieving very little'. In many villages, even the tiny family farms are spatially fragmented. The villagers demanded that land distribution should be fair and equal. Consequently, one family might end up with some high-grade plots on one end of the village, some low-grade plots on the other end, and some medium-grade plots somewhere else, posing further difficulties for integrated management. Some villages attempt a different scheme: each family is allocated one chunk of land, and the plots are rotated over the years. But this creates another problem: farmers lose incentives to invest in land and soil for long-term gain.[7]

Figure 1 presents China's total grain production and per capita grains production between 1978 and 2003. Total production rose steadily throughout the 1980s and much of the 1990s. However, between 1998 and 2003 grain production fell sharply. Although the total production has recovered somewhat over the last two years, per capita production has now fallen back to the levels of the early 1980s. Declining grain production poses a serious challenge to the country's long-run food security.[8]

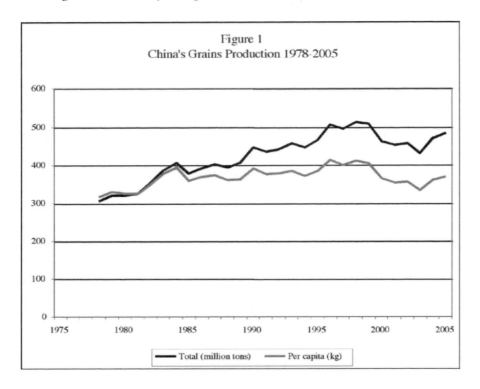

Figure 1
China's Grains Production 1978-2005

4. CHINA'S ENVIRONMENTAL CRISIS: AIR, WATER AND LAND

Due to its huge population of about 1.3 billion, China's natural resources endowment per capita is small. Currently, China's per capita arable land is only one-third of the global average, its water resources one-fourth, and oil deposits one-eighth. According to the World Wide Fund for Nature's *Living Planet Report* (2002), China's biological capacity is only 1.04 global hectares per person, or 55 per cent of the global average.[9] Yet even this limited natural endowment is not under good stewardship. China is paying a heavy environmental price for its economic boom.

Air pollution

According to a World Health Organization report, seven of the ten most polluted cities in the world are located in China. Air pollution claims 300,000 lives prematurely per year. China accounts for over 40 per cent of the total deaths caused by air pollution in developing countries, at more than twice the rate of South Asia, which has a comparable population. Acid rain impacts about one-third of the country.[10]

While a transition from coal to oil or natural oil has reduced urban air pollution, a large-scale transition from bicycles and mass transit toward private automobiles in recent years has offset all the benefits and further exacerbated the problem. While many multinational car companies have taken this as an opportunity to sell 'clean vehicle technology' to China, the whole premise of automobile-oriented growth and urban planning needs to be called into question. The majority of urban residents still rely on bicycles and public transport and have to suffer from the filthy air and increasing traffic jams brought about by the explosion of vehicles. For example, the average bus speed in Beijing was 10 miles per hour in the 1980s. It decreased to 5 miles per hour in the 1990s, and today has fallen to a crawling 2.5 miles per hour. In 2004, China became the world's fourth largest producer and third largest consumer of automobiles. The number of automobiles in China is growing at 19 per cent per year. Cleaner technology cannot deliver cleaner air if this trend is not abated.

Water scarcity and water pollution

China is facing one of the world's worst water shortages. The country is divided into two regions: the 'dry North', referring to all areas north of the Yangtze basin, and the 'humid South', which includes the Yangtze River basin and everything south of it. The north has a population of 550 million, two-thirds of the country's cropland, and one-fifth of the water. The South has a population of 700 million, one-third of the cropland, and four-fifths of the water.

The water shortage is most serious in the Yellow River basin in Northern China, which is generally considered the birthplace of Chinese culture. The river flows though the Loess Plateau, where the planet's most extensive soil erosion is to be found. After several thousand years of continuous cultivation much of the natural vegetation has been stripped away. This is compounded by the fact that the soil on the Loess Plateau is noted as being among the most erosion-prone on the planet. The river is laden with yellow sediments, which give it its name.

In the last several decades the deteriorating ability of local vegetation to conserve water, and the over-pumping of ground water, have shrunk the river's water supply. In 1972, for the first time, the river failed to reach the sea. In 1997, a year of severe drought, the river failed to reach its last 700 kilometres for 226 days; for its last 136-kilometer stretch the dry period was 330 days.

The dry runs have severely affected the normal life and production of people along the river's middle and lower reaches and led to a further deterioration in the local ecology. There is fierce and bitter competition for water between the mainly agricultural upstream provinces and more industrialized coastal provinces.

Due to water shortages and the widespread pollution of surface water, more cities and villages are increasingly tapping into underground aquifers. Under the North China Plain, a region that produces 40 per cent of China's grain, the water table is dropping by an average of 1.5 metres per year. In 1999, the water table under the capital city Beijing dropped by 2.5 metres. Since 1965, the water table under the city has fallen by some 59 meters. What will people do when the aquifers are depleted?[11]

About 60 per cent of the water in seven major river systems – the Yangtze, Yellow, Huai, Songhua, Hai, Liao, and Pearl Rivers – are classified as grade IV or worse – meaning, not suitable for human contact. 75 per cent of the lakes suffer from various degrees of eutrophication. The culprits are often agricultural runoff and untreated wastewater from both municipalities and industry. Chinese farmers use 2.3 times as much chemicals (fertilizers and pesticides) as US farmers. About one-third of industrial wastewater and two-thirds of municipal wastewater is released into waterways without any treatment.[12]

In 1994 the government began a massive clean-up campaign for the Huai River, one of the most polluted in China. After billions of dollars have been poured into the clean-up effort, improvement of the water quality remains an illusion. China's State Environmental Protection Administration has so little authority that the fines they levy are often less than the cost of using water treatment equipment where it has been installed, so naturally many manufacturers choose to pay fines instead. According to government estimates, while water treatment facilities have been installed in most major industrial plants under government mandate, one-third of these are not being operated at all and another one-third are being operated only occasionally.[13]

Pollution is exacerbating the water scarcity problem. In the previously water-rich Pearl River Delta and Yangtze River Delta regions water shortages have emerged in recent years, and much water has been rendered unusable due to heavy pollution. Contamination is spreading to underground aquifers as well – it is estimated that 25 per cent of aquifers are being polluted.

Land degradation and soil pollution

According to the monitoring results of China's State Forestry Administration in 1999, China has 2.67 million square kilometres of desert land, accounting for 27.9 per cent of its total territory; and this area is still expanding at an average rate of 10,400 square kilometres a year. 37 per cent of the total territory (3.56 million square kilometres) suffers from various degrees of soil erosion.[14]

Due to soil erosion, salination, pollution and other factors 40 per cent of the country's arable land is degraded. In recent years, rapid industrialization and urbanization have been claiming farmland at an alarming speed. In order to protect the already scarce arable land, the government has passed an 'arable land balance' law: for any farmland converted to industrial, commercial or construction use, the responsible party has the financial obligation to create the same amount of arable land somewhere else. While this act has slowed down the emergence of landless farmers, the net effect is that more and more marginal lands are reclaimed for cultivation while fertile farmlands are converted for other uses.

The remaining farmlands suffer from pollution caused by agricultural chemicals, mining activities, and industrial pollution. Chemical pesticides have polluted some 13-16 million hectares of farmland. 20 million hectares of farmland (about one-fifth of the arable land) are contaminated by heavy metal (cadmium, arsenic, lead, chromium, etc.). It is estimated that about 12 million tons of grain are contaminated (i.e., harmful for human consumption) and that pollution is responsible for more than 10 million tons of reduced grain production.[15]

The Yangtze River and Pearl River Deltas, two prosperous regions thanks to recent rapid export-oriented growth, serve as examples. For centuries, the fertile and water rich river deltas were China's rice and fish baskets. They still supply the country with a considerable amount of agricultural products. But probably unknown to most consumers, or even the growers themselves, the farmland in these regions is suffering from extensive contamination from heavy metal and persistent organic pollutants, much of it from polluting industries outsourced from the advanced capitalist countries, or even from electronic wastes imported illegally from the US.

From 1999 to 2002, Guangdong Province carried out a geological survey of 10,000 square kilometres of farmland in the Pearl River Delta region. They found that only 10.6 per cent of the land can be classified as clean, 35.9 per cent is moderately or heavily polluted, and the rest is lightly polluted. 46 per cent of the land is contaminated by cadmium and 12.6 per cent by mercury.[16]

The Yangtze River Delta exhibits a similar situation. Scientists have found 16 kinds of PAHs and more than 100 kinds of PCBs, both highly carcinogenic persistent organic pollutants.[17] In a 2002 survey by Nanjing Agriculture University, more than 70 per cent of the soil samples were found to have above-normal levels of heavy metal. Highly contaminated grains including 'mercury rice', 'lead rice', and 'cadmium rice' have been found in the market.[18]

5. CHINA, THE GLOBAL ENERGY CRISIS
AND CLIMATE CHANGE

According to the International Energy Agency, China accounted for 7.2 per cent of the world's total primary energy consumption in 1973 and 13.5 per cent in 2003. Between 1973 and 2003, the world energy consumption expanded at an average annual rate of 1.9 per cent and China's energy consumption expanded at an average annual rate of 4.0 per cent.[19] If China's energy consumption keeps growing at this rate it will double in less than twenty years. In recent years, China's energy demand actually accelerated. From 2000 to 2004, China was responsible for 40 per cent of the world's total increase in energy consumption.

Coal accounts for about three-quarters of China's primary energy consumption. Oil and natural gas account for about one-fifth. Nuclear and renewable energies together account for less than 6 per cent and their share has not increased in recent years. The recent explosion of private vehicles (an increase of 19 per cent a year) has led to a rapid increase in oil consumption. China currently imports 32 per cent of its oil and the need for imported oil is expected to double between now and 2010. By 2020, China's dependence on imported oil could exceed 50 per cent; by 2050 it could exceed 80 per cent.[20]

It might be argued that China uses its energy much more wastefully than OECD countries, and that there is therefore great potential for China to fuel its rapid economic growth by improved energy efficiency rather than rising energy consumption. The argument is, however, based on flawed statistics. China does appear to have much lower energy efficiency if its GDP is measured by the market exchange rate. But measured by purchasing power parity, which better reflects the material flows of goods and services, China's energy consumption per dollar of GDP is higher than the world average by only about 10 per cent, and higher than the OECD countries by about 20 per cent. This suggests that there is only limited scope for China to improve energy efficiency in the future. Table 1 compares China's energy consumption in relation to population, economic output and greenhouse gas emissions with selected regions in the world.

Table 1: Energy Consumption, Population,
and Economic Output (2003)*

Region	TPES/ population	TPES / GDP	TPES / GDP (PPP)	CO_2 / TPES
China	1.10	0.92	0.23	2.64
OECD	4.67	0.20	0.19	2.37
Middle East	2.52	0.66	0.38	2.48
Former USSR	3.36	2.12	0.51	2.38
Non–OECD Europe	1.89	0.76	0.27	2.56
Asia (ex. China)	0.61	0.72	0.19	1.91
Latin America	1.07	0.32	0.16	1.83
Africa	0.66	0.87	0.30	1.36
World	1.69	0.32	0.21	2.36

* TPES stands for total primary energy supplies measured by tons of standard oil, which equal consumption. CO_2 stands for carbon dioxide emissions measured by tons. PPP stands for purchasing power parity, which estimates the long-run equilibrium exchange rates of different currencies.
Source: International Energy Agency, *Key World Energy Statistics*, 2005.

China's growing demand for energy and especially its thirst for oil must be seen in the context of a developing global energy crisis. The world currently depends on oil and gas for 56 per cent, and on all forms of fossil fuels for 80 per cent, of its total primary energy consumption. There is growing evidence that global oil and gas production could reach a peak and start to decline in the coming decade. A growing dependence on coal would accelerate the depletion of coal and greatly worsen the impact on global warming. In the foreseeable future it is highly unlikely that the various forms of renewable energy can replace fossil fuels to sustain current levels of world energy consumption and future economic growth. The current Chinese growth pattern could greatly accelerate the global energy crisis and lead to potentially very dangerous geopolitical situations.[21]

China's per capita emission rate of greenhouse gases is only about one tenth of that of US. But due to its huge population of 1.3 billion people, the total emission is considerable. After the USA, China is already the world's second largest greenhouse gases emitter. With the current GDP growth trend, it is estimated that China may exceed the US as the top emitter in 2020.

Climate models predict that global warming will cause less rainfall in northern China and more in southern China. This is consistent with the pattern of recent years. There has been continuous drought in the North China

Plain since the 1980s, while flooding disasters have happened frequently in southern China. This impact has been especially severe since the 1990s. According to a report published in September 2004 by the Chinese and British governments, climate change could lead to a drop of between 20 and 37 per cent in China's yield of rice, wheat and maize over the next 20 to 80 years. In short, climate change may greatly exacerbate China's water crisis and threaten its food security.[22]

6. ENVIRONMENTAL INJUSTICE AND ENVIRONMENTAL UNREST: CLASS ISSUES IN THE ENVIRONMENTAL CRISIS

In recent years there has been growing environmental awareness among China's urban residents. In 1999 the Social Survey Institute of China surveyed households in Beijing, Shanghai, Tianjin, Guangzhou, Chongqing, Wuhan and other cities on the issues that most concern citizens. Environmental protection was the second highest priority, second only to corruption. Thanks in part to increasing public pressure, the capital city Beijing and a handful of other big cities are being cleaned up. For example, Beijing has moved nearly 130 factories out of the city. Cleaner, gas-fuelled power stations are being built while older ones are being retrofitted with scrubbers. Many environmental NGOs in Beijing have been instrumental in this process.[23]

One progressive Chinese scholar, however, commented on this as follows: 'It is not clear to me whether these organizations are practicing environmentalism or environmental imperialism'. While the comment may sound harsh, and it is not fair to lay all the blame on environmental NGOs, the criticism is not totally unwarranted. Instead of being retrofitted to reduce pollution, many polluting factories are simply being relocated to poorer areas. Instead of treating wastewater, many cities are digging long ditches to send the water away. While Beijing and Shanghai are increasingly supplied with natural gas from western China, many people and factories in the gas-producing areas have to purchase coal (sometimes from other areas far away) for their own energy needs, because most of the cleaner fuel is reserved for distant big cities. As a consequence of these unfair practices, the rural population suffers disproportionately from environmental degradation.

Heavy metal pollution serves as an example. Farmers play no part in creating it; profit-making capitalist industry does. Yet the farmers bear the consequences, often without any form of compensation. Roughly 20 million hectares of farmland is contaminated by heavy metals. Given the average size of a family farm, that translates into about 130 million farmers who are negatively impacted. In some of the worst hot-spots, pollution has become a life and death issue. In Shaanxi Province, in a small village of only 154 people, there have been 30 deaths due to cancer over the past 27 years.[24] In Huangmengying, a village of about 2,400, there have been 114 cancer deaths over the past 14 years. The nearby Shaying River is so polluted by industrial waste that the water is sometimes as black as soy sauce. According to Huo Daishan, an independent environmentalist, there are more than 20 cancer villages along the river in Shenqiu County alone.[25] Along some stretches of the Huai River, the death rate is one third higher than and the cancer rate twice the provincial average.

While farmers may initially be ignorant of the environmental impact of the polluting industries, it is obvious to them that something is wrong when the river runs black or when young children die from cancer one after another. Yet local officials are often deaf to the cries and petitions of the rural victims. Their performance is evaluated on the basis of GDP figures, and environmental degradation is not taken into account at all. And local government depends on the taxes and revenues generated by the factories. In some cases, the officials themselves are big shareholders in the polluting factories, and thus have a direct interest in keeping the factories running and keeping costs as low as possible.

When the victims have no legitimate means of addressing their grievances, social unrest is unavoidable. In the eastern province of Zhejiang there have been three big pollution-related protests since April 2005. Each involved thousands or even tens of thousands of protesters. In the April 2005 event in Huaxi village more than 20,000 villagers confronted and drove off 3,000 police who were sent in to break up a protest against an industrial park. In the event of August 2005 protesters set fire to the buildings of a battery manufacturer that was believed to be responsible for lead poisoning in the region. It is noteworthy that Zhejiang is a prosperous coastal region and in recent years it has enjoyed one of the highest economic growth rates of all provinces. Yet the local people are increasingly saying 'no' to this model of development.

7. CONCLUSION

The current model of economic growth in China is not sustainable. If the current growth pattern continues, in the not very distant future China may have to struggle with a major energy crisis, drastic declines in food production, the exhaustion of usable water resources and an uncontrollable public health crisis, as well as catastrophic natural disasters. Not only could the Chinese economy stop growing, and the existing social structure collapse; the potential consequences for the population could be too horrific to imagine.

On the other hand, it is very unlikely that either China's or the world's environmental problems can be effectively addressed within the existing institutional framework, geared towards economic globalization and hyper-growth. The pursuit of profit and accumulation, as well as the operations of the global financial market, are driving China inexorably along a path of environmental self-destruction.

To prevent this from happening it is necessary to fundamentally transform the entire existing social and economic structure. The economy must be oriented towards meeting the population's basic needs rather than the pursuit of profit and capital accumulation. To stabilize and improve China's environmental conditions, China needs first of all to stabilize its overall consumption of energy, water, and land resources, and then gradually reduce the consumption of these resources to sustainable levels.

This raises the question of how to meet the population's basic needs at relatively low levels of consumption of energy and resources. Both historical evidence and theoretical arguments indicate that this can not be accomplished within a market- fundamentalist system. The only hope lies in a more egalitarian economy based on economic democracy, and the recovery and cultivation of the commons. In this respect, despite all the problems with Maoist China we identified at the beginning of this essay, its successes in addressing people's basic needs with limited material resources are likely to be taken by many as providing valuable lessons in the conflicts to come over China's future direction.

NOTES

Disclaimer: this paper is the result of a collaboration. The two authors do not agree totally with each other, or with every idea contained in these pages.

1   On the social consequences of China's market-oriented reform as well as the impact of neoliberal globalization on China, see Dale Wen, 'China Copes With Globalization: A Mixed Report', San Francisco: International Forum on Globalization, 2005; Minqi Li and Andong Zhu, 'China's Public Services Privatization and Poverty Reduction: Healthcare and Education Reform (Privatization) in China and the Impact on Poverty', United Nations Development Programme Briefing Paper, 2004.

2   On China's performance in healthcare and education in the Maoist era and the era of market-oriented reform as well as international comparison, see Li and Zhu, 'China's Public Services'.

3   On how China's market-oriented reform gradually but inescapably led to development of capitalist economic and social relations, see Martin Hart-Landsberg and Paul Burkett, 'China and Socialism: Market Reforms and Class Struggle', *Monthly Review*, 56(3), 2004.

4   On the limits of technical solutions to the environmental problems, see John Bellamy Foster, *Ecology against Capitalism*, New York: Monthly Review Press, 2002.

5   'The Chinese Miracle Will End Soon', *Der Spiegel*, 7 March 2005.

6   Data are from *Zhongguo Nongcun Jingji Tongji Nianjian* (China Rural Economy Statistical Yearbook), Beijing: Zhongguo Tongji Chubanshe, 1992.

7   On the economic, social, and environmental impact of China's agricultural privatization, see Mobo C.F. Gao, *Gao Village: A Portrait of Rural Life in Modern China*, Honolulu: University of Hawaii Press, 1999.

8   Data for figure 1 are from China's State Statistical Bureau, *China Statistical Yearbook*, 2004.

9   World Wide Fund for Nature, *Living Planet Report 2002*, Washington: WWF International, 2002.

10   On China's environmental performance in international comparison, see Hua Wang, 'Environmental Performance Rating and Disclosure: China's GreenWatch Program', World Bank Policy Research Working Paper 2889, September, 2002.

11   On China's water shortages, see Ma Jun, *China's Water Crisis*, Norwalk: EastBridge, 2004.

12   '30 per cent of water in the seven major river system is classified as Grade V', *Guangmin Ribao* (Guangmin Daily), 24 March 2005.

13   The State Environmental Protection Administration, *China's Environmental Situation Brief*, 2004.

14   On statistics of China's land degradation and soil erosion, see ibid.

15   Fang Xuanchang, 'How Much "Dirty Earth" is There in China?', *China Newsweek*, 4 July 2005.

16   Liu Liying, 'The Pearl River Delta: Poisoned Land', *China Newsweek*, 4 July 2005.

17   The full chemical names for these compounds are Polycyclic Aromatic Hydrocarbons (PAHs) and Polychlorinated biphenyls (PCBs).

18   Chen Jiang, 'The Yangtze River Delta: The Dangerous Metal Land', *China Newsweek*, 4 July 2005.

19   On international energy statistics, see International Energy Agency, *Key World Energy Statistics*, Paris: International Energy Agency, 2005.

20   On a survey of China's energy demands and supply potentials, see Shao Zhen, *Nengyuan* (The Energy), in Zheng Yisheng and Wang Shiwen, eds., *Zhongguo Huanjing yu Fazhan Pinglun* (China Environment and Development Review), Beijing: Shehui Kexue Wenxian Chubanshe (China Social Science Literature Press), 2001, pp. 191-203.

21   On the evidence and issues related to the global peak of oil production, see Andrew Mckillop with Sheila Newman, eds., *The Final Energy Crisis*, London: Pluto Press, 2005. On the limits of nuclear and renewable energies, see Ted Trainer, 'Renewable Energy: What Are the Limits?', unpublished manuscript.

22   Chinese Academy of Agricultural Sciences & the Chinese Agrometeorology Institute, *Investigating the Impacts of Climate Change on Chinese Agriculture*, Report

on Phase I of a China-UK collaboration project, 2004. Published online only and available from http://www.defra.gov.uk.

23   On the growing environmental awareness of China's urban residents, see Elizabeth Economy, *The River Runs Black*, Ithaca: Cornell University Press, 2005.

24   In early June 2001 a report titled 'Heavy Metals Make Village Cancer Rates Soar' appeared in *Gongren Ribao* (Worker Daily).

25   Wang Jiaquan, 'Riverside Villages Count Cancer Cases', *China Daily*, 19 October 2004.

AFRICA: ECO-POPULIST UTOPIAS AND (MICRO-) CAPITALIST REALITIES

HENRY BERNSTEIN AND PHILIP WOODHOUSE

Of all the world's regions today, sub-Saharan Africa is seen as most emblematic of 'disaster' and 'tragedy'. All that can go wrong in the human condition seems to be concentrated with particular bleakness here, in an apparent combination of the effects of the worst of nature and the worst of society. The former is registered in images of 'overgrazing and the "desertification" of drylands, the widespread existence of a "woodfuel crisis", the rapid and recent removal of once pristine forest, soil erosion, and the mining of natural resources caused by rapidly growing populations'.[1] These images connect with those of social disintegration and desperation: intensifying poverty and insecurity, the ravages of HIV/AIDS, endemic and vicious ('tribal') conflict with its displacements and other brutalizations of whole populations, political regimes and warlords predatory on an anonymous mass of victims.

This essay aims to probe some of the realities behind such widespread generalities which are uniformly negative, and frequently pejorative too, conveying the sense of a place where the miseries of the human condition are self-inflicted. We first sketch some issues of environmental change in Africa and perspectives in the debates they have generated. While the 'new ecology' of African environments, and how African farmers use them, has much to commend it, it is called on to support an eco-populism that ignores the dynamics and effects of 'actually existing capitalism' in Africa. This includes commodity relations in the countryside (and in urban areas, with which they are so closely bound up), and the class and other social inequalities they inevitably generate. In particular we focus here on petty production in savanna environments, for reasons explained below, after first sketching some global forces in environmental change in Africa.

GLOBAL FORCES

The major sources of today's global environmental problems are concentrated in the advanced centres of capitalist production *and* consumption (and
rapidly industrializing zones such as in China) with respect to both sides
of the environmental equation: depletion of non-renewable resources and
degradation of renewable resources, and dealing (or not dealing) with the
massive pollution and waste generated, both of which have effects for other
parts of the world. Given our focus on petty production by African farmers,
here we only note briefly some of the ways in which global environmental
dynamics – and their political economy and politics – 'mark and constrain
the lives of [Africa's] inhabitants at every turn'.[2]

First is the continuing, or accelerated, large-scale extraction of Africa's
mineral resources, hardwoods, fisheries, and agricultural and horticultural
commodities, for export. The global economy draws from Africa over half its
supply of diamonds, platinum, cobalt and chromium, and more than a third
of its requirements of many more minerals, including rare and strategic metals (e.g. Vanadium, Zirconium, Manganese).[3] Extraction of other materials
often has disastrous environmental effects. For example, in the rich east Atlantic fisheries off the coast of Senegal, the weight of fish caught per hour of
fishing effort in the late 1990s had declined to less than half, and in the case
of more valuable fish species to less than a tenth, of that achieved in the early
1980s.[4] An example of environmental stress imposed by large-scale export
horticulture is the lucrative trade in cut flowers from Kenya, air-freighted to
supermarkets in northern Europe and worth over US$80 million by 1998.
Production is dominated by three farms, two of which employ over 5,000
workers each, and their intense horticulture is depleting the water resources
of Naivasha. Another East African agricultural example is a large company
engaged in 'sun coffee' production (versus shade-grown) which clears new
land for coffee planting every five to seven years, abandoning existing plant-
ings exhausted by deforestation and the depletion of soil nutrients.[5]

Second are the effects for Africa of global ecological dynamics generated
by concentrations of industrial production and of consumption elsewhere.
While the science of global warming remains contested, its likely consequences include increasing variability in rainfall, hence the increasing incidence of drought, in certain parts of Africa and notably the South and East.

Third is carbon trading. Africa is a favoured location for 'mitigation' efforts, such as tree-planting on large areas – from which human populations
and their needs to make other uses of the land are necessarily excluded – to
'sequester' carbon from the atmosphere to compensate for carbon emissions

in Europe and North America. Such 'carbon emission reductions' are also commodities recognized under UN climate change treaties (e.g. the Kyoto Protocol), and may be sold by those investing in such projects. In effect, land used for forest designated for carbon sequestration becomes the property of 'carbon traders'.

Fourth is 'green imperialism', including the exercise of what Joan Martinez-Alier calls 'environmental conditionality' applied by aid agencies.[6] Low levels of industrialization and the small scale of most farming, coupled with its association in the 'North' with 'charismatic megafauna' ('big game'), means that Africa provides an attractive global site for international efforts to conserve 'pristine' environments. At the close of the colonial period sub-Saharan Africa accounted for nearly half of the world's formally conserved areas, with a further increase of 63 per cent (1.5 million square kilometres) in 'protected areas' in sub-Saharan Africa since 1970. Recent examples include trans-border wildlife parks extending the Kruger Park from South Africa into Mozambique and Zimbabwe, and even suggestions for a 'Cape to Cairo green corridor'. In East and Southern Africa, the proportion of land classified as 'protected' now stands at over 16 per cent, a higher proportion than in North America, Europe, or Australia (15, 13, and 10 per cent respectively).[7] The enclosure of such areas as necessary to global environmental well-being, with consequent displacement of local populations, is driven directly by major international conservation agencies. Moreover, the rate of expansion of 'protected areas' (e.g. nature reserves) has risen with the increasing dominance of neo-liberalism. This can be understood in terms of a perception of 'protected nature' as a commodity for a new set of purchasers: corporations wishing to create eye-catching environmental associations for PR purposes; governments seeking to expand assets available for commercial tourism concessions; international conservation organizations seeking to raise their profile and assets for fund-raising.

Finally, but not least, is the long history of 'rural development' policies and projects aimed at boosting the productivity of African farming and, in the current discourses of 'caring' neo-liberalism exemplified by the World Bank, of 'empowering the [rural] poor' (through facilitating their greater participation in markets) as well as achieving environmental sustainability. Here we only note that such interventions impact on, and feed into, typically intricate and contested politics of control over land at local levels and beyond, with outcomes that confound the stated good intentions of their designers and funders.[8]

During colonial rule and since, property rights over most natural resources in Africa have been vested in the state. However, the strength of international capital relative to African governments today is evident in the distribution of the benefits from both large-scale exploitation of resources and the 'environmental services' sought from Africa: as a sink for industrial waste, as a site for mitigation of climate change, and as location for biodiversity conservation. In some instances the property rights of African states (however flimsy in any meaningful 'public' or 'national' sense) might depend on the capacity of international capital to defend particular mineral or forest resources or vast 'conservation' areas from those states' own citizens seeking land to cultivate and to graze their livestock on. Similarly, the weaknesses of African governments – and lack of democratic pressure on them – means that aid donors, and the interventions by NGOs that they license, often have major (if unintended) impacts on local land arrangements and the conflicts increasingly associated with them, which we come back to.

THE SCIENCE OF SAVANNA ECOLOGY

International concern over environmental change in the 'South' is most readily identified with deforestation in the humid tropics. Due to high rainfall and temperatures, the underlying rocks and the soils that form over them in tropical forest zones are subject to high rates of release and loss of plant nutrients; in effect, the principal stocks of nutrients are in the trees themselves. Removing trees (deforestation) is thus an unambiguous, as well as visible, impoverishment of the environment, which can be partially mitigated by planting land with tree crops (cocoa, oil palm, banana/plantains) or by relatively long recovery (fallow) periods to enable forest re-growth.

While equatorial Africa has its share of these threatened forests, with some of the highest recorded deforestation rates in the world,[9] we focus here on the 'savanna' environments that predominate to the north, south and east of the equatorial forest belt below the Sahara and cover some two-thirds of the African continent. Their wide extent is in part due to the broad definition of savannas as 'tropical/subtropical ecosystems characterised by continuous... cover of ...grasses that show seasonality related to water, and in which woody species are significant but do not form a closed canopy...'.[10] This definition covers a great range of grassland types with widely differing densities of trees, reflecting the principal underlying influence of rainfall. Where rainfall is higher (800-1200 mm annually) 'savanna woodlands' are characteristic of 'Sudanian' vegetation north of the equator, while south of the equator they include the *miombo* systems in Tanzania, Zambia, Zimbabwe and northern Mozambique, and *mopane* woodlands in Namibia and the Limpopo basin (Botswana, Southern Zimbabwe, and South Africa). Where rainfall is less, trees tend to be more sparse and dominated by *Acacia* species, as in 'savanna parklands' (e.g. the West African 'Sudano-sahelian' zone: 600–800 mm) or 'low tree savanna' (e.g., the 'Sahelian'zone: 400–600 mm). These broad classifications based on rainfall are heavily modified by underlying geology and its influence on soil fertility, and by the climatic effects of altitude. At a smaller scale still, variations in topography cause differential drainage and accumulation of water within the landscape, forming a mosaic of patches of different levels of productivity. The effects of greater water availability in low-lying patches of the landscape may vary, in some instances giving rise to dense 'gallery' forest along river banks, but in others creating waterlogged conditions resulting in grasslands in which tree growth is suppressed altogether.

Meteorological records, and evidence of climate change before such records (notably from the levels and sediments in Africa's great lakes), show historic shifts and cycles, producing wetter or drier periods. Within these longer-term climatic changes, savanna ecosystems are subject to extreme annual variations in rainfall. This means, first, that overall biomass productivity varies greatly from one year to the next, so much so that ecologists have suggested these may be ecosystems which never reach 'equilibrium' but are naturally in a state of constant adjustment between drier and wetter conditions, with large and erratic shifts in local plant and animal populations consequent on periodic 'extreme' events (drought, floods, fire, storm damage, etc.). Second, variations in rainfall affect the relative productivity of different patches of the savanna. For example, higher parts of the landscape are more drought-prone in dry years, but lower-lying patches may experience flooding in wetter years. However, since water is the main factor limiting plant productivity in savannas, and rainfall is restricted to four or five months of the year, the potential biomass production over any given year tends to be higher in the wetter patches of the landscape.

All this signifies high levels of uncertainty for crop or livestock production dependent on rainfall in savanna environments; the positive contribution of the 'new ecology' is to problematize how environmental change, and degradation, in African farmed landscapes is defined, identified and measured. While scientific knowledge of African savanna environments and how and why they change over time is still very incomplete, and strongly contested, it has also been advanced by recent research that introduces human agency into the account, and within a historical perspective.

MANAGING SAVANNA ENVIRONMENTS

It is now evident that the balance of tree and grass species in savanna landscapes has been profoundly shaped by cultivators and herders, whose management has taken many forms, increasing tree cover in some circumstances and reducing it in others. In the nineteenth century pastoralists' herds were important in suppressing trees (and thus tsetse infestation) in East African savannas. Conversely, expansion of settlement and cultivation in parts of the West African savanna has been associated with an increase of tree cover. In drier savannas in southern and eastern Africa, heavy grazing is believed to encourage the replacement of grasses by woody shrubs or 'thicket'.

Recent research has also illuminated how cultivators and herders on the African savannas managed environmental uncertainty by using risk-minimizing and 'opportunistic' management strategies. Rather than seeking to maintain a constant level of production at every site in every year, they recognized the need to modify planting or grazing patterns according to the variation in productive potential determined by rainfall. For herders of livestock on Africa's savannas this meant accepting fluctuation of herd sizes following cycles of wetter and drier years. While conventional agronomic science argued that small-scale farming in Africa degrades soils, because fertilizer usage is too low to replace plant nutrients lost from the soil, advocates of 'indigenous knowledge' contest this. They argue that agronomic measurements are not made at the relevant scale, nor do they take account of the complexity of small farmers' practices in Africa that adapt to, and spread risks between, precarious environmental conditions (not least those of rainfall) and the localized diversity of micro-environments in many African landscapes. Well-known examples include the intercropping of many plant species, and dividing cultivation between different sites (upland/lowland, localized wetlands/drylands, heavier/lighter soils, and so on) in ways that trade off the security of overall harvests, and hence household food supply, against the optimal yields of particular crops or fields.

A proper understanding of 'indigenous knowledge' – as socially produced, developed and transmitted – connects with another topic of much current interest: how various kinds of customary regime regulated access to and the use of arable and grazing land, water, forest, and so on, as 'common property resources' (i.e. in the absence of private property rights). The notion of common property 'regimes', and the legitimacy and effectiveness of their authority over their areas of jurisdiction, often has affinities with notions of strongly cohesive African rural communities, bound together by ties of cooperation, reciprocity, interest – and identity, expressed in the idioms of common descent and shared locale.

Recent recognition of the technical and social knowledges and skills developed by African cultivators and pastoralists to deal with the environmental uncertainties they face was much needed, and indeed has helped (some) scientists to develop an understanding of the 'non-equilibrium' character of savanna (and forest) environments. At the same time, how far the social conditions still exist in Africa which once made possible indigenous knowledge and innovation, effective (self-governing) common property regimes and cohesive rural communities, is a more tricky question, to which we will return.

DEBATING ENVIRONMENTAL CHANGE TODAY: THE SPECTRE OF MALTHUS

Until the 1990s environmental understanding of the impacts of natural resource use by small producers in Africa reflected the predominant 'limits to growth' perspective and focused largely on the aggregate impact of 'population pressure' on natural resources (land and its fertility, water, forest). This view, evident in much of the international commentary on African droughts and famines in the 1970s and 1980s, was informed by two basic assumptions: (a) that farming technologies were 'primitive' and farmers resistant to change; and (b) that social institutions were unable to control individually rational strategies of increasing family size and area cultivated, or numbers of livestock grazed, on land held as 'common property'. A notorious and highly influential expression of this was Hardin's 'tragedy of the commons'; Hardin proposed that under 'common' or 'communal' property regimes it is in every individual's interest, and in the interest of as many individuals as possible, to exploit as much as possible the resources made available as common property, leading inexorably to their depletion and degradation.[11] In Hardin's argument the possession of private property rights gives owners of land (and other resources) the incentive to manage them efficiently, so as to conserve or enhance their economic value, thereby bringing individual and social rationality into harmony – a familiar enough bourgeois dream. In mainstream policy agendas the solutions proposed to avoid the 'tragedy of the commons' were either centralized state regulation of natural resource use, or reform of social institutions to ensure that private property rights are allocated via market mechanisms to more 'efficient' resource users. The latter was increasingly advocated in the neo-liberal era from the 1980s onwards.

The Malthusian position that increasing population reduces capacities to maintain the productivity of natural resources (land, wildlife, forest, pasture, fisheries) has been countered by several lines of argument. One draws in part on Ester Boserup's influential thesis that historically population growth was the driver of technological change which increased agricultural productivity.[12] The logic of Boserup's argument informs the most influential recent counter-Malthusian statement applied to African farming and environment, albeit cast in a 'market-friendly' mould (in contrast to Boserup) – the study of Kenya's densely-populated Machakos district by Tiffen, Mortimore and Gichuki, to which we return below.[13]

Another line of argument, just noted, counterposes the sophistication and adaptability of indigenous technical knowledge to inherited assumptions of African farmers' technical 'backwardness' and 'conservatism', which are rooted in very static conceptions of 'tradition', 'traditional' culture, and the like, reminiscent of the worst of colonial anthropology.

A third response is more ambiguous. Those in favour of 'common property regimes' argue that Hardin's notion of 'the commons' misunderstands these regimes, so that their historic role in managing savanna environments has been devalued or simply denied. The evidently declining ability of such regimes to prevent degradation in contemporary conditions is attributed to the subversion of their control by states and markets, and especially by 'urban', 'elite', and 'foreign' business interests – all signifiers of what is alien and external to rural producers and their communities. On this view, environmental degradation by small-scale farmers, forest users and other petty producers registers a breakdown in local social institutions and a shift from a previously socially-regulated common property regime in arable, grazing or woodlands to an 'open access' free-for-all. This interpretation gives rise to a populist environmentalism which advocates reclaiming/re-establishing common property rights over resources on behalf of small-scale users and rural communities, viewed as the legitimate custodians of nature.

ENVIRONMENTAL CHANGE TODAY:
PROBLEMS OF EVIDENCE

One reason why it can be so difficult to identify clear environmental effects or outcomes is that ideas about the environment are value-laden and open to contestation. For example, the conversion of wildlife habitat to farmland may be regarded as environmental degradation. For those less concerned with wildlife and its welfare, the criterion of environmental sustainability might be the continued productivity of land now cultivated and/or grazed by livestock. Many concerns expressed about environmental deterioration in Africa relate simply to reductions in wildlife numbers or habitats, and typically originate in the environmental agencies of the 'international community'. This suggests the need for a firmer recognition that modern environmental arguments hinge on issues of the 'ownership' of nature, and therefore on the dynamics of commoditization in specific historical and social conditions.

This applies equally to considering the contemporary impact of petty production on the environment, for which there is a range of fragmentary evidence (from indisputably negative to highly contentious). The most unambiguous impacts, for example, mercury contamination of rivers by artisanal gold miners, are arguably worse than those of their large-scale equivalents, due to lower investment levels. There may also be bigger problems in regulating the polluting impact of large numbers of small-scale industrial units than those of fewer large-scale enterprises (e.g. tanning in India and coal mining in China, and gold mining in Latin America as well as Africa). Set against this is the notion that artisanal (indigenous) knowledge/technology allows petty producers in extractive or processing activities to achieve lower environmental costs for each unit of output – analogous to the 'poor but efficient' model of small-scale farmers' use of land.

Beyond the above instances, defining and measuring the effects of a wide range of petty production in diverse and unstable savanna environments, and assessing whether (and for whom) those effects represent environmental 'degradation', is unavoidably contentious. Routine assertions by UN agencies that 'over 45 per cent of Africa is affected by desertification'[14] are simply not supported by a framework of evidence or analysis that addresses the diversity of African savannas outlined above. While the lack of clear evidence of any general trends of environmental degradation, and notably of soil erosion, may seem frustrating, we provide some examples (and indicate some explanations) of more localized instances below. Moreover the problem of adequate and reliable knowledge is hardly unique to knowledge of patterns of environmental change. Another example, relevant to this discussion, is the extreme variation of statistical evidence (guesstimates) of food production in Africa at any significant level of aggregation. Such extreme variations of data on food production (and their subsequent 'corrections') are rarely accidental or innocent. In some cases they conceal marked gender biases. In addition, sensationalist 'crisis narratives' concerning food availability often serve the interventionist interests of aid agencies and of NGOs that compete for aid funding, as well as the appetite of African state classes and accumulators for foreign aid.[15] There is a further aspect to the difficulties of environmental accounting, as there is in accounting for food production (and many other important measures), which is that Africa's fluid and contradictory social realities continuously elude the kinds of (ostensibly) clear categories through which scientific evidence is constructed and organized. What both sides of the 'Malthusian' debate tend to neglect is that different outcomes (say, soil degradation or soil conservation) can and do occur simultaneously and in related ways, in part due to social differentiation among petty commodity producers. Next we address the challenge of analyzing those fluid and contradictory social dynamics that both eco-populists, who take the side of (undifferentiated) farmers and 'communities', and environmental scientists, who see 'population pressure' in aggregate quantitative terms, are poorly equipped to take on.[16]

SOCIAL DYNAMICS: THE SPECTRE OF MARX

For some, then, the source of the problem is the assault on an indigenous Africa by capitalism (or simply modernity?) as the great 'other', registered in a trajectory of alien intervention from colonial conquest through the statist developmentalism of late colonialism and political independence to the current agendas of global neo-liberalism. The ambiguities of social relations in sub-Saharan Africa today include commoditization without (complete) dispossession of small farmers, and the way notions of 'community' based in descent and/or locale permeate political discourse. Such ambiguities provide ideological spaces in which thrive varieties of ecological populism that celebrate either or both (a) the small scale of farming and its generally 'low-input' character, and (b) the ties, wisdoms and capacities of (rural) 'community' to protect and manage natural resources constituted as 'common property'. The latter typically embodies, more or less explicitly, views of the virtues of indigenous African society and culture, including environmental values and knowledges deemed to have resisted and, in varying degrees, survived the depredations of colonialism, capitalism, and developmentalism.

For others, across a wide range of ideological positions, underlying the images of Africa's current problems are notions that the continent's failures of development are the effect of a lack of 'enough', 'full' or 'proper' capitalism. For example, in something of an echo of Marx's dictum about regions that 'suffer not only from the development of capitalist production, but also from the incompleteness of that development', two veteran progressive scholars of Africa propose that 'predominant social relations (in Africa) are still not capitalist, nor is the prevailing logic of production. Africa south of the Sahara exists in a capitalist world, which marks and constrains the lives of its inhabitants at every turn, but is not of it...'.[17]

At the same time, John Saul and Colin Leys would be the first to acknowledge that the vulnerability of Africa makes it a kind of ideological free-fire zone in which discursive insult is piled upon, and helps to reproduce, the injuries of material existence. Africa is the region of the 'South' most exposed, as laboratory or playground, to the latest fashions in neo-liberal experiment with structural adjustment, market-led 'poverty reduction', state reform, and indeed tropical environmental management. If the agendas of the World Bank and others to 'develop' and 'democratize' Africa on liberal capitalist lines, and to 'sustain' its environments, manifest an ideological fantasy, the responses to them of nationalism and populism are hardly adequate. Nationalism can generate its own fantasies in defence of African sovereignty as represented by its current political regimes, and populism tends to idealize peasantries, including notions of their intrinsic, and egalitarian, 'community-ness' and folk wisdom.

Our principal interest here in understanding petty commodity production, and its role in the social reproduction of Africa's classes of labour, is how it might contribute to analyzing and assessing patterns of environmental change. For most Africans some form and degree of petty (commodity) production involving direct appropriation of nature – predominantly through farming but also, for example, fishing, artisanal mining and logging – is a key element of the bundles of activities (including wage labour) that they pursue to secure their reproduction ('livelihoods'). Moreover, and *pace* Leys and Saul, we contend that contemporary Africa is characterized by its own forms of 'actually existing capitalism', in which commodity relations are generalized and internalized in the circuits of social reproduction – even though this has not generated accumulation and development of the productive forces on the scale implied by their reference to the 'logic' of capitalist production (at the level of national economy?). Even if 'actually existing capitalism' is experienced by most Africans as 'relentless micro-capitalism', in Mike Davis's term, it is still capitalism.[18] And it is still capitalism when commodity relations, not least in the countryside, are often mediated by ostensibly 'traditional' cultural forms and claims to 'customary' authority through which land is allocated and labour mobilized (and exploited).

African societies and savanna environments are much too diverse to allow any simple generalizations, and we have no ambition to propose an encompassing 'model' of degradation or conservation, of environmental vice or virtue, as eco-populist approaches do. Moreover, as suggested above the evidence concerning processes of environmental change is simply too incomplete, inconclusive and debatable to allow such conclusions. At the same time, the fragmentation of labour, pressures on its reproduction, (intensified) commoditization, social inequality, and competition for land in conditions of contested property rights, are key dynamics in any satisfactory account and understanding of environmental change in sub-Saharan Africa today.

SOCIAL DYNAMICS: 'ACTUALLY EXISTING CAPITALISM' IN CONTEMPORARY AFRICA

We prefer the term 'classes of labour' to the vocabulary of proletarianization/proletariat (and semi-proletarianization/semi-proletariat), as it is less encumbered with problematic assumptions and associations, both historical and ideological.[19] Classes of labour comprise 'the growing numbers...who now depend – directly *and indirectly* – on the sale of their labour power for their own daily reproduction'.[20] The emphasis we have added links to our notion of the 'fragmentation of labour'. We use this term to encapsulate the effects of how classes of labour in global capitalism, and especially in the 'South', pursue their reproduction. That is typically through insecure and oppressive – and in many places increasingly scarce – wage employment, often *combined with* a range of likewise precarious small-scale farming and insecure 'informal sector' ('survival') activity. In turn, such activity is subject to its own forms of differentiation and oppression along intersecting lines of class, gender, generation, caste and ethnicity. In short, most people have to pursue their means of livelihood/reproduction across different sites of the social division of labour: urban and rural, agricultural and non-agricultural, wage employment and self-employment.

This has implications for understanding the dynamics, forms and effects of class relations. First, petty commodity production in farming and other ('informal sector') activities always contains the possibility of social differentiation because the social basis of petty commodity production within capitalism is a contradictory combination of the class places of capital and labour. Petty producers are only able to employ themselves (labour) because they have access to means of production (capital), and hence have to reproduce themselves as both labour and capital. A strategic way in which they try to do this is by combining petty production with selling their labour power, in an important sense a further index of 'fragmentation' as relative success or failure in labour markets and salaried employment is typically key to the viability (reproduction) of petty commodity production in farming, as in other activities.[21] In short, both petty production and wage labour have their own, intersecting, circuits (and disciplines) of reproduction.

Second, the fragmentation of labour – and its deepening impoverishment, for the vast majority of people in sub-Saharan Africa today – suggests that relatively few are successful in surmounting the pressures on their reproduction as labour by accumulating sufficient capital to secure a viable base of livelihood principally in farming and/or other petty production.

Third, commoditization can generate relatively stable petty commodity production in farming (the idealized 'middle peasant' or 'yeoman' model) in particular places at particular times, as exemplified by some cash cropping areas of Africa, especially from the 1920s to the 1970s: cocoa and oil palm in the forest zones of West Africa; groundnuts, cotton and tobacco in savanna regions across the continent; coffee in suitable upland environments; as well as the specialized commodity production of such food staples as rice, plantains and, pre-eminently, maize. However, what is typically overlooked is that relatively stable forms of commodity production in African farming, as elsewhere, reflect and/or generate processes of social differentiation.[22] Their entry and reproduction costs can be met by mobilizing land and labour by 'customary' means (not least by chiefs and 'big men'), and by the remittances and savings of (better paid) migrant workers. The development of cash cropping was also often promoted and supported by the agricultural development schemes of late colonialism and the early years of independence.

Fourth, an effect of the very precarious material and social conditions in which labour pursues means of livelihood in Africa is that, in addition to structural constraints, quite idiosyncratic or fortuitous factors can rapidly and radically change the individual fortunes in farming and/or labour markets of those whose reproduction combines 'hoe and wage'. Life is highly unpredictable.

None of these processes is novel in recent African history, but the resulting pressures have undoubtedly intensified in the last 30 years or so, with the interconnected onset of contemporary globalization and the implosion of the statist development project. In particular, the neo-liberal onslaught of structural adjustment has undermined the fiscal and institutional basis on which many branches of petty commodity production in agriculture rested, notably for export crops.[23]

In addition to the cumulative and overwhelming evidence of increased poverty and insecurity, and of how globalization weakens African economies, the pressures on the reproduction of classes of labour have some paradoxical effects. These are partly explicable by the desperate pursuit of any means of livelihood, and partly by how they are experienced by different categories of people (women and men, 'natives' and 'strangers', old and young) in different circumstances and different places. First, there is a marked trend of what Deborah Bryceson terms 'de-peasantization' or 'de-agrarianization', registered in the growing dependence of rural household on sources of income outside their own farming.[24] This also links to the scale of urbanization (or more precisely, urban migration). The pursuit of survival by many Africans involves a high degree of mobility between countryside and towns, between different rural zones, and across borders between African countries and beyond (for example as migrant workers to the horticultural zones of southern Europe).

Second, there is a kind of scissors effect at work here, as the difficulties of securing a livelihood from farming push rural people increasingly towards wage work and 'informal sector' activity, although formal wage employment in cities has declined drastically, as have real wages, while the informal sector is 'over-crowded', immensely competitive, and provides only highly precarious and meagre sources of livelihood for the great majority.[25]

Third, a paradoxical outcome of this scissors effect is that 'de-agrarianization' is accompanied by an *intensification* of struggles and conflicts over land rights, and access to land, across much of Africa.[26] These struggles encompass a wide range, and mix, of social actors, who confront each other in a range of circumstances. Those circumstances include the officially sanctioned appropriation of land for development and conservation schemes on behalf of international capital and aid agencies; other forms of appropriation and enclosure by individual members of the state class and their clients; attempts to acquire land by retrenched industrial workers and miners and by an urban-based middle class, many of whom also experience severe pressures on their reproduction in the conditions of Africa's generalized economic crisis; the desire for land by migrant (ethnic) 'strangers', who are often refugees from civil wars and drought, by adjacent rural communities, by neighbours within the same locales, and indeed by kinsfolk; and the increasing distribution of land (and especially good land) through growing transactions in 'vernacular land markets'. A striking aspect of the complex dynamics of competition and conflict in some rural areas is the reassertion by 'traditional authorities' (chiefs) of their rights to allocate land. In the forest zones of Ghana, resistance to chiefs and the local state is offered by those whom Kojo Amanor calls 'night harvesters, forest hoods and saboteurs'.[27] In Namibia and South Africa, recent and highly contentious legislation has given 'traditional leaders' a central statutory role in the administration and allocation of 'communal' lands.[28]

Underlying these observations are, first, the fluid and contradictory social categories that those who labour for their living inhabit, combine and move between, and that defy the inherited assumptions and conventions of fixed (and uniform) notions of 'worker', 'peasant', 'pastoralist', 'trader', 'artisan', 'rural', 'urban', and the like. Second, while this very fluidity of social categories and activities, as well as mobility between them, hinders any evident appearance of clear-cut social classes, social reproduction is shaped by the effects of class dynamics inherent in commoditization. For example, livelihood 'diversification', another concept currently fashionable in development discourse, is in practice strongly patterned along class lines. For the labouring poor, it means seeking out and seizing, or inventing and improvising, various sources and combinations of means of livelihood, including dangerous and badly-paid wage work, for example, in mining and construction. For those in the countryside with greater resources (i.e. capital, and hence the ability to command labour), accumulation is often based not on improved farming but on investment in crop processing, trading and transport, and other mercantile enterprises, as well as in (urban) housing and education of their sons and, increasingly, their daughters too. In populist views of Africa there is a fashionable notion that vibrant 'social networks' rooted in kinship or community support their poorer members. But such 'social networks' are continuously created and recreated in ways that are as likely (or more likely) to manifest pervasive inequalities: they are hierarchical and often amount to patron–client relations; they are means of accumulation and mobilization of labour, land and political support by the powerful; money is required to maintain (or 'buy into') authority and to command followers; they operate on the ability of their powerful members to exclude others, and so on – all of which is represented in (typically) patriarchal idioms of common descent and identity.[29]

Third, intensified commoditization does not affect everyone in the same way. For example, the rapid growth of urban populations means growing demand for staple foods, presenting opportunities to farmers who are well located and with sufficient command of resources to produce for urban markets. Indeed, declines in export crop production can reflect a switch by farmers to growing 'fast crops' for domestic food markets, which provides a more regular and timely source of cash income.[30] Finally, in conditions of intensified commoditization and its class and other social inequalities, the desperation of most people presents opportunities to some, neatly expressed by a local (village) capitalist in northern Uganda in the early 1980s: 'what helped us [to accumulate] was the famine of 1980. People were hungry and they sold us things cheaply [including land and cattle]. That is when we really started buying'.[31]

The dynamics of social reproduction, commoditization and social differ- entiation, and their connections with land and farming, that we have briefly and selectively sketched, have important implications for the issues of envi- ronmental change, of degradation/conservation and ecological management, that we presented earlier.

A remarkable theoretical essay by Mahmood Mamdani on the 'extreme but not exceptional' nature of the agrarian question in Uganda, informed by village fieldwork in the early 1980s, deployed a very different take on the mo- tif of individual rationality and social irrationality to that of Hardin (above).[32] Instead of seeing the problem as caused by the form of property rights (the 'tragedy of the commons'), Mamdani proposed a kind of Malthusian effect *in class terms*: the rural poor, confronted with crises of reproduction, respond by [over-]exploiting the only assets at their disposal, namely such land as they are able to access, hence leading to its degradation, and their ability to produce children, leading to relative surplus population (over-population). Mamdani located this in the class structure established by and inherited from colonialism, and subsequent social dynamics and state aggrandisement after independence. He pointed to processes, both overt and hidden, of enclosure of 'common' lands and sources of water, especially by the state class (and its local allies), as an aspect of 'accumulation from above' through extra-economic coercion, as distinct from 'accumulation from below' arising from the ('normal') capitalist economic process of class differentiation of the peasantry. We would suggest that enclosure has increased in the current period, and partly explains the growth and intensity of conflicts over land noted above. Mamdani also found that poor peasants with access to areas of land of comparable size to those farmed by middle and rich peasants cultivated much less of it because they lacked adequate implements (instruments of labour, in Marx's term) to do so. This ties in with his argument that poor peasants exploit their procreative powers, since having more 'hands' to do the work in a sense substitutes for other means of cultivation (i.e. it substitutes labour for capital); and the use of child labour in household farming 'releases' men for migration to find paid work.

This also has a wider relevance in relation to the often neglected syndrome of being 'too poor to farm' – or to farm more, or farm better, whether due to lack of enough (good quality) land, or of adequate implements and inputs, or enough labour. Of these conditions, Mamdani identified the second – lack of inputs – as the key factor for poor villagers in the areas of Uganda he studied at that time. In many circumstances and places in Africa today, any or all of these three factors commonly applies to those who try to satisfy part of their reproduction needs through farming: access to land is often limited by processes of enclosure and commoditization through 'vernacular land markets'; access to instruments of labour is limited by the available cash to buy them; access to labour is often constrained by the absence of adult men seeking work elsewhere, by the 'flight' from the countryside of many young people, and by the gender barriers to women commanding the labour of others.

Our own studies, of highly-prized 'wetlands in drylands' in Mali, Botswana, South Africa and Kenya, highlight the importance of water management as a defining constraint to unlocking productive potential in the African savannas. They also inform our view that combinations of (i) increasing population pressure on land, (ii) intensified commoditization of scarce resources of (good quality) arable and grazing land, water and forest, and (iii) social inequality, generate tendencies to environmental degradation in some cases. And this includes the degradation of the energies and health of the rural poor, who leave for the urban slums or have to intensify their toil on small, less fertile, plots of land, typically with inadequate 'instruments of labour' (both implements and biochemical inputs), for uncertain harvests. Nor is it enough to safeguard against (irresponsible) 'crisis narratives' simply by invoking (geographical) diversity, as in the observation that 'problems take different forms for different people in different places'.[33] Rather social differentiation and the dynamics of inequality mean that problems take different forms for different people in *the same places.*

This is the logic of Mamdani's social analysis, of which we provide a final illustration in relation to the influential counter-Malthusian study by Tiffen, Mortimore and Gichuki, mentioned earlier. They suggest that in Machakos, a semi-arid environment with a prior history of degradation, population growth from 250 thousand people in 1930 to 1.5 million in 1990 was associated with an improvement in soil conservation and farm productivity, registered in an aggregate four-fold increase in agricultural output per head of population and an eleven-fold increase in yield per hectare cultivated over the period. They demonstrate the capacity of African farmers to increase productivity, in this case through constructing terraces on sloping land to increase rainfall capture and cultivating higher value crops (coffee and horticultural commodities) on those terraced fields. They also demonstrate the key role of non-farm income – earnings from urban employment in Nairobi, 50km to the north – in funding this investment. Did the increasingly numerous residents of Machakos benefit equally? John Murton's subsequent study in the same area investigated the *distribution* of non-farm income, of investment in conservation and farming, and of land, which revealed aspects of social differentiation missed (or ignored) by Tiffen, Mortimore and Gichuki. Murton found that 57 per cent of households lacked the means to invest in cash crop production; that 20 per cent of households with the highest non-farm incomes had purchased more land than they had inherited; and that in the previous 30 years the 20 per cent of households with the largest holdings had increased their share of total land from 40 to 55 per cent, at the expense of the 40 per cent of households with the smallest holdings whose share had declined from 21 to 11 per cent. We thus have a snapshot of a Boserup-type increase in investment and productivity by the locally wealthy, together with a Malthus-type crisis of the poor, who experience 'a detrimental and involutionary cycle of declining yields, declining soil fertility and diminishing returns to labour, as first phase [historic] conservation and productivity gains are overtaken by population growth'.[34]

AFRICA'S CRISES OF REPRODUCTION CONFRONT
GREEN POPULISM

As in so much else concerning Africa, the diagnosis of its environmental ills, and prescriptions for their treatment, are often dominated by interests and priorities originating elsewhere. Recent re-assessments of the understanding of African ecologies have begun to question arguments from environmental science that underpin some of these prescriptions, and claims for the control of Africa's landscapes in the name of a greater 'global' environmental good. In particular, the diagnosis of degradation in the savanna ecologies that predominate in Africa needs to give less priority to the conservation of notionally 'pristine' environments. More attention needs to be paid to the question of how any activity based on the appropriation of nature can sustain its productivity in the longer term, without any ecologically-mediated negative effects on other people (for example, depletion and/or pollution of water sources, or lack of wood for fuel).

While we share green populism's distaste for 'green imperialism', we have already suggested the inadequacy of any alternative that puts its faith in 'traditional' (egalitarian) African institutions as a means to achieve environmental salvation. Whatever the ecological skills developed by African farmers over their long history, there is little convincing evidence that pre-colonial land regimes were concerned with conservation of forest, pasture or water, as distinct from ensuring that 'outsiders' did not gain access to them without approval by the controlling authority. Processes and patterns of social differentiation and inequality generated by commoditization pervade the everyday conditions of life in Africa today, albeit in the absence of more familiar forms of 'capitalist relations of production', such as self-evident classes of capital and labour. It follows that we are sceptical about any scheme to reclaim (or re-create) customary systems of property rights and common resource management, which fails to confront the fact that the 'customary' (and the rural 'community') are permeated by the class dynamics of commodity relations.

We are also sceptical about the assumptions and plausibility of the common populist panacea for the problems of small farmers and the rural poor of 'withdrawal from the market'. One of the more accessible reviews of land productivity in Africa identified a number of areas – for example, in parts of the Ethiopian highlands, Rwanda, and Malawi – with good rainfall and soil fertility that favour agricultural productivity and population growth, but which lack access to agricultural and labour markets. In the absence of access to markets or alternative employment opportunities for existing agricultural labour, the review concludes that 'these farming systems will continue to provide low levels of income and livelihood for their populations, continuing vulnerability to food deficit, and exposure of soils to increasing levels of exhaustion'.[35]

In environmental terms, only investment will stabilize productivity in Africa. For much of the savanna, that means managing the supply of water, which typically requires collective action beyond the scale of most individual land holdings. However, to achieve anything like this in ways that benefit more than a few, the hierarchies and unequal power relations of customary institutions, and their submerged class dynamics and purposes, have to be more effectively challenged than has mostly been the case in local conflicts over land and chiefly authority. This leaves us with a sequence of questions.

Given the commitments contained in most African constitutions, including those concerning stewardship of national resources, what might induce governments to exercise that responsibility, and notably what kinds of pressure might come from movements from below? What forms of democratic collective action are there, potentially or actually, to contain the environmental degradation that results from over-exploitation of land and other resources, whether through the extractive activities of international capital, the activities of (would-be) African accumulators or the strongly constrained petty production of those who populate the classes of labour? Are there inherited ideas, institutions, and forms of practice, that can be adapted and/or invented, that advance collective and democratic action to resist the individualization of 'survival', in this context in relation to access to the means of livelihood and environmental regulation?[36] What are the prospects for alternative ways of farming, and managing the environment, that could address the socio-ecological contradictions of commoditization in African countrysides?

John Iliffe has recently suggested that the mobilization of people with HIV/Aids in Africa 'not only introduced patient power into medical systems but was a major step towards the repoliticization of Africa after the long stagnation of one-party rule'.[37] Struggles over access to land may similarly give rise to a 'politics of the commons' that connects with other struggles around the wider social conditions of their reproduction waged by Africa's classes of labour.[38]

NOTES

We are grateful to comrades at the *Socialist Register* workshop in Oxford, organized by Barbara Harriss-White, for their comments on an early draft. In order not to (over-) burden this short essay with endnotes, we refer interested readers to the following work for bibliographies of the many empirical studies we draw on, both historical and contemporary, as well as expositions of the theoretical reasoning we simply state here in abbreviated fashion, for example, in relation to the analysis of petty commodity production and 'actually existing capitalism': Henry Bernstein, '"The Peasantry" in Global Capitalism: Who, Where and Why?', *The Socialist Register 2001*; 'Considering Africa's Agrarian Questions', *Historical Materialism*, 12(4), 2004; 'Rural Land and Land Conflicts in Sub-Saharan Africa', in Sam Moyo and Paris Yeros, eds., *Reclaiming the Land. The Resurgence of Rural Movements in Africa, Asia and Latin America*, London: Zed Books, 2005; 'Land Conflicts in Sub-Saharan Africa: Political Economy and Moral Economy', *Afriche e Orienti*, forthcoming; Philip Woodhouse, 'African Enclosures: A Default Mode of Development', *World Development*, 31(10), 2003; Philip Woodhouse, Henry Bernstein and David Hulme, *African Enclosures? The Social Dynamics of Wetlands in Drylands*, Oxford: James Currey, 2000; Henry Bernstein and Philip Woodhouse, 'Telling Environmental Change Like It Is? Reflections on a Study in Sub-Saharan Africa', *Journal of Agrarian Change*, 1(2), 2001; Admos Chimhowu and Philip Woodhouse, 'Customary vs. Private Property Rights? Dynamics and Trajectories of Vernacular Land Markets in Sub-Saharan Africa', *Journal of Agrarian Change*, 6(3), 2006.

1   Melissa Leach and Robin Mearns, 'Challenging Received Wisdom in Africa', in Leach and Mearns, eds., *The Lie of the Land*, Oxford: James Currey, 1996, p. 1. Their list does not mention water as a critical resource, nor is it addressed by any of the contributors to their influential collection.

2   In the words of John S. Saul and Colin Leys, 'Sub-Saharan Africa in Global Capitalism', *Monthly Review*, 51(3), 1999, p. 13; reprinted in John S. Saul, *The Next Liberation Struggle. Capitalism, Socialism and Democracy in Southern Africa*, Toronto: Between The Lines, 2005.

3   L. Taylor, T. Brown, A. Benham, P. Lusty and D Minchin, *World Mineral Production, 2000-2004*, Nottingham: British Geological Society, 2006.

4   United Nations Environment Programme report: *Fisheries and the Environment. Fisheries Subsidies and Marine Resources Management. Lessons Learned from Argentina and Senegal*, UNEP.ch/etb/publications, Geneva: United Nations Environment Programme, 2001, pp. 39-43.

5   On Kenyan flower exports, see Alex Hughes, 'Accounting for Ethical Trade: Global Commodity Networks, Virtualism and the Audit Economy', in Alex Hughes and Suzanne Reimer, eds., *Geographies of Commodity Chains*, London: Routledge, 2004; the coffee example is from Benoit Daviron and Stefano Ponte, *The Coffee Paradox. Global Markets, Commodity Trade and the Elusive Promise of Development*, London: Zed Books, 2005, p. 178.

6   Joan Martinez-Alier, *The Environmentalism of the Poor. A Study of Ecological Conflicts and Valuation*, Cheltenham: Edward Elgar, 2002.

7   We are indebted to Daniel Brockington for his estimates drawn from the *World Database on Protected Areas*, 2005 edition, and for advice on current trends in Africa's protected areas.

8   In his compelling study, *From Enslavement to Environmentalism: Politics on a Southern African Frontier*, Seattle: University of Washington Press, 2006, David McDermott Hughes shows how current conservationist models and interventions reproduce the 'native questions' of colonialism.

9   See, for example, the FAO's *Global Forest Resources Assessment 2005*, Rome: FAO, 2005, and UNEP's *Global Environmental Outlook*, Geneva: United Nations Environment Programme, 2006, available at http://www.unep.org.

10   M.E. Adams, 'Savanna Environments' in William M. Adams, Andrew S. Goudie and Antony R. Orme, eds., *The Physical Geography of Africa*, Oxford: Oxford University Press, 1996, p. 196.

11   Garrett Hardin, 'The Tragedy of the Commons', *Science*, 162, 1968. Eric B. Ross's lively *The Malthus Factor. Poverty, Politics and Population in Capitalist Development*, London: Zed Books, 1998, contains information about Hardin's unsavoury political views and connections.

12   Ester Boserup, *The Conditions of Agricultural Growth: The Economics of Agrarian Change Under Population Pressure*, London: Allen and Unwin, 1965. Colin Clark and Margaret Haswell, *The Economics of Subsistence Agriculture*, London: Macmillan, 1964, was one of a number of counter-Malthusian, and indeed natalist, texts by the Roman Catholic Clark, a pioneering economic statistician and development economist.

13   Mary Tiffen, Michael Mortimore and Francis Gichuki, *More People, Less Erosion. Environmental Recovery in Kenya*, Chichester: John Wiley, 1994; Mary Tiffen and Michael Mortimore, 'Malthus Controverted: the Role of Capital and Technology in Growth and Environmental Recovery in Kenya', *World Development*, 22(7), 1994.

14   United Nations Environment Programme, *Global Environment Outlook GEO-3 Factsheet Africa*, Geneva: United Nations Development Programme, 2006.

15   Jane Guyer, 'Women's Work and Production Systems: A Review of Two Reports on the Agricultural Crisis', *Review of African Political Economy*, 27, 1983, pointed out that tubers and root crops cultivated by women, an important staple source of carbohydrates in forest zones, tend to be ignored in estimates of aggregate food production. On the problematic nature of food production data, and how they are (mis)used, see also the pointed accounts by Sara Berry, 'The Food Crisis and Agrarian Change in Africa: A Review Essay', *African Studies Review*, 27(2), 1984; Philip Raikes, *Modernising Hunger. Famine, Food Surplus and Farm Policy in the EEC and Africa*, London: James Currey, 1988; Stephen Wiggins, 'Interpreting Changes from the 1970s to the 1990s in African Agriculture through Village Studies', *World Development*, 28(4), 2000.

16   As William Beinart suggested in the African context: 'Environmental history which systematically builds in perspectives from political economy as well as ecology has hardly begun'. 'Environmental Destruction in Southern Africa', in Leach and Mearns, *The Lie of the Land*, p. 71.

17   Karl Marx, *Capital*, Volume 1, translated by Ben Fowkes, Harmondsworth: Penguin Books, 1976, p. 91; Saul and Leys, 'Sub-Saharan Africa', p. 13.

18   Mike Davis, *Planet of Slums*, London: Verso, 2006, p. 181.

19   For example, notions of semi-proletarianization – not least in the historical context of migratory labour systems in Southern Africa and elsewhere in Africa – are often (if not inevitably) deployed in functionalist reasoning about 'peripheral capitalism'.

20   Leo Panitch and Colin Leys, 'Preface' to *Socialist Register 2001*, p. ix.

21   As more nuanced work on systems of labour migration in Southern Africa has long shown, in contrast to views of 'semi-proletarianization' as generating a homogeneous mass of the labouring poor.

22   Outside the historical settler colonies where capitalist landed property emerged from dispossession, processes of the commoditization and social differentiation of farming in most of sub-Saharan Africa have only rarely been registered in the formation of evident classes of (large) landed property, although labour markets permeate the zones of specialized petty commodity (petty capitalist) production, supplying the farms of middle and rich 'peasants'.

23   For example, state-provided credit, subsidized inputs, technical assistance, and marketing. The delivery of these services as public goods often left much to be desired but their removal has left many farmers worse off. One of the clearest indicators of the effects of market 'liberalization', of particular salience in agricultural productivity, is the drastic reduction of fertilizer use by small farmers.

24   Deborah Bryceson, 'Deagrarianization and Rural Employment in Sub-Saharan Africa: A Sectoral Perspective', *World Development*, 2(1), 1996, and 'African Rural Labour, Income Diversification and Livelihood Approaches: A Long-term Development Perspective', *Review of African Political Economy*, 80, 1999.

25   On which see Mike Davis's *Planet of Slums*, published as we were completing this essay. Although its subject area is very different from ours (as is the vitality of his prose) we are struck by many parallels between his analysis of what he calls the 'informal working class' and 'relentless micro-capitalism' and a number of our themes and ideas concerning the fragmentation of labour (including some of its axes of differentiation), classes of labour, and their crises of reproduction.

26   As Pauline Peters has documented and argued persuasively – 'Inequality and Social Conflict Over Land in Africa', *Journal of Agrarian Change*, 4(3), 2004.

27   Kojo Sebastian Amanor, 'Night Harvesters, Forest Hoods and Saboteurs: Struggles over Land Expropriation in Ghana', in Sam Moyo and Paris Yeros, eds., *Reclaiming the Land. The Resurgence of Rural Movements in Africa, Asia and Latin America*, London: Zed Books, 2005.

28   See Ben Cousins, 'The Zimbabwe Crisis in its Wider Context: The Politics of Land, Democracy and Development in Southern Africa', in Amanda Hammar, Brian Raftopoulos and Stig Jensen, eds., *Zimbabwe's Unfinished Business: Rethinking Land, State and Nation in the Context of Crisis*, Harare: Weaver Press, 2003. Critics of South Africa's Communal Land Rights Act of 2004 include the country's leading activist organization in this field, the National Land Committee.

29   Two examples are ostensibly 'traditional' forms of cooperation in the activities of cultivation (clearing land, planting, weeding, harvesting) and ostensibly 'traditional' practices of 'lending' land and livestock, both of which often conceal the appropriation of the labour of the rural poor by their richer neighbours.

30   See Stefano Ponte, *Farmers and Markets in Tanzania. How Policy Reforms Affect Rural Livelihoods in Africa*, Oxford: James Currey, 2002. Given that food production has generally performed much better than export crop production in the period of neo-liberalism, Bryceson's view that 'African peasant agriculture's

inability to compete in today's global market' is a fundamental cause of 'de-agrarianization' ('African Rural Labour', p. 185) needs more nuance on agrarian trends in African and a more critical stance on how 'competition' in world markets for agricultural commodities is structured.

31   Quoted in Mahmood Mamdani, 'Extreme but not Exceptional: Towards an Analysis of the Agrarian Question in Uganda', *Journal of Peasant Studies*, 14(2), 1987, p. 208.

32   Ibid.

33   Leach and Mearns, 'Challenging Received Wisdom', p. 3.

34   John Murton, 'Population Growth and Poverty in Machakos District, Kenya', *Geographical Journal*, 165(1), 1999, p. 44. Before Murton, Dianne Rocheleau had questioned aspects of Tiffen and Mortimore's historical and spatial-environmental account, as well as its lack of attention to processes and patterns of inequality. Their reply suggested that there is 'simply not enough information to make definitive statements' about social differentiation (but then their research did not even pose the question) and also that 'there always have been, and always will be, individuals and families who do better than others' – a view of inequality as inherent in the human condition, hence not peculiar to colonial capitalism and commoditization more generally. This exchange was published as 'More on Machakos', *Environment*, 37(7), 1995.

35   Ian Scoones and Camilla Toulmin, *Policies for Soil Fertility Management in Africa*, London: Department for International Development (DFID), 1999, p. 51.

36   For an elucidation of this question more broadly, see Mahmood Mamdani's seminal *Citizen and Subject. Contemporary Africa and the Legacy of Late Colonialism*, Cape Town: David Philip, 1996. In his earlier article that we have drawn on, 'Extreme but not Exceptional', p. 419, Mamdani commented that 'the politics of patronage has a disintegrating effect …The poor are atomised as each seeks a personal advantage against another, as each looks for a private solution to a social problem'.

37   John Iliffe, *The African Aids Epidemic. A History*, Oxford: James Currey, 2006, p. 156.

38   Hughes, *From Enslavement to Environmentalism*, p. 172, suggests that the 'studied parochialism' of the pervasive discourses of rural community, including 'community-based conservation', among governments, aid donors and NGOs, helps 'to frustrate the possibility of wide-scale rural mobilization'.

FEEDING THE WORLD: AGRICULTURE, DEVELOPMENT AND ECOLOGY

PHILIP MCMICHAEL

Under present political arrangements feeding the world is a pipe-dream. Although more than enough food is produced for the world's population, its distribution is strikingly unequal. Three principal reasons for this are: (1) industrial and bio-engineered agricultures systematically displace farmers who supply food for the poor; (2) markets respond to people with incomes, not people as such; and (3) agro-exporting, a structural imperative of the state system, exacerbates these tendencies. Ironically, while technology, markets and trade are touted as essential conditions of development and prosperity, these forces have combined, under the banner of 'development', to create 'hunger amidst abundance'.[1] The irony is compounded by the way technology, markets and trade further compromise the ecological conditions for future food production.

How and why does 'development' privilege a global agricultural system that is socially limited and ecologically unstable? This essay examines the ways in which 'development' has been represented and applied to the task of feeding the world, and its ecological consequences. 'Development', a term with universal appeal, has been appropriated as an ideological expression of capitalist development.[2] It actually represents the political relations of global capitalism, though not of course without being contested. This essay frames capitalist development in terms of three successive historical 'projects':[3] the colonial, development, and globalization projects. The contradictions of each successive project condition the one that follows, just as the crisis-ridden globalization project is today shaping an emerging, unstable, 'imperial project', focused on securing resources to sustain US military power and the global consumption relations of a minority class.[4]

The colonial project ruptured age-old systems of agro-ecology by creating colonial monocultures in the service of European capitalist development, and its successor projects deepened the scale and scope of this rupture. The

early twentieth century crisis (world wars, protectionism, and the mobilization of labour) combined with the world-wide struggle for decolonization
after World War II to dismantle the colonial project; the US then reconstructed the world economy under the aegis of an international 'development
project', promoting 'inner-directed' growth as a model of capitalist regulation
for the world of newly-independent states. This model, a Fordist-Keynesian
compromise responding to the political mobilization of industrial labour and
agro-industrialization, represented development as a national/public responsibility, with trade as the servant of the state. It also mirrored the state-centred
accumulation regime pursued in the Soviet Union and its empire.

The international dimensions of the development project were condi-
tioned by Cold War containment policies, which operated as a vehicle for
US capitalism to secure global resources from, and extend its reach into,
the post-colonial world, in the guise of foreign aid and military protection.
The maturing relations of the US empire (the deepening of global supply chains by transnational corporations, the associated explosion of offshore
money markets, and intervention in key states such as Iran, Indonesia and
Chile) eventually overrode the ideology and practice of economic nationalism, prefiguring the successor 'globalization project'. The latter redefined
development as a private outcome. States now acted as the servants of trade,
cross-border investment, deepening agro-exporting and the construction of
an ecologically-invasive 'world agriculture'.

Across all these periods capitalist agriculture has matured, from colonial
plantations to bio-engineered agricultures, via social and ecological relations
specific to each set of political relations. That is, capital's need to convert
natural processes into value relations is realized politically, and in each case
this generates specific new social and ecological barriers to further development. In attempting to overcome these barriers, but always within the limits
of its specific agro-industrial narrative, capital constantly deepens the developmental crisis, and it is out of this crisis that alternatives emerge. The current proliferation of agro-ecological alternatives shows that modernity does
not need to marginalize farming based on ecologically-based knowledge,[5]
and that a modern, post-capitalist society can replenish modes of agriculture
that are both socially and environmentally sustainable, and arguably capable
of equitably feeding the world.[6]

FEEDING THE WORLD?

The goal of 'feeding the world' emerged within the Cold War context, addressing postwar and colonial deprivations via the politics of containment,
as communist movements threatened Western interests. In the context of

food shortages and famines in the early 1940s, the United Nations Food and Agriculture Organization (FAO) was established with a mandate to stabilize world agriculture and establish global food security. The FAO's role was to foster and manage international trade in foodstuffs to this end. At its Second Session, in 1946, the FAO put forward a vision:

> The raising of the levels of living of rural populations calls for the improvement of agriculture, rural industrialization, large-scale public works, and social and educational services in the country-side, and the raising of the levels of living of many different races and peoples. This in turn requires a reorientation of world agriculture and of world trade in which food will be treated as an essential of life rather than primarily as merchandise.[7]

This vision interpreted 'feeding the world' as an international endeavour to transcend the colonial-era extraction of food from the colonies for export to Europe. It conformed to the stipulations of the UN's Universal Declaration of Human Rights (1948), which informed the 'development project',[8] and echoed the demands of organized labour for improved levels of consumption.[9] At the same time, this vision was founded in reductionist scientific representations of agricultural modernization: 'new imaginations of people, places and food were premised on the acceptance of a scientific approach that permitted the comparison of otherwise distinct contexts and subjected local knowledges to the supremacy of scientific images of, and universal claims for, food and agriculture'.[10]

These claims were manifest in agro-technologies and dietary and nutritional sciences,[11] which were premised on the continuation of class-based relations of food production and consumption, realized through the operation of global food markets – i.e. a premise opposed to the FAO's vision of de-commodified food.[12] And, just as 'feeding the world' licensed a universal 'scientific agriculture', so 'development' licensed representing post-colonial societies as 'underdeveloped' and 'poor', and rationalized all manner of neo-colonial interventions to gain access to strategic resources and markets within the context of the Cold War.[13] As a result, the FAO (and its mother organization, the UN) facilitated the expansion of the US capitalist empire, sabotaging in the process its public vision of food 'as an essential of life rather than as merchandise'.

Early on, the US overrode a 1946 proposal of the FAO and UN Relief and Rehabilitation Administration (UNRRA) to establish a World Food Board, preferring to develop its own network of bilateral aid programs. Thus in 1954 the US government instituted the PL-480 food aid programme, which recycled food surpluses from its domestic commodity stabilization programmes as concessional food subsidies to selected states on the Cold War perimeter in Asia (including occupied Japan), the Middle East and Latin America. The PL-480 programme anchored a 'food aid regime',[14] which resolved the over-production tendencies of petro-farming[15] by subsidizing Third World national industrial development with cheap food, and extended the scope of agro-industrial production through the export of 'green' revolution (intensive farming) technologies to key Third World states, including Mexico, Brazil, Argentina, Venezuela, the Philippines, Indonesia and India.

The postwar food aid regime reinforced the US policy of containing the Soviet empire, and establishing the new capitalist world order based on the reconstitution of states within an informal US empire.[16] Methods of political legitimation included state-building via military and economic aid – notably the introduction of petro-farming via the Marshall Plan in Europe, and the 'green' revolution in regions of the Third World, with the US consumption model as the development standard. This, in turn, drove Cold War rivalry, under which the political legitimacy of the competing systems depended to some extent on expanding meat-intensive agriculture and a meat-intensive diet – both of which the US exported to its neo-colonial clients through a variety of aid programmes, including PL-480, under which the 'counterpart funds' made available by the recipient countries were spent on agribusiness initiatives, laying the foundations of an ecologically-intensive 'livestock revolution'.[17]

While the postwar food aid regime lasted, agricultural commodity prices remained relatively stable because of the publicly-regulated trade in foodstuffs.[18] This regime collapsed when US 'détente' with the Soviet Union in 1972–73 cleared surplus grain stocks for the first time in the post-war period; the price of grains and oilseeds tripled, generating the 1974 world food crisis.[19] The FAO convened a World Food Summit in 1974, as 'billions of people were defined as "food insecure" by the disappearance of US surplus stocks and a surge in world grain prices'.[20] 'Food security' now became an explicit policy goal of the UN, through its member governments, linking food production and distribution. The mercantilist practices of the food aid regime were now replaced by a dual approach: food aid became explicitly 'humanitarian' (with grants replacing concessional sales), while food trade relations were institutionalized via the Uruguay Round of the General Agreement on Tariffs and Trade (GATT), in order to stabilize what had developed into a US-EU competition for market outlets for their domestic food surpluses generated by petro-farming.[21] But separating public, humanitarian food aid from commercial sales led to 'food security' becoming identified with the operation of food markets, and this in turn helped to shape a re-definition of 'development', in 1980, as 'participation in the world market'.[22] This in turn anticipated the 'globalization project'; development was finally recast as a matter of private initiatives in and through global markets.

The 1980s, in fact, were a political dress rehearsal for the wholesale corporate globalization of the 1990s. Management of the debt crisis by the IMF/World Bank nexus via Structural Adjustment Programs forced states in the South to open their markets and resources to Northern business, and to give much higher priority to agro-exporting relative to the production of staple food crops, while austerity measures and the privatization of previously public systems of food subsidies and distribution led to a wave of 'IMF riots' across the South during this decade.[23] The corporate solution to the food crisis was agro-exporting, which gave rise to a global livestock complex supplied by international chains of feedstuffs, alongside growing shipments of fruits, vegetables and seafood. The resulting expanded, and energy-intensive, circulation of food on a global scale was institutionalized in the WTO's 1995 Agreement on Agriculture, which 'prescribes a model for agriculture that has basically only one dimension: increasing agricultural production for exports, importing what cannot be produced without tariff protection or subsidies to producers'.[24] As the Indian policy analyst Devindar Sharma noted, 'whereas for small farmers the subsidies have been withdrawn, there is a lot of support now for agribusiness industry … The result is that the good area under staple foods is now shifting to export crops, so we'll have to import staple food'.[25] Simultaneously, the WTO's Trade-Related Investment Measures (TRIMs) protocol has facilitated cross-border investments and mergers in the food sector, so that agriculture across the world is increasingly enveloped by corporate relations, including a recent 'supermarket revolution',[26] notably in Latin America and Asia.

Through the Uruguay Round the United States redefined food security as 'best provided through a smooth-functioning world market',[27] in order to secure a competitive advantage for US agribusiness. This definition became the organizing principle of the 1995 Agreement on Agriculture; under its provisions Southern states, in particular, were compelled to open up their domestic markets to cheap food imports and thus deepen their food dependency in the name of 'food security'. The WTO's political asymmetry, protecting indirect subsidies to agribusiness in the North and opening food markets in the global South, maximizes the impact of artificially-cheapened prices for agricultural commodities in world trade.[28] In the last few years of the twentieth century agricultural commodity prices fell 30 per cent or more, reaching in 1999 the lowest level in 150 years.[29] Low prices deepen the subjection of agriculture to capitalist relations, with food dumping undermining peasant agriculture, and driving displaced peasants into unstable forms of contract farming, onto plantations (*agro-maquilas*), or into urban slums or *maquilas*.

A 1997 FAO study claimed that the overall impact of liberalization was to induce concentration in farming and the marginalization and dispossession of small producers.[30] In West Africa, for example, cheap tomato concentrate imported from Europe undermines local tomato production and processing; in Jamaica and the Mercosur region (Uruguay, Brazil, Argentina and Paraguay), where dairy farms and coops are concentrating and transnational firms such as Nestlê (Swiss) and Parmalat (Italian) are reorganizing milk processing, subsidized EU dairy products are undercutting milk producers and coops.[31] In Mexico almost two million *campesinos* have been dispossessed as a consequence of a torrent of corn imports from the US, enabled by NAFTA.[32] While the FAO study does not measure dispossession directly, it is estimated that between twenty and thirty million people have lost land through the impact of trade liberalization.[33] A related trend is the 'semi-proletarianization' of farmers. In Africa, some late 1990s evidence has suggested that between 60 and 80 per cent of rural household income was derived from off-farm sources,[34] with the poorest households being the most heavily dependent on off-farm, informal and piecework labour.[35] For Asia, between 30 and 40 per cent of rural household incomes are supplemented from off-farm sources,[36] while in Latin America the great majority of the peasantry are semi-proletarianized, with 'subfamily farmers...now increasingly complementing [60 per cent of] their incomes with rural non-agricultural employment'.[37]

In sum, the combination of Northern mercantilism and Southern liberalization of farm sectors and food markets subjects producers everywhere to a punishing world price. The effect is to institutionalize national food dependency and create a market in food that excludes and starves rural peoples who formerly grew their own food.[38] The neo-liberal mantra of feeding the world with cheap food conceals an unequal subsidy structure favouring corporate farming in the North, and destabilizing agriculture in the South.

ECOLOGY IN THE AGE OF DEVELOPMENT

The colonial project established specialized agricultures in the colonies for the export of raw materials and foodstuffs to the metropolitan centres. The tropical sugar plantation was an early prototype of modern, land-depleting monoculture. It was matched during the nineteenth century by the relocation of temperate agriculture (grains and livestock farming) to European settler regions of the world economy, as provisioning the European proletariat required increasingly large volumes of food staples.[39] The relocation of temperate agriculture supplied cheap food to Europe and so cheapened the wage-costs of European capital, but it depended on the intensive exploitation of virgin soils in the New World via mono-cropping with increasingly complex farm machinery. Native grasses were systematically displaced by the plough and the introduction of non-native grasses, in a process of 'ecological imperialism' that was later reproduced and generalized via the globalization of the US model of agribusiness. While there are 10,000 grass species, 99 per cent of pastures sown depend on just 40 of them, the development of which was closely associated with domestication of cattle over the centuries.[40] Britain's outsourcing of its grain supplies and its beef culture was accomplished through a double rupture that governs global agri-food relations to this day: on the one hand the 'metabolic rift', and on the other the generalization of a 'world agriculture', and dietary patterns abstracted from place-based cuisine.

Ecological rupture: the metabolic rift

The first rupture was with the 'high farming' of the Victorian era, whereby ecologically-sustainable biological methods of crop rotation and the management of livestock sustained 'the condition of the land indefinitely, even while production levels climbed'.[41] On the American plains, however, farmers 'ripped open enormous areas of prairie grasslands'[42] and enjoyed high yields so long as crops drew down 'a vast storehouse of accumulated organic fertility just below the surface'; once this resource was consumed the frontier was simply extended until the process reached its ecological limits in the 'dustbowl' crisis of the 1930s. As already indicated above, the US solution to this crisis was publicly-supported capital-intensive agro-industrialization, centered on commodity stabilization programmes. While these programmes secured the farm belt as a political constituency, the intensive agricultural methods involved also had political origins. The agri-chemical revolution of the 1950s depended on the conversion of war-time nitrogen production (for bombs) to inorganic fertilizer, which displaced the nitrogen-fixing legumes and manure used previously. Along with mechanization, the use of inorganic fertilizer increased farm demand for fuel oils, gasoline and electricity, 'thus increasing agricultural dependence on the energy sector and thereby converting the latter more than ever into a part of agribusiness'.[43] Subsequently, the FAO agreed to an industry plan, in the name of the UN's Freedom from Hunger campaign (1960), to provide extension services for the dispersal of surplus inorganic fertilizer across the Third World, intensifying agricultural dependence on the energy sector still more widely.[44]

The US exported its agro-industrial model first to Europe via the Marshall Plan, and then to Third World regions via the PL-480 programme and 'green' revolution initiatives. This model responded in part to class-based insurgencies in various parts of the Third World. While the ideology of the development project encouraged the stable provision of 'wage foods' for urban populations by national agro-industrial complexes,[45] dependence on 'green' technology laid the foundations for a long-term process of marginalization of agro-ecological farming.

The 'metabolic rift',[46] then, refers to the process whereby the agronomic methods of agro-industrialization abandon agriculture's natural biological base, reducing the possibility of recycling nutrients in and through the soil and water. Thus, the progressive subordination of agriculture to capitalist production relations can also be seen as a metabolic rift between countryside and city.[47] Petroleum plays a central role in widening this rift, through industrializing agriculture while also serving as a major input for the production of inorganic fertilizer, pesticides, herbicides and seed varnishes, as capital attempts to sustain productivity on a deteriorating ecological base. The subordination of agriculture to capital reinforces an abstract representation of agriculture 'as an input-output process that has a beginning and an end',[48] rather than as a complex embedded in local biological cycles that replenish the soil through the maintenance of biotic diversity. Seen in this light, agriculture appears eminently available for abstraction, and relocation, with appropriate chemical inputs and bioengineered seeds, to specialized locales: 'as artificial, off-farm inputs come to matter more and more, so the former intrinsic qualities of the land matter less'.[49] Colin Duncan underlines the significance of capitalist politics in amplifying the perversity of industrial agriculture:

> ...the 'West' now relies on a chronically overproductive industrialized agriculture that is quite bereft of economic rationale, however politically convenient it may be...For once industrialized agriculture became the technical norm, price-support systems originally intended to keep farmers from poverty actually encouraged the excessive use of inputs produced by industry (where previously they had been a contributory cause of the use of excessive areas for crops).[50]

The contradictions of industrial agriculture – soil erosion, salination and deformation, toxic chemical pollution, and unsustainable water practices – are noted by Marc Reisner in *Cadillac Desert: The American West and Its Disappear-*

ing Water. 'Westerners call what they have established out here a civilization, but it would be more accurate to call it a beachhead.... And if history is any guide, the odds that we can sustain it would have to be regarded as low'.[51] In the US, a million acres disappear annually to urbanization and 2 million acres of farmland are lost to erosion, soil salinization, and flooding or soil saturation as a result of intensive agriculture, which consumes groundwater 160 per cent faster than its replenishment rate.[52] The likely consequence is an acceleration of offshore production.

Here corporate food regime dynamics are decisive, as agriculture moves offshore to escape degraded environments and exploit cheap land and labour. While British capitalism outsourced agriculture in the mid-nineteenth century to cheapen 'wage-foods', in the twenty-first century, food corporations outsource production via TRIMS-related liberalization mechanisms. For instance, when the Doux group, the foremost French and European poultry producer, purchased Frangosul, the fourth largest poultry producer in Brazil (which had lower wage costs and weaker environmental regulations), and relocated poultry production there, it reduced its production costs by two-thirds.[53] In the US, several decades of minimal returns on investment in agriculture (1.5 per cent) have led to the concentration of agricultural production.[54] The result has been a wholesale exodus of small and medium farmers,[55] an intensification of production technologies – deepening the metabolic rift – and a relocation of commercial food production offshore.

The outsourcing of food depends on the availability of cheap land and labour in the global South. Such resources are not naturally available, rather, they are *made* available by expelling rural populations from agriculture by importing cheap food and agro-technologies from the North. For example, after a decade of neo-liberal policies threatening India's tens of millions of small farmers, the Indian Ministry of Agriculture noted in 2000: 'The growth in agriculture has slackened during the 1990s. Agriculture has become a relatively unrewarding profession due to an unfavourable price regime and low value addition, causing abandoning of farming and migration from rural areas'.[56] One consequence, a social experiment underway in Andhra Pradesh state, Vision 2020, is to consolidate agro-industrial estates, 'farmed on a contract basis for corporations', using genetically-modified seeds to produce agro-exports of vegetables and flowers, and requiring the displacement of upwards of 20 million small farmers.[57]

Combine this effect with WTO-driven cross-border investment of agribusiness capital, and structural adjustment requirements to expand agro-exporting in order to service Southern debt, and the conditions are ripe for a steady relocation of industrial (and increasingly transgenic) agriculture to the

South. Recent satellite land cover images show that about 40 per cent of the surface of the planet has been converted to crop or pasture lands, compared with 7 per cent in 1700. While intensive farming has slightly reduced crop-land in the US and Europe, agricultural conversion is intensifying in tropical forest regions, in particular through the expansion of soyfields in Brazil and Argentina for agro-exports to China and the EU.[58]

The relocation of agriculture also implies a dramatic increase in 'food miles'. Food transport, the cost of which fell 70 per cent for sea freight be-tween 1980 and 2000, and continues to fall for air freight by 3-4 per cent annually, is one of the fastest-growing sources of greenhouse gas emissions. National accounting systems do not include these emissions and they are also absent from the Kyoto Protocol targets. As a result, a damaging amount of 'food swapping' exacerbates the 'food miles' problem, exemplified by the milk trade. As Millstone and Lang note, 'Until recently most people con-sumed milk produced locally, but from 1961 to 1999 there was a five-fold increase in milk exports, with many countries both importing and exporting large quantities, resulting in millions of extra food miles'.[59] Analogous to the extension of the Southern land frontier for offshore food production is the rising fossil fuel consumption involved in the global fishing industry: with the depletion of fish stocks, boats venture farther out to sea, using 12.5 times as much energy catching fish as the fish provide to consumers. An ecologist claims that 'it's the wide application of fuel that has allowed fleets to expand and really has underpinned much of the overfishing of stocks and deteriora-tion of aquatic ecosystems'.[60]

Deepening the ecological rupture: 'world agriculture'

The second rupture overlays the first. It is symbolized in the beef culture, spawned by British capitalist expansion into the Americas, and reaching into the twenty-first century as a key stress on the environment. Not only was the international cattle complex a financial frontier for English and Scot-tish firms in the second half of the nineteenth century, but it also converted South American land into an offshore pasture, laying the foundations for the twentieth century development project's identification of beef with dietary modernity. Then as now the beef culture was differentiated by class: 'While Argentina provided much of the beef for the British aristocracy and mid-dle class, Uruguayan cattle were used to make the famed "Liebig extract" of meat, a cheap beef spread sold primarily to the English working class. For many Englishmen, the extract served as their main source of animal protein' – prefiguring today's class gap between beef steak and hamburger.[61] Central America became a source of hamburger meat while whole regions of South

America have been converted into off-shore platforms for supermarket-organized exports of beef to Europe and the Middle East. South America has also become a major source of soybean exports to Asia, whose consumer class is larger than that of North America and Europe combined, and which has also become the leading edge of the global livestock revolution.[62] Two-thirds of the increase in meat consumption is taking place in the global South, sourced primarily with Brazilian soybeans. China, once a net exporter of soybeans, is now the world's largest importer of soybeans and oils.[63]

The rising levels of consumption of animal protein (beef, poultry, pork, fish and shrimp), by global consumers divided into high- and low-incomes, demanding specialty cuts (including fresh fish and shrimp) and processed meats respectively, have a multi-layered ecological impact. Both cattle and shrimp farming have irreversible ecological effects on soil and forests and on coastal mangrove swamps in South America and South and Southeast Asia respectively. In the case of shrimp, as mangroves have been depleted, running down their fragile biodiversity and therefore the habitat for local fishermen, shrimp aquaculture has proliferated, along with new ecological vulnerabilities ranging from fresh water pollution and depletion to the disease outbreaks familiar in other forms of industrially-farmed livestock.[64]

In addition to the direct environmental impact of livestock, its symbolic dietary function skews resource use along class lines. Cattle consume more than one-third of the world's grain, and animal protein consumption in general bids cereals and land away from the majority of the world's population. Roughly 95 per cent of global soybean production and a third of commercial fishing is consumed by animals rather than humans, and a 'quarter of the earth's landmass is used as pasture for livestock farming. Half of all US farmland, directly or indirectly, is devoted to beef production. In the EU, 75 per cent of agricultural land is used for growing animal feed'.[65] In its recent report, 'Eating up the Amazon', Greenpeace notes that 'Europe buys half the soya exported from the Amazon state of Matto Grosso, where 90% of rainforest soya is grown. Meat reared on rainforest soya finds its way onto supermarket shelves and fast food counters across Europe'.[66]

Under the constraints of trade and foreign exchange needs, states encourage this pattern of indirect consumption of cereals by relatively affluent global consumers.[67] The grain fed to US livestock roughly equals the amount of food consumed by the combined populations of India and China.[68] The substitution of feed crops for food crops, known as the 'second green revolution', is part of the globalization of high-value production that intensifies monocultures and redistributes food from low- to high-income populations, undermining the staple food systems upon which a large proportion of the world's population depends.[69] While noting the importance of roots and tubers as a key staple for poor farmers around the world, and the recent increased production of potatoes and yams, in particular, the International Food Policy Research Institute (IFPRI) reports that a 'rapid expansion in the demand for roots and tubers for livestock feed has been under way for some time, particularly in Asia, and is likely to continue as demand for meat products grows rapidly in coming years'. Meanwhile, IFPRI predicts that demand for maize in the South 'will overtake demand for rice and wheat' and that about '64 per cent of the maize demand will go toward feeding livestock, compared with 8 per cent of wheat and 3 per cent of rice in 2020'.[70] During the 1990s, while food cereals production in Brazil and China remained constant, feed cereals production almost doubled.[71]

In transforming the food landscape, corporate-led factory farming has unleashed a bio-war against the environment and the human body. In the US, for example, 'animal factories produce 1.3 billion tons of manure each year. Laden with chemicals, antibiotics, and hormones, the manure leaches into rivers and water tables, polluting drinking water supplies and causing fish kills in the tens of millions'.[72] In addition to contaminating the natural environment, the ecological crisis also has direct impacts on human health. To quote Millstone and Lang again: 'Animals in cramped conditions easily catch and transmit bacteria, which may then be passed to humans. Farmers routinely use antibiotics to combat infectious diseases, but in so doing may be contributing to growing antibiotic resistance among humans'.[73] The related global threat of an avian flu pandemic is rooted in the ecology of rising densities of urban populations and factory farming systems, and transnational human mobility. In *The Monster at Our Door* Mike Davis chronicles how the spread of factory farming is actually being intensified by East and Southeast Asian governments' attempts to control virus outbreaks by culling backyard chicken flocks, rather than corporate chicken factories. Although poultry conglomerates claim that their industrial farming is impregnable to viral outbreaks and epidemics, factory farming, says Davis, is more likely to 'maximize the accumulation of viral load and subsequent antigenic drift...In an epidemiological sense, the outdoor flocks are the fuse, and the dense factory populations, the explosive charge'.[74] Affirming the politics of the corporate food regime, GRAIN charges that the FAO, like the WHO, has allowed the targeting of small-scale poultry farming, after years of promoting it: 'Its technical advisor on bird flu to Viet Nam recently told Agence France-Presse that it made both public health and business sense for the country to shift from family poultry farms to large-scale factory farms. Such thinking goes right to the very top of the organisation. Samuel Jutzi, the FAO's Director of

Animal Production and Health, told a Swiss newspaper that small farms are behind the spread of bird flu, not the large factory farms that he describes as "highly protected"'.[75]

Rising animal protein consumption is perhaps the key indicator of the 'nutrition transition', involving a declining consumption of cereals and legumes and a rising consumption of meat and dairy fats, salt and sugars.[76] This transition is not an evolutionary process; rather it expresses the power relations of successive food regimes that have promoted forms of animal protein, and over-production, such as artificially cheapened surplus corn stocks that underwrite 'supersizing' in the fast food industry.[77] Across the world, North and South, the nutrition transition is contributing to rising incidences of obesity, described by the World Health Organization as 'one of the greatest neglected public health problems of our time'. The WHO estimates that 50 per cent of the world's population suffers from malnutrition of one kind or another – indeed, 'a survey of U.N.-sponsored studies indicates that hunger afflicts at least 1.2 billion people, while another 1.2 billion consume more than they need, becoming overweight with harmful consequences'. Most of these 2.4 billion people, both the hungry and the obese, are deficient in essential vitamins and minerals, which are lacking in both impoverished and affluent diets, a fact that is significantly linked to the effects of the global animal protein complex.[78] The conversion of the natural world to service a livestock-based food system stresses both environments and bodies, and, in the context of private solutions to public health problems that privilege care over prevention, promotes a scientific and institutional complex geared to ameliorating, and thereby in practice deepening, the effect.

At the same time a 'nemesis effect' unfolds, as eroding ecosystems interact in unpredictable ways. The UN World Commission on Environment and Development has noted that 'major unintended changes are occurring in the atmosphere, in soils, in waters, among plants and animals, and in relationships among these…The rate of change is outstripping the ability of scientific disciplines and our capabilities to assess and advise'.[79] These changes foretell threats to global public health, such as immune system suppression by ultraviolet radiation, indirect health consequences of climate change on food production and the spread of infections, and the loss of biological and genetic resources for producing medicines – all arising from 'planetary overload, entailing circumstances that are qualitatively different from the familiar, localized problem of environmental pollution'.[80] Broadly, human cultural evolution, distorting ecological relationships, has caused four types of health hazard: 'First came infectious diseases. Then came diseases of industrialization and environmental pollution by toxic chemicals. Simultaneously, in rich populations, various "lifestyle" diseases of affluence (heart disease, assorted cancers, diabetes, etc.) emerged. Today we face the health consequences of disruption of the world's natural systems'.[81]

One form of disruption is genetic engineering, by which capital reinforces its attempt to convert nature to a system of expanded reproduction of value relations. Genetically-modified seeds become a commercial input whose current use-value is principally designed to reduce barriers to chemical agriculture. Commodification of seeds via commercial patenting 'steal(s) nature's harvest by destroying biodiversity, increasing the use of herbicides and pesticides, and spreading the risk of irreversible genetic pollution'.[82] Genetic engineering of foods, rationalized as essential to global food security, deepens the metabolic rift by replacing biodiversity with uniformity based on the control of the biology of agronomic species, via corporate intellectual property rights institutionalized in the WTO.[83] The resulting genetic erosion contributes to the ecological crisis: 'the U.S. soy crop, which accounts for 75 per cent of the world's soy, is a monoculture that can be traced back to only six plants brought over from China... of the seventy-five kinds of vegetables grown in the United States, 97 per cent of all the varieties have become extinct in less than eighty years'.[84] Vandana Shiva warns of 'a clear narrowing of the genetic basis of our food supply. Currently, there are only two commercialized staple-food crops. In place of hundreds of legumes and beans eaten around the world, there is soybean. In place of diverse varieties of millets, wheats, and rices, there is only corn. In place of the diversity of oil seeds, there is only canola'.[85]

Where the 'green' revolution increased yields on staple foods through the monoculture of rice, wheat and maize, the current gene revolution focuses on herbicide resistance – 54 per cent of the expansion of transgenic crops is aimed at improving herbicide resistance rather than food increases.[86] In other words, the 'gene giants' (Astra-Zeneca, DuPont, Monsanto/Pharmacia, Novartis and Aventis) deploy their monopolizing technology to expand control of the food chain, to resolve problems exacerbated by 'green' revolution monocultures (plant disease, soil depletion and pest/weed infestation)[87] and to capture competitive advantages on the transgenic frontier, rather than to address the distributional issues behind world hunger.[88] As a leading chemical industry analyst with Lehman Brothers noted: 'Let's stop pretending we *face* food shortages. There is hunger, but not food shortages. GM food is for the rich world. The money for GM is in developed countries'.[89] The current focus of the 'gene giants' on 'functional foods' confirms this view: the new generation of 'agbiotechnology' includes 'nutriceuticals'. designed to address health concerns ranging from obesity, body development, cancers, diabetes and gastrointestinal functions.

The other segment of the new generation of agbiotechnology, 'terminator' technology, is designed to eliminate traditional seed saving, and compel farmer dependence on annual seed renewal via non-renewable commercial seed. To this end, the biotechnology industry expands its investment in crop development in the South, purchasing local seed companies and relocating over 60 per cent of the production of transgenic crops, mainly soybean, canola, corn and cotton. Recent research discloses that there are 132 genetic patents on crops originating in the South, now grown worldwide – 68 for maize genes, 17 for potato, 25 for soybean, and 22 for wheat, suggesting that biotechnology firms are targeting control of staple foods and feeds.[90] Transgenic technology threatens the foundational biodiversity of intercropped seed varieties across the world, expropriating farmers, who lose control of their land and/or seed, or converting them into 'bioserfs'. Genetic reductionism forecloses possibilities of agro-ecological futures through instituting a 'world agricultural' corporate empire.

CONCLUSION: AGRO-ECOLOGY FUTURES?

In addition to deepening the metabolic rift and, therefore, the ecological crisis, twenty-first century corporate agriculture privileges biotechnological solutions over the possibility of sustaining food cultures or reforming land relations to overcome hunger via democratic forms of social reproduction. It is in this nexus that social opposition arises, combining the classical questions of land and bread with the green question.[91] Since the expanded reproduction of corporate agriculture depends on either eliminating or incorporating pre-existing agro-ecologies, it gives rise to opposition in the shape of proliferating land reclamation and food sovereignty movements, the most notable being the Vía Campesina.[92] This organization is waging a global struggle against the socially exclusionary and de-naturing effects and implications of corporate agriculture. Formed in 1992, the several million-strong Vía Campesina unites some 140 local and regional chapters of landless peasants, family farmers, agricultural workers, rural women and indigenous communities across 56 countries in Africa, Europe, Asia, and North, Central and South America. At the Rome World Food Summit in 1994, Vía Campesina introduced the concept of 'food sovereignty' into global discourse in the following way:

> Food sovereignty is the right of peoples to define their own agriculture and food policies, to protect and regulate domestic agricul-

tural production and trade in order to achieve sustainable development objectives, to determine the extent to which they want to be
self reliant, and to restrict the dumping of products in their markets.
Food sovereignty does not negate trade, but rather, it promotes the
formulation of trade policies and practices that serve the rights of
peoples to safe, healthy and ecologically sustainable production.[93]

In the Vía Campesina vision trade is not ruled out; rather there should
be alternative multilateral institutions to regulate it, including a Convention
on Food Sovereignty and Trade. The anti-capitalist resistance represented by
the Vía Campesina does not retreat into 'the local' but seeks to re-politicize
'the global' in ways that support democratic conditions of food production
and distribution. For example, in the conflict between the French Farmers' Confederation and McDonalds in 1999, Jose Bové and his colleagues
destroyed transgenic corn produced by global firms 'not because the seeds
are produced by "others" but because of the way they are produced'.[94] Bové
and the Vía Campesina emphasize two central premises: first, that the international tensions surrounding the politics of food ultimately derive not
from conflict between states, but between models of production and rural
development – 'a conflict that exists in both the North and the South';[95] and
second, that the struggle is global but decentralized in content and leadership: 'The strength of this global movement is precisely that it differs from
place to place…The world is a complex place, and it would be a mistake to
look for a single answer to complex and different phenomena. We have to
provide answers at different levels – not just the international level, but local
and national levels too'.[96]

Answers in themselves are easy enough – clearly building sustaining food
systems means drastically reducing 'food miles' and 'food swapping', reducing fossil fuel dependence (via alternative energy sources such as wind, solar,
bio-fuels), and democratizing agriculture (which would return more of the
value-added in marketed foods to the farmers). We know that sustainable
agriculture almost doubles productivity per hectare while simultaneously
conserving scarce water, and can be many times more productive than mo-
nocultural farms.[97] But the question is, how to move towards a post-capitalist
agriculture. Not only is the entrenched power of the agribusiness complex,
evident in Northern intransigence and failed WTO Ministerials, unmistak-
ably strong, but it also threatens to appropriate alternative technologies[98] –
from organic foods[99] to bio-fuels – that are needed for a democratic and ecologically sustainable agriculture. While these may yield some environmental
and health benefits, such solutions, in catering to class purchasing power

(e.g., bio-fuel crops for cars vs. hunger, are likely to deepen social inequality globally at the expense of peasants and poor consumers.[100]

There are perhaps three inter-related paths toward a post-capitalist agriculture: (1) public education regarding the rethinking of food relations via a new 'ecological-public health' paradigm,[101] raising awareness of 'ecological footprints' and the impact of industrial foods on human and environmental health, and including long-term strategies for alternative energy, de-urbanization/re-localization, and the de-commodification of food; (2) class and peasant mobilizations around land and food rights, prefiguring alternatives to the corporate food regime, generating new fair-trade conventions, and based on cooperative (rather than comparative) advantage principles (as in the Bolivarian Alliance for the Americas);[102] and (3) using the crisis, and eventual collapse, of the industrial food system (in the form of food-borne illnesses, water shortages, the shortage of fertile land for intensive farming, peak oil, climate change/remedies vs food production, etc.), to advance alternative development models of farming and of the political regulation of food provision.

There is, of course, no 'magic bullet', and it is most likely that industrial and ecological food systems will coexist in uneasy tension for some time. In the meantime a practical necessity is to reverse the wholesale movement of farmers off the land. The 'food sovereignty' movement addresses that issue directly. It is a very long-term strategy of reversing the social, cultural and environmental damage of a privatized food security system. Some of its movements, such as the MST, engage strategically with urban forces, but remain preoccupied with consolidating the 'struggle on the land' as a social project. Longer-term questions about linking sustainable, cooperative models of agriculture to large-scale urban provisioning schemes are yet to be resolved, but their resolution is not impossible given an appropriate political climate (and indeed, there are already smaller-scale urban provisioning models, such as that in Brazil's Belo Horizonte: 'the only city…in the capitalist world that has decided to make food security a right of citizenship').[103] Beyond promising experiments with urban gardens (which provision 35 million people in the US alone) and community-supported agricultures,[104] securing the legitimacy of 'peasant spaces' is vital to surviving the crisis of industrial and transgenic agricultures.[105]

In this sense, the transnational peasant movement represents a strategic intervention to broaden future possibilities through its diverse organizations. Within the European Confédération Paysanne, Bové practices the artisan model of specialty cheese production in France, but on the other side of the world in Brazil another chapter of the Vía Campesina, the Landless Workers

Movement (the MST, occupying over 15 million hectares of land) combines staple food production for Brazil's working poor with organic agriculture and fair trade, 'transforming the economic struggle into a political and ideological struggle'. Joao Pedro Stedile, the MST president, declares: 'We are convinced that nowadays it is necessary to reorganize agriculture on a different social base, democratize access to capital, democratize the agro-industrial process (something just as important as landownership), and democratize access to know-how, that is, to formal education'.[106] Rather than conceding to a corporate agro-industrial future, or viewing land redistribution as a solution to surplus labour, the food sovereignty movement envisions an agrarian trajectory that would reintegrate food production and nature in an alternative culture of modernity.

There are countless other, and just as significant, movements practising agro-ecology, seed saving, and other sustainable practices in the interstices and on the margins of the corporate system. The Slow Food movement, originating in Italy but now global, builds on similar principles to those of fair trade: localizing food-sheds, retaining local cuisines, and protecting food heritage in general. The Slow Food Foundation for Biodiversity was formed in Italy in 2003 to 'know, catalogue and safeguard small quality productions and to guarantee them an economic and commercial future'. In relation to this, COOP-Italia, a consortium of over 200 consumer co-operatives, co-ordinates the production and sale of quality food products traceable to their socio-spatial origins, with the aim of protecting links between consumers and producers within a broader ethical engagement that includes supporting fair trade initiatives and supplying people with water in Africa, and contesting the diffusion of genetically-modified organisms.[107] Alternative Food Networks also contribute to the proliferation of new rural development practices, such as agro-tourism, energy production, and landscape management.

As globally-networked movements Vía Campesina and Slow Food, despite their quite distinct class compositions, are *paradigmatic* in combining a strategic, single-point perspective to challenge corporate 'food security' with 'food sovereignty', and corporate 'fast food' with 'slow food', while yet embodying the kind of multi-perspectival politics and practice called for by a world needing to transcend its fixation on accumulation.[108] Of course, neither movement is focused specifically on 'feeding the world'. But stemming dispossession and reclaiming the right to farm are critical to provisioning the 2.5-3 billion rural poor who are being starved under the corporate food regime. And reconnecting urban consumers with rural producers under an ecological regime, whether in France, Italy, Brazil or India, is a precondition of alternative methods of feeding the world for the future. The international ethics of such movements are also preconditions (certainly requiring development) for constructing these methods around global social needs rather than national economic accounts. These kinds of interventions champion biodiversity and the reversal of the catastrophic ecological impacts of industrial and biotechnological monoculture. They reformulate the idea of 'development' as the art of democratic self-reliance, as opposed to a singular, centralized dynamic of unbridled accumulation. And they model methods of feeding a diverse world that are inherently more sustainable than the corporate method of feeding a global minority who happen to have purchasing power.

NOTES

I am grateful to Marion Dixon for research support in the preparation of this essay, as well as to Elmar Altvater, Henry Bernstein and Harriet Friedmann for thoughtful feedback on previous drafts.

1   Farshad Araghi, 'The Great Global Enclosure of Our Times: Peasants and the Agrarian Question at the End of the Twentieth Century', in Fred Magdoff, John Bellamy Foster and Frederick H. Buttel, eds., *Hungry for Profit: The Agribusiness Threat to Farmers, Food and the Environment*, New York: Monthly Review Press, 1999.

2   See Gilbert Rist, *The History of Development: From Western Origins to Global Faith*, London: Zed, 1997.

3   The term 'project' refers to the ideological and political relations through which dominant structures of capital accumulation are represented and implemented, although not without contradiction or contestation.

4   For an elaboration of the political-economic principles of these projects, see Philip McMichael, 'Globalization and Development Studies', in Richard P. Appelbaum and William I. Robinson, eds., *Critical Globalization Studies*, New York: Routledge, 2005.

5   'Marginalizing farming' means displacing farming as a culture/knowledge with industrial agricultures abstracted from local ecologies. See Colin Duncan, *The Centrality of Agriculture. Between Humankind and the Rest of Nature*, Montreal: McGill-Queen's University Press, 1996.

6   Jules Pretty makes the case for the reality of sustainable agriculture projects across the world that, on average, produce a 93 per cent increase in agricultural yields, and represent 'novel ways in which to feed the world and to save biodiversity', in *Agri-Culture*, London: Earthscan, 2002, pp. 84-95.

7   Quoted in Lynne Phillips and Suzan Ilcan, '"A World Free From Hunger": Global Imagination and Governance in the Age of Scientific Management', *Sociologia Ruralis*, 43(4), 2003, pp. 433-53.

8   Note that in naming states as the exclusive guardians of rights, the UN declaration regarding the social contract sanctioned a form of biopolitics and sovereignty originating under colonialism. See Rajeev Patel and Philip McMichael,

'Third Worldism and the Lineages of Global Fascism: The Regrouping of the Global South in the Neoliberal Era', *Third World Quarterly*, 25(1), 2004, p. 241.

9   In the US, the 'growth of working class power in the 1930s and during the war forced capital to meet urban worker demands for cheap and plentiful food, just as it was forced to provide full employment and rising wage levels. This required a significant increase in farm productivity, which could only be accomplished by keeping farm income up through price supports – without the guarantee of which farmers would refuse to invest in productivity-raising new technologies'. Harry Cleaver, 'Food, Famine, and the International Crisis', *Zerowork*, 2, 1977, p. 16.

10   Phillips and Ilcan, 'A World Free From Hunger', p. 436.

11   Tim Lang, 'What is Food and Farming For? – The (Re)emergence of Health as a Key Policy Driver', in Frederick H. Buttel and Philip McMichael, eds., *New Directions in the Sociology of Global Development*, Oxford: Elsevier, 2005.

12   See Philips and Ilcan, 'A world Free from Hunger'.

13   Some regions were more equal than others within the early Cold War context, so that the introduction of industrial agriculture and the administration of food aid followed predictable containment patterns: heavily focused on Asia, Latin America and the Middle East.

14   Harriet Friedmann, 'The Political Economy of Food: The Rise and Fall of the Postwar International Food Order', *American Journal of Sociology*, 88 (Special Supplement), 1982, pp. 248-86.

15   Richard Walker defines 'petrofarming' as '…not one thing – machinery, water or petrochemicals – but a whole complex of farming practices, technologies, and inputs'. Walker, *The Conquest of Bread. 150 Years of Agribusiness in California*, New York: The New Press, 2005, p. 151. I would add that this definition should extend to the circulation of agri-capital in the transport of food products ('food miles').

16   Leo Panitch and Sam Gindin, 'Global Capitalism and American Empire', *Socialist Register 2004*.

17   Harriet Friedmann, 'Distance and Durability: Shaky Foundations of the World Food Economy', in Philip McMichael, ed., *The Global Restructuring of Agro-Food Systems*, Ithaca: Cornell University Press, 1994. In Egypt, for example, US and Egyptian government subsidies encouraged a dietary shift from legumes and maize to wheat and meat, thereby expanding the market in Egypt for American feed grains: 'From 1970 to 1980, while crop production grew in real value by 17 per cent, livestock production grew almost twice as much, by 32 per cent. In the following seven years, crop production grew by 10 per cent, but livestock production by almost 50 per cent'. Timothy Mitchell, 'America's Egypt. Discourse of the Development Industry', *Middle East Report*, March-April, 1991, p. 21.

18   Laurence Tubiana, 'World Trade in Agricultural Products: From Global Regulation to Market Fragmentation', in David Goodman and Michael Redclift, eds., *The International Farm Crisis*, New York: St. Martin's Press, 1989.

19   Harriet Friedmann, 'From Colonialism to Green Capitalism: Social Movements and Emergence of Food Regimes', in Frederick H. Buttel and Philip

McMichael, eds., *New Directions in the Sociology of Global Development*, Oxford: Elsevier, 2005.

20   Ibid., p. 245.

21   Ibid.

22   From the World Bank, *World Development Report*, Washington DC, 1980.

23   John Walton and David Seddon, *Free Markets & Food Riots: The Politics of Global Adjustment*, Oxford: Blackwell, 1994.

24   Sophia Murphy, 'WTO, Agricultural Deregulation and Food Security', *Globalization Challenge Initiative*, 4(24), 1999, http://www.foreignpolicy-infocus.org.

25   Quoted in John Madeley, *Hungry for Trade*, New York: Zed Books, 2000, p. 79.

26   Thomas Reardon, C. Peter Timmer, Christopher B. Barrett and Julio Berdegue, 'The Rise of Supermarkets in Africa, Asia and Latin America', *American Journal of Agricultural Economics*, 85(5), 2003, pp. 1140-46.

27   Quoted in Mark Ritchie, *Breaking the Deadlock. The United States and Agricultural Policy in the Uruguay Round*, Minneapolis: Institute for Agriculture and Trade Policy, 1993.

28   For an extended discussion of how this works, see Emelie Peine and Philip McMichael, 'Globalization and Governance', in Vaughan Higgins and Geoffrey Lawrence, eds., *Agricultural Regulation*, London: Routledge, 2005.

29   Mark Ritchie, 'The World Trade Organization and the Human Right to Food Security', Presentation to the International Cooperative Agriculture Organization General Assembly, Quebec City, 29 August 1999. http://www.wtowatch,org. *The Economist*, 17 April 1999, p. 75.

30   Madeley, *Hungry for Trade*, p. 75.

31   J. Bailey, 'Agricultural Trade and the Livelihoods of Small Farmers', *Oxfam GB Discussion Paper - 3/2000*, http://www.oxfam.org.uk; Madeley, *Hungry for Trade*, pp. 75, 87.

32   Laura Carlsen, 'The Mexican Farmers' Movement: Exposing the Myths of Free Trade', *Americas Program Policy Report*, Silver City, NM: Interhemispheric Resource Center, 2003. Available at: http://www.americaspolicy.org.

33   Ibid., p. 75.

34   Deborah Bryceson, 'Agrarian Vista or Vortex? African Rural Livelihood Policies', *Review of African Political Economy*, 31(102), 2004, pp. 618-9.

35   Henry Bernstein, 'Rural Land and Land Conflicts in Sub-Saharan Africa', in S. Moyo and P. Yeros, eds., *Reclaiming the Land. The Resurgence of Rural Movements in Africa, Asia and Latin America*, London: Zed Books, 2005; Rachel Bezner-Kerr, 'Informal Labor and Social Relations in Northern Malawi: The Theoretical Challenges and Implications of *Ganyu* Labor for Food Security', *Rural Sociology*, 70(2), 2005, pp. 167-87.

36   N. Kabeer and Tran Thi Van Ahn, 'Leaving the Rice Fields, but not the Countryside. Gender, Livelihoods Diversification, and Pro-poor Growth in Rural Vietnam', in S. Razavi, ed., *Shifting Burdens. Gender and Agrarian Change under Neoliberalism*, Bloomfield, CT: Kumarian Press, 2002.

37   Moyo and Yeros, *Reclaiming the Land*, pp. 28-9.

38   The experience of the Philippines is instructive, as outlined in 1999 by the Hon. Wigberto Tanada, a member of the Philippines' House of Representatives:

'Under the globalized trading rules, our rice imports grew more than ten times from 1993 to 1998, from 201,000 metric tons to 2.2 million metric tons; corn imports swelled by close to 500 times, from 640 metric tons to 462,000 metric tons; beef imports by almost 4 times; and pork, 164 times. Mr. Speaker, it is obvious that under the WTO, we have become a major agricultural importer and have lost all hopes of becoming self-sufficient in, if not a net exporter of, agricultural products. We are now importing everything – rice, corn, sugar, beef, pork, poultry, fruits and fishery products. Our food security is now completely dependent on the availability of importable agricultural products, particularly cereals. The annual growth rate of agricultural production in the country is one of the lowest in the region – 0.23 per cent from 1994 to 1998, which is indeed devastatingly low compared to our annual population growth rate of 2.4 per cent'.

'Are we ready for the Millennium Round of Trade Liberalization?', *Integrated Rural Development Foundation*, 1999, available from Mark Ritchie at mritchie@iatp.org.

39   Harriet Friedmann, 'What on Earth is the Modern World-System? Food-Getting and Territory in the Modern Era and Beyond', *Journal of World-Systems Research*, VI(2), 2000, pp. 480-515.

40   Alfred W. Crosby, *Ecological Imperialism*, New York: Cambridge University Press, 1986, p. 288.

41   Duncan, *The Centrality of Agriculture*, p. 65. Cf. Foster and Clark's comments on British high farming guano dependence in John Bellamy Foster and Brett Clark, 'Ecological Imperialism: The Curse of Capitalism', *Socialist Register 2004*. Richard Walker notes that guano was a nitrogen supplement for plant growth, Richard Walker, *The Conquest of Bread. 150 Years of Agribusiness in California*, New York: The New Press, 2005, p. 181.

42   Ibid., p. 102.

43   Harry Cleaver, 'Food, Famine, and the International Crisis', *Zerowork*, 2, 1977, p. 17.

44   Ibid., p. 28.

45   Alain de Janvry, *The Agrarian Question and Reformism in Latin America*, Baltimore: The Johns Hopkins University Press, 1981.

46   This concept is attributed to Marx. See, for example, Foster and Clark, 'Ecological Imperialism', p. 188.

47   Jason W. Moore, 'Environmental Crises and the Metabolic Rift in World-Historical Perspective', *Organization & Environment*, 13(2), 2000, p. 123.

48   Duncan, *The Centrality of Agriculture*, p. 123.

49   Ibid., p. 122.

50   Ibid., p. 114.

51   Quoted in Mark Briscoe, 'Water: The Untapped Resource', in Andrew Kimball, ed., *The Fatal Harvest Reader. The Tragedy of Industrial Agriculture*, Washington: Island Press, pp. 182-3.

52 Roger Segelken, 'Fewer Foods Predicted for Crowded Future Meals', *Cornell Chronicle*, 23 February 1995, p. 5.

53 Patrick Herman and Richard Kuper, *Food for Thought. Towards a Future for Farming*, London: Pluto Press, 2003, pp. 21-2.

54 Steven C. Blank, *The End of Agriculture in the American Portfolio*, Westport, CT: Quorum Books, 1998.

55 See Public Citizen, *Down on the Farm: NAFTA's Seven-Year War on Farmers and Ranchers in the U.S., Canada and Mexico*, 26 June 2001, Washington, DC: Public Citizen, http://www.citizen.org.

56 R-P. Paringaux, 'The Deliberate Destruction of Agriculture. India: Free Markets, Empty Bellies, *Le Monde Diplomatique*, 1-9 September 2000, p. 4.

57 Katherine Ainger, 'The Market and the Monsoon', *New Internationalist*, 353(January/February) 2003, pp. 25-6.

58 Kate Ravilious, 'Food Crisis Feared as Fertile Land Runs Out', *Guardian Weekly*, 16-22 December 2005, p. 21.

59 Erik Millstone and Tim Lang, *The Atlas of Food*, London: Earthscan Publications, 2003, p. 66.

60 Peter H. Tyedmers, quoted in Cornelia Dean, 'Fishing Industry's Fuel Efficiency Gets Worse as Ocean Stocks Get Thinner', *The New York Times*, 20 December 2005, p. F3.

61 Jeremy Rifkin, *Beyond Beef. The Rise and Fall of the Cattle Culture*, New York: Penguin, 1992, p. 147.

62 Hilary French, 'Linking Globalization, Consumption, and Governance', in Linda Starke, ed., *State Of the World, 2004: The Consumer Society*, Washington, DC: The World Watch Institute, 2004, p. 148.

63 Larry Rohter, 'Relentless Foe of the Amazon Jungle: Soybeans', *The New York Times*, 17 September 2003, p. 3.

64 Derek Hall, 'The International Political Ecology of Industrial Shrimp Aquaculture and Industrial Plantation Forestry in Southeast Asia', *Journal of Southeast Asian Studies*, 34(2), 2003, pp. 251-64.

65 Millstone and Lang, *The Atlas of Food*, p. 34.

66 Greenpeace, 'Eating up the Amazon', 2006, p. 5, available at http://www.greenpeace.org.

67 As Frances Moore Lappé pointed out in her *Diet for a Small Planet* a quarter of a century ago, the mass production of animal protein is an inefficient *and* inequitable use of world grain supplies, using seven times as much grain for livestock feed as for human food. To illustrate: 'The U.S. beef industry… generate(s) close to $40 billion per year, (but) leaves less than 10% of planted forage crops to feed people in the U.S. and elsewhere. Chemical companies also benefit greatly from having land farmed to feed animals, since animal feed carries far less stringent pesticide tolerances than does feed intended for human consumption. The net result of using transgenic crops to feed animals is that more chemicals can be used'. Frances Moore Lappé and Britt Bailey, *Against the Grain. Biotechnology and the Corporate Takeover of Your Food,* Monroe, ME: Common Courage Press, 1998, p. 87.

68   Nicholas Hildyard, 'Foxes in Charge of Chickens', in Wolfgang Sachs, ed., *Global Ecology*, London: Zed, 1993, p. 30.

69   Billie DeWalt, 'Mexico's Second Green Revolution: Food for Feed', *Mexican Studies/Estudios Mexicanos*, 1, 1985, pp. 29-60.

70   Per Pinstrup-Andersen, R. Pandya-Lorch and M.W. Rosegrant, *World Food Prospects: Critical Issues For the Early Twenty-First Century*, Washington, DC: IFPRI, 1999, pp. 12-14.

71   FAO Statistical Tables, 2000.

72   Andrew Kimbrell, *The Fatal Harvest Reader. The Tragedy of Industrial Agriculture*, Washington: Island Press, 2002, p. 16.

73   Millstone and Lang, *The Atlas of Food*, p. 38.

74   Mike Davis, *The Monster at Our Door. The Global Threat of Avian Flu*, New York: The New Press, 2005, p. 107-8.

75   GRAIN, 'The Top-Down Response to Bird Flu', April 2006, available at http://www.grain.org.

76   Tim Lang, M. Heasman and J. Pitt, 'Food, Globalisation and a New Public Health Agenda', *International Forum on Globalisation,* San Francisco, 1999.

77   Richard Manning, 'The Oil We Eat', *Harpers Magazine*, February, 2004, p. 43.

78   Gary Gardner and Brian Halweil, *Underfed and Overfed. The Global Epidemic of Malnutrition*, WorldWatch Paper #150, March, 2000, p. 7.

79   World Commission on Environment and Development, *Our Common Future*, Oxford: Oxford University Press, 1987, p. 22.

80   A.J. McMichael, *Planetary Overload. Global Environmental Change and the Health of the Human Species*, Cambridge: Cambridge University Press, 1993, p. 336.

81   Ibid.

82   Vandana Shiva, *Stolen Harvest. The Hijacking of the Global Food Supply*, Boston: South End Press, 2000, p. 95.

83   Debi Barker, 'Globalization and Industrial Agriculture', in Andrew Kimbrell, ed., *The Fatal Harvest Reader*, Washington: Island Press, 2002, p. 261.

84   Jeremy Rifkin, *The Biotech Century. Harnessing the Gene and Remaking the World*, New York: Tarcher/Putnam, 1998, p. 110-11.

85   Vandana Shiva, *Stolen Harvest. The Hijacking of the Global Food Supply*, Boston: South End Press, 2000, p. 104.

86   Ibid, p. 103.

87   In fact, most of the food products (milk, soybeans, animal feed, canola, sugar beets, corn and potatoes) targeted by Monsanto for transgenic development enhance their chemical business rather than address the issue of supplying food to the world's hungry. Kenny Bruno, 'Monsanto's Failing PR Strategy', *The Ecologist*, 28(5), 1998, p. 293.

88   Philip McMichael, 'Biotechnology and Food Security. Profiting on Insecurity?' in Lourdes Benería and Savitri Bisnath, eds., *Global Tensions. Challenges and Opportunities in the World Economy*, London: Routledge, 2004.

89   Sergey Vasnetsov, quoted in John Vidal, 'Global GM Market Shows Signs of Wilting', *Guardian Weekly*, September 20-26, 2001, p. 26.

90   ActionAid, 'Crops and Robbers. Biopiracy and the Patenting of Staple Food Crops', p. 9, available at http://www/actionaid.org.

91   Philip McMichael, 'Rethinking Globalization: The Agrarian Question Revisited', *Review of International Political Economy*, 4(4), 1997, pp. 630-62.

92   Annette Desmarais, 'The Via Campesina: Consolidating an International Peasant and Farm Movement', *Journal of Peasant Studies*, 29(2), 2002, pp. 91-124.

93   Vía Campesina, 'Our World Is Not For Sale. Priority to Peoples' Food Sovereignty', Bulletin, 1 November 2001, http://www.viacampesina.org.

94   Judit Bodnar, 'Roquefort vs Big Mac: Globalization and Its Others', *European Journal of Sociology*, XLIV(1), 2003, pp. 133-44.

95   Vía Campesina, 'Statement on Agriculture after Cancun', Bulletin, 15 December 2003, p. 5, http://www.viacampesina.org.

96   Jose Bové and Francois Dufour, *The World Is Not For Sale*, London: Verso, 2001, p. 168.

97   Jules Pretty, *Agri-Culture. Reconnecting People, Land and Nature*, London: Earthscan, 2002, p. 84; and Helena Norberg-Hodge, Peter Goering and John Page, *From the Ground Up. Rethinking Industrial Agriculture*, London: Zed, 2001, p. 61.

98   'Unilever, one of the largest food businesses in the world, is developing policies and processes that will eventually allow it to source all primary agricultural produce from sustainable systems', ibid., p. 124.

99   See Laura Raynolds, 'Re-embedding Global Agriculture: The International Organic and Fair Trade Movements', *Agriculture and Human Values,* 17(3), 2000, pp. 297-309.

100 Cf. Harriet Friedmann, 'From Colonialism to Green Capitalism: Social Movements and Emergence of Food Regimes', in Frederick H. Buttel and Philip McMichael, eds., *New Directions in the Sociology of Global Development*, Oxford: Elsevier, 2005.

101 For an extended discussion of this, see Tim Lang and Michael Heasman, *Food Wars. The Global Battle for Mouths, Minds and Markets*, London: Earthscan, 2004.

102 Emir Sader, 'Free Trade in Reciprocity', *Le Monde diplomatique*, February, 2006, p. 7.

103 Frances Moore Lappé and Anna Lappé, *Hope's Edge. The Next Diet for a Small Planet*, New York: Jeremy P. Tarcher/Putnam, 2002, p. 93.

104 Jules Pretty, *Agri-Culture. Reconnecting People, Land and Nature*, London: Earthscan, 2002, pp. 117 and 185.

105 Philip McMichael, 'Peasant Prospects in a Neo-liberal Age', *New Political Economy*, 11(3), 2006.

106 Quoted in Orlanda Pinnasi, Maria Fatima Cabral and Miriam Claudia Lourencao, 'An Interview with Joao Pedro Stedile', *Latin American Perspectives*, 27(5), 2000, pp. 46-52.

107 Maria Fonte, 'Slow Foods Presidia: What Do Small Producers Do with Big Retailers?', in Terry Marsden and Jonathan Murdoch, eds., *Between the Local and the Global: Confronting Complexity in the Contemporary Agri-Food Sector*, Research in Rural Sociology and Development, Oxford: Elsevier, 2006.

108 Cf. John Gerard Ruggie, 'Territoriality and Beyond: Problematizing Modernity in International Relations', *International Organization*, 47(1), 1993, pp. 139-74.

WATER, MONEY AND POWER

ERIK SWYNGEDOUW

> We are witnessing something unprecedented: Water no longer flows downhill. It flows towards money.
>
> Robert F. Kennedy Jr.[1]

> What we call man's power over nature turns out to be a power exercised by some men over other men with nature as its instrument.
>
> C.S. Lewis[2]

Providing safe and clean water to communities is not exactly rocket science: the basic technologies and engineering principles are known and mastered, management systems understood, aquatic bio-chemical and physical processes reasonably well comprehended. Despite the relative technological and managerial ease of providing clean water for all, and of evacuating and treating wastewater, it is remarkable that more than one billion people worldwide are still suffering from inadequate, unreliable (both in quantity and quality) and/or difficult access to clean water, and almost two billion from unsatisfactory sanitation. While the humanitarian and socio-economic costs of inadequate water and sanitation services are well known, progress in alleviating water problems remains excruciatingly slow. The annual number of premature deaths and the persistence of debilitating conditions actually suffered by the poor of the world as a result of inadequate water supply far outweigh even the most pessimistic estimates of the current human costs of global warming. The World Health Organization estimates that 1.8 million people die each year prematurely of water-related diseases. Every day, more than 4,500 children under five die as a result of inadequate water and sanitation services.[3] This compares with, for example, the 150,000 people who, according to Greenpeace, are dying each year as a result of climate change.[4]

Yet it would be remarkably easy to remedy this water problem. With the possible exception of very arid regions, conditions of problematic water access have little, if anything, to do with water availability or absolute scarcity. It is primarily a problem of access to, and of equitable distribution of, the available resources. What needs to be understood better, therefore, is not how to bring water to people, but, rather, why it is that some social groups do not have adequate access to water and sanitation, while others do. While the Millennium Development Goals are committed to a significant increase of the number of people with access to clean water and adequate sanitation, it can be confidently predicted that conditions will only have improved marginally, if at all, by 2015. Despite rhetorical commitment and political support, eradicating water poverty meets with significant barriers and difficulties.

The WHO's estimates of 1.1 billion people without water, and 2.5 billion without basic sanitation, are almost certainly underestimates, particularly for urban areas. There is a high per centage of urban residents who do not have indoor piped water and are consequently dependent on standpipes, wells, and, most often, informal private water vending. This makes the urban water problem particularly acute as both quality and quantity is limited and the cost (in terms of time as well as price) is very high. Moreover, unreliable or difficult access to water has very little if anything to with absolute scarcity. This is abundantly clear with respect to urban areas. With a few possible exceptions, all major cities produce sufficient volumes of potable water to satisfy the health and sanitation needs of their populations. Average per capita water consumption in Latin American cities, for example, is comparable to the average per capita consumption of water in cities in the developed world.[5] But a relatively small per centage of the population consumes most of the available water. The share consumed by the great many poor people who depend on water vending is very small indeed. Moreover, the price charged by water venders who are always local micro-entrepeneurs, selling water which usually comes from the urban water system, is invariably significantly higher than the tariff of the official water company.

Of course, rural populations too have highly problematic and uneven access to water for consumption and for agriculture. There are various reasons for this. Under particular geo-climatic conditions, local or regional problems of scarcity may arise. Most often, however, the cost of infrastructure and the average cost of supplying clean water to sparsely settled communities are prohibitively high. The latter holds true, of course, for both public and private provision. The fixed capital investment cost is high while potential returns are rather low, uncertain and unreliable. The problem of water access and water control is thus primarily a question of purchasing power, available capital and the direction of capital investment. Or, in other words, access to water reflects the social power relationships through which money and capital are appropriated, organized and distributed.

If anything, the relationship between social power and water access is even more acute for agricultural systems that are dependent on hydraulic infrastructures and irrigation. As large-scale hydraulic infrastructures are primarily planned and organized through the state there is close relationship between capital investment, state power, and the distribution of and access to irrigation waters. In addition to the obvious conflicts between different water uses, and between local residents and dam constructions, with their inevitable displacements of people, the subsequent distribution of the irrigation waters also reflects social power relations. Not only do dams and irrigation channels radically change the previous flows of water (and their uses) but they also produce new uses, new structures of access, and new patterns of water distribution. While access is massively improved for some, it is often made worse for others. The grand hydraulic works that produced California's agricultural success in the twentieth century are a case in point, as is the hydro-modernization that characterized the rapid economic development of Spain during the second half of the twentieth century.[6] None of these changes is ever power-neutral.

WATER AND THE STATE

Only in the most exceptional of circumstances, caused by unexpected events, do powerful social groups lack access to water, while ownership of, or control over, water and its distribution and allocation are formidable sources of social power. The first theoretically sophisticated analysis of the relationship between social power and water was Karl Wittfogel's thesis on political power hierarchies in Hydraulic Societies, in his seminal book *Oriental Despotism*.[7] He argued that in ancient empires like those of China or Egypt, sophisticated irrigation-based societies developed which exhibited an extraordinary degree of stability; a strict hierarchical social and political organization characterized by a despotic 'emperor', surrounded by an elite stratum of bureaucrats and scientists; a military arm to maintain (or expand) territorial integrity; a small army of tax collectors; and a peasant population whose socio-ecological sustainability was dependent on an intricate and sophisticated irrigation engineering system and a regulated water distribution system that demanded some form of centralized control and organization. Although Wittfogel recognized that not all societies living under arid or semi-arid conditions necessarily develop despotic forms of social organization with an all-powerful political elite and a disempowered and politically excluded peasantry, his analysis was widely taken to assume such a necessary link between water management and authoritarian political regimes. And of course the despotic forms of water engineering and control that characterized not only some ancient political regimes, but also some 'modern' ones, like the those of the USSR and modern China, seemed to fit Wittfogel's argument.

Wittfogel's analysis was also mobilized to theorize and understand hydro-social power relationships under capitalist forms of development. For example, Donald Worster in *Rivers of Empire* takes an explicitly Wittfogelian perspective to theorize the 'conquest of the West' in the USA.[8] The US Corps of Engineers and the Bureau of Reclamation became, according to Worster, a powerful elite with 'despotic' bureaucratic institutions that combined political and technological power to push through and implement a particular hydro-social project and associated development model:'The American West can best be described as a modern hydraulic society... based on the intensive, large-scale manipulation of water and its products in an arid setting.... [It is] increasingly a coercive, monolithic, and hierarchical system, ruled by a power elite based on the ownership of capital and expertise'.[9]

The transformation of the Californian waterscape, and especially the political-economic power struggles and conflicts associated with bringing sufficient volumes of water to Los Angeles to permit its continuous growth and expansion, have also been analyzed in a similar way and became canonical examples of how control or ownership of water, the mobilization of water's flows, and political and economic power, come together and produce simultaneously unequal power relations between different social groups. The interests of land speculators, urban developers, land managers and water bureaucrats fused together throughout Los Angeles's twentieth century history (immortalized, for example, in Roman Polanski's movie *Chinatown*), consolidating or reinforcing their economic and or political power through mobilizing, controlling and engineering ever larger watersheds. In the process, of course, water access, water rights, and water control were re-assigned and re-distributed.[10] Neither Los Angeles's rapid urbanization nor California's spectacular hydro-agricultural development[11] could have occurred without changing water distribution, water access and socio-ecological power relations. As Joaquin Costa, a Spanish intellectual, had already remarked at the beginning of the twentieth century, 'to irrigate is to govern'.

It has now been generally accepted that there is no necessary link between aridity or relative scarcity of water and authoritarian political and economic power relations, but a variety of social power relations do operate around the power/water nexus everywhere. Complex hydro-engineering systems, for example, that require a detailed technical and social division of labour and sophisticated management structures at the level of entire river basins

or watersheds are accompanied by large, hierarchically organized, bureaucratic organizations, whose top cadres have considerable political, social and
cultural power, and who are usually well networked with other centres of
private and/or state power.

Speaking generally, although I do not suggest that arrangements in the
developed and the developing world follow the same pattern, all hydrosocial
configurations are centrally constructed through political and social power
and conflict, configurations that produce regimes of access and of exclusion as well as the registers and frames for water entitlements. Engineering
practices, technological systems and political regimes are not socially neutral,
but embody particular social and economic visions that are associated with
particular social elite formations, and are vitally important arenas for gaining
or maintaining social power.

Yet the relationship between state development models on the one hand
and the mobilization of water resources on the other has been seriously
neglected in considering the modalities of water access or water distribution. The hierarchical bureaucratic state organizations through which hy-
dro-technical edifices are constructed, maintained and shaped also produce
a stratification of access to and exclusion from water. While this suggests a
relation between state power, political project, and hydraulic interventions
and transformation, a relationship that is present in most countries around
the world, the fundamental axis around which the water nexus is organized
is the availability of and access to capital. And this is closely related to the
process of commoditization of nature, a process that has accelerated rapidly
over the past decades as neo-liberal solutions for socio-environmental issues
have become more and more prominent.

WATER, MONEY AND THE CITY

It is not surprising that the world's urbanization processes have been marked
by intense social and political struggles around water, from the formation of
urban landscapes to aquatic eco-systems around reservoirs. Water has always
possessed powerful urban connotations and conveyed important symbolic
messages. 'Naturalness', virginity, healing and purification have often been
associated with water, while water spectacles have testified to the power and
glory of various kinds of (urban) elites.[12] At the same time water became a
commodity, and uneven social power relations became etched into the hydro-social cycle. In Mexico City, for example, 3 per cent of households have
60 per cent of all urban potable water, while 50 per cent make do with 5 per
cent. In Guayaquil, Ecuador, 65 per cent of urban dwellers receive 3 per cent
of the produced potable water at a price that is at least two hundred times

higher (20,000 per cent) than that paid by a low-volume consumer connected to the piped urban water network. While middle and upper classes have
usually unlimited access to cheap, and generally subsidized, potable water, the
poor have to make do with a limited supply of often insalubrious yet generally very expensive water sold by private water vendors.[13]

The urbanization of water necessitated both ecological-metabolic transformation (capturing water from underground aquifers or distant watersheds, engineering its flow, negotiating geo-political relations, transforming
its chemical and biological properties and so forth) *and* social transformation.
'Potable' water became legally defined and standardized. Bio-chemical and
physical treatment (adding or extracting substances) was required to homog-
enize water according to politically and socio-culturally defined 'scientific'
norms enshrined in binding legislation. Homogenization, standardization
and legal codification are essential to the commodification process.

The 'modern' engineering systems through which water becomes commodified demand large capital investments with installations with a long life-
span (sometimes 50 to 100 years) and an immense infrastructure that guides
the circulation of water in an interconnected way on a large scale, often
covering entire regions.[14] It is clear that such a system requires some form of
central control and a coordinated, combined but detailed division of labour.
In addition, the quantity, quality and regularity of the circulating waters are
determined by the weakest link in this detailed technical and social division of labour. Sufficiently large amounts of capital have to be amassed and
sunk into the construction of fixed infrastructure systems with long turnover
times and relatively low returns. While expanding water availability was vital
both to assure social reproduction and as a key means of production in the
accumulation process, early private capital-based urban 'watering' initiatives
were gradually replaced by primarily state-funded investments in public water works, managed by large public or mixed public-private companies.[15]

Producing and providing water is essentially and necessarily a deeply localized activity, while transporting bulk water is a difficult – and costly – process. This double aspect of modern water systems – centralized control on the
one hand, and a necessarily localized circulation process on the other – works
itself out in very contradictory and conflicting ways. Although geo-climatic
conditions, such as the availability and type of natural water resources and
pluvial regimes, and settlement patterns, are of great importance for the organization of water management systems, these physical characteristics cannot be separated from the organization of human relations.[16]

In short, the urbanization of water and the social, economic and cultural
processes associated with its domestication brought access to water squarely

into the realm of class, gender and cultural differentiation, and various patterns of cooperation, competition and conflict. The commodification of water, in turn, placed the circulation of water directly in the sphere of money circulation, which consequently made access to water dependent on positions of social power. For each expanding city, the physical-territorial basis on which the successful watering of the city rests needs to expand as the city grows. Either new untapped water reserves have to be incorporated in the urban water cycle or existing water supplies must be used more intensively. In the case of aquifer water this leads either to a problem of generalized over-pumping which outstrips the natural recharge capacities of aquifers, or to a gradual decline in the quality of aquifer waters (as, for example, in the case of Mexico City[17]). The geographical expansion of the 'ecological footprint' of urban water not only transforms places and environments often far removed from the city, but also intensifies conflicts with other users over limited water supplies. From the vantage point of the early twenty-first century, there is increasing evidence that the sustainability of urban development has been bought at the expense of an expanding water frontier and of geographically widening the sphere of impact of the urban water cycle, leading to socially conflicting and socio-ecologically unsustainable practices of expanding resource extraction, and intensified struggle for control or access.

A DANGEROUS LIAISON:
FINITE RESOURCES AND PRODUCED 'SCARCITY'

Because of growing awareness of the central importance of water for human development, water issues have risen high on the environmental agenda in recent years, while being simultaneously subjected to market logic. In fact, these two dynamics are mutually intertwined. Increasing attention is paid to demand management, mainly as a result of the growing environmental awareness and the assumed risk of dwindling water resources.[18] This has intensified the political and social debate about the 'scarcity' of water.[19] As Maria Kaïka has pointed out, this discursive build-up of a particular water narrative and ideology – particularly noticeable, for example, during the drought-related crisis conditions in Athens in the early eighties – serves specific political and economic objectives and policies.[20] Similar tactics emerged in the summer of 2002 in Sicily, in the context of a local drought that intensified debate over the need for more infrastructure, a political process that re-enforced existing local power geometries, in which, for example, organized crime plays an important role.[21] A climate of an actual, impending or imagined water crisis – i.e. the discursive production of the imminence of a hydro-socio-ecological disaster – not only serves to facilitate further investment in the expansion of the water-supply (as in the case of Athens, Guayaquil, Delhi or Seville) but also fuels and underpins the drive towards privatization.[22] As the price signal is hailed as a prime mechanism to manage 'scarcity' and the market as the preferred mechanism for allocating all 'scarce' goods, the discursive construction of water as a 'scarce' good becomes an important part of strategies of commodification and privatization.

In this context, strange and often unholy political alliances are forged between advocates of the market and parts of the environmental movement.[23] To the extent that the latter's concern about the increasing, but socially constructed, scarcity of water has become more effective in reaching the wider public it leads to a greater 'willingness-to-pay' and an acceptance of the market as the best, if not the only available, mechanism for allocating it. While environmentalists keep on insisting that water is a scarce and finite good and, consequently, needs careful handling, the private water sector and governments at all geographical scales embrace this discourse of 'scarcity'. A market economy, of course, requires 'scarcity' to function. If need be, therefore, 'scarcity' will be effectively 'produced', i.e. socially engineered.[24] Moreover this manufactured scarcity is invariably presented as residing in nature, even to the point of 'blaming' nature for the social conflicts that arise over water. In fact, water is one of the least finite resources in the world. It is plentiful and virtually non-exhaustible. There may be local or regional limits and problems with quality (itself usually negatively affected by human use and pollution) and reliable availability, but there is no evidence of global shortages.

The management of the hydro-social cycle and, in particular, the management of demand, operates largely via a combination of campaigns aimed at raising public awareness about saving water and attempts to reduce water consumption by means of a variety of technological fixes.[25] Generally speaking, the cost-effectiveness of water-saving devices depends on the price of the technology and the price of water. If the price of water is low water-saving devices are often not cost-effective. Although it is still disputed what the aggregate effect of water saving is (most studies indicate a slow-down in the growth of water demand, but not a reversal of upward trends), a technological fix for water-related problems requires significant investment. Private water companies remain reluctant to invest in such technologies (given the cost implication), while public subsidies may be seen as a subvention to the private sector (in the case of a privatized water sector), or run against the dominant ideology of 'full cost recovery' (in case of public companies). Despite the availability, therefore, of a wide range of water-saving devices and technologies, uptake remains limited and is not likely to have a major impact in the near future. More importantly, the displacement effects (in terms of the environmental implications associated with the development and production of new technologies) is almost invariably completely ignored and not part of the environmental audit. Yet it is abundantly clear that environment-friendly technologies when applied in one sector may have adverse effects in another, arising from their own production processes. A total environmental audit would be required in order to assess the net environmental benefit derived from any technological fix.

THE GLOBAL WATER NEXUS

The supply of water is increasingly embedded in processes of economic globalization. Whether publicly or privately owned, water businesses are expanding their operations geographically and they have become involved in an international competitive process. In the case of privatized water service companies, furthermore, their capital structure is also becoming increasingly internationalized. For example, when the UK government sold its 'golden share' in the country's water companies in December 1994 it opened the way for a frenzied spree of mergers and international takeovers. Many UK water companies are actively acquiring water operations elsewhere in the world, while British companies have been subject to takeover by foreign competitors. For instance Thames Water (London's water supply company) was acquired in September 2000 by the German multi-utility RWE. The part-privatization of the Athens water company turned EYDAP into a stock market-listed company and, hence, made it subject to the vagaries of national and international capital markets.

At a global scale, an accelerated process of concentration and consolidation is taking place that is rapidly leading to a fairly oligopolistic economic structure of water utility companies.[26] As Table 1 shows, only two French companies, Ondeo (Suez) and Vivendi, have an overwhelming share of the water market, with Thames Water (part of the German multi-utility RWE) and SAUR trailing far behind in third and fourth place respectively. The dominance of the French is related to their long-term preferential access to the French water market. This gave them a competitive edge in international markets once they became more deregulated. Moreover, the French tradition has always combined state investment in infrastructure with private management of water delivery services. This is evidently more profitable for the private sector and French companies have successfully exported the model. The Anglo-Saxon model is instead based on full privatization (infrastructure as well as delivery) and the export of this model has resulted in several failures or under-performing utilities. Moreover for the top companies water is often only a relatively small part of their operations. Water-related activities are usually integrated with larger multi-utility service provision activities, such as consultancy, engineering and the like.

Table 1: The Global Water Companies (2001)

Company (water subsidiary)	Country base	People served with water (Million)	Water Business Revenues (Billion euro)	Total Revenues (Billion euro)
Vivendi (Vivendi Water)	France	110	12.8	26.48
Suez (Ondeo)	France	115	10.1	42.36
RWE (Thames Water)	Germany	43	1.69	62.9
Bouygues (SAUR)	France	30	2.5	20.5
American Water Works	US	10	1.44	1.44
Anglican Water Group	UK	4.1	0.892	1.29
Severn Trent	UK	8	0.887	1.68
Kelda Group (Yorkshire Water)	UK	4.5	0.62	0.775
United Utilities	UK	7	0.2	1.78

Source: Public Services International Research Unit (http://www.world-psi.org). Data were also obtained from Corporate Reports 2001 and corporate websites. Data for Vivendi are for 2000 and Data for Anglian Water Group are for 1999.

One of the four top companies is involved in nearly every urban privatization scheme in the world. Moreover, for big projects it is not unusual for the big four or five to share the spoils and either to manage water systems jointly or to carve up the concession into two geographical areas, each controlled by one of the global players. In Budapest, for example, Vivendi has a joint venture with RWE Aqua, and in Sidoargo, Indonesia, RWE runs one half of the system while Vivendi controls the other. These joint ventures and joint bids for contracts further erode whatever limited 'competition' exists in the market. The market for privatizing urban water is far removed from the competitive 'environment' that neo–liberal pundits hail as the saviour of ailing economies in the third world. Needless to say, such oligopolistic control provides considerable leverage for the corporate mandarins when negotiating terms with local or national states.

Servicing urban residents with reliable potable water services is a complex operation. It requires significant long term investment, and sophisticated organization and management arrangements. And profitability is by no means assured, particularly in urban environments where many people have a low ability to pay and problematic access conditions. In short, only some urban water systems are likely to generate the prospect for long-term profitability, while others will continue to require subsidies and support if they are to continue to improve service delivery. Recent experience has indeed shown that global private companies only really go for the nice bits, those that have some meat on the bone, so that only big city water works are considered worthy of privatization. And within those cities, areas with high-income residents with proven ability to pay offer, of course, the most valued customers. This leads to strategic 'cherry-picking'.[27] The 'promising' utilities (in terms of prospects for profit making) are cleared for privatization; the smaller and usually less profitable utilities remain in public hands and require continuous subsidization. Moreover, contractual obligations have to be written into concession arrangements to force companies to expand service provision in poorer areas. Rarely, however, do private service providers fulfill all the terms of their contractual obligations.

Strategic cherry-picking is just a variation on a recipe long proven successful in capitalism: privatize profitable business and let the taxpayer cough up the subsidies for unprofitable, but essential, services, and the latter are invariably those on which the sustainability of the poorest groups of the population crucially depends. Moreover, the inevitably strong link between the state and the private sector in privatization schemes opens them up to all manner of corrupt practices. They may be illegal, but more often than not they are in the standard arsenal of agreed practices and accepted procedures. Bribery, under-the-table deals, greasing palms to facilitate certain contractual arrangements and making financial contributions to political allies, are all in the standard tool-kit of privatized water utilities. The concession contract for Jakarta with Thames Water (now RWE) had to be renegotiated after allegations of corruption. Bribery scandals were also associated with the concessions in, among others, Grenoble, Tallinn, Lesotho and in Kazakhstan. Vivendi, Suez and the now defunct Enron have all been accused of making payments to political parties in return for favours.

No more subtle but fully legal inducements for privatization are offered by national states and international organizations. For example, World Bank loans to the water sector are generally conditional upon spending a considerable share of the loan on managerial and other streamlining measures to prepare the groundwork for water privatization. In the case of Guayaquil, Ecuador, for example, the Inter-American Development Bank provided a $40 million loan on condition that almost half of it would be spent on preparing the public water utility for privatization.[28] At the 4th World Water Forum in Mexico City in March 2006, the World Bank representatives continued to insist that full privatization provided the most secure way of improving water access, while the representatives of the major water companies insisted that recent experience suggested otherwise. In their view, not surprisingly, private sector participation in the water sector is increasingly dependent on public involvement, public investment and a regulatory environment that secures short and medium-term profitability.

COMMODIFICATION AND PRIVATIZATION: THE PUBLIC AND THE PRIVATE

Transforming H_2O into a useful 'thing' requires remodelling and re-organizing the socio-hydrological cycle so that it serves particular socio-physical ends (irrigation, recreation, sanitation, etc). The resulting hydro-social cycle is embedded in and organized through the commodification of water. The central issue, then, is one that revolves around (a) the allocation and control over investment capital, (b) the ownership of the infrastructure and of water, and (c) the distribution of the capital and of the socialized waters produced with it.

A considerable discussion has emerged over the past two decades or so around the question of commodification and the structures of ownership. A common misunderstanding is to equate public ownership with free goods and a non-commodified form of service delivery. Irrespective of the public or private nature of service delivery, large-scale water distribution (in the form of irrigation or urban water) is fully commodified and has been for a long time. The crucial questions, therefore, are not about water's commodification (i.e. that it is exchanged for money), but about who pays for the investment cost and for the use of the water, and who organizes its allocation and distribution. These are of course eminently political questions. Large-scale urban water infrastructures demand large capital investments. The provision of such capital has to be a central concern. Investment decisions are directly related to the source of capital and the distribution of the returns of that capital investment, and these issues cannot be addressed independently of the ownership rules, water allocation decisions and the political distribution of decision-making powers.

It is here that a vital distinction appears between private and public sector involvement. In a purely privatized environment, investment decisions are decided by considerations of profitability. This requires the exclusive right to appropriate and distribute water, and the right to set the price of water so that at least an average return on capital investment is achieved. This necessarily limits the range of private investment options to those that are directly profitable, whereas the public organization of water supply and delivery can (and generally does) distribute the cost of investment, and the return on it, in politically and/or socially motivated ways; who pays and who benefits then reflects the configuration of the state and the balance of class forces. Such redistribution processes always entails socio-spatial flows from certain social groups to others, and from some places to others.

In addition, as Karen Bakker has pointed out, water is an un-cooperative commodity.[29] For a number of fairly evident reasons – water is bulky, non-substitutable, heavy, socially and economically contested, inherently monopolistic, and requires long-term fixed investment – it does not make obvious sense to subject it to pure market logic. Recent experience with water privatization experiments that have attempted to subsume water formally within the logic of capital accumulation has shown abundantly that turning water services into profitable and socially acceptable businesses is not an easy task. Moreover, to demand 'full cost recovery' in water-related activities reduces the possibilities of cross-financing and cross-subsidization. It is of course evident that all capital investment costs need to be recovered by someone, somewhere; the key question is a political one, that is, who will be responsible for the recovery of what kind of costs.

When 'full cost recovery' is discussed in the context of water projects it invariably refers to the view that the cost of investment should be borne completely by the consumers. This precludes subsidies and, thus, the financing of projects from local, regional, national tax revenues, or through development aid that is itself derived from tax revenues or capital raised elsewhere. Yet the use of tax revenue has been the only way through which successful development of large scale water works with comprehensive coverage has been achieved, or large irrigation schemes implemented, in the developed world. There is no evidence that this can be achieved in any different way in the developing world. Therefore 'full cost recovery' needs to be replaced by a principle that permits water provision to be based on various forms of financial re-distribution. Achieving the Millennium Development Goals for water thus necessarily implies a major redistribution of capital resources.

Guaranteeing access to clean and safe water for the 1.3 billion people who do not have it will necessitate the investment of very considerable amounts of capital whose cost will have to be carried by the wealthier members of the world's population.

This is independent of the question of whether the management of water supply and delivery should be publicly or privately organized. Insofar as this is a question of effective management, both public and private (or mixed) companies around the world have proved that they can be effective and efficient. However the public/private debate should not overshadow, as it has done in recent decades, the question of the origin of the required investments to secure access to water. The private sector, because it requires at least a normal return on investment, cannot and will not guarantee access to water to social groups with insufficient effective buying power (or, in some cases, willingness to pay), or invest in projects with an uncertain return. The only way that can provide a mass solution is one based on subsidies and, thus, on redistribution of capital and income.

But while inter-spatial and inter-social cross-subsidization is an absolute necessity if the Millennium Goals are to be taken seriously, this should be considered separately from the private or public character of the management of water services understood in a narrow sense, even though the public organization of water distribution, as well as investment, may permit a wider range of technological, organizational, ecological and managerial options to be considered. However, the question of subsidization and cross-subsidization is a political one that poses clear social, political, ecological and economic choices. These issues need to be addressed at local, national and transnational levels, within appropriate institutional frameworks where they can be discussed democratically and openly. Since no one has ever voted to die of thirst, political empowerment is vitally important for achieving a more equitable and sustainable distribution of water.

WATER AND CAPITAL:
FINANCING THE MILLENNIUM DEVELOPMENT GOALS

The financial resources required to reach the Millennium Development Goals are indeed considerable. Agenda 21 (the report of the 1992 Rio Conference on Environment and Development) estimated the annual additional investment needed to achieve global water security at US$ 56 billion.[30] However, more recent estimates suggest that a much more significant effort is needed. The World Water Council's *World Water Vision* report estimated that in the run-up to 2025, US$180 billion will be required *annually* to achieve good water access for all.[31] This includes an investment of US$550 billion in dams and irrigation schemes to, assuming a 40 per cent increase in world food production and a 1.5 billion increase in the world's population, half of whom will live in cities. Combined with the existing deficiencies of water access (1.5 billion people) and ongoing rural-to-urban migration (0.5 billion), the total number of people that need to be serviced rises to 3 billion. At a conservative estimate of US$600 per person for urban water supply and sanitation, the total cost would be US$1.8 trillion. In addition, industrial water use will expand, while urgent replacement investment is required in the developed world and in the former socialist states.

In addition to the quite staggering magnitude of the investment required, the World Water Council report expects 70 per cent of the total to be raised by the private sector. It asserts that 'private actors can thus provide the main source of infrastructure investment'. The World Bank accepted this view, which supported their push for privatization as the main means through which to elicit private sector participation.[32] However, after some serious difficulties (exemplified by the cases of Atlanta, Cochabamba, Jakarta and Manila) many international operators are strategically withdrawing from major investments (Buenos Aires is the most recent example).[33] The recent report of the World Panel on Financing Water Infrastructure (the Camdessus Report), in considering the modest contributions of the private sector to financing water projects thus far, concluded that 'multilateral financial institutions will be the pillars of the new water financial architecture. They should do everything to reverse the recent decline in their water lending and make every effort to expand their use of guarantees and insurance'.[34] The latter would include establishing a 'Devaluation Liquidity Backstop Facility'. This rather fancy name refers to the establishment of an international public body that would 'effectively guarantee the foreign loans and finance the additional debt service incurred from devaluation to be reimbursed by the authority responsible for setting the tariffs'.[35] In straightforward language, this would mean that private investment risk would be transferred to the international public sector, which would then recoup any losses from the public in the developing country concerned, if its currency was devalued. In other words, the public is to carry the brunt of unfavourable national and international political economic conditions; this will hardly improve the situation of the poor and disempowered. As Amann-Blake attests, 'through a review of the historical record we see that infrastructure…was not primarily financed by the private sector'. He therefore 'questions why this would be different in developing countries today as they face rapid urbanization, unstable economies, and population growth'.[36]

Indeed, even with privatization, private sector participation in the water sector remains limited and the prospects for future private sector investment remain rather dim. This leaves no other alternative than public financing to cover the bulk of the required investment. It would be a mirage, if not worse, to believe or assert that the Millennium Development Goals can be achieved on the basis of greatly increased private sector investment in the water sector. Without massively enhanced national and international public support, the Goals will remain an empty promise. The fundamental policy question that the world is faced with is only whether this public investment will take the form of direct investment in public utilities, or financial mechanisms to make operations safe and profitable for the private sector.

But more than 'policy' is also involved here. Socio-ecological 'sustainability' can only be achieved by means of a democratically-controlled and organized process of socio-environmental construction. This in turn can only be realized through fundamental shifts in the power geometries that link money and the state along the lines identified in this essay, a shift that can only be brought about through a range of class, gender, ethnic and other struggles. How to strategically connect the struggles for a more equitable distribution of social power with a more inclusive mode of the production of nature is the key challenge that needs to be taken up by a programme of political-ecology which seeks to enhance the democratic content of socio-environmental construction.

NOTES

1   Quoted in Anita Roddick, ed., *Troubled Waters*, White River Junction: Chelsea Green Publishing Company, 2004, Introduction.
2   *The Abolition of Man*, New York: Macmillan, 1965, p. 69.
3   World Health Organization, *Water for Life – Making it Happen*, WHO/UNICEF Joint Monitoring Programme for Water Supply and Sanitation, Geneva: World Health Organization, 2005. World Health Organization, *Meeting the MDG Drinking Water and Sanitation Target – A Mid-Term Assessment of Progress*, Geneva: World Health Organization and United Nations Children's Fund, 2004.
4   From the 'Climate Change' report of the Asia Energy Revolution Ship Tour 2005, published on the Greenpeace web site, SE Asia section: http://www.greenpeace.org.
5   Erik Swyngedouw, *Social Power and the Urbanisation of Water. Flows of Power*, Oxford: Oxford University Press, 2004.
6   Erik Swyngedouw, 'Technonatural Revolutions: Scalar Politics and Paco Rana's Wet Dream for Spain, 1939-1975', 2006 (forthcoming).
7   Karl Wittfogel, *Oriental Despotism: A Comparative Study of Total Power*, New Haven: Yale University Press, 1957.

8   Donald Worster, *Rivers of Empire. Water, Aridity, and the Growth of the American West*, New York: Pantheon, 1985.

9   Worster, *Rivers of Empire*, p. 7.

10   See, for example, Mike Davis, *City of Quartz: Excavating the Future in Los Angeles*, London: Verso, 1990; Robert Gottlieb, *A Life of its Own: The Politics and Power of Water*, London: Harcourt Brace Jovanovich, 1988; Robert Gottlieb and Margareth Fitzsimmons, *Thirst for Growth*, Tucson: The University of Arizona Press, 1991; Norris Hundley Jr., *The Great Thirst*, Los Angeles: University of California Press, 1992; Marc Reisner, *Cadillac Desert: The American West and its Disappearing Water*, London: Secker & Warburg, 1990.

11   See Richard A. Walker, *The Conquest of Bread – 150 Years of Agribusiness in California*, New York: The New Press, 2004.

12   Charles Moore and Jane Lidz, *Water and Architecture*, London: Thames and Hudson, 1994.

13   See Swyngedouw, *Social Power*.

14   Iraïdes Margarita Montano and Henri Coing, *Le Service d'Eau Potable dans les Villes du Tiers-Monde. Modes de Gestion et d'Organisation*, Paris: Ecole Nationale des Ponts et Chaussées, Centre d'Enseignement et de Recherches, 1985.

15   Dominique Lorrain, *Gestions Urbaines de l'Eau*, Paris: Economica, 1995.

16   See, for example, Danilo Anton, *Thirsty Cities – Urban Environments and Water Supply in Latin America*, Ottawa: International Development Research Centre, 1993. Iraïdes Margarita Montano and Henri Coing summarize this succinctly in *Le Service d'Eau Potable*: 'The management of water is, therefore, always the result of the social relationships which crystallize around its appropriation and its usage. It varies in function of both the geo-climatic constraints and the relationships of power between users'. The social struggle around water is evidently the result of the deeply exclusive and marginalizing political, economic, and ecological processes that drove the expansion of the city.

17   See, for example, Esteban Castro, *Water, Power and Citizenship: Social Struggles in the Basin of Mexico*, New York: Palgrave, 2006.

18   See, for example, Karen Bakker, 'Deconstructing Discourses of Drought', *Transactions of the Institute of British Geographers, New Series*, 24(3), 1999; Graham Haughton, 'Private Profits – Public Drought: the Creation of a Crisis is Water Management for West Yorkshire', *Transactions of the Institute of British Geographers, New Series*, 23(4), 1998.

19   Leonard Nevarez, 'Just Wait until there's a Drought: Mediating Environmental Crises for Urban Growth', *Antipode*, 28(3), 1996.

20   Maria Kaïka, *City of Flows*, London: Routledge, 2005.

21   Ilaria Giglioli, 'Let's Drink to the Great Thirst! An Investigation into the Nature of Sicilian Water Politics', Dissertation, School of Geography, University of Oxford, Oxford, 2006.

22   See, for example, Karen Bakker *An Uncooperative Commodity – Privatizing Water in England and Wales*, Oxford: University Press, 2003.

23   Erik Swyngedouw, Ben Page and Maria Kaïka, 'Sustainability and Policy Innovation in a Multi-Level Context: Crosscutting Issues in the Water Sector', in Panyotis Getimis, Hubert Heinelt, Grigoris Kafkalas, Randall Smith and Erik

Swyngedouw, eds., *Participatory Governance in Multi-Level Context: Concepts and Experience*, Opladen: Leske & Budrich, 2002, pp. 107-131.

24   Mike Davis, *Ecology of Fear: Los Angeles and the Imagination of Disaster*, New York: Metropolitan Books, 1998.

25   Giorgos Kallis and Harry Coccossis, *Water for the City: Critical Issues and the Challenge of Sustainability*, METRON Research Project, European Commission DG-Research, Environment and Climate Programme, Mytilini: University of the Aegean, 2001.

26   See, among others, David Hall, *The Water Multinationals*, Public Services International Research Unit, London: University of Greenwich, 1999; David Hall 'The Private Water Industry – a Global Assessment from the Perspective of Trade Unions', Paper read at Conference on Achieving Participatory Governance: Sustainability and Innovation Policies in a Multi-Level Context, 29-30 October 2001, Athens; Ann-Christin Sjölander Holland, *The Water Business – Corporations versus People*, New York: Zed Books, 2005; The Centre for Public Integrity, *The Water Barons*, Washington: Public Integrity Books, 2003.

27   Steven Graham and Simon Marvin, *Splintering Urbanism – Networked Infrastructures, Technological Mobilities and the Urban Condition*, London: Routledge, 2001.

28   David Hall and Emanuele Lobina, *Water Privatisation in Latin America,* Paper read at PSI Americas' Water Conference, San José, Costa Rica, July, 2002; Swyngedouw, *Social Power.*

29   Bakker, *An Uncooperative Commodity.*

30   UN Conference on Environment and Development, *Agenda 21,* Rio de Janeiro, 3-14 June 1992.

31   *World Water Vision: Commission Report. A Water Secure World: Vision for Water, Life and the Environment*, Marseille: World Water Council, 2000; William Cosgrove and Frank Rijsberman, *World Water Vision*, London: Earthscan, 2000.

32   George Pitman, *Bridging Troubled Waters: Assessing the World Bank Water Resources Strategy,* Washington: Operations Evaluation Department, The World Bank, 2002.

33   Peter Gleick, *The World's Water 2004-2005 – The Biennial Report on Freshwater Resources*, Washington: Island Press, 2004; Corporate Europe Observatory, *Reclaiming Public Water*, Amsterdam: TransNational Institute (TNI), 2005.

34   James Winpenny, *Financing Water for All. The Report on the World Panel on Financing Water Infrastructure (chaired by Michel Camdessus)*, Marseille: World Water Council, Global Water Partnership, 2003.

35   See Ibid.

36   Nataniel Amann-Blake, 'Turbid Waters: Globalization, Water, Development.... and Private Capital?', mimeographed, paper available from author, 2006, p. 16.

THE POLITICAL ECONOMY
OF THE KYOTO PROTOCOL

ACHIM BRUNNENGRÄBER

Climate change is regarded as one of the central problems which humanity has to solve in the 'century of the environment'.[1] Negatively formulated we usually speak of a global environmental problem; this can be positively formulated with regard to the atmosphere as a public good which should be globally protected, a 'global public good'.[2] In order to illustrate the natural limits which societies come up against due to the over-strained consumption of resources and too high emissions of pollutants, the Wuppertal Institute speaks of a limited 'global environmental space'.[3] It has been said of this space that 'mutual interests in security, economic and social development and global environmental policy' are derived from the 'multiplication of risks which affect all societies'.[4] The messages which are based on this perception of the problem are intended to lead to 'new' strategies: they unequivocally demand coordinated action by the 'community of states' against the serious ecological damage which is being done in the course of rapid and resource-intensive globalization.[5]

But such a view of the problem and the way in which it should be dealt with, which is often tied to strategic goals, is analytically short of the mark. It implies a uniform definition of the problem, it focuses on international politics for dealing with the problem and it often assumes that recognition of the problem will lead automatically to structural change and sustainability. The achievement of international regulations for the protection of the climate does not depend on any one government. What is needed depends on the increasingly frequent extreme weather conditions experienced around the globe. From this point of view the Kyoto Protocol is the result of an almost inevitable development, and what the 'correct' answer to climate change should look like is therefore no longer questioned: primarily economic and 'flexible' instruments, such as emission trading (ET), the clean development mechanism (CDM) and joint implementation (JI) are to counteract the trend towards an increasing greenhouse effect. The fact that in this way only *one* of the possible forms of the regulation of the ecological crisis – although certainly the dominant one – has become established is no longer questioned.

The actual problem is much more complex than it appears at first sight. First, the reactions and the development of opportunities in societies are not unequivocally determined by 'nature'. The scientific uncertainties which exist regarding climate change and its effects contribute to this. It is possible to prove with certainty a causal link with regard to the melting of glaciers or the rising of the sea level, but not with regard to droughts or flooding. Climate change is therefore also a part of the communication of society about nature and about what in nature is regarded as worthy of protection and what is to be given over to exploitation. The various approaches to the issue are themselves power-forming discourses, and together with the representation by the media of what is defined as a crisis, they are decisive elements in the perception of climate change.[6] This helps ensure that it is not the crisis of capitalism but the ecological crisis that is foremost in our perception.

Second, climate change and climatic catastrophes are not purely natural phenomena but caused by humans.[7] Climate change results from the economic processes involved in valorizing fossil energy, social behaviour and the resulting ecological, i.e. material changes. This leads to a conflict-laden and contradictory network of relationships and forms of behaviour between individuals, institutions, society and nature. The greenhouse effect thus dissolves the separation between nature and society.

Third, climate policy is dependent on powerful interests which are inscribed in each of the policy sectors – energy, transport, trade and finance – in very specific ways. Climate policy is a multiple policy field because it calls into question the fossil – and global – energy regime as a whole. Its subject is the permanent crisis of capitalism, which is, however, regulated in a form that allows it to remain workable despite the finite nature of fossil energy sources and the negative effects of greenhouse gas emissions.

To summarize and formulate all this pointedly: climate change is a profound crisis of society and of the capitalist mode of production to which there can be no simple reaction which is adequate to the problem or without contradiction. Nevertheless, hegemonic forms of the regulation of the crisis emerge which correspond to neoliberal political concepts. Measures which fit into the existing economic system are more successful than those which call into question the existing fossil energy system. In climate policy these mechanisms are the result of diplomatic negotiations, technical-control optimism and a political-economic strategy which follows a 'win–win' logic. The mechanisms are constructed in a 'flexible' form, so that within the framework of a skilful CO_2 bookkeeping balance-sheet the reductions appear to take place, when in absolute terms no reduction at all has in fact occurred.[8]

DISPUTED ASSESSMENTS

Assessments of the international answers to climate change vary considerably, as each of the annual UN Climate Conferences which have taken place to date has shown (Conference of the Parties, or COPs). Certain results are celebrated as 'a victory for the climate' or 'success for multilateralism'. These emphatic reactions directly following the COPs are based mainly on the drawn-out negotiations, the blocking strategies and divergences of interest which characterize even a weak consensus as a great success. In contrast to this, there are voices which describe the partial results as 'Pyrrhic victory' or 'pulling the wool over our eyes'. Critics point to the slow speed of negotiations, the meagre reduction targets and their sluggish implementation. Both positions are inadequate.

Although no 'great breakthrough' in international climate policy for truly far-reaching climate protection has been achieved, regulation of the crisis certainly has. This also explains why the Kyoto Protocol is clung to – for in the foreseeable future the 'world community' will not have a better set of international instruments for dealing with the greenhouse effect and its human-made catastrophic consequences. It was wearisome and conflict-laden enough to establish this set of regulations based on a partial consensus of the international community of states – and to defend it against all the attempts to dismantle it which have accompanied climate policy since the first Conference of the Parties in 1995. A new beginning or a fundamental change in direction would be politically risky and strategically clumsy against this background. Meanwhile, the fossil fuel form of capitalism is legitimized and stabilized in spite of its tendency to crises because the Kyoto process has made it seem possible to find what looked like answers to the crisis. This is the case despite the fact that the Kyoto Protocol will remain a fragile contract for a long time.

Just how fragile was shown when, not long after his election, US President George W. Bush questioned whether the greenhouse effect actually existed. The apparent consensus of the community of states on this issue, which appeared to be scientifically indisputable, was thus annulled. Even when a committee of experts from the National Academy of Sciences called into being by the Bush administration itself subsequently confirmed that the greenhouse effect was already in full swing and was caused by humans,[9] this did not hinder Bush in formulating his position quite clearly: 'I oppose the Kyoto Protocol'.[10]

Up to the present the US administration – and the fossil fuel industry behind it – have continued to try to undermine the agreements laboriously reached in the Conferences of the Parties. At the same time Bush undertook bilateral efforts to convince other parties to the agreement to abandon the Kyoto process. In 2005 the USA and Australia allied themselves with Japan, China, India and South Korea in the 'Asia–Pacific partnership for clean development and climate' (AP6) with the goal of taking voluntary climate measures outside the Kyoto Protocol and of cooperating closely in this with private industry. The importance of this alliance should not be underestimated: they consume almost one half of energy production worldwide and are responsible for about 50 per cent of the emissions of greenhouse gases. Although this initiative was presented as not intended to be an alternative to Kyoto, a severe tension between the multilateral and the bilateral approach has been created.

Despite the exit of the USA and the hesitant behaviour of some other states, the Kyoto Protocol came into force in 2005.[11] According to the agreement, by 2012 the industrial countries must have reduced their emissions by 5.2 per cent on average compared with 1990. They are far from achieving this target, however. CO_2 emissions in the OECD countries increased by 8–9 per cent over the 1990s.[12] In certain countries the growth was even more dramatic. From 1990 to 2003, they rose by 24.2 per cent in Canada, 41.7 per cent in Spain, 21.5 per cent in Portugal and Finland, 16.5 per cent in Austria – and 12.8 per cent in the country that gave the Protocol its name, Japan. France succeeded in reducing its emissions by 1.9 per cent and Germany by 18.2 per cent.[13] In addition to the problem of the growing emissions in most of the industrial countries, there is the undermining of the reduction target via the role played by sinks and carbon trading.[14] Nor do the forecasts show any signs of an improvement. The US Energy Information Administration (EIA) expects a worldwide increase of 75 per cent in CO_2 emissions by 2025 compared to 1990.[15] The German Institute for Economic Research (DIW) forecasts that the CO_2 emissions of the OECD countries will increase by 53 per cent in the same period. In the developing countries CO_2 emissions will increase threefold.[16]

The growth in emissions is due to the increasing use of fossil energy sources. The rapid growth in energy requirements of 1.8 per cent per annum, and forecasts of future demand for fossil fuels (an increase of up to 70 per cent by the year 2030) are alarming from a climate policy point of view. The share of fossil energy sources in energy production worldwide has been over 80 per cent for decades, and according to the forecasts of the European

Commission will reach as much as 88 per cent by 2030 (with the share of oil at a continued 34 per cent remaining the largest component of this).

Growing demand combined with ever scarcer resources explains the long-term geostrategic calculation and the military presence of the oil-importing countries, above all the USA, in the producing regions. The Iraq war and the militarization of oil appropriation as a whole must be seen against this background. Demand for gas and coal will also grow rapidly, however: gas consumption, primarily for the production of electricity and heat, will grow worldwide by 2-3 per cent per annum and coal consumption by 2 to 2.5 per cent, up to the year 2030. At the same time, the European Commission forecasts an increase in the share of renewable energy sources in total energy consumption to just 8 per cent by the year 2030.[17] These figures show clearly that no significant change in the energy industry's dependence on fossil energy sources can be expected in the near future.

All this explains why the Kyoto Protocol will remain fragile. While official negotiators argue on the terrain of 'high diplomacy' that the process of international climate policy-making must be continued, external observers ask themselves to what extent this still has to do with climate protection. Does Kyoto only amount to a regulation of capitalism's ecological crisis rather than a solution to it? In order to be able to answer this question, we will first show that climate change is not a clearly defined global environmental problem which requires specific strategies for its solution, but a terrain of conflict on which social struggles are taking place over the interpretation of the problem and the 'correct' plan for solving it.

IMMANENT RISKS

Environmental protection and environmental policy in the industrial countries, emerging in the 1960s and 1970s, aimed at the identification of nature reserves, the rescuing of birds, effluent-control technologies, and the repair or limitation of the damage which humans had caused to the physical environment such as forests, rivers and soil. The risks were at least partly controllable; they could be interpreted as *external risks* from a more or less controllable environment. This was a manifestation of the pretension of modernity to rationally shape the relationships between humans and the objective, external world. This pretension of technological controllability is less valid today than ever. This can be shown using the example of human-made climate change.[18]

The ubiquitous greenhouse effect no longer allows a demarcation between the concepts of environment and society. Humans themselves, especially those in the rich industrial countries, contribute to the greenhouse effect through the utilization of fossil energy sources. Floods, storms and droughts are therefore risks immanent to the system, or *internal* risks. To put it more drastically: humans and societies are threatened by the spirits which they themselves have called up. Ecological problems rebound on humans in the form of damage to the foundations of their lives and to their health, or as additional costs.[19]

The contradictory interrelationships between nature and society must be understood as a central dimension of the ecological crisis: humans articulate demands for the protection of nature yet are themselves – through their own modes of production and consumption – continually changing and destroying nature. There are, however, considerable inequalities both among those who do the damage and among those affected. Whereas in Germany the CO_2 emissions per capita per annum are around 10 tonnes, in the USA the figure is 20 tonnes. In contrast, the per capita emissions in China are 2.7 and in India 1.2 tonnes CO_2. The social and economic expressions of climate change are therefore anything but globally uniform. Poor people in developing countries are the chief victims of climate changes, while people in the industrialized countries can (still) protect themselves relatively well by various means of adjustment. The situation in industrialized countries is also becoming precarious, however, as hurricane Katrina dramatically showed.

LIMITED ENVIRONMENTAL SPACE?

The assimilative capacity of the world's oceans, plants and forests for human-made climate-damaging emissions has been exceeded, i.e. the 'natural' equilibrium with regard to the material composition of the atmosphere, which remained unchanged for millions of years, has been disturbed. Ultimately, exceeding nature's capacity to assimilate climate-damaging gases is expressed in an increase in average world temperature. The Intergovernmental Panel on Climate Change (IPCC) assumes that in the course of the twenty-first century it will increase by between 1.4 and 5.8 degrees centigrade.[20] This still does not define a limit, however, which could prevent the increasing concentration of climate-damaging gases in the atmosphere. On the contrary: in the coming decades millions of tonnes of CO_2 and other climate-damaging gases will be 'deposited' there. In a purely scientific sense there is therefore no limit such as is assumed by the 'limited environmental space' approach.[21] The 'limit' is to be understood as a symbol with which it can be made clear that humans – certainly in quite different ways and to differing extents – are in the process of robbing themselves of their own basis of life.

Because there are no absolute limits – or because these limits are discursively constructed – the WBGU (German Advisory Council on Global

Change), the World Wide Fund for Nature and the Climate Action Network also follow the strategy of defining limits beyond which climate change is no longer tolerable. These bodies consider any increase in world temperature of more than 2 degrees Celsius to be unacceptable.[22] But the effects of the climate change that has already occurred are presumably already unacceptable to those affected, such as those experiencing the unusually violent storms sweeping over the slums in many developing countries, and the geographical shifts in vegetation zones which further impoverish rural populations, not to mention the inhabitants of the South Sea state of Tuvalu with its atolls and islands which are sinking beneath the water.[23] The definition of limits to environmental space leads to a foreshortened view of the problem, because '...it abstracts from societies, i.e. from the interlacing of institutions, power and importance, into which every treatment of nature is incorporated, with the result that the environmental problems appear as a crisis of nature and not as a crisis of society'.[24]

Climate change is in fact a societal crisis, related to a crisis of the capitalist mode of production. It is dealt with, perceived and symbolized in a socialized form, i.e. the crisis is socially, politically, economically and culturally characterized.[25] But the congruence between fossil energy use and capitalism has not (yet) been broken by the finiteness of these resources or the limits to an increase in world temperatures. At least for the time being, that congruence remains secured by economic power, geo-political strategies and military means, as Elmar Altvater's essay in this volume shows.

THE NEOLIBERAL CLIMATE

The discovery of 'the climate problem', and the attempts to explain and make public the causes of the greenhouse effect, were made by natural scientists and environmental associations, and for a long time they were not taken particularly seriously. It was not until the late 1980s that a strong politicization of the phenomenon took place. The early discussions were about issues concerning justice between North and South, about the equal worldwide distribution of per capita emissions, about the connection between poverty, wealth and the destruction of the environment, or about the historical responsibility for climate change and the case for a substantial transfer of funds from the industrialized to the developing countries.[26] Climate policy in this phase was thus certainly concerned with societal relationships with nature. But after the parties to the Framework Convention on Climate Change in 1997 had agreed on the Kyoto Protocol, with its reduction targets for the industrialized countries, this phase came to an end. It has been replaced by the narrow focusing of climate negotiations on economic issues because the fossil fuel industry has suddenly recognized the importance, or the danger, of the Protocol for its business interests.

Economic policy measures, new technologies and financial instruments now dominate the negotiations. The Kyoto Protocol is regarded as one of the most far-reaching economic agreements which has been signed under the auspices of the United Nations for many years.[27] Under its aegis, a *hegemonic* treatment of the problem took shape. The dominant interests of governments and the business lobby prevailed, producing a specifically capitalist form of regulation. The solution was to be found in the opening up of new markets. Through the participation of NGOs a broad societal consensus for this was achieved, although they did not agree to every individual measure in detail. The necessity of a broad regulation of societal relationships with nature, the search for alternative solutions, and questions of justice, are no longer part of the international climate negotiations.

THE SELLING OF INDULGENCES

The Joint Implementation provision and the Clean Development Mechanism of the Kyoto Protocol may be a modern version of the selling of indulgences. The idea behind these two instruments is simple: governments or firms that are forced to reduce their emissions can meet their obligations by carrying out climate protection measures in another country. *Joint Implementation* (JI) refers to projects involving investments in an industrial country from one or more other industrial countries, while the *Clean Development Mechanism* (CDM) refers to projects involving investment in a developing country from industrial and/or developing countries. Examples are investments in the construction of power stations and wind power, or forestation projects. The emissions which are saved (or in the case of the forestation projects trapped), as a result can be credited to the account of the investing country and subtracted from its international reduction obligations. In this way inexpensive climate protection is made possible for these countries, since it is regarded as irrelevant in which country the greenhouse gases are emitted or reduced. On the contrary, it is considered economically efficient to implement the measures in those countries and regions in which the greatest emission reductions can be achieved with a given budget.

Initially a pilot phase was agreed upon during which reductions would not be credited. For this pilot phase no explicit targets were named, nor were specific reporting criteria laid down which would have allowed the comparison of different projects. There was simply a common form for reports, without any clear means of measuring success.[28] Many scientific, technical and procedural details also remained unclarified. For example, the required methods of calculation have not yet been standardized, which is why it cannot be decided unequivocally how many emissions are saved by a particular project.

Later on it was at least decided – and this was an open question for a long time – that nuclear power stations would not be taken into account in the CDM and JI. In addition, in order to allow CDM projects to begin, a CDM executive board was constituted which decides on the guidelines and methodologies of projects and registers and examines project applications. In the case of JI, on the other hand, a supervisory body only becomes active if a 'guest' (investing) country does not fulfil its obligation to present a report. Otherwise it can conduct the process of registration and examination itself. As of June 2006, 190 CDM projects had been registered, 860 were in the application process and 112 JI projects were in the revision process. CDM and JI projects must be regarded sceptically, not only because of the weakness and flexibility of these regulations, but also simply because the volume of the expected savings is too small in relation to the total amount of (expected) emissions. CDM serves more to promote foreign trade than to reduce emissions. 31 per cent of CDM projects are hosted by India, 20 per cent by Brazil and 7 per cent by Mexico. Other countries in Africa or Latin America or in the Asia Pacific have not been seen as very attractive for CDM projects.

TRADING IN AIR

Without the clause on emission trading, which makes international trade with emission certificates possible in principle, the USA would scarcely have committed itself at the climate negotiations in Kyoto to an emission reduction of 7 per cent (a commitment which is of course now out of date). At Buenos Aires in 1998 the leading negotiator for the USA made it unmistakeably clear that the ratification of the Kyoto Protocol would otherwise not take place. Other industrialized countries were prepared to accept this demand because it meant that it might be possible to achieve the agreed reductions, at least on paper.

Basically, the trade in emission certificates means that all states get certificates which correspond to their assigned amount of emissions. Trading is planned for 2008 onwards, according to the Protocol. The countries with unused emission rights can then offer these quantities for sale to countries which exceed their assigned emission amounts. The buying country can add the shares bought to the amount initially assigned to it and thus compensate for any failure to reduce its own emissions. The trade in emission quotas is convenient above all for central and eastern European 'transition' countries. Thus, it was agreed in Kyoto that by 2012 Russia and the Ukraine must only stabilize their emissions at their 1990 levels. Due to the collapse of their economies, however, there have been real emission reductions, which makes it possible for these two countries to auction their excess emission rights on the certificate futures market (in this case we speak of trade in *hot air*). In 2001 in Bonn, and then again a few months later in Marrakech, Russia even succeeded in acquiring sink potentials (Russian forest air) which it can add to the trade in hot air. Russia did not have to struggle long in order to have this demand accepted. After the USA had announced its withdrawal from the Kyoto Protocol, ratification by Russia was essential for the Protocol to come into force. Russia's ratification of the Protocol at the end of 2004 was thus bought dearly.

The Kyoto Protocol specified vaguely that trade in emission rights should take place in addition to the national measures, and upper limits for emission trading were discussed (*caps* or *concrete ceilings*), but the demand brought forward mainly by developing countries and supported by the EU, that at least 50 per cent of the emission reductions should take place at home, had no chance of success. Here, too, the USA took on the role of hard-liner, and prevailed in combination with other industrialized countries. As a result, the Protocol merely states that a 'significant share' should take place at home.

The UK, the Netherlands and Denmark soon began pilot projects in emission trading. In Germany, by contrast, there was considerable resistance by industry because of fears of obstacles to growth and additional financial burdens; accordingly voluntary commitments to reduce emissions at home were preferred. This position was still held in Germany even when emission trading within the EU had long been intensively under negotiation. It is an irony of history that the European Union – and Germany in particular – which for a long time were outspoken opponents of emission trading as a climate protection measure, in contrast to the USA, established emissions trading *de jure* in January 2005, while the USA did not ratify the Protocol.

Throughout the EU 12,000 electricity producers and industrial plants now need a certificate for every tonne of CO_2 emitted. At the beginning of emission trading a total of 2.19 billion certificates were distributed, largely free, to industry. Since this volume corresponded roughly to the current level of emissions and the certificates were distributed generously by the governments, the price of CO_2 certificates collapsed in May 2006, falling from 30 euro per tonne of CO_2 to less than half of that. CO_2 savings are, however, only to be expected if the certificates are scarce and the price is high. Missing the target in the sense of climate protection is therefore inherent in the market economy. The door is open wide for balance-sheet tricks using a combination of emission trading, CDM and JI. These tricks, as we shall now see, are made even easier by sinks.

SINKS: THE GREAT UNKNOWN

The term 'sinks' refers to the 'trapping' of CO_2 by plants, forests or seas. For example, by means of forestation projects CO_2 is trapped in the timber. Vice versa, the burning of biomass sets CO_2 free, which is designated as a source. Clearing by fire thus leads to CO_2 emissions, while growing forests absorb CO_2 and therefore contribute to climate protection. The advantages are obvious: forestation and forest maintenance projects are relatively cheap in comparison to many other projects, such as those based on technology transfer for example, and are particularly suitable for public relations purposes. The French car manufacturer Peugeot protects the Brazilian rainforest, the chemical firm Henkel protects the forest in Argentina, and New Zealand hopes to achieve 80 per cent of its emissions reduction by forestation.[29]

Due above all to pressure from states such as the USA, New Zealand, Australia and Norway, a limited sinks provision was included in the Kyoto Protocol in 1997. Four years later in Bonn the geographically large states and Japan demanded the unlimited recognition of sinks as climate protection measures – and largely got what they wanted. Japan, as well as several other countries, will in future be able to realize a considerable share of its reduction targets through sink activities, although an upper limit was set for forest sinks. The escape hatch is agricultural land, which can be used as a sink without limit. In the CDM, however, only forestation and reforestation are allowed. Formal agreement was achieved on the technical questions of definition, the method of calculation and of monitoring, but fundamental problems of calculating sink potentials have still to be solved. These are, first, that there is no reliable method of determining whether CO_2 has in fact been absorbed by the vegetation; yet, according to the Bonn decisions arable land and grassland farming as well as the sowing of wasteland can now also be counted as climate protection measures. Second, the sink approach creates incentives for the creation of timber plantations (e.g. eucalyptus) which are ecologically very questionable and could be in contradiction to the goals of the Biodiversity Convention; nor is it clear how the absorbed amounts of carbon dioxide are to be balanced against the carbon dioxide which will be released by the later utilization of the timber or in the construction of the planned timber plantations. Third, there is a danger that the inclusion of sinks will offer a further cheap alternative and thus delay or even prevent the development and application of technologies for low CO_2 energy production and use in the industrial countries themselves.[30]

The criticism by developing countries expressed on the subject of JI is again being heard in relation to sinks. In particular the representatives of indigenous peoples speak of carbon dioxide colonialism, because sink activity will take place predominantly in developing countries while the industrialized countries themselves remain inactive. In addition, these critics object to the fact that the focus on sinks and other flexible instruments revives a concentration on development projects which has long been under criticism in North-South relationships, rather than on changes in trade and investment structures. For a long time it was assumed that, against the background of the ecological crisis, the developing countries now had greater power to advance their own interests in international negotiations. The industrialized countries had been diagnosed as 'over-developed' because of their high CO_2 emissions, so they would have to recognize that from ecological perspectives further economic growth should take place in the South. Moreover, the environmental crisis could not be tackled without the active support of the developing countries because their rates of increase of greenhouse gas emissions considerably affect the global ecosystem. But any hopes that developing countries entertained that this logic would give them greater power in climate negotiations proved unfounded, and they were unable to establish their interests in international climate policy.[31]

THE DEVIL IN THE DETAILS

The climate policy targets of the Kyoto Protocol were set low, the instruments were weak, the question of financing was anything but satisfactorily solved and the unjust North-South relationships have not changed. The instruments, which above all promise solutions in which everybody wins, are the expression of a 'creative' carbon dioxide bookkeeping. Whether they will do anything much for the climate is doubtful. A number of famous climate experts such as Tom Wigley of the IPCC and Patrick Michaels, an adviser to the US Senate, share this opinion. Even if the Protocol were implemented, the warming of the earth's atmosphere would neither be stopped nor even be markedly influenced.[32] That would require much more far-reaching and more ambitious measures and prohibitions than have presently been agreed at the COPs. Therefore the fact that in Marrakech a compliance system was agreed, and established in March 2006, foreseeing consequences if a state does not fulfil its obligations under the Protocol and containing detailed procedural regulations for decision-finding, must be seen in this context.

The official documents alone now comprise several thousand pages. The devil is either in the detail or in the design of the economic instruments. In this way the debate on climate protection has been moved increasingly out of the everyday world into the hands of 'global resource managers'.[33] The escape hatches which the documents leave open can hardly be identified by the experts themselves, never mind by the broad public. This is quite apart from the question of whether Kyoto is consistent with the agreements of the World Trade Organization or the Convention on Biological Diversity. It is often argued that a partitioning off of climate negotiations from negotiations on other issues was necessary in order to come to internationally agreed climate regulations at all. Sectoralization was necessary in order to prevent the emergence of conflicts between various international institutions, or at least to defuse them.

The 'control optimism' which finds its expression in a narrow focus on the economic instruments and intergovernmental negotiations obscures the uncertainties about the implementation and effects of the Protocol, and at the same time it obscures the specifically capitalist dimensions of the problem. It opens up a secondary global arena in which the causes of the risks produced by climate change and capitalism's destructive relationship with nature are no longer discussed. It narrows the search for solutions to system-specific perspectives, concepts and methods. In other words, what is really important about Kyoto is what has been 'neglected, postponed, left out, omitted and lost since the beginning of the conference series'.[34]

If control is defined as a means whereby economic rationality is taken into account and regulatory intervention remains as low as possible, then current climate policy can be described as making a contribution to sustainability. If, however, the target of a sustainable climate policy is taken to be the reversal and avoidance of the climate change caused by humans, the situation looks rather different. In view of the ever-increasing unsustainable consumption of resources, and the increase in CO_2 emissions connected with this, we are heading towards a climate collapse rather than a sustainable policy of climate protection.

The Kyoto climate policy is supported by powerful interest groups from the coal, gas and oil lobby; after all, 80 per cent of the emission of climate-relevant gases stems from these energy sources (with the addition of a small amount of uranium). Measures which affect the market economy and are regarded as damaging to it are to be prevented; market access, efficiency and ecological modernization are to be guaranteed. State decisions support this goal because for them international competitiveness is in the foreground. A field of activity is thus opened up to actors from the private sector of the economy to develop, test and implement market instruments. There are, of course, differences of opinion, as the discussions concerning emission trading in Germany and the European Union showed, but in the final analysis for today's governments – especially via the 'strategic detour' of the international level – national energy business interests and economic growth targets are the priority.[35] Even most NGOs in the industrial countries do not take a fundamentally opposed position here, but see their task above all in the presentation of detailed pragmatic solutions (such as the underground sequestering of CO_2), and thus as contributions to control. Most Southern NGOs are rather more critical, but they are usually underrepresented at the international climate negotiations.[36]

CONCLUSION

The actors involved in the climate negotiations are certainly not guided by the socio-ecological consequences that would inevitably follow from the climate catastrophes that today's 'sustainable globalization' must more or less necessarily give rise to. Instead, climate policy is pervaded 'by two contradictory and overlapping tendencies: the politicization of forms of utilization in relationships with nature and the overdetermination of ecological problem definitions by relationships of power and domination'.[37] In this connection a major difference between climate and biodiversity policy must be pointed out: with regard to biodiversity policy the direct appropriation of nature in the form of its economization under conditions of competition is in the foreground of the controversies.[38] In climate policy, because there can be no direct economic utilization, artificial steps are necessary: the atmosphere is valorized through emission trading. In this way decisions are taken on the future of society, i.e. certain development paths are opened and others are not supported (notably renewable energy), or tend to remain closed.

Climate policy has thus led to a regulation of the ecological crisis which is characterized by three essential shortcomings: first, by its emphasis on economic instruments, which largely excludes alternative approaches to solving the problem, such as a far-reaching structural change in energy production and use; second, by defining the problem in apparently 'objective' scientific terms and deriving the treatment of the problem from this; and third, by concentrating on the international level of policy-making, even though at this level the consensus required for action is very weak and allows for only very limited agreements. It has not yet been possible to specify and implement the mechanisms for the reduction of greenhouse gases in such a way that a reduction of CO_2 measured in absolute figures can be guaranteed. Moreover, the sectoralization of climate protection policy within the UN is significant. It takes place in the shadow of the much more important neo-imperial appropriation of the oil reserves by the powerful industrial countries.

In the meantime newly developing countries such as Brazil, India and China are advised to leapfrog. They should bypass the climate-damaging development paths of the twentieth century and place their bets directly on renewable energies. Leaving aside the fact that the enormous energy requirements of these countries could not possibly be met in this way, renewable energies and capitalism are not in contradiction with each other, as is seen from the fact that renewable energies are already a field of capitalist investment and the drive for international competitiveness. What is missing is a public debate beyond Kyoto – and not *after* 2012 – through which the dimensions of global justice and North-South conflict again become central. But it is also necessary to bring national and local interests – and resistances to them – into the climate debate and to treat climate problems as part of a larger, comprehensive socio-ecological crisis. The thematic opening and repoliticization of the climate issue is a precondition for this.

NOTES

This paper was written as part of the research project 'Global governance and climate change' at the Free University of Berlin. Thanks are due to the Federal Ministry of Education and Research (BMBF), which made this project possible under its 'Framework Programme of Socio-ecological Research'. The author also wishes to thank Uli Brand and Leopold Aaron for their helpful comments.

1   E.U. von Weizsäcker, *Das Jahrhundert der Umwelt. Vision: Öko-effizient leben und arbeiten*, Frankfurt am Main: Campus Verlag, 1999. Cf. also J.N. Rosenau, 'Globalization and Governance: Bleak Prospects for Sustainability', *Internationale Politik und Gesellschaft*, 3, 2003, on global governance of the environmental crisis.

2   I. Kaul, P. Conceicao, K. L. Goulven and R. U. Mendoza, eds., *Providing Global Public Goods. Managing Globalization*, Oxford: Oxford University Press, 2003.

3   BUND and Misereor, eds., *Zukunftsfähiges Deutschland. Ein Beitrag zu einer global nachhaltigen Entwicklung*, Basel: Wuppertal Institut für Klima, Umwelt, Energie, 1996.

4   D. Messner and F. Nuscheler, *Global Governance. Herausforderungen an der Schwelle zum 21*, Jahrhundert, Bonn: Stiftung Entwicklung und Frieden, 1996. Wissenschaftlicher Beirat der Bundesregierung Globale Umweltveränderungen (WBGU), *Climate Protection Strategies for the 21st Century: Kyoto and Beyond*, Berlin: WBGU, 2003.

5   Worldwatch Institute, ed., *Zur Lage der Welt 2005: Globale Sicherheit neu denken*, Münster: Westfälisches Dampfboot, 2005.

6   The lack of discussion of environmental issues is also a problem in this context. It is important to differentiate here between local, national and global 'blind spots'. Local and national environmental problems can be 'externalized' and contribute to the 'NIMBY syndrome' (not in my backyard).

7   Intergovernmental Panel on Climate Change (IPPC), *Climate Change 1995. Impacts, Adaptations and Mitigation of Climate Change: Scientific-Technical Analyses. Contribution of Working Group II to the Second Assessment Report of the Intergovernmental Panel on Climate Change*, Cambridge: Cambridge University Press, 1996.

8   In the following I concentrate on the international political process, although this is not independent of the controversies at the national and local levels. The existing local and regional relationships of power, and interpretations of problems and forms of dealing with the problems which are recognized as legitimate, may be similar to those at the international level, but they are not necessarily so. We cannot deal systematically here with the entanglements which result from the forms of multilevel governance, however. For the analysis of a specific example see A. Brunnengräber, 'Warming Up in Queensland? Climate Change and Policy Responses on a Multi-Level Playing Field', Discussion Paper 02/05, BMBF-Project 'Global Governance and Climate Change', Berlin: Free University of Berlin, 2005.

9   See also the Pentagon Report by P. Schwartz and D. Randall, *An Abrupt Climate Change Scenario and its Implications for United States National Security*, Emeryville: Global Business Network, 2003.

10   Cf. U.E. Simonis, 'Präsident Bushs klimapolitische Wegfahrsperre', in G. Altner, B.M.-v. Meibom, U.E. Simonis and E.U. von Weizsäcker, eds., *Jahrbuch Ökologie 2002*, München: C.H. Beck, 2001.

11   For this to happen at least 55 states had to ratify the Protocol, and these had to be responsible for at least 55 per cent of worldwide CO_2 emissions. This clause was met when Russia ratified the Kyoto Protocol at the end of 2004.

12   DIW, *Wochenbericht*, 6, 2001.

13   http://www.unfcc.int.

14   F. Jotzo and A. Michaelowa, 'Estimating the CDM market under the Bonn Agreement', HWWA Discussion Paper 145, Hamburg: HWWA, 2001.

15   EIA, *International Energy Outlook*, Washington: Energy Information Administration, 2003.

16   DIW, *Wochenbericht*, 37, 2004.

17   European Commission – Directorate-General for Research, ed., *World Energy, Technology and Climate Policy Outlook 2030*, Luxemburg: Office for Official Publications of the European Communities, 2003.

18   The catastrophe of Chernobyl on 26 April 1986 also demonstrated clearly the non-controllability of our own technologies.

19   C. Görg, *Gesellschaftliche Naturverhältnisse*, Münster: Westfälisches Dampfboot, 1999, p. 10.

20   IPCC, *Third Assessment Report, Climate Change 2001: Impacts, Adaptations and Vulnerability*, Cambridge: Cambridge University Press, 2001.

21   BUND and Misereor, *Zukunftsfähiges Deutschland*, 1996.

22   See for example the WBGU's assessment in *Climate Protection Strategies for the 21st Century: Kyoto and Beyond*, Berlin: WBGU, 2003.

23   H.-J. Schellnhuber, M. Schulz-Baldes and B. Pilardeaux, 'Umweltveränderungen und ihre Folgen', in Bundesakademie für Sicherheitspolitik, ed., *Sicher-*

heitspolitik in neuen Dimensionen. Kompendium zum erweiterten Sicherheitsbegriff, Hamburg: Mittler, 2001.

24   BUND and Misereor, *Zukunftsfähiges Deutschland,* 1996.

25   In the emerging global change research, which is in the process of extending or replacing classical national environmental policy, this aspect is completely ignored. The ecological crisis of society is even terminologically stripped of its drama. The global change is to be dealt with using pragmatic management concepts, technological innovations and new global institutions. See D. Harvey, *Justice, Nature and the Geography of Difference,* Cambridge: Blackwell Publishers, 1996, p. 131 and C. Görg, *Gesellschaftliche Naturverhältnisse,* Münster: Westfälisches Dampfboot, 1999.

26   A. Missbach, *Das Klima zwischen Nord und Süd. Eine regulationstheoretische Untersuchung des Nord-Süd-Konflikts in der Klimapolitik der Vereinten Nationen,* Münster: Westfälisches Dampfboot, 1999.

27   A. Taalab, *Stimmen gegen den Treibhauseffekt,* Frankfurt am Main: IZE, 1998, IV.

28   A. Michaelowa, 'Klimapolitik fünf Jahre nach Rio: zwischen Ernüchterung und Konsolidierung', *Nord-Süd aktuell,* 2, 1997, p. 259. A. Herold, 'Kopfgeburt oder praktikables Konzept? Öko-Institut beurteilt Pilotprojekte für Joint Implementation im Klimaschutz skeptisch', *epd-Entwicklungspolitik,* 1, 1998, pp. d1-d2.

29   Michaelowa, 'Klimapolitik fünf Jahre nach Rio', p. 245.

30   A special report of the WBGU deals with the problem of the sinks. Although the Advisory Council supports the idea of a connection between climate and sink protection, it evaluates the way in which activities in the area of land use changes and forest economy in the Kyoto Protocol are calculated 'as inadequate and in need of improvement... The present method of calculation can lead to negative incentives both for climate protection and for the protection of biodiversity and the soil', cf. WBGU, *Die Anrechung biologischer Quellen und Senken im Kyoto-Protokoll: Fortschritt oder Rückschlag für den globalen Umweltschutz? Sondergutachten 1998,* Bremerhaven: WGBU, 1998, p. 1. For the WBGU's position on sinks see also *Die Chance von Johannesburg – Eckpunkte einer Verhandlungsstrategie. Politikpapier 1/2001,* Berlin: WGBU, 2001, p. 8.

31   B.-O. Linnér and M. Jacob, 'From Stockholm to Kyoto and Beyond: A Review of the Globalization of Global Warming Policy and North-South Relations', *Globalizations,* 2(3), 2005. J. Paavola, 'Seeking Justice: International Environmental Governance and Climate Change', *Globalizations,* 2(3), 2005.

32   *Wirtschaftswoche,* 9 August 2001.

33   M. Goldman, 'Allmacht und Allmende. Die "Commons" – Debatte und der Aufstieg der globalen Ressourcenmanager', in M. Flitner, C. Görg and V. Heins, eds., *Konfliktfeld Natur. Biologische Ressourcen und globale Politik,* Opladen: Leske & Budrich, 1998.

34   H. Scheer, 'Klimaschutz durch Konferenzserien: eine Fata Morgana', *Blätter für deutsche und internationale Politik,* 9, 2001.

35   On the cooperation of state and private economic interests see D.L. Levy and D. Egan, 'A Neo-Gramscian Approach to Corporate Political Strategy: Conflict and Accommodation in the Climate Change Negotiations', *Journal of Management Studies,* 40(4), 2003.

36   H. Walk and A. Brunnengräber, *Die Globalisierungswächter. NGOs und ihre transnationalen Netze im Konfliktfeld Klima*, Münster: Westfälisches Dampfboot, 2000, pp. 141ff.

37   C. Görg, 'Schutz durch nachhaltige Nutzung? Der Konflikt um die biologische Vielfalt', in K.-W. Brand, ed., *Nachhaltige Entwicklung. Eine Herausforderung an die Soziologie*, Opladen: Leske & Budrich, 1997, p. 112.

38   U. Brand and C. Görg, 'Neue Akteure der Biopolitik. Nichtregierungsorganisationen und ihr Beitrag zum "Netzwerk internationaler Regulation"', in M. Flitner, C. Görg and V. Heins, eds., *Konfliktfeld Natur. Biologische Ressourcen und globale Politik*, Opladen: Leske & Budrich, 1998; U. Brand and C. Görg, *Access & Benefit Sharing. Zugang und Vorteilsausgleich – das Zentrum des Konfliktfelds Biodiversität*, Bonn: Germanwatch/Forum Umwelt & Entwicklung, 2001.

GARBAGE CAPITALISM'S GREEN COMMERCE

HEATHER ROGERS

In American capitalism today, more than ever, the mass consumption of commodities lies at the heart of social life and economic growth, and intrinsic to consumption is garbage. In the United States over the last 30 years, rubbish output has doubled.[1] Today almost 80 per cent of US products are used once, and then thrown away.[2] While comprising just 4 per cent of the global population, the US churns out almost 30 per cent of the wastes generated by Organization of Economic Cooperation and Development member nations (the world's most developed countries).[3] Unfortunately, the mess does not remain confined within national borders; today, the Pacific Ocean contains six times more plastic waste than zooplankton.[4] These unprecedented levels of rubbish are not the outcome of some organic process connected to human nature. The most developed countries create torrents of trash because waste and destruction are the necessary analogues of consumer society. Indeed, for capitalism to continue to grow – as it must – consumers are obliged to keep buying, which means they are destined to throw ever more mterials into the trash pile.

Since the years after World War II, when the US began mass production and consumption in earnest, industry has exerted tremendous effort to manage public perceptions of waste and, beginning in the late 1960s, the more far-reaching ecological impacts of a high-trash system. Garbage is a miniature version of production's destructive aftermath, which inevitably ends up in each person's hands; it is proof that all is not well. Since rubbish has the power to reveal to consumers the realities of an economy that pushes many of its costs onto the environment, garbage has become a key site for corporate 'greenwashing'. Manufacturers neither pay the full price for the raw materials they use in production, nor do they accurately account for the costs of pollution, energy use and the future environmental impacts of their activities. To maintain their relatively unfettered access to nature, as both a resource and a dumping-ground, US companies have had to convince the public that the castoffs they can see – and, by extension, wastes they cannot see, like those created by industry – are benign, and not an indication of crisis.

The roots of corporate greenwashing in the United States lie in two previous episodes, one in the 1950s, the other in the 1980s, both relating to consumer products (and not to energy, or other products and services). In the 1950s the group Keep America Beautiful was formed by industry to pre-empt legal restrictions on disposable goods, namely packaging. Through an elaborate public relations campaign the organization generated a popular narrative about garbage that shifted responsibility from industry to the individual. Then, in the 1980s, manufacturers exploited the rise of recycling to further ingrain a sense of personal culpability for increasing levels of trash, and to crack open new consumer markets. This later effort was more explicitly 'green', but both campaigns had the goal of protecting production from restrictive interventions and keep commodities flowing.

These two episodes help explain today's popular acceptance that individual consumer choices are the source of environmental destruction – and salvation. The form this now takes is referred to as 'green capitalism' or 'green commerce'. The latest development in greenwashing, green commerce, is being greeted with mounting enthusiasm by many in the environmental movement as well as in business circles, and by growing numbers of consumers; they are all embracing the idea that the planet can be saved simply by buying and selling environmentally friendly products.

According to its boosters this market-based solution – referred to by some as the 'investment' phase of the environmental movement – bypasses the need for legal restrictions on the use of natural resources since, the theory goes, demand will create incentives for industry to adopt ecologically sound practices of its own accord.[5] As the track record reveals, however, unregulated capitalist industry devotes its efforts not to protecting natural resources, but to seeking out its goal – surplus value. Just because a business professes its devotion to the health of natural systems, or makes an environmentally friendly product, doesn't mean it has transformed its relation to nature. The 'greening' of business without concomitant changes in the economic structure, and in the role of the state – including planning, a more democratic use of natural resources, and giving priority to human and environmental health over profits – permits the continuation of practices destructive to the earth's ecosystems.

KEEPING IT BEAUTIFUL

To a large extent, American capital's elaborate green offensive began with the earliest effort to restrict disposables in 1953. A measure passed by Vermont's legislature – coming not from nascent environmentalists, but disgruntled dairy farmers – banned the sale of all throwaway bottles throughout the state. According to a newspaper report: 'Farmers, who comprise nearly one-third of the House membership, say that bottles are sometimes thrown into hay mows and that there is need to prevent loss of cows from swallowing them in fodder'.[6] Their livelihoods on the line, the husbandmen politicians ratified the law.

Within a few short months the packaging industry concocted a lavishly funded nonprofit body called Keep America Beautiful (KAB). This was the first of many greenwashing corporate fronts to come, and its goal was to distract people from questioning the viability of an increasingly trash-reliant marketplace. KAB's founders were the powerful American Can Company and Owens-Illinois Glass Company, inventors of the single-use disposable can and bottle, respectively. They linked up with more than twenty other industry heavies – all connected to the disposables industry – including Coca-Cola, the Dixie Cup Company and Richfield Oil Corporation (later Atlantic Richfield), as well as the National Association of Manufacturers with whom KAB shared members, leaders and interests. Still a major player today, KAB urgently funnelled vast resources into a nationwide, media-savvy campaign.[7]

The centerpiece of the organization's strategy was its great cultural invention: *litter*. This category of debris existed before, but KAB masterfully transformed its political and cultural meaning to shift the terms of the debate over an unprecedented surge of waste in the post-World War II years. KAB wanted to turn any stirrings of concern over the larger ecological effects of so much production and consumption away from industry's massive and supertoxic destruction of the natural world, reducing the problem to the eyesore of litter and singling out the real villain – the 'litterbug'.[8] Taking this tack, KAB could defend disposability and obsolescence. The problem wasn't the rising levels of waste, it was all those heathens who failed to put their discards in the proper place.

By 1970, when the mainstream environmental movement emerged, KAB had already helped industry successfully navigate what the trade magazine *Modern Packaging* called the 'awesome challenge' of managing rubbish without restricting packaging production.[9] KAB entered the eco-era a seasoned anti-environmentalist, an old hand at turning the tables. On the second Earth Day on April 22, 1971, KAB premiered the first of its now-iconic television advertisements starring the buckskin-clad longtime Hollywood actor Iron Eyes Cody. This commercial represented a growing sophistication in the industry's messaging about environmental issues.

The haunting ad was seared into the guilty consciences of Americans young and old: after stoically canoeing through a wrapper- and can-strewn delta, past a silhouetted factory puffing smoke, Cody dragged his canoe onto a bank sprinkled with litter. Hiking to the edge of a freeway clogged with cars, the stereotypical Native American (who was posthumously discovered to be of Italian ancestry) was abruptly hit on the moccasins with a fast-food bag tossed out the window by a freewheeling blond passenger. Cody then looked straight into the camera as he shed a single tear. The accompanying music was stirring, the voice-over solemn: 'Some people have a deep, abiding respect for the natural beauty that was once this country. But some people don't. People start pollution. People can stop it'.[10]

The TV spot's inclusion of smokestacks and a traffic-choked highway marked a shift for KAB; maintaining its litter-is-the-root-of-all-evil position was getting more difficult as the organization confronted the main-streaming of ecological awareness. To uphold its legitimacy KAB was obliged to acknowledge issues like air and water pollution, against protests from its board of directors.[11] However, neither this commercial nor subsequent spots featuring Cody in similar dirty, tear-soaked scenarios departed from KAB's constant refrain – the responsibility for pollution lay with the individual. Environmental devastation was the bitter consequence of each person's own selfish disregard for nature.

The key tactic of blaming individuals – as one American Can executive insisted, 'Packages don't litter, people do' – obfuscated the real causes of mounting waste.[12] KAB paved the way in sowing confusion about the environmental impacts of mass production and consumption, today a favourite tool in the corporate greenwashing world. If the public believes that industry is responsibly handling natural resources, if they think production under a free market system is sustainable, and if average consumers accept that they are to blame when waste gets out of control, then laws will not be enacted, government will not intervene, and production can continue on industry's terms.

TECHNICALLY GREEN

The next wave of garbage-related greenwashing accompanied the rise of mandatory recycling programmes, which were a product of a major landfill crisis and public pressure – often from the diverse groups that started the environmental justice movement – to reprocess rather than dispose of wastes.

The vast majority of landfills from the postwar era through the late 1980s accepted a wide range of hazardous materials and lacked control systems for their harmful by-products of leachate (liquid runoff) and gas. Over time, even the best-managed sanitary fills poisoned the soil, contaminated ground-water and polluted the air. By the late 1980s so many former dumps had been declared toxic that they comprised half of all 'Superfund' sites – places designated by the federal government as among the most hazardous in the US.[13]

In this context, a provision from a 1976 law – the Resource Conservation and Recovery Act (RCRA), the first federal effort to regulate waste facilities – was finally implemented. It required minimum safety standards for land disposal sites and forced aging facilities to clean up or shut down, with dramatic effect. In the mid- to late-1980s, 90 per cent of US wastes were disposed of on land and an estimated 94 per cent of those sites were not up to standard.[14] As a result, U.S. landfills were closed by the hundreds, their numbers plummeting by two-thirds.[15] At the same time, garbage output was exploding; between 1960 and 1980 the amount of solid waste in the United States quadrupled.[16] Municipalities had to find other solutions, and find them fast.

With measures that would restrict the generation of rubbish, like manda-tory deposit laws and source reduction (requiring manufacturers to make less wasteful products) dying at the hands of industry lobbyists, in the 1980s and early 1990s recycling underwent a renaissance.[17] Across the country, school-children put down their construction paper and crayons to learn the virtues of 'closing the recycling loop'. Suburban housewives made room in their kitchens for extra bins to separate paper from cans and bottles. Community activists and neighbourhood groups were revitalized, sparking renewed inter-est in recycling from politicians as municipalities began experimenting with and implementing recycling programmes.

In the 1980s curbside recycling systems were adopted – many of them mandatory – in Connecticut, New Jersey, New York, Rhode Island and Mar-yland, while dozens of American cities and counties passed their own meas-ures.[18] By the late 1980s there were more than 5,000 municipal recycling programmes in the United States, up from just 10 in 1975.[19] And in 1993, almost a quarter-century after the first Earth Day, the US Environmental Protection Agency reported that domestic recycling had tripled by weight, from 7 per cent to almost 22 per cent.[20] As more cities adopted voluntary and mandatory recycling measures, growing numbers of Americans welcomed recycling into their daily routines.

Rather than resist all this recycling, the highest levels of industry appeared to undergo a green conversion. Very soon manufacturers began feverishly stamping their packaging with the 'chasing arrows' recycling symbol, and proudly advertising more enlightened, eco-friendly ways. But the reality was not so simple. Industry accepted recycling in lieu of more radical changes like bans on certain materials and industrial processes, production controls, minimum standards for product durability, and higher prices for resource extraction. Faced with all these potential regulations capital recognized that recycling had an advantage that other options lacked. Unlike reduction and re-use, remanufacturing single-use materials into new containers and packages would not impinge on consumption levels and would have the least impact on established manufacturing processes. It meant producers could keep making and selling disposable commodities in much the same way they had for decades. As American Can Company executive William May put it a few years earlier, when discussing the potential garbage tidal wave from so much disposable packaging: 'We must comprehend, as a nation, that the solutions also lie, to a very large degree, in technology...We oppose any reduction in productivity'.[21] In industry's eyes, recycling was a lesser evil.

Leading up to this, during the peak of 1970s environmentalism, many US firms, fearing the tide had turned against them, lobbied state, local and national politicians for policies that favoured recycling, as a bulwark against the adoption of more rigorous measures mandating reduction and re-use. Writing at the time, Environmental Action's Patricia Taylor observed that, in contrast to efforts that would curtail trash production, recycling had 'a frightening potential for institutionalizing waste generation'.[22] Her assessment was right; recycling did allow for maintaining and further ingraining high levels of production, consumption and waste.

Recycling also delivered another dividend. As the practice spread during the 1980s and '90s, promoted by some in industry and many environmentalists, manufacturers of all kinds began to comprehend the valuable PR and marketing opportunities that could spring from recycling and green branding. With greater numbers of Americans identifying as environmentalists, why shouldn't big business do the same? As it turned out, recycling helped industry in two ways: it distracted the public from making more radical demands while offering a means to connect to a new consumer base. This played out most strikingly in the plastics packaging sector.

An important resin greenwashing episode occurred in 1988, when the Society of Plastics Industries (SPI) took up the chasing arrow symbol. Since its creation in 1970 the recycling symbol had been in the public domain, and could therefore be used by anyone without any restrictions or oversight.[23] The SPI altered the image slightly by inserting numerals in its center, which assigned various plastics grades 1 through 9, and then promoted this to state governments as a 'coding system' that could be used in lieu of bans, deposit laws and mandatory recycling standards. The industry-backed Council on

Plastics and Packaging in the Environment explained in a 1988 newsletter that some state legislatures which had adopted the coding system had done so 'as an alternative to more stringent legislation'.[24] At the time almost $1 of every $10 Americans spent on food and beverages paid for packaging; with such a tremendous market, the fast-growing plastics industry was doing all it could to shut out regulation.[25]

Once states adopted the plastics codes, resin packaging was stamped according to its grade, but, significantly, it was also embossed with the recycling symbol. Indicating nothing specific about recycling, the triangular symbol on plastic packaging misleadingly telegraphed to the voting consumer that the packaging was recyclable and perhaps had even been manufactured with reprocessed materials. But often neither was the case.

While the code numbers did indicate various types of plastics in the broadest sense, there were (and are) so many critical variations within those categories that the coding system's efficacy was (and remains) questionable. Crucially, the grades did not create a useful sorting system for producers, who need to categorize discarded plastics based on how they're made, regardless of their code number.[26] By the early 1990s some recycling centres were criticizing the code-stamps for creating public confusion over what was actually recyclable and driving up costs for local waste-handling facilities.[27]

In 1993 the Environmental Defense Fund claimed that the rate of recycling 'did not even come close to keeping up with increased production of virgin plastic...'.[28] Just four years later, in 1997, the output of new resins exceeded the recycling of plastics by nearly 5 to 1.[29] Thanks to the polymer trade's exploitation of recycling as green marketing, however, most Americans believed otherwise.

The packaging industry undermined the expansion of recycling even as producers were extracting favourable public relations from it. In collaboration with another key plastics sector organization, the American Plastics Council, during the mid-1990s the SPI vigorously talked up recycling while simultaneously opposing the passage of some 180 regulatory and legislative proposals in thirty-two states.[30]

Individual firms adopted the same tactics. Coca-Cola pledged a 25 per cent recycling target in the early 1990s, when much public attention was concentrated on the issue. As political pressure and consumer focus shifted, without any government accountability and no restrictions on the use of the recycling symbol, Coke found that it did not need to actually recycle to maintain a green image with the eco-sensitive customer. In this permissive climate, the company stopped using recycled plastic entirely in 1994 and suffered no consequences, or at least none that were legal or lasting. In 2001 the company was faced with renewed public calls for more recycling, but feeling little pressure to aim high, it promised to use a meagre 2.5 per cent of reprocessed resin.[31] In addition, Coca-Cola's biggest plastic bottle supplier, South Eastern Container, upgraded two factories to enable them to produce 60,000 brand-new half-litre soda bottles every hour, 'which the company is claiming as a world first'.[32]

As the 1990s wore on, the chasing arrows and printed appeals to 'please recycle' adorned every type of bottle, jar, can, envelope and wrapper, as if they were endorsed by Mother Nature herself. The social and political impact of all this pro-recycling PR was much like that of anti-littering efforts in previous decades. Regardless of industry's actions, the rhetoric of recycling targeted individual behaviour as the key to the garbage problem, steering public debate away from the regulation of production. However, municipal waste – which includes discards from households, local businesses and institutions like schools – accounts for less than one in every 70 tons of garbage; the rest is generated by industrial processes in manufacturing, mining, agriculture, and oil and gas exploration.[33] Merely putting litter in its place does nothing to curb rubbish output, and recycling as it exists today does little to reshape industrial production in such a way as to diminish the largest category of waste.

While recycling offers certain benefits, and is far better than burning or burying discards, it has not proven to be the cure-all it initially seemed. Although recycling rates grew considerably over the previous twenty years, in the mid-1990s they began to stagnate, and toward the end of the decade reprocessing levels in some places actually declined.[34] With a recycling bin in the corner of the kitchen people often believe that their trash has become benign. Today it is likely that more Americans recycle than vote – yet greater amounts of rubbish are going to landfills and incinerators than ever before.[35]

The phenomenon of recycling is a good indicator for future 'greening' reforms. It demonstrates that attempts to mitigate the environmental fallout of capitalism's need for constant growth can easily be eroded by the political and economic force of that expansion. Because capital is so often able to remedy its contradictions through crisis, it can manipulate greening efforts to actually stoke the fires of consumption. In the case of recycling, this manipulation has played out as recuperation; political pressure to factor in environmental costs pushed capital toward further commodification, with business and industry taking advantage of recycling to create green branding. Capital's interpretation of recycling has helped keep legislative controls at bay and maintain the discourse of individual responsibility for environmental health, all the while camouflaging increasing consumption.

All this was made possible through massive spending on public relations. As Marx pointed out: 'I am ugly, but I can buy for myself the most *beautiful* of women. Therefore I am not *ugly*, for the effect of ugliness – its deterrent power – is nullified by money...Money is the supreme good, therefore its possessor is good'.[36] If money can make the ugly beautiful, and the bad good, it can also make the ecologically destructive green.

DOING GOOD BY BUYING RIGHT

After four decades of cultural messages hammering home the idea that the individual, not industrial production, was the cause of environmental decay, the public was primed for the next phase of greenwashing: 'green capitalism'. Also called 'natural capitalism' and, most recently, the more benign-sounding 'green commerce', this concept is currently gaining popularity among policy wonks, entrepreneurs, yuppies, corporate executives, environmentalists and New Agers alike. A product of the early 1990s (and a kindred spirit to 'corporate social responsibility'), green capitalism attempts to forge new approaches to production that on their face aim to keep business and industry from poisoning the planet. 'Green commerce' also entails the selling and buying of products that are described as 'environmentally friendly' (chemical-free, sustainably sourced, organic, etc.), as well as the multi-faceted marketing of an environmentally responsible image. Leasing commodities instead of buying them is another proposal advanced by some 'natural capitalists'; if manufacturers have to take back used products, the logic goes, they will be motivated to make units that are more recyclable and less toxic. Central to this 'next industrial revolution', as its proponents call it, is the principle of no government intervention and a belief that with the right tweaking, growing consumption levels can continue unabated.

But, while the idea seems to prioritize the much-needed goal of reshaping production, green capitalism is not a solution to the environmental devastation wrought by mass waste. First, because the changes that green commerce is supposed to engender are strictly voluntary, the results are dubious. Since eco-business is based on internalizing some of the costs that historically have been pushed onto the environment, it comes at a higher price. But in a free market system green firms must hold their own against non-green rivals, which most often leads in one of two directions: either eco-firms go out of business because they cannot keep costs low enough to compete; or they end up making higher- end goods for a niche market. This means that only those shoppers with the biggest pocketbooks can afford to buy green. Second, being unregulated 'green capitalism' can easily be exploited to obscure business practices that remain environmentally destructive; yet like recycling it reduces the pressure for regulation and lets business interests continue to pursue high growth levels and expanding markets. It can also allow companies to get away with poor labour practices; if a firm is seen as environmentally responsible people will be likely to think it is also socially responsible. Given these issues, it is worth exploring what lies behind the current surge in eco-capitalism, and whether or not it can deliver on its promises.

Some of green capitalism's most vigorous promoters are the upscale gardening chain-store founder Paul Hawken and the eco-minded architect William McDonough. Both have published books outlining their ideas and strategies for creating greener business, at the center of which lies *design*. Capitalism is not the cause of environmental decline, green capitalists proclaim. The real problem is poor product and manufacturing design, which leads to huge amounts of wasted natural resources. Shunning government intervention, green commerce's goal is for individual companies to voluntarily back-engineer the production and circulation of commodities so that wastes and toxicity are designed out of the process. Under such a system, markets can theoretically continue expanding, bypassing the perceived threat to business of reduced consumption. And with the prospect of regulatory laws nowhere in sight in the US, green commerce is getting a lot of play. The computer maker Dell now takes back its obsolete machines. The fast-food giant McDonald's dispenses napkins that use less paper. Toyota cannot fill orders fast enough for its hybrid cars. Firms that make and sell environmentally friendly products are also doing a booming trade. Whole Foods, the organic supermarket chain, is growing so fast even the *Wall Street Journal* is drooling over its stock prices. Firms like the beauty products maker Aveda, and Seventh Generation, a manufacturer of chemical-free cleaning supplies, are thriving.

This more sophisticated form of greenwashing is gaining ground because the old methods – the patriarchal voice of authority telling the public what to do with its wastes in the 1950s and '60s, and the eco-labelling of the '80s and early '90s – have lost their potency as environmental crisis has deepened.[37] Consequently, cultivating a green appearance has become more complex. A 2003 poll revealed that 80 per cent of those asked said their purchasing decisions are influenced by whether or not a product is safe for the environment. The same survey also found that 70 per cent of respondents are more likely to buy a product from a company that is known to have environmentally friendly practices. And while the poll reported just 57 per cent actually bought recycled or environmentally safe products in 2003, more recent figures reveal a shift.[38] In 2005 nearly two-thirds of US consumers bought organic foods and beverages, up from about half the previous year.[39]

In another survey, roughly 50 per cent of those questioned said they would pay more for environmentally superior goods including cars, energy, homes and appliances. Yet that does not always translate into eco-sales. With power companies offering 'green pricing' at a premium to almost half of all energy customers nationwide, fewer than one per cent of those eligible take part.[40] People purport to care about the environmental impacts of the things they buy, but they may not necessarily make purchasing decisions on that basis. Furthermore, as the 2003 poll revealed, the vast majority of respondents – 94 per cent – said they do not regularly investigate a company's environmental record.[41]

The implication of these findings is that it is in business's interest to come across as green, because so many people profess to care about the planet; but, because fewer consumers actually buy eco-safe products, and an even smaller number delve into the reality of a company's practices, there is no need to truly transform production. Firms can cash in by merely jumping through the right hoops, which today include environmental claims certi-fied by a third party, corporate investment in 'green' projects in partner-ship with non-profit environmental organizations, and offering eco-oriented consumer products.[42] As *Advertising Age* put it: 'That means less "greenwash-ing" – wherein marketers just throw ad dollars at environmental causes – and more tie-ins that ring of authenticity'.[43]

In 2003, the Ford Motor Company unveiled its newly rebuilt River Rouge plant. Designed by William McDonough, the factory featured a grass roof and skylights, and was surrounded by a constructed wetland system to filter storm water. The Rouge's green makeover was one of the initial steps the company's new CEO Bill Ford (grandson of Henry) took in charting a more environmentally sophisticated direction for the firm. In 2005, when Ford rolled out its first hybrid vehicle, the Escape SUV, using the slogan 'I guess it is easy being green', they also announced a larger eco-vision for the company. Via a high-profile but top-secret project dubbed 'Piquette' the firm is devising what it promises will be a green future in auto-making. According to *Time* magazine, Piquette involves a massive retooling of Ford's manufac-turing systems and product lines with the goal of 'making a recyclable, reus-able car'. Ford's new agenda also includes a projected annual 250,000 new hybrid autos on the road by 2010, and a pledge to be a leader in alternative-fuel technologies.[44] With Bill Ford leading the media push, the auto giant is busy asserting that it has a grasp on the big environmental picture. But what's beneath this race toward environmentalism?

Green capitalism allows a corporation like Ford which makes highly polluting products to recast itself as an advocate of environmental health. This helps to stimulate greater consumer interest and keep government controls at bay. Since the River Rouge plant reopened, Ford has exploited the facility to hype its green credentials; the 'eco-effectiveness' (McDonough's phrase) of the factory can eclipse the fact that some of the world's least fuel-efficient vehicles roll off Ford's assembly lines, like the F-150 truck, and the Explorer SUV (which gets between 10 and 15 miles to the gallon). With global warming taking centre stage in the unfolding environmental crisis, and with vehicle emissions a major contributor to climate change, Ford has serious reason to watch its back. Since the company loses money on its smaller cars that get better mileage, and earns its biggest profits from the gas-guzzlers, it is no wonder the firm is trying to distract consumers from the environmental realities of its business.

Ford is also facing a serious crisis of profitability and growth. Despite the top-selling Explorer, over the last five years Ford has seen its market share in the US nosedive, leading in 2005 to its shares being downgraded to junk-bond status. In 2006, along with his new green vision, Bill Ford also announced a massive restructuring in which as many as 10 of its 43 US plants will be closed, laying off one-fifth of its 123,000-strong North American workforce.[45] So by rebranding itself as being on the environmental cutting-edge the firm is also trying to divert attention from its labour policies. In writing about the re-done Rouge factory, McDonough says that through the architectural changes, especially the new skylights, the company was demonstrating its 'commitment to social equity as well as to ecology...'.[46] Greater social and ecological equity would more likely be achieved by the firm ceasing its lobbying against higher fuel efficiency standards. Instead, Ford is using its greening efforts to convince consumers that the company cares about the earth to fend off pressure for regulation.

Another case in point is Wal-Mart, the world's largest corporation, which is currently making a surprise turn toward environmental sensitivity. In 2005 the discount retailer suddenly unveiled an environmental programme including selling organic foods, reducing its stores' energy consumption, switching to more fuel-efficient trucks, and aiming for 'zero waste' − no trash coming out of its doors − by 2016. And, clearly responding to market research, the discounter also announced, with much fanfare, a partnership with the National Fish & Wildlife Foundation to spend $35 million over ten years conserving one acre of wildlife habitat for every acre of the company's 'footprint'.[47]

But behind the scenes Wal-Mart has been fending off serious threats to growth. In 2005 it was slapped with the biggest sex discrimination class action lawsuit ever filed in the US when 1.6 million of its current and former female employees sued the firm for unfair treatment.[48] It was also recently convicted of employing children, as well as undocumented immigrants. And unable to meaningfully crack the large consumer market in the northeastern US, just as sales in its older stores are slumping, the firm sees working the ecological angle as a way to protect its interests.[49]

Significantly, waste handling firms are also reinventing themselves as environmental guardians. The largest garbage corporation in North America, Waste Management Incorporated (WMI), has deftly deployed green marketing to keep the public believing all is well. It repainted its dumpsters and collection truck fleet a deep forest green, and over the past decade has engaged in a PR offensive to promote its earth-friendly virtues, including a partnership with KAB in 'community programs and educational initiatives'.[50] A message from WMI's CEO on its website reads: 'We're proud of our company and the many ways we Think Green® every day. Think Green® is more than a theme line. It is the attitude we take toward our landfill operations, our innovative recycling programs… and our ongoing role as stewards of the environment in the thousands of communities we serve'.[51]

As is true in the waste treatment industry overall, WMI's profits climb in direct proportion to the amount of trash it can bury, so the firm needs to convince the public that environmental health is a top priority. This will ease the way for them to keep expanding their market share without the pinch of stricter laws mandating waste reduction. A lot is on the line; as of 2003, WMI had revenues topping $11.5 billion.[52] The firm earns far more profits from landfilling discards than from waste diversion efforts like recycling. According to Peter Anderson, executive director of the Center for a Competitive Waste Industry, for corporations like WMI, recycling has a 5 per cent profit margin while landfills yield 25 per cent.[53] Consequently, it is in WMI's interest to get as much into the ground as possible, which means the firm consistently sidelines rubbish reduction and alternative uses for discarded materials like composting and meaningful recycling. Nevertheless, WMI diligently promotes itself as an upstanding eco-citizen that tirelessly protects the environment.

While trade with an ecological bent is used by the biggest corporations like Wal-Mart, Ford and WMI, smaller companies that may not have paid much attention to environmental issues in the past can also adopt a green image to use for similar PR and marketing purposes. However, there are still other companies that practise green commerce in a slightly different manner.

For the latter kind of enterprise, environmentalism is an organizing principle of their business model. Although their definitions of environmentalism may vary widely, to some degree they all share an interest in reinventing production to take ecosystems more fully into account.

The beauty products maker Aveda was started in 1978 with the idea of using natural ingredients like herbs and wildflowers for its shampoos, soaps and cosmetics. Today Aveda continues to be guided by an overall environmental ethos. According to the company's president, Dominique Conseil, 'Aveda believes in conducting business in a manner that protects the Earth, conserves resources and does not compromise the ability of future generations to sustain themselves'.[54] Indeed the firm tracks its energy use, carbon dioxide output and waste generation in order to rethink manufacturing and distribution. Its website explains some of its efforts: 'Because air shipping emits 73 times more carbon dioxide than shipping by sea, Aveda uses sea ships rather than airfreight whenever possible. From July 2001 through June 2002, Aveda reduced its air shipments by 50%'. Additionally, Aveda has pioneered some of the least exploitative sourcing practices in the industry, uses between 25-45 per cent post-consumer recycled materials in its packaging, and has its own environmental sustainability department.[55]

The catch is that Aveda's products are among the priciest on the market. Cost can create significant barriers, even for a 'prestige brand' like Aveda. Speaking at a waste reduction conference in the spring of 2005, Mary Tkach, Executive Director of Environmental Sustainability for the company, gave a Powerpoint presentation with lists of what the company would like to achieve, among them its pathway toward creating zero waste. When pressed by a member of the audience over what the firm was actually able to achieve, Tkach confessed that there were limits. 'Aveda wants to get to zero waste, but it just gets too expensive', she explained. For example, packaging that could be reused was out of the question because no affordable technology exists to sanitize containers like squeeze tubes.[56]

Even though they are more green than many other companies, Aveda still gets caught between doing right by the planet and doing right by its shareholders. The firm, bought by the cosmetics giant Estée Lauder in 1998, operates within the free market system, and is therefore subject to its rules. If Aveda's products are excessively expensive they will not sell; spending too much on environmental sustainability would drive them out of business. While the firm's practices may help to create a sense of ecological responsibility among other producers, and contribute to a larger culture within which the stewardship of natural resources is respected, on their own these moves will not foment a green conversion of industrial practices.

Companies that operate as environmentally friendly endeavours will inevitably struggle with high prices. Sean Twomey is the owner of a retail store in Ottawa, Ontario, that sells green products – everything from chemical-free cleaning supplies and composting toilets to organic cotton sheets and self-published books on biofuels. Because of his experience in the trade he understands that these commodities are not accessible to everyone: 'If we weren't in a wealthy neighbourhood, there's no way we'd still be in business'.[57] Consumers who can afford the ecologically sound stuff are the shoppers with bigger budgets. Most working families – even in North America – cannot afford to buy green.

According to green capitalism's advocates, abundant consumer interest in green products is precisely what should spark the voluntary shift in production toward more environmentally sustainable and responsible ways. However, something different seems to be taking shape. The organic food industry offers a useful example. Just inside the front door of one of the newest upscale Whole Foods grocery stores, on New York City's Union Square, track-lit aisles are packed with organic breads, cookies, meats, produce, milk and cheese, not to mention a vast array of non-toxic personal care products. The natural foods chain has successfully tapped into the lucrative organics industry, which has grown by a stunning 20 per cent each year for the past decade. Whole Foods has seen its stock price surge from $2.92 in 1992 to $64.92 today.[58] Having started as a single vegetarian market in Austin, Texas, in 1978, Whole Foods is now the largest natural grocery retail corporation in the world, successfully making the move from hippie ghetto to urban mainstream. In 2004 the *Financial Times* described the company as 'the fastest growing mass retailer in the US'.[59]

As demand for eco-products like organics swells, green businesses are enticed to expand, and large corporations are lured into the market. This can, not surprisingly, involve significant trade-offs; instead of industrial production being remade, capital is remaking what is considered green. So, a product labelled organic may contain chemical-free ingredients, but its production and distribution may be environmentally destructive.

To keep its shelves piled high with organic produce, Whole Foods imports fruits and vegetables from as far away as New Zealand. Silk, the number one brand of soymilk in the US, does not always use domestically produced inputs; the firm is known to import organic soybeans all the way from Brazil and China.[60] The entire organics sector had revenues of $15 billion in 2004; last year imported organics accounted for a sizeable chunk of that market, $1.5 billion.[61] While chemical-free foods from overseas may be raised without synthetics, their transportation consumes non-renewable hydrocarbons and pollutes the atmosphere with carbon dioxide, a leading contributor to global warming.

And as the market grows, selling organics gets trickier. Chemical-free foods cost on average 50 per cent more than 'conventional' edibles grown with substances like fertilizers, pesticides, antibiotics and hormones.[62] The higher price for organics stems from a greater outlay for production. Costs are pushed up, for instance, by the increased labour required when workers pull up weeds by hand instead of spraying crops with chemicals. Industrial farmers spend about $50 per acre on herbicides, while organic farmers can dole out as much as $1,000 per acre to control weeds.[63] Also, organic crops often have much lower yields than their pumped-up 'conventional' counter-parts. One organic citrus farmer in Florida assesses that yields can fall by as much as 30 per cent without the use of chemicals.[64]

Breaking out of the high-end niche retailing of stores like Whole Foods, in recent years organics have hit the shelves in mainstream supermarket chains, including Wal-Mart. This might indicate that healthier foods are becoming more affordable, but that's not quite the case. What is happening is a con-solidation of the industry, as firms owned by corporations like Coca-Cola, ExxonMobil, Unilever and Monsanto buy up small organic producers.[65] This shift in ownership is leading to the pursuit of lower prices, but not necessarily through better ecological practices. As Peter Skelton, an agronomy researcher at the University of Nebraska, explains, industrial food production is still hard on ecosystems, even if that intensive farming is technically chemical-free: 'On an organic dairy farm, instead of giving the cows conventional feed, you're giving them organic feed. But you're still trucking in inputs to the farm with all the environmental impacts that entails. Whereas, if you had a grass fed system [a small-scale farm] you wouldn't need all those external inputs'.[66]

It's not that small-scale farms do not aim to be profitable just as agribusi-ness does, but the demands of shareholders and constant growth drive big producers to constantly search out greater efficiencies. The operations at Ho-rizon Dairy, the largest organic milk producer in the US, illustrate the push to get around maintaining expensive organics standards. Owned by Dean Foods, the country's biggest dairy processor, Horizon is known to keep cows confined in outdoor corrals instead of letting them graze primarily in open fields. As *Consumer Reports* noted, 'Current federal regulations state that or-ganically raised animals must have access to pasture and may be "temporarily confined only for reasons of health, safety, the animal's stage of production, or to protect soil or water quality". But that vague language allows large producers to cut corners and compromise on what consumers expect from organic food...'.[67] Companies like Horizon can also take advantage of other loopholes. Established guidelines are unclear as to whether cows could have been treated with antibiotics or feed containing genetically modified grain and animal by-products prior to becoming part of an organic dairy herd. According to Ronnie Cummins, the national director of the Organic Consumers Association, a Minnesota-based advocacy group, this allows for Horizon's practice of 'regularly importing calves from industrial farms and simply calling them organic'.[68]

As the largest conglomerates move into the organics trade, they are not turning into truly green producers. On the contrary, ever since the passage of the US Department of Agriculture organic labelling standards in 2002, powerful corporations have lobbied for eased regulations. One Georgia chicken producer persuaded his state representative to tack on to a 2003 Federal Appropriations bill an amendment that softened organics standards. According to one account, 'The amendment stated that if the price of organic feed was more than twice the cost of regular feed – which can contain heavy metals, pesticides, and animal by-products – then livestock producers could feed their animals less costly nonorganic feed but still label their products organic'. The amendment was repealed after much uproar from consumers and organic farmers, but the attack on organic standards continues. In 2005, Congress voted to weaken the organic labelling law, allowing synthetic ingredients to be included in some foods labelled 'organic'.[69] As Ronnie Cummins explains, 'Consumer spending on organics has grown so much that we've attracted big players who want to bend the rules so that they can brand their products as organic without incurring the expenses involved in truly living up to organic standards'.[70]

Green commerce makes sense to so many individuals and businesses because it fits into the existing economic order, allowing the 'social relations of consumption' to stay intact (as did anti-litter and recycling campaigns in the past). According to the green commerce-promoting non-profit organization Co-op America, on average each US household spends $17,000 on necessities like food, clothes, and home and personal care products. 'Now imagine that every dollar spent went toward promoting healthy, organic food; ending sweatshops and promoting Fair Trade; and creating a national marketplace for green products. That's what buying green is all about. It's about making purchasing decisions that help create a better world to leave to our children and children everywhere'.[71]

Sounds great, but although future ecological damage might be mitigated to some degree by green commodities, such goods still course through a system that relies on maximum production, maximum consumption, and, therefore, maximum waste. And capitalism is expansionary; within it businesses must continually grow, even firms that are green. However much proponents of eco-commerce imagine we can consume our way out of the problems of consumption, green capitalism is not capable of solving the problems embedded in capitalist social relations of production and in capitalist production's exploitative relation to nature.

CONSUMPTION AS POLITICS

Green commerce is thus only the latest chapter in the long story of US companies seeking to shape public perceptions of the environmental fallout from industrial capitalism. Eco-commerce is a means for capital as a whole to avoid truly remaking itself, while giving the opposite impression. This misperception helps capital continue cultivating the ideology of individual responsibility linked to a market-based solution, pre-empting government regulation. And, as with greenwashing in the past, green commerce has the potential to distract people from becoming meaningfully involved in creating political change to protect ecological health. It assists capital in papering over the grim realities the environmental movement has exposed and lets companies make the continued exploitation of nature seem acceptable in the midst of serious ecological crisis. According to James O'Connor, 'corporations construct the problem of the environment…[as] the problem of how to remake nature in ways that are consistent with sustainable profitability and capital accumulation. "Remaking nature" means more access to nature, as a "tap" and "sink"… the green movement may be forcing capital to end its primitive exploitation of precapitalist nature by remaking nature in the image of capital…'.[72]

As capitalism spreads across the globe nature ceases to exist independently of humans; now even the remotest nature is affected by the actions of people whose lives are structured around the social relations of the free market system. However historically true it may be, Neil Smith's observation that 'human beings have produced whatever nature became accessible to them' certainly applies to life under green commerce.[73] Even though the practice appears to factor environmental health into the decisions made during production, what is actually transpiring is a recreation of nature for the purpose of removing obstacles to the accumulation of wealth

Green commerce belongs to the wider cultural discourse of what Toby M. Smith calls 'productivist hegemony', which construes capitalist production as a utopian project that invariably improves quality of life while fostering a belief in competition and growth as a way out of environmental crisis. As Cindi Katz says, 'clean capitalism is better than dirty to be sure – but other issues are at stake. Politics as consumption (and vice versa) works to individualize environmental problems and their solutions in ways that repeatedly forestall and mystify any meaningful ways of dealing with them'.[74]

With green commerce there is a two-fold con game afoot: first, people are induced to accept individual, personal responsibility for cleaning up the environment and are lulled into a sense of complacency by the idea that they are actually doing something effective. And, secondly, because the solution is said to be personal, people avoid confronting those in power and are distracted from tackling the inequities and exploitation inherent in the current economic system.[75] Eco-capitalism draws energy away from the struggle required to secure real political solutions, such as restricting raw materials extraction, regulating manufacturing, and reducing consumption and waste.

Green commerce also has the potential to derail the important work of the environmental justice movement. According to Co-op America's website, 'Our mission is to harness economic power – the strength of consumers, investors, and businesses – to create a socially just and environmentally sustainable society'.[76] Green capitalists imply that by virtue of being environmentally-minded a business's other policies will also be socially and economically responsible. But just because a company pledges allegiance to trees does not mean it will be fair to its workers, as is clear from the notoriously anti-union policies of both Wal-Mart and Whole Foods.

Green capitalism also reinforces the longstanding tendency of the mainstream environmental movement to treat the ecological crisis as something separate from the economic system in which it arises. Unlike the environmental justice movement, the environmental establishment has avoided confronting the role of the state in supporting ecologically destructive business practices through direct subsidies, tax breaks, and pro-waste legislation.[77] The eco-mainstream refuses to connect the dots between environmental degradation, the exploitation of people (workers and those most often subjected to pollution), and the economic, political and social forces that foster both. The health of natural systems cannot be protected and improved by ignoring the economic context of environmental destruction.

NOTES

Timothy Duggan provided research assistance for this essay.

1   Office of Solid Waste and Emergency Response, *Municipal Solid Waste in the United States: 2001 Facts and Figures*, Washington: US Environmental Protection Agency, 2003, pp. 3-4.

2   Neil Seldman, 'Recycling – History in the United States', in Attilio Bisio and Sharon Boots, eds., *Encyclopedia of Energy Technology and the Environment*, Hoboken: John Wiley, 1995, p. 2352.

3   Heather Rogers, 'Titans of Trash', *The Nation*, 281(21), 2005, p. 22.

4   Hillary Mayell, 'Ocean Litter Gives Alien Species an Easy Ride', *National Geographic News*, 29 April 2002, electronic version; Paul Gottlich, 'The Sixth Basic Food Group', 16 November 2003, see http://www.mindfully.org/.

5   On 'investment', see Eliza Strickland, 'The New Face of Environmentalism', *East Bay Express*, 28(4), 2005, p. 17.

6   John H. Fenton, 'Vermont's Session Has Budget Clash', *New York Times*, 1 February 1953.

7   Heather Rogers, *Gone Tomorrow: The Hidden Life of Garbage*, New York: New Press, 2005, pp. 141-2.

8   Bernard Stengren, 'What Makes a Litterbug?', *New York Times*, 5 December 1954.

9   'The Waste-High Crisis', *Modern Packaging*, 41(11), 1968, p. 102.

10   Keep America Beautiful website, see http://www.kab.org; see the entry on 'Iron Eyes Cody' at the Snopes website: http://www.snopes.com.

11   Peter Harnik, 'The Junking of an Anti-Litter Lobby', *Business and Society Review*, 21(Spring), 1977, p. 50; Daniel Zwerdling, 'Iron Eyes', *All Things Considered*, National Public Radio, 10 January 1999.

12   Quoted in Louis Blumberg and Michael Gottlieb, *War on Waste: Can America Win Its Battle with Garbage?*, Washington: Island Press, 1989, p. 19.

13   Seldman, 'Recycling – History in the United States', p. 2354.

14   Center for Investigative Reporting and Bill Moyers, *Global Dumping Ground: The International Traffic in Hazardous Waste*, Washington: Seven Locks Press, 1990, p. 7.

15   Travis W. Halleman, *A Statistical Analysis of Wyoming Landfill Characteristics*, Master's Thesis, Department of Civil and Architectural Engineering, University of Wyoming, August, 2004, electronic version.

16   Seldman, 'Recycling – History in the United States', p. 2352.

17   By 1976 every US state legislature and numerous town, city and county councils – more than 1,200 in all – had proposed some form of restrictive packaging law. But at the end of the decade only 8 states had adopted beverage container measures, due to harsh industry pressure. See Thomas W. Fenner and Randee J. Gorin, *Local Beverage Container Laws: A Legal and Tactical Analysis*, Stanford: Stanford Environmental Law Society, 1976, p. 3; Harnik, 'The Junking of an Anti-Litter Lobby', pp. 49-51.

18   Blumberg and Gottlieb, *War on Waste*, p. 208.

19   Seldman, 'Recycling – History in the United States', p. 2356.

20   Susan Strasser, *Waste and Want: A Social History of Trash*, New York: Henry Holt, 1999, p. 285.

21   Quoted in Lerza, 'Administration "Pitches In"', *Environmental Action*, 6(2), 1974, p. 5.

22   Patricia Taylor, 'Source Reduction: Stemming the Tide of Trash', *Environmental Action*, 6(7), 17 August 1974, p. 11.

23 The recycling symbol was designed by Gary Anderson for the Container Corporation of America, a paper products manufacturer. See 'The History of the Recycling Symbol', *Dyer Consequences!*, available from http://www.dyer-consequences.com.

24 Ecology Center, *Report of the Berkeley Plastics Task Force*, Berkeley, California, April, 1996, p. 7.

25 Cynthia Pollock, *World Watch Paper 76: Mining Urban Wastes: The Potential For Recycling*, Washington: Worldwatch Institute, 1987, p. 8.

26 From an interview with Neil Seldman, 20 January 2005.

27 Ecology Center, *Report of the Berkeley Plastics Task Force*, pp. 6–7.

28 Cited in ibid., p. 7.

29 Neil Seldman and Brenda Platt, *Wasting and Recycling in the United States 2000*, Athens, Georgia: GrassRoots Recycling Network, 2000, p. 12.

30 Ecology Center, *Report of the Berkeley Plastics Task Force*, p. 6.

31 'Setting the Record Straight', available from the Container Recycling Institute website, http://www.container-recycling.org.

32 Des King, 'Calling the Shots', *Packaging Today International*, 25(9), 2003, electronic version.

33 Seldman and Platt, *Wasting and Recycling in the United States 2000*, p. 13.

34 Ibid., p. 10.

35 Ibid., p. 9.

36 Karl Marx, 'Economic and Philosophic Manuscripts of 1844', *The Marx-Engels Reader*, Robert Tucker, ed., New York: W.W. Norton, 1978, p. 103.

37 Data from the early 1990s reveal that shoppers were often confused by eco-labelling, and were uninformed about the meaning of terms like 'biodegradable'. Consumers also considered a company's own claims about the environmental benefits of their products to be misleading and deceptive. See Lucie I. Ozanne and Richard P. Vlosky, 'Certification from the U.S. Consumer Perspective: A Comparison from 1995 and 2000', *Forest Products Journal*, 53(3), 2003, electronic version.

38 Rebecca Gardyn, 'Eco-friend or Foe?', *American Demographics*, 25(8), 2003, electronic version. Similar numbers were found in a 1993 poll, see E. Howard Barnett, 'Green with Envy: the FTC, the EPA, the States, and the Regulation of Environmental Marketing', *Environmental Lawyer*, February, 1995, electronic version.

39 'Start the Year Right: When it Pays to Buy Organic', *Consumer Reports*, 71(2), 2006, electronic version.

40 Cait Murphy, 'The Next Big Thing', *Fortune Small Business*, 13(5), 2003, p. 64.

41 Gardyn, 'Eco-friend or Foe?'.

42 Ibid.

43 Dale Buss, 'Eco-efforts Rely on Authenticity', *Advertising Age*, 76(24), 12 June 2005, electronic version.

44 Dorinda Elliott, 'Can This Man Save The American Auto Industry?', *Time*, 167(5), 2006, pp. 38–48.

45 Elliott, 'Can This Man Save The American Auto Industry?', pp. 41–44.

46   William McDonough and Michael Braungart, *Cradle to Cradle*, New York: North Point Press, 2002, p. 163.

47   Buss, 'Eco-efforts Rely on Authenticity'.

48   Liza Featherstone, *Selling Women Short: The Landmark Battle for Workers' Rights at Wal-Mart*, New York: Basic Books, 2004, p. 4.

49   Kris Hudson, 'Wal-Mart Sticks With Fast Pace of Expansion Despite Toll on Sales', *Wall Street Journal*, 13 April 2006.

50   Waste Management Inc. website, see http://www.wm.com/WM/ThinkGreen/Community/kab.asp.

51   Waste Management Inc. website, see http://www.wm.com/WM/ThinkGreen/ceo.asp.

52   'The 2004 Waste Age 100', *Waste Age*, 1 June 2004, electronic version.

53   From an interview with Peter Anderson, 15 September 2005.

54   Aveda website, see http://www.aveda.com/customerservice/ourmission.tmpl.

55   'Company Profile: Aveda', *GreenMoney Journal*, online version, http://www.greenmoneyjournal.com/.

56   From the Zero Waste conference in New York City, May, 2005.

57   From an interview, February, 2006.

58   Steven Shapin, 'Paradise Sold', *The New Yorker*, 15 May 2006, p. 84.

59   Quoted in ibid.

60   'The Rotten Side of Organics: The *Satya* Interview with Ronnie Cummins', *Satya*, April, 2006, p. 10.

61   On the 2004 figure, see Shapin, 'Paradise Sold', p. 84. On the 2005 figure, see Matt McKinney, 'Demand Up for Organic Milk', *Grand Forks Herald*, 22 May 2006, electronic version.

62   'The Rotten Side of Organics', p. 10.

63   Kymberlie Adams Matthews, 'Defining Organic', *Satya*, April, 2006, p. 14.

64   Pallavi Gogoi, 'Going Organic, the Profits and Pitfalls', *Business Week Online*, 25 May 2006, electronic version.

65   'Food Guide: Who Owns What', *Satya*, April, 2006, p. 11.

66   From an interview with the author, 2 June 2006.

67   Ibid.

68   Quoted in 'The Rotten Side of Organics', p. 10. See also, 'Start the Year Right'.

69   'Start the Year Right'.

70   Ibid.

71   Coop America website, 'Buying Green', http://www.coopamerica.org/.

72   James O'Connor, *Natural Causes: Essays in Ecological Marxism*, New York: The Guilford Press, 1998, pp. 238-39.

73   Neil Smith, *Uneven Development: Nature, Capital and the Production of Space*, Oxford: Basil Blackwell, 1984, p. 57.

74   Cindi Katz, 'Whose Nature, Whose Culture?', Bruce Braun and Noel Castree, eds., *Remaking Reality: Nature at the Millennium*, London: Routledge, 1998, p. 52.

75   Toby M. Smith, *The Myth of Green Marketing: Tending Our Goats at the Edge of Apocalypse*, Toronto: University of Toronto Press, 1998, p. 107.

76   Co-op America website, see http://www.coopamerica.org/cabn/.

77   One recent example in the US is the 2005 energy bill that provided over $1 billion in subsidies to the petroleum industry, which at the time was earning the highest profits of any business in US history.

WORKING MORE, SELLING MORE, CONSUMING MORE: CAPITALISM'S 'THIRD CONTRADICTION'

COSTAS PANAYOTAKIS

S cholars and environmentalists have long pointed out that the consumer-ist living standards of rich capitalist countries cannot be universalized without inflicting irreparable damage on the planetary ecosystem.[1] This re-alization spells the end of any doubt as to whether the small island of 'high mass-consumption' that used to be held up as a model for the 'underdevel-oped' world to emulate could be said to have resolved the contradictions stemming from the class nature of capitalist society.[2] As Silver and Arrighi point out: 'Here, ultimately, lies the great challenge that will face workers in the twenty-first century: that is, the challenge to struggle, not just against ex-ploitation and exclusion, but for consumption norms and secure livelihood standards that can be generalized to all and for policies that actually promote this generalization'.[3]

Although many scholars and social critics have in the past questioned whether growing levels of economic output and consumption lead to a rich-er and happier human life,[4] very few have approached this question from the standpoint of the social and ecological contradictions that capitalist social structures tend to generate. This essay analyzes the futility of consumerism and the compulsive pursuit of economic growth under capitalism as a mani-festation of a 'third contradiction' of capitalism.

SETTING THE STAGE: O'CONNOR'S 'SECOND CONTRADICTION' THESIS

One of the more distinctive contributions of ecological Marxism to the body of Marxist theory is James O'Connor's conceptualization of a 'second contradiction' of capitalism, understood as an addition to the first contradic-tion that has always been a central focus of Marxist analysis.[5] In particular, O'Connor uses the term 'first contradiction' to refer to the tendency of capitalist economic development to be punctuated by economic crises triggered by the difficulty of realizing the surplus value generated by capital's exploitation of labour.[6] In this respect, O'Connor views the first contradiction as a manifestation of the tension between forces and relations of production that the traditional Marxist theory of history has identified as the driving force of historical development.[7]

By contrast, O'Connor's 'second contradiction' is one 'between capitalist production relations (*and* productive forces) and the *conditions* of capitalist production'. According to O'Connor, Marx was aware that capitalist production presupposed conditions that were not produced as commodities and even identified three distinct types of production conditions.

> The first is 'external physical conditions', or the natural elements entering into constant and variable capital. Second, the 'labor power' of workers was defined as the 'personal condition of production'. Third, Marx referred to 'the communal, general conditions of social production, for example, 'means of communication'.[8]

Despite Marx's recognition of capitalism's dependence on these conditions, O'Connor argues that he did not draw the full implications of this.[9] This is what O'Connor tries to do by drawing on Polanyi's analysis in *The Great Transformation*.[10] In that work Polanyi examined the attempt in nineteenth-century Britain to institute a free market social order based on the subordination of 'fictitious commodities' like labour, land and money to the vicissitudes of market forces. According to Polanyi, this attempt inevitably failed as the degradation of labour and natural conditions made it clear that fictitious commodities like labour, land and money were too important for the integrity of social life to be regulated by unadulterated market forces. The result was a series of social reforms that circumscribed the play of market forces.

Similarly O'Connor argues that the operation of capitalist economy tends to degrade the production conditions that are not produced as commodities. This tendency makes it imperative for these conditions to be regulated by a non-market agency, such as the capitalist state. Since these conditions are very broad, encompassing areas as diverse as regulation of natural conditions, the reproduction of a relatively healthy and skilled labour force, and the building of the cultural and urban infrastructures essential to capitalist production, O'Connor goes as far as to suggest that '[i]n terms of domestic policy, the state does little more than regulate capital's access to production conditions, and often participates in the production of all three, for example, in the form of wetlands policy, urban zoning policy, and child care policy'.[11]

Like Polanyi, moreover, O'Connor argues that the degradation of the conditions of production tends to give rise to social movements challenging the terms under which these conditions are appropriated by capital. 'In Polanyi's terms', O'Connor argues, 'new social movements can be defined as "society" fighting the commodification of production conditions...[o]r...the specific forms of capitalist restructuring of already commodified conditions of production'.[12] Although O'Connor recognizes that the second contradiction thesis cannot exhaust the meaning of new social movements, he does point out that 'new social movements seem to have an objective referent in production: ecology and environmentalism in natural conditions; urban movements ...in urban infrastructure and space; and movements such as feminism that pertain to (among other things) the definition of labour power, the politics of the body, the distribution of child care in the home, and similar issues, in the "personal condition of production"'.[13]

Thus the second contradiction leads O'Connor to interpret new social movements as potential agents within a more broadly redefined socialist project. In O'Connor's view, the second contradiction may represent a second path to socialism, with new social movements potentially playing the role with respect to the second contradiction that traditional Marxism has long assigned to the working class with respect to the first contradiction.[14]

EVALUATING THE SECOND CONTRADICTION THESIS

One of the important contributions of the second contradiction thesis and its analysis of the conditions of production is that it opens up Marxist theory to the importance of natural and cultural factors and processes. By integrating such factors and processes into the analysis of capitalism's crisis tendencies, O'Connor contributes to the emancipation of Marxist theory from its often economistic past.[15] At the same time, however, O'Connor's treatment of the second contradiction as a supplement that can be added on to traditional Marxism's analysis of capitalist contradictions is neither critical enough of the traditional analysis nor appreciative of the extent to which this analysis has to be reconceptualized in view of the 'second contradiction' thesis.

To begin with there is an element of uncritical teleology in O'Connor's speculation that we may be 'engaging in a long process in which there occur different yet parallel paths to socialism, hence that Marx was not so much wrong as he was half-right'.[16] In interpreting the two contradictions as 'parallel paths to socialism', O'Connor does not of course appeal to any kind of inexorable economic necessity. On the contrary, he emphasizes that whether capitalist crises lead to a restructuring of capitalism or a move towards socialism 'depends on the ideological and political terrain, degree of popular mobilization and organization, national traditions, and the like, including and especially the particular world economic and political conjuncture'.[17] Nonetheless, O'Connor does believe that, even when crises are resolved through the restructuring of capitalist society, this restructuring tends to lead to 'more cooperation or planning', thus 'making production more transparently social, meanwhile subverting commodity and capital fetishism, or the apparent "naturalness" of capitalist economy. The telos of crisis is thus to create the possibility of imagining a transition to socialism'.[18] In other words, O'Connor's analysis is teleological to the extent that it suggests that the economic crises generated by capitalism's first and second contradictions point in the direction of socialism, even though it may be true that whether these crises lead to socialism depends on a multiplicity of political and ideological factors.

There are compelling reasons to reject the teleological assumptions underlying O'Connor's account of the first contradiction. As O'Connor recognizes, crises play an important function in the capitalist accumulation process insofar as they constitute 'an economic disciplinary mechanism'.[19] In particular, capitalist economic crises stem from the fact that the reproduction of class relations in capitalist society is mediated by market competition. This fact also accounts for the economic and technological dynamism that, as Marx points out in the *Communist Manifesto*, differentiates capitalism from the class societies that came before it. In this respect, the economic crises that traditional Marxism has analyzed could very well be viewed as manifestations of capitalism's vitality rather than disruptive events promising to set humanity on the path to socialism. As Marshall Berman has pointed out,

> Marx appears to believe that these crises will increasingly cripple capitalism and eventually destroy it. And yet, his own vision and analysis of bourgeois society show how well this society can thrive on crisis and catastrophe … given the bourgeois capacity to make destruction and chaos pay, there is no apparent reason why these crises can't spiral on endlessly.[20]

Marx's theory of history can help to explain this paradox. As I have discussed elsewhere, Marx's theory of history elevates the structural logic of capitalist society into a trans-historical principle of social change and then projects it forward to anticipate the replacement of capitalist society by socialism.[21] If the cyclical character of capitalist development becomes transformed in Marx's theory of history into a succession of modes of production and capitalism is viewed as one of these modes of production, then the logical next step is to assume that capitalism is as likely to reach its limits as previous modes. To the extent that the increasingly crippling effect of economic crises would signify the onset of a stage where capitalism's limits became increasingly felt, it is clear that Marx's answer to the question posed by Berman may, at least in part, stem from the ideological impact of the structural logic of capitalist society on Marx's theory of history.

Marx's theory of history appears in O'Connor's work in the form of an assumption that the contradiction between capitalist forces and relations of production points in the direction of socialism. Once it is recognized that Marx's theory of history was built upon an implicit and dubious homology between capitalist development and human history as a whole, traditional Marxism's teleological interpretation of the relation between forces and relations of production becomes clearly problematic. In its place emerges a recognition of the possibility that capitalism may be more capable of advancing productive development and economic growth than traditional Marxism assumed. In fact, as O'Connor himself recognizes, its ability to do just that has contributed to capitalism's ability to neutralize political challenges in the past.[22]

Thus, although the first contradiction does entail an opposition between capital and labour, it was Marx's theory of history, with its discounting of capitalism's long-term ability to promote productive development, that encouraged a teleological interpretation of this contradiction. At the same time, the fact that, as noted in the beginning of this essay, the neutralization of capitalist contradictions through economic growth may not be ecologically sustainable suggests the need to view the first and second contradictions not as setting up parallel paths to socialism but as interacting moments within a larger capitalist totality. The nature of the interaction between these two contradictions may vary depending on the economic, political, and ideological conjuncture. It is also this conjuncture that helps to determine whether each of these contradictions will tend to aggravate or contain the impact of the other.

O'Connor himself recognizes that the question of 'the relationship between the first and second contradictions of capitalism' is a legitimate one and goes on to conceptualize it as a question of whether these contradictions 'compound or offset their respective effects on profits'.[23] O'Connor also provides an example of the relationship between the two contradictions when he points out that 'the relatively slow rate of growth of worldwide market demand since the mid-1970s',[24] which for O'Connor is a manifestation of the first contradiction,[25] has led capital to attempt to restore profits both by 'raising the rate of exploitation of labor, by depleting and exhausting resources, and by subverting the integrity of local community'.[26] These responses are likely to aggravate both the first and the second contradictions, since intensified exploitation and growing inequalities would be likely 'to reduce the final demand for consumer commodities',[27] while the externalization of 'social and environmental costs'[28] would tend 'to reduce the "productivity" of the conditions of production, and hence to raise average costs'.[29]

There is a neat symmetry underlying this description of how the two contradictions of capitalism reinforce each other. According to O'Connor, the second contradiction illuminates the threats to capitalist profitability that come from the 'supply side',[30] while traditional Marxism's concern with the first contradiction has tended to focus on the demand side. O'Connor does not, however, recognize the implications of the fact that different types of crises may call for different types of policy responses.

Working with a similar distinction between demand- and supply-side crises, Bowles, Gordon and Weisskopf have pointed out that, from the point of view of the functional requirements of the capitalist system, these two types of crises may call for diametrically opposite policy responses.[31] While the most appropriate response to demand-side crises would be redistributive measures and government spending that boost aggregate demand, supply-side crises are likely to build pressure for policies, such as deregulation and lower government spending, that are likely to reduce the costs faced by capital. Bowles, Gordon and Weisskopf's insight into the policy implications of different kinds of economic crisis can also be used to analyze the implications of economic crises for the second contradiction.

Indeed, in the same way that a demand-side crisis could, as it did after the depression of the 1930s, lead to progressive policies aimed at reducing economic inequalities, it could also lead to measures that alleviate the impact of the second contradiction. Thus, for example, government projects designed to respond to a demand-side crisis could be, at least in part, focused on the repair of natural conditions of production, the development of labour power through investments in education, and the building of urban and public infrastructures. Government projects during the New Deal provide an illustration of how the attempt to alleviate a demand-side crisis could also help to reduce the threat of a supply-side crisis generated by the degradation of the conditions of production.

The different types of policies needed to address the different types of economic crises also suggest that any move towards policies that make 'production more transparently social, meanwhile subverting commodity and capital fetishism, or the apparent "naturalness" of capitalist economy' could be reversed if the problems afflicting capitalist economies change.[32] Thus, as O'Connor himself recognizes, the continuing relevance of the first and second contradictions has not prevented the neoliberal move towards, rather than away from, reasserting fetishism and the primacy of the capitalist market as well as 'defang[ing] national states once capable of effective social and environmental regulation at a time when more effective regulatory and control mechanisms are essential'.[33] Once again, a teleological conception of the first and second contradictions as triggering changes that 'create the possibility of imagining a transition to socialism' seems problematic.[34] Analyzing the two contradictions as moments within a capitalist totality that keeps changing partly as a result of the ways that the interaction of the two contradictions either aggravates or helps to contain their respective impacts seems more appropriate. An examination of the third contradiction of capitalist society further reinforces this conclusion.

THE THIRD CONTRADICTION OF CAPITALISM

Simply put, the third contradiction of capitalism stems not from an inability of capitalist social relations to continue advancing technological and productive development but rather from an inability to translate such development into a richer and more satisfying life for all human beings. In discussing the second contradiction, O'Connor points out that capitalism's degradation of the conditions of production raises 'the possibility not only of an economic crisis for capital but also of a legitimation crisis for the state'.[35] The third contradiction too has both an economic and a legitimation dimension.

On the one hand, capitalism's irrational use of the technological potential it brings forth generates a virtually universal human interest in a democratic, non-capitalist society capable of putting this potential to a better use. The more people become conscious of this interest, the more likely it becomes that this interest will give rise to a legitimation crisis for capitalist society. That such a legitimation crisis is a concrete possibility is shown by the fact that the demands advanced by radical movements in the 1960s did not just involve social justice and political rights but also a more 'utopian' quest for an alternative to the poverty of everyday life that is endemic to capitalist societies around the globe. On the other hand, we will see that the third contradiction could also have an economic dimension if it were to give rise to social movements pushing for reforms that addressed its sources.

The rest of this essay will undertake two tasks: first, it will provide a sketch of how the structure of capitalist social relations gives rise to the third contradiction; and, second, it will discuss some of the ways in which this contradiction may interact with the two contradictions analyzed by traditional Marxism and O'Connor. The purpose of this discussion is to show that the eco-socialist project that O'Connor seeks to advance has to be as cognizant of the third contradiction of capitalism as of the two contradictions treated in O'Connor's work. I will defend this claim by focusing on two major sources of the third contradiction, capitalism's bias for production rather than free time and its systematic cultivation of consumerist aspirations.

CAPITALISM'S PRODUCTIVIST BIAS

A number of scholars have discussed the significance of the fact that, beyond a certain level of income, the average reported level of life satisfaction in a given country does not increase with economic growth.[36] Existing accounts have not, however, offered a systematic treatment of the ways in which the structural features of capitalist economy may contribute to this disconnect. Instead, they have more often focused on consumption races that are triggered by individual pursuit of 'positional goods' and the existence of a conflict between individual self-interest and social outcomes.[37]

Robert Frank, for example, convincingly demonstrates the waste generated by the spread of consumerist patterns and the missed opportunity for enhanced human welfare that such waste entails. One manifestation of this missed opportunity, according to Frank, is the fact that Americans have been overworking themselves to sustain consumerist lifestyles even as studies suggest that, once a level of material comfort has been attained, non-positional goods, such as free time, make a greater contribution to human welfare than additional consumption of material goods.[38]

Other authors have investigated the economic and historical reasons why labour productivity increases in the last hundred years have overwhelmingly been translated into growing economic output and consumption rather than shorter work hours.[39] These accounts do make reference to the differences between the interests and perspective of labour and those of capital but often understate the degree to which a bias against free time is inherent in capitalist society.[40] For example, the historical overview of the trade-off between economic growth and free time in *capitalist* society leads Gary Cross to a pronouncement concerning *industrialism's* supposed bias 'toward producing goods rather than leisure'.[41] This pronouncement obscures the ways in which the productivist bias stems from the capitalist nature of our socio-economic system, and thus also obscures the possibility of a non-capitalist alternative that would redress the imbalance between production and free time.

The claim that the productivist bias of our economy is linked to its capitalist nature can be defended on both empirical and theoretical grounds.

On the empirical side, Pietro Basso's work on the European working hours regime casts doubt on Schor's presentation of European capitalism as having attained a more balanced relationship between economic growth and free time.[42] Basso's analysis suggests that instead of representing a viable alternative to the American model, European countries are converging towards the 'flexible' American model that intensifies exploitation and reduces free time.

On the theoretical side, the fact that the trade-off between production and free time has, in recent decades, been resolved in favour of the former and that this development 'did not occur as a result of public debate' bears witness to the power of capital to shape social developments in accordance with its interests.[43] Schor has discussed a number of reasons for the appeal that long hours continued to have for employers even after workers started to get paid hourly wages.[44] There is, however, another important reason why capital would prefer the translation of increased productivity into economic growth rather than a shorter work day.

If all the productivity gains were taken in the form of shorter hours, all of the benefits of increased productivity would go to workers. In the absence of economic growth, it would be hard for profits to grow and, although this would be true for consumption as well, workers would at least be getting the benefit of more free time. The reverse is true when productivity becomes translated into economic growth. Then it becomes easier for capital to benefit from productivity growth and this benefit comes at no cost for the owners of capital. As returns on capital are not the result of work, capital's partiality towards production does not represent capital's answer to a tradeoff facing everyone involved. This partiality is an attempt, on the part of capital, to buy higher profits through the sacrifice of other people's free time.

Thus, it is not an accident, as Hunnicut points out in his discussion of the factors responsible for the slowdown of 'the drive for shorter hours', that the opposition of American capital to shorter hours hardened with the emergence of 'business doubts about the link between increased productivity and shorter hours'.[45] From the point of view of capital, if shorter hours cannot themselves be a source of productivity gains, they are undesirable because they siphon off productivity gains in the direction of workers. Hunnicut also traces the historical forces in the early twentieth century through which work came to be viewed as an end in itself. Although the experience of the Depression contributed to this outcome, capital and its representatives also played a role in this remarkable discursive development:

> Businessmen also defended work against the threat of shorter hours by attacking the notion that work was unpleasant – some kind of trial or a negative part of living. They spoke of work as a "joy"…In contrast to the previous two decades, when work as a social value was undergoing a 'crisis', in this decade [1920s] few such doubts remained, at least in business and trade publications.[46]

The ability of capitalists to use their economic resources to influence public debate shows another limitation of those non-Marxist accounts of our economic system's irrational productivism and consumerism that downplay the significance of the power relations inherent within capitalism. For Robert Frank, for example, consumerist patterns that do not advance our welfare as effectively as more free time would are due to ignorance, and to our failure to understand both the sources of these patterns 'and how painless it would be to change them'.[47] Like Galbraith, then, Frank places his hopes on the market of ideas and the long-term capacity of good ideas to prevail, ignoring how a highly unequal capitalist society lends an inherently productivist bias to the market of ideas.[48] No market of ideas can be expected to perform its function properly when it is embedded in a highly unequal capitalist society.

Capital's ability to translate productivity increases into growing production rather than reduced working hours for all is supported by another feature of capitalist society that is usually neglected by mainstream economics. For mainstream economics the amount of time people devote to work tends to reflect their preferences between free time and income. Juliet Schor, however, identifies an important obstacle to people's ability to pursue a satisfying life when she points out that in the United States, for example, there is no true market for free time since workers usually do not have the option 'to trade off income gains for a shorter work day' and cannot shift to part-time work without incurring a heavy 'economic penalty' in the form of lower pay rates.[49] Another reason for long work hours in the United States is that overtime pay legislation does not cover salaried workers. As their pay does not vary with amount of work, their marginal cost to employers is zero, who can, for that reason, push them to '[toil] at nineteenth-century schedules'.[50]

All of this points to the difference between the abstract models of a market economy that neoclassical economists work with and the realities of a capitalist economy that involves power relations that inevitably shape the way markets operate. The degree to which labour markets provide workers with the possibility to select the optimum for them mix of free time and income depends on social and labour legislation. The fact that recent moves towards economic and labour 'flexibility' have catered more to the needs of employ-ers than those of workers reflects the disproportionate level of economic power and political influence that capitalist inequalities accord capital and its representatives.[51] As Schor points out, the absence of a market for free time is consistent with capital's interest in long hours, so that a challenge of this absence would inevitably represent a challenge to capital. It would also represent, however, a challenge to a socio-economic system that accords disproportionate power to a privileged minority with a stake in policies that frustrate the translation of growing productive and technological potentials into a richer and more satisfying human life.

Individual choice between income and free time is distorted by capitalism's bias for growth and consumption in yet another way. As Conrad Lodziak has pointed out, the unnecessarily long days that most people have to work in capitalist societies drain them of their energy. This means that long workdays tend to leave people under-resourced to pursue, in their free time, creative activities, which might be demanding and challenging, but which also would increase the satisfaction that they could derive from the use of their free time. Instead, people are more likely to pursue less demanding activities, such as watching TV or going to the mall, which are either consumption-intensive or expose them to endless advertisements.[52] Thus a vicious cycle is generat-ed: capitalism's bias for growth and consumption shapes people's preferences in ways that devalue free time while increasing the appeal of commodities; then these distorted preferences further reinforce capitalism's translation of productivity increases into growing consumption rather than reduced work time. Capital's ability to accumulate is thus predicated on a stagnation of the human enjoyment that can be derived from the immense technological and productive potentials that capital accumulation also generates.

'THE SALES EFFORT' AND CAPITALISM'S CULTIVATION OF CONSUMERISM

Another way in which contemporary capitalism systematically frustrates hu-man enjoyment is through the growing importance of 'the sales effort'. As critically oriented economists and scholars have long pointed out, one of the most important developments in twentieth-century capitalism was the emergence of a rapidly growing apparatus for marketing commodities.[53] This apparatus relies on scientific research, employs the creative talent of a grow-ing army of design, advertising and marketing professionals, and oversees the investment of commodities with meanings that are culturally valued and play on the consuming public's deepest longings, aspirations and fears.

The rising importance of the sales effort has been just one aspect of the project, more or less consciously pursued by twentieth-century capitalist elites, to build a consumer culture capable of reducing labour resistance in the workplace, containing capitalism's economic crisis tendencies and turning people's discontent with the problems of life in a capitalist society into fuel for further capital accumulation.[54] The mobilization of cultural meanings by the 'commodity sign industry' parasitically feeds on the cultural creativity of diverse contemporary subcultures.[55] In attempting to associate standardized commodities with images and subcultures that are accorded 'social and cultural value', contemporary capitalism often trivializes the meanings it employs.[56]

Nonetheless, the endowment of commodities with culturally valued meanings simultaneously implies the increasing association of cultural values with the appropriate commodities. As capitalist consumer culture continues to liquidate non-commercialized local cultures, the 'migration of meanings and values from relationships with people to relationships with market goods and spectacles' channels people's consumption preferences and conceptions of the 'good life' in a consumerist direction.[57] The result is not just the already discussed bias against free time, but also a systematic alienation of people from their ability to pursue enjoyment through an autonomous creation of meaning.

This alienation is an outgrowth of the alienation at the basis of capitalist society, namely that of producers from the means of production. Beyond forcing the majority of the population to sell their labour power for survival, this alienation also makes it possible to organize the social construction of meaning in ways that favour capital accumulation. Indeed, one of the functions of the separation of producers from the means of production is to reduce the time working people can devote to the task of gaining the information they need in order to be less vulnerable to the seductions of advertising and to the ability of capital to subordinate the creation of meaning to its quest of profitability.[58] The separation of producers from the means of production does not just undercut the autonomy of individuals qua consumers but also gives capital access to the time, ingenuity and creativity of the workers who specialize in the appropriation, processing and subordination of cultural meanings to the quest of capitalist profitability. A growing number of workers are engaged in this type of activity, ranging from workers carrying out traditional advertising and marketing functions to the 'cool hunters' who scour inner cities and assorted subcultural milieus to investigate and exploit the ever-changing conceptions of culturally valued traits.[59]

The consumerist conception of the good life that capitalism engenders undercuts human enjoyment in more than one way. Apart from distorting people's relative valuation of income and free time, this conception interacts with the meritocratic illusions capitalism engenders to separate people into 'winners' and 'losers'. In particular, the fact that the reproduction of class relations in capitalist society is mediated by market competition and a certain degree of socio-economic mobility lends credence to the ideological portrayal of those at the top as worthy individuals who owe their success to nothing but their talent and hard work. As the labels 'winner' and 'loser' are invested with intense emotional content, moreover, conforming to consumption norms becomes a source of pleasure in its own right. As satisfaction increasingly becomes a function of relative rather than absolute levels of consumption, satisfaction increasingly becomes a positional good, the availability of which does not change with ever growing average levels of consumption. Thus the consumerist conception of the good life that capitalism encourages also gives rise to the kind of wasteful consumption races that Robert Frank attributes to fanciful causes, such as the biological evolution of the human species.[60]

It is possible to imagine ways in which capital's ability to subordinate cultural meanings to the imperatives of capital accumulation could be curbed. Imagine an alternative regulatory framework in which advertising, on behalf of businesses, was carried out by independent public bodies that had as their mandate not the persuasion of consumers but the provision of reliable information. In this framework, advertising might include an objective comparison of the advertised commodity to close substitutes. Companies seeking to advertise their products could also be required to make substantial contributions to a fund devoted to the advertising of non-commodified public goods, so that the problem of social balance discussed by Galbraith could also be redressed.[61]

What would be the effects of such a regulatory framework? Advertising would lead to more reliable information for consumers. Instead of distorting people's choice between consumer goods and free time and contributing to consumerism and the waste of the productive and technological potential of our society, advertising could save people time by making consumer choice easier and less uncertain. The amount of resources devoted to advertising would also probably decrease, since such a framework would give only companies with high quality products an incentive to advertise.

Modest as such a proposal may sound, it would be a challenge to capital's preference for a consumerist society that leads to a stagnation of human satisfaction through its systematic bias for economic growth and against free time.

Once again, the disproportionate power that capitalism accords capital and its representatives becomes an obstacle to policies that could increase human satisfaction and enrich human life. This does not mean, of course, that pursuing such policies is impossible. What it does mean is that to the extent that social movements were successful in their pursuit of the type of labour market and advertising reforms sketched in this essay, capital profitability might be affected negatively. In this respect, what O'Connor says about the second contradiction also applies to the third contradiction. This contradiction has both a legitimation and a profitability dimension. Just as the existence of this contradiction threatens to delegitimize capitalism by exposing its fundamental irrationality, the social reform movements that this contradiction can potentially give rise to could undercut capitalist profitability.

CONCLUSIONS

The three contradictions addressed in this essay should be treated as analytical tools that can be used to illuminate specific social, economic and political conjunctures and the challenges and possibilities that such conjunctures pose for emancipatory movements. Thus, instead of a teleological interpretation of these contradictions as parallel paths to socialism, the conception advanced here would lead us to focus on the ways in which the ever-changing articulation of these contradictions becomes a constitutive element of specific historical conjunctures.

The status of economic growth as an unquestioned ideal of capitalist society speaks to the relationship between the first and the third contradictions. The appeal of economic growth in capitalist society is due to the fact that economic growth functions both as a substitute of economic redistribution and a means to averting unemployment and the chronic material insecurity confronting large parts of the population in capitalist economies.[62] Thus, economic growth helps to contain two implications of the first contradiction, the potential for class struggle against the rule of capital, and the precariousness of the position of working people within capitalist society. This means, however, that an effect of the first contradiction may be to strengthen the bias in favour of growth that is central to the third contradiction. At the same time, however, the urgency of the demand for material security may also obscure the irrationality of capitalist society that becomes manifest in the third contradiction. Capitalism's inability to translate productive and technological advances into a richer, more satisfying life may seem as a secondary, and relatively abstract, concern to anyone struggling to secure basic material survival.

In encouraging a blind faith in economic growth, the first contradiction can also aggravate the impact of the second contradiction. This also means that the second contradiction places limits on capitalism's ability to contain the negative impacts of the first contradiction through economic growth. O'Connor's formulation of the second contradiction suggests that the degradation of the conditions of production can be the result of capital's adoption of cost-cutting measures.[63] Provided that such measures are a response to economic pressures generated by the first contradiction, the first contradiction can aggravate the impact of the second contradiction. O'Connor also suggests that the first contradiction itself can be the result of capital's cost-cutting measures.[64] Provided that such measures are the result of a supply-side crisis generated by the second contradiction, and that the cost-cutting measures undercut wages and employment to the point of triggering a demand-side crisis, the second contradiction can add to the economic crisis potential generated by the operation of the first contradiction.[65] As pointed out above, however, it is also true that the first contradiction could alleviate the impact of the second contradiction if it led to Keynesian government projects that sought to boost aggregate demand by repairing the conditions of production degraded by the operation of the capitalist economy.

Just as it places limits on capitalism's ability to contain the impacts of the first contradiction through economic growth, the second contradiction also makes the compulsive productivism and consumerism associated with the third contradiction harder to sustain. At the same time, the compulsive consumerism associated with the third contradiction can help to contain economic crisis tendencies emanating from the first contradiction. Thus, for example, the recognition of this possibility led to the conscious project by capitalist elites to address the threat of overproduction facing the American economy in the 1920s through the construction of a consumerist culture and the formulation of what Hunnicut has aptly described as a 'gospel of consumption'.[66]

However, things look very different today when we look at the current conjuncture of global capitalism, which like any other is in large part defined by the articulation of capitalism's three contradictions. As capitalism continues to aggravate global environmental problems, not least global warming, the third contradiction does provide some cause for optimism. If the compulsive productivism and consumerism generated by our social system does not, beyond a certain level of affluence, add to people's life satisfaction, then the drastic revision of consumerist lifestyles is not so much a sacrifice that present generations have to make for the sake of future generations, but a matter of self-interest for present and future generations alike.

Such a revision would only be possible as part of a transition to a fundamentally different society which would facilitate the translation of increasing technological potential into greater human happiness. It would also make possible a global redistribution of resources that would address the social injustice at the core of the first contradiction, while also reducing the impact of economic activity on the planet. As the curse of capitalism's second contradiction was lifted, it would become possible to place technology at the service of human development without, at the same time, degrading the natural, cultural and human 'conditions of production'.

NOTES

1   See, for example, Herman Daly, 'Steady-State Economics', in C. Merchant, ed., *Key Concepts in Critical Theory: Ecology*, Amherst: Humanity Books, 1994, and Saral Sarkar, *Eco-socialism or Eco-capitalism? A Critical Analysis of Humanity's Fundamental Choices*, New York: Zed Books, 1999.

2   Cf. W.W. Rostow, *The Stages of Economic Growth: A Non-communist Manifesto*, New York: Cambridge University Press, 1965.

3   Beverley Silver and Giovanni Arrighi, 'Workers North and South', *Socialist Register 2001*, p. 72.

4   See Alan Durning, *How Much is Enough?*, New York: W.W. Norton & Company, 1992 and Robert E. Lane, *The Loss of Happiness in Market Democracies*, New Haven: Yale University Press, 2000.

5   See James O'Connor, 'The Second Contradiction of Capitalism', in Ted Benton, ed., *The Greening of Marxism*, New York: Guilford, 1996.

6   Ibid, p. 202.

7   Ibid, p. 200.

8   Ibid.

9   See James O'Connor, *Natural Causes*, New York: Guilford, 1998, p. 307.

10   Karl Polanyi, *The Great Transformation*, Boston: Beacon Press, 1957.

11   O'Connor, *Natural Causes*, p. 307.

12   Ibid, p. 308.

13   Ibid.

14   O'Connor, 'The Second Contradiction', p. 211.

15   See, for example, 'Culture, Nature and the Materialist Conception of History' in *Natural Causes*.

16   O'Connor, 'The Second Contradiction', p. 211.

17   Ibid, p. 205.

18   Ibid, p. 203.

19   Ibid.

20   Marshall Berman, *All that is Solid Melts into Air: The Experience of Modernity*, New York: Simon and Schuster, 1982, p. 103.

21   Costas Panayotakis, 'A Marxist Critique of Marx's Theory of History: Beyond the Dichotomy Between Scientific and Critical Marxism', *Sociological Theory*,

22(1), 2000. The rest of the paragraph provides a brief summary of the argument advanced in this article.

22   O'Connor, *Natural Causes*, p. 10.

23   Ibid, p. 176.

24   Ibid, pp. 272-73.

25   On the first contradiction as a 'demand crisis', see James O'Connor, 'Is Sustainable Capitalism Possible?', in Martin O'Connor, ed., *Is Capitalism Sustainable? Political Economy and the Politics of Ecology*, New York: Guilford, 1994, pp. 160 and 162.

26   O'Connor, *Natural Causes*, pp. 272-73.

27   O'Connor, 'The Second Contradiction', p. 160.

28   O'Connor, *Natural Causes*, p. 272.

29   O'Connor, 'Is Sustainable Capitalism Possible?', p. 165.

30   Ibid, p. 162.

31   See Samuel Bowles, David M. Gordon and Thomas E. Weisskopf, *After the Waste Land: A Democratic Economics for the Year 2000*, Armonk: M.E. Sharpe, 1991, p. 28.

32   O'Connor, 'The Second Contradiction', p. 203.

33   O'Connor, *Natural Causes*, p. xiii.

34   O'Connor, 'The Second Contradiction', p. 203.

35   O'Connor, *Natural Causes*, p. 150.

36   See, for example, Richard A. Easterlin, 'Does Satisfying Material Needs Increase Human Happiness?', in Richard A. Easterlin, ed., *Growth Triumphant: The Twenty-First Century in Historical Perspective*, Ann Arbor: The University of Michigan Press, 1996; and Lane, *The Loss of Happiness*.

37   See, for example, Robert H. Frank, *Luxury Fever: Why Money Fails to Satisfy in an Era of Excess*, New York: Free Press, 1999; and Fred Hirsch, *Social Limits to Growth*, Cambridge: Harvard University Press, 1976.

38   See, for example, Frank, *Luxury Fever*, p. 92.

39   See, for example, Juliet B. Schor, *The Overworked American: The Unexpected Decline of Leisure*, New York: Basic Books, 1991 and Gary Cross, *Time and Money: The Making of Consumer Culture*, London: Routledge, 1993.

40   In *The Overworked American* Schor rightly points out that 'it is capitalism, not industry, that has been responsible for expanding work schedules' (p. 164). By the time Schor writes *The Overspent American*, however, a subtle shift in her tone is detectable as a systemic critique of capitalism's bias against free time is replaced by a discussion of European capitalism as an attractive model capable of reaching a better balance between economic growth and free time. See, Juliet B. Schor, *The Overspent American: Upscaling, Downshifting, and the New Consumer*, New York: Basic Books, 1998, pp. 171-73.

41   See Cross, *Time and Money*, p. vii.

42   See Pietro Basso, *Modern Times, Ancient Hours: Working Hours in the Twenty-First Century*, edited and translated by Giacomo Donis, London: Verso, 2003.

43   Schor, *The Overworked American*, p. 3.

44   These reasons included 'mechanization in the second half of the nineteenth century, the use of long hours and the concept of employment rent to promote

workplace discipline, by the twentieth century, and the bias created by the structure of fringe benefits since the Second World War'. See Schor, *The Overworked American*, p. 59.

45   See Benjamin Kline Hunnicutt, *Work Without End: Abandoning Shorter Hours for the Right to Work*, Philadelphia: Temple University Press, 1988, p. 310.

46   Ibid, p. 47.

47   Frank, *Luxury Fever*, p. 278.

48   See John Kenneth Galbraith, *The New Industrial State*, Fourth Edition, New York: New American Library, 1985, pp. 200–01, and Frank, *Luxury Fever*, p. 279.

49   Schor, *The Overworked American*, pp. 3; 133–34.

50   Ibid, p. 68.

51   See Basso, *Modern Times*, and Carmen Siriani, 'The Self-Management of Time in Postindustrial Society', in Karl Hinrichs, William Roche and Carmen Siriani, eds., *Working Time in Transition: The Political Economy of Working Hours in Industrial Nations*, Philadelphia: Temple University Press, 1991, p. 263.

52   See Conrad Lodziak, *The Myth of Consumerism*, London: Pluto Press, 2002.

53   See, for example, Galbraith, *The Affluent Society* and *The New Industrial State*; and Paul A. Baran and Paul M. Sweezy, *Monopoly Capital: An Essay on the American Economic and Social Order*, New York: Modern Reader Paperbacks, 1968, ch. 5.

54   For useful accounts of the historical process through which a consumer culture was created in the twentieth century, see Cross, *Time and Money*; Hunnicut, *Work Without End*; Stuart Ewen, *Captains of Consciousness: Advertising and the Social Roots of the Consumer Culture*, New York: McGraw-Hill, 1977; and Richard H. Robbins, *Global Problems and the Culture of Capitalism*, Third Edition, Boston: Allyn and Bacon, 1999, ch. 1.

55   Cf. Robert Goldman and Stephen Papson, 'Advertising in the Age of Accelerated Meaning', in Juliet B. Shor and Douglas B. Holt, eds., *The Consumer Society Reader*, New York: The New Press, 2000, p. 85.

56   Ibid, pp. 81, 91.

57   Douglas B. Holt, 'Does Cultural Capital Structure American Consumption?', in Schor and Holt, *The Consumer Society Reader*, p. 247.

58   Even neoclassical economists, such as Staffan Linder, have recognized the link between scarcity of time and vulnerability to advertising. According to Linder: 'People can be made the victims of persuasion, not because they are irrational, but because they are rational….[T]o obtain complete information, one would have in fact to…spend all one's time reading consumer reports, and otherwise acquiring information on economic matters. The majority of people will find, on calculation and reflection, that this would be an uneconomic way of allocating their time…By accepting a number of mistakes, one will gain more than sufficient time to offset these mistakes by greater income from work. But as soon as one lacks complete information, one is also exposed to the possibility of being influenced by advertising.' (See Staffan Burenstam Linder, *The Harried Leisure Class*, New York: Columbia University Press, 1970, pp. 73-4.) As this quotation indicates, Linder assumes that people's vulnerability to advertising is an outgrowth of their fundamentally rational allocation of time to different

uses. Thus, Linder does not even consider the possibility, discussed earlier in this essay, that, in cultivating a consumerist conception of the good life, advertising may contribute to a sub-optimal allocation of time between work and free time. He also does not consider the fact that scarcity of time is aggravated by the fact that capitalist society forces individuals to devote an unnecessarily large part of their life to the pursuit of basic survival.

59   Cf. Malcolm Gladwell, 'The Coolhunt', in Schor and Holt, *The Consumer Society Reader*.

60   See Frank, *Luxury Fever*.

61   See Galbraith, *The Affluent Society*.

62   See Galbraith, *The Affluent Society*, pp. 98-9 and Frithjof Bergmann, 'Ecology and New Work: Excess Consumption and the Job System', in Juliet B. Shor and Douglas B. Holt, eds., *The Consumer Society Reader*, New York: The New Press, 2000, pp. 489-90.

63   O'Connor, 'Is Sustainable Capitalism Possible?', p. 165.

64   Ibid, p. 160.

65   Ibid, p. 162.

66   See Hunnicut, *Work Without End*.

SOCIAL METABOLISM AND ENVIRONMENTAL CONFLICTS

JOAN MARTINEZ-ALIER

Ecological economics, which views the economy as a metabolic system of materials and energy flows, has a long tradition which arose alongside and, as we will see, close to, that of historical materialism. Ecological economists do not see the environment as one more sector of the economy, in the sense of the economics of agriculture or the economics of transport; they see the economy as a subsystem embedded in the environment, a subsystem open to the entry of energy and materials, and to the exit of waste (e.g. carbon dioxide). This 'metabolic' perspective implies that capital accumulation does not take place by itself, and it is not only based on the exploitation of labour and technical change. Economic and population growth lead to increased use of materials and energy, and therefore to greater waste production. Because of unequal property rights, and inequalities of power and income among humans (both international and within each country), pollution burdens and access to natural resources are also unequally distributed.

Capitalism (or, in general, the industrial system) advances into commodity frontiers because it uses more materials and energy, therefore it produces more waste, undermining the conditions of livelihood and existence not only of future generations but also of contemporary peripheral peoples, who complain accordingly. Such movements for environmental justice cannot be subsumed under the conflict between capital and labour. They may become a strong force in favour of sustainability and eco-socialism, and also against market-fundamentalism, because conflicts over the use of the environment are expressed in many languages of valuation. For instance, we know that economic growth goes together with increased emissions of greenhouse gases. Some social actors see climate change as an 'externality', the (damage or abatement) costs of which can be calculated in economic terms and compared to the benefits of economic growth. Others will appeal instead to the livelihood and rights of local peoples and/or future generations, or to the sacredness of nature, or to ecological and landscape values measured in their own units, or to the equal dignity of all humans when confronted by 'environmental racism'. Why should all evaluations of a given conflict (e.g. over gold or bauxite extraction in Peru or Orissa, over hydro-electrical dams in the North-East of India, over mangroves in Bangladesh or Honduras sacrificed to shrimp exports, or over the determination of an acceptable level of carbon dioxide emissions by the European Union), be reduced to a single dimension?[1] People who are poor, and whose health and lives are cheap, often appeal to non-monetary languages of valuation. It is only capitalism, with its fetishism of commodities (even fictitious commodities, as in the 'contingent valuation' methods of neoclassical environmental economics), that sees only one way to value the world. Ecological economics rejects such a simplification of complexity, favouring instead the acceptance of a plurality of incommensurable values. By rejecting money-reductionism in favour of value pluralism, ecological economics can contribute to the success of struggles over distribution. For instance, Via Campesina denies that modern agriculture really achieves productivity increases, pointing to its decreased efficiency of energy use, chemical pollution, loss of seed varieties, and loss of local cultures.[2]

INTELLECTUAL BACKGROUND

Contemporary authors working on social or industrial metabolism look at the economy in terms of energy and material flows.[3] This 'metabolic' view of the economy has roots not in economics but in the work of nineteenth century natural scientists. It was not until the 1960s that a few dissident economists (Nicholas Georgescu-Roegen, Kenneth Boulding, K.W. Kapp, Herman Daly) began to look at the economy as a subsystem embedded in a physical system of materials and energy flows.

This approach, however, deserves to be taken as seriously by socialists today as it was by Marx himself. His interest in the relations between the economy and the environment, particularly as regards capitalist agriculture, was expressed in the use, in his own drafts after 1857-58, and in *Capital,* of the notion of 'metabolism' (*Stoffwechsel*) between the economy and Nature. Marx became so keen on the concept of metabolism that in a letter to his wife (21 June 1856), he wrote charmingly that what made him feel like a man was his love for her, and not his love for Moleschott's metabolism or for the proletariat.[4] Marx was one generation younger than both Liebig (1803-73) and Boussingault (1802-87) who from 1840 onwards published their research on the cycles of plant nutrients (phosphorous, nitrogen, potassium) in the context of debates on decreasing agricultural yields. Their analyses of the composition of guano, and of other manures and fertilizers used by farmers, laid the foundations for agricultural chemistry. New agricultural rotations and new fertilizers made it impossible to assume that in Britain the produce of the land would increase more slowly than the number of workers employed on it; at the time production was increasing while the number of agricultural labourers was undergoing an absolute decline.[5] This was part of the reason why Marx was not worried about crises of subsistence. He attacked Malthus' belief in decreasing returns, and also Malthus' thesis that improving the situation of the poor was counterproductive because they would have more children. In February 1866 Marx wrote to Engels that Liebig's chemistry was more important than all the economists put together in order to dismiss the notion of decreasing returns in agriculture.[6] Later, around 1900, there were debates on 'how many people could the Earth feed'.[7] Some Marxists (e.g. Lenin) attacked not only Malthus but also late nineteenth century Neo-Malthusians, who were often radicals and feminists – e.g. Paul Robin and Emma Goldman.[8]

In his published writings, however, Marx did not consider energy flows, although the link between material metabolism (*Stoffwechsel*, exchanges of materials) and the flow of energy at the level of cells and organisms had been made in the 1840s. It was then also understood that agriculture meant changes in energy flows, and not only in the cycling of plants nutrients (J.R. Mayer, 1845, used '*Stoffwechsel*' to refer to energy flows).[9] Materials could to some extent be recycled, but energy could not. Heat could be transformed into movement, and also movement into heat, but much energy was dissipated in the latter process. The theory of the direction of the flow of energy was developed after the Second Law of thermodynamics was established in 1850.

Marx and Engels were keen on new sources of energy. One example will suffice. Under discussion at the time was the question whether hydrogen could be a net source of energy, depending on how much energy was required by electrolysis. In April 1866 Marx wrote to Engels that a certain M. Rebour had found a way of separating oxygen from hydrogen in water for very little expense. One intriguing point arises from Engels' unwillingness to accept that the First and Second Laws of thermodynamics could apply together: the 'dialectics of Nature' failed him there. As Engels became aware of Clausius' concept of entropy, he wrote to Marx: 'In Germany the conversion of the natural forces, for instance, heat into mechanical energy, etc., has given rise to a very absurd theory – that the world is becoming steadily colder... and that, in the end, a moment will come when all life will be impossible... I am simply waiting for the moment when the clerics seize upon this theo-

ry...'.[10] But Engels' dislike of the Second Law was not only motivated by its religious abuse. He thought (together with other contemporary authors) that ways would be found to re-use the heat irradiated into space.

Another interesting point is Engels' negative reaction, in letters to Marx written in 1882, to the work of S.A. Podolinsky.[11] Podolinsky had studied the law of entropy and the economic process, and he tried to convince Marx that this could be brought into the Marxist analysis. Politically he was not a Marxist but a Ukrainian federalist narodnik, and he complained of Marx's overbearing behaviour at the 1872 congress of the International, praising the anarchist James Guillaume. Nonetheless he saw his work on agricultural energetics as a contribution to Marxism. Writing to Marx in April 1880 he said: 'With particular impatience I wait for your opinion on my attempt to bring surplus labour and the current physical theories into harmony'. Podolinsky's analysis started out from the proposition that the Earth was receiving enormous quantities of energy from the sun, and would continue to do so for a very long time. All physical and biological phenomena were expressions of the transformations of energy. He was hoping (as he had written to Marx on 30 March 1880, when sending his work to him) to develop applications of energy flow accounting to different modes of production. He explained that plants assimilated energy, and animals fed on plants and degraded energy. This formed the *Kreislauf des Lebens*:

> We have in front of us two parallel processes which together form the so-called circle of life. Plants have the property of accumulating solar energy, but animals, when they feed on vegetable substances, transform a part of this saved energy and dissipate this energy into space. If the quantity of energy accumulated by plants is greater than that dispersed by animals, then stocks of energy appear, for instance in the period when mineral coal was formed, during which vegetable life was preponderant over animal life. If, on the contrary, animal life were preponderant, the provision of energy would be quickly dispersed and animal life would have to go back to the limits determined by vegetable wealth. So, a certain equilibrium would have to be built between the accumulation and the dissipation of energy.[12]

Not only plants but also human labour had the virtue of retarding the dissipation of energy. Human labour achieved this by agriculture, although the work of a tailor, a shoemaker or a builder would also qualify as productive work, since they afforded 'protection against the dissipation of energy into space'. The energy available for humankind came mainly from the sun. Podolinsky gave figures for the solar constant. He explained how coal and oil, wind energy and water power, were all transformations of solar energy. He mentioned tides as another possible energy source. He then began his analysis of agricultural energetics, remarking that only a tiny proportion of solar energy was assimilated by plants. Human labour, together with the work of animals directed by humans, was able to increase the availability of energy by agricultural activity.

Podolinsky went on to explain the capacity of the human organism to do work – otherwise 'it would be difficult to explain the accumulation of energy on the surface of the earth under the influence of labour'. Quoting from Hirn and Helmholtz, he concluded (correctly) that 'man has the capacity to transform one-fifth of the energy gained from food into muscular work', giving to this ratio the name of 'economic coefficient', and remarking that man was a more efficient transformer of energy than a steam engine. He then used a steam-engine metaphor to propose a general theoretical principle concerning the minimum natural conditions of human existence, from an energy point of view. He wrote that humanity was a 'perfect machine', in Sadi Carnot's sense: 'humanity is a machine that not only turns heat and other physical forces into work, but succeeds also in carrying out the inverse cycle, that is, it turns work into heat and other physical forces which are necessary to satisfy our needs, and, so to speak, with its own work turned into heat is able to heat its own boiler'.[13] Taking into account that not everybody is able to work (children, old people), and that there are other energy needs apart from food, a proper discussion of the demographic question had to take into account the relation between the quantity of energy on earth and the quantity of people who live on it, and this was a more relevant view than the Malthusian prognosis.

Podolinsky interpreted capital accumulation not as increasing the produced means of production in financial terms, but as increasing the availability of energy (and of course also its dissipation). He emphasized the difference between using the flow of solar energy and the stock of coal energy. The task of labour was to increase the accumulation of solar energy on earth, rather than simply to transform energy already accumulated on earth into work, especially since work involving the use of coal was accompanied by a great dissipation of heat-energy into space. The energy productivity of a coalminer was much larger than that of a primitive farmer, but this energy surplus from coal was transitory. Podolinsky was not, however, pessimistic about the prospects for the economy. He was hopeful about the direct use of solar energy for industrial purposes. He could envisage that one day solar energy would be used directly to make chemical syntheses of nutritive sub-stances, by-passing agriculture.[14]

The link between the use of energy and the development of human cul-ture, in the form of 'social energetics', became well established and debat-ed in Europe around 1900. Some Marxist authors (Bogdanov, 1873-1928; Bukharin, 1888-1938) adopted this outlook, and their work has been seen as an anticipation of Bertalanffy's systems theory, which grew out of the links between thermodynamics and biology.[15] There is, however, no Marxist his-toriography that provides quantitative studies of material and energy flows, emphasizing their highly unequal distribution.

OTTO NEURATH

In my 1987 book, *Ecological Economics*, the relationship between Marxism and ecological economics was discussed mainly by looking at Engels' nega-tive reaction to Podolinsky's agricultural energetics. But it also looked at Otto Neurath's contribution to the Socialist Calculation debate of 1919 and the following years, already acknowledged by K. W. Kapp. Otto Neurath (1882-1945) was a famous analytical philosopher of the Vienna Circle; he was also an economist or economic historian, and a Marxist in at least two senses. First, in the Socialist Calculation debate he defended a democratically planned economy based on accounting in energy and material terms (*Natu-ralrechnung*), following Popper-Lynkeus' and Ballod-Atlanticus' quantitative, realistic 'utopias'. He introduced the idea of incommensurable values in the economy.[16] Second, some years later, in the context of the Vienna Circle's project for an Encyclopedia of Unified Science, Neurath defended a dialec-tical view of history (although he did not like the word 'dialectics') as the putting together of the findings of the different sciences on concrete proc-esses or events. The findings of one science with regard to a given particular process or event should not be contradicted by the assumptions or the find-ings of another science also included in the Encyclopedia. An attempt should be made to remove the contradiction. To use Edward Wilson's later word, 'consilience' should be the rule of the Encyclopedia.

To grasp the relevance of Otto Neurath one must realize that Hayek's strong critique of 'social engineering' was, as John O'Neill noted, direct-ed not only against thinkers like Saint-Simon but also against the tradition, now called ecological economics, which attempts to understand the ways in which economic institutions and relations are embedded within the physical world and have real physical preconditions, and which is consequently criti-cal of economic choices founded upon purely monetary valuation.[17] While Hayek rudely dismissed Patrick Geddes, Wilhelm Ostwald, Lancelot Hogben, Frederick Soddy and Lewis Mumford, his main targets were Neurath's *Naturalrechnung* and planning.

SOCIAL METABOLISM TODAY

The use of energy in the economy is more relevant than ever, as we contemplate the patterns of economic growth of India, China and other countries and their effects on oil and gas prices, the increased human use of biomass as fuel to the detriment of other species, the imminence of 'peak oil', the increased use of coal and its influence on the greenhouse effect, and the growth of nuclear power.[18] At the global level the use of all sources of energy is increasing. The consumption of biomass energy (food, feedstock and fuelwood), is estimated to have increased more than four-fold in the twentieth century, coal six-fold, and oil many times more. The notion of 'energy return on energy input' (EROI): that is, the energy cost of obtaining energy (in different systems: wind energy, tar sands, fuel-biomass, etc.), was applied to the economy by Charles Hall and other ecologists in the 1970s, raising questions about its economic implications.[19]

Since then research on material flows has made much progress. Eurostat statistics follow an agreed methodology developed through a debate in the 1990s.[20] In that framework, a complete balance for an economy can be carried out in the form of a Material Flow Analysis or MFA.[21] Metabolic profiles are established in terms of energy flows as well as material flows. Fossil fuels and biomass will show up both in the material and energy statistics, but nuclear energy and hydroelectricity are not included in the material flows. Here we focus on material flows.

In the Eurostat methodology (Figure 1), material flows are classified into three main material groups (minerals, fossil fuels and biomass) and into four main categories (domestic extraction, imports, exports and waste). Waste is in part recycled outside markets by natural cycles. A small part is recycled by markets (some paper, metals). The net accumulation of materials can be calculated as the difference between what enters the system and what goes out.

This kind of analysis yields a very different picture of an economy from that presented by conventional or Marxist economics. Taking, for instance, the MFA of Spain between 1980 and 2000, the conclusion is reached that Spain's nice trend towards convergence of per capita income within the European Union is matched by its 'race to the top' in material metabolism.[23] The materials moved by the Spanish economy (i.e. DMI = domestic extraction plus direct material imports) increased by 85 per cent from 1980 to 2000, whereas GDP increased by 74 per cent. While in other European countries there has been relative dematerialization (i.e. increased resource productivity), Spain followed a trend typical of developing economies. The growth of building

Figure 1: Economy-wide material balances (excluding air and water)[22]

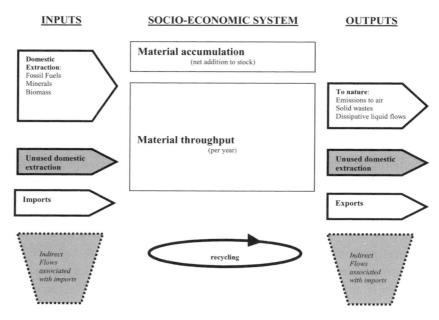

materials is remarkable, as is also the increase in energy-carrying materials, despite the decline of domestic coal extraction. The Spanish economy has become increasingly dependent on international trade. Imports are twice as large as exports in terms of weight: net imports have reached 3 tons per capita/year, displacing environmental loads elsewhere. Imports of biomass and particularly of oil and gas have increased. Also, metals that were domestically produced are now imported.

Taking all materials together (energy carriers, minerals, biomass), the European Union as a whole is importing about four times more tons than it is exporting, while Latin America appears to be exporting six times more tons than it imports.[24] Moreover, the South's exports carry heavier 'ecological rucksacks' than its imports, as shown by research on the energy and carbon-intensities of Brazil's trade – i.e. the energy dissipated, and the carbon dioxide produced, by each dollar of exports and imports – and by research on the 'environmental pollution terms of trade' for several metals.[25] Pengue has computed the hidden flows in the soybean trade of Argentina, in the form of loss of nutrients (this would have pleased Liebig and Marx), soil erosion, and 'virtual water'.[26] Will Argentina and Brazil now become large fuel-biomass exporters?

Pérez-Rincón gives figures for Colombia of 70 million tons of exports per year compared to 10 million tons of imports.[27] The periphery extracts and exports resources to satisfy the requirements of the centre. The theory of the deterioration of terms of trade in peripheral countries was formulated in parallel by Prebisch and Singer: an increased quantity of primary exports is needed to obtain the same amount of imported goods. Marxists pointed out that exports from poor countries were labour-intensive and produced by cheap labour, so there was also unequal exchange in terms of human labour.[28] Moreover, the centre-periphery division involves not only monetary exchanges but also physical exchanges in which Southern regions provide materials and energy so that the North can maintain and develop its socio-economic metabolism. In the United States oil imports are now over 10 mbd, i.e. 500 million tons or 2 tons per person per year. However, not all developing countries are net physical exporters: India and China are probably net importers (because of oil imports). Internally, some regions in India and China provide coal and other minerals. India exports much iron but also exports outsourced services. On the other hand, some rich countries with low populations (and high material and energy use per capita) are net resource-exporters (Canada, Australia), successfully following the path of Harold Innis' 'staples' theory of growth, contrary to much of Latin America, Africa and Indonesia. Whatever the historically changing positions of different countries or regions, the metabolic processes that maintain the world system's centres are underpinned by ecologically unequal exchange, deteriorating terms of trade for natural resources, exploitation of labour and, if necessary, by military force.

To summarize: economies today can be accurately described in terms of their metabolic profiles, as well as in terms of economic indicators such as growth of GDP, savings ratio, budget deficit as percentage of GDP, current account balance in the external sector, unemployment rate; or in terms of the social dimensions included in the Human Development Index (which, however, leads to a ranking not very different from that arrived at by GDP per capita). 'Metabolic profiles' of countries or regions are to be found in the statistics provided by MEFA (Material and Energy Flow Accounting) and by HANPP (human appropriation of net primary production of biomass).[29]

Economic, social and physical indicators give non-equivalent descriptions.[30] For example, a given economy may be described in the following non-equivalent terms: it provides 240 GJ of energy per person/year, material flow amounts to 21 tons per person/year of which fossil fuels account for 6 tons. Of the material flows, 5 tons are imported, one ton is exported. Income per capita is 25,000 US$. Of another economy, we may say that it provides only 25 GJ person/year, while its materials flow amounts to only 3.5 tons person/year. Income per capita is US$1,200 (in purchasing power parity). Different classes of people could also be classified according to their metabolic profiles. We could study the different trends in the various components of the metabolic flows as the economy grows.

METABOLIC PROFILES AND ECOLOGICAL CONFLICTS

It is in the context of such thinking that political ecology studies conflicts over access to natural resources and services, and the burdens of pollution or other environmental impacts. Externalities are not so much market failures as cost-shifting successes. There are links between each society's metabolic profile and conflicts at local, regional, national and global scales. If an economy were 'dematerializing' in an absolute sense (and not only, as in some countries, relative to GDP), then many such conflicts would be less pervasive and intense. Ecological conflicts are classified here according to the points in the 'commodity chains' where they occur. Given space limits, only a few examples are cited.

Conflicts over the extraction of materials and energy:

1. Mining and Oil extraction conflicts. Complaints about mines and smelters because of water and air pollution, and land occupation by open-cast mining and slag. Many such conflicts have long histories (e.g. Ashio in Japan or Rio Tinto in Southern Spain around 1900). Likewise conflicts over oil and gas extraction. (Networks active in 2006: Mines and Communities / Oilwatch). For instance, in the growing economy of India, there are disputes over the mining of coal, iron ore, uranium, bauxite, mainly in Orissa and Jharkhand, by national public or private companies or by transnational companies (e.g. the Alcan and Vedanta projects in Orissa).[31] There are conflicts over building materials, including some involving the deaths of officials who try to stop quarrying of sand by 'sand mafias' in Tamil Nadu.[32]

2. Biopiracy. The appropriation of genetic resources ('wild' or agricultural) without adequate payment or recognition of peasant or indigenous knowledge and/or ownership (including the extreme case of the Human Genome project). The term 'biopiracy' was introduced by Pat Mooney, of Rural Advancement Foundation International (RAFI), in 1993. The fact is old; the new name reveals a new sense of injustice.

3. Land Degradation. Soil erosion caused by unequal land distribution, or by pressure of export production. For instance, in some areas of Ecuador, poor peasants farm the mountain slopes while the valley bottoms are used for flowers for export. The crucial distinction between pressure of population and pressure of production on the sustainable use of land was first made by Blaikie and Brookfield in 1987.[33]

4. Plantations are not forests.[34] All over the world complaints are made against eucalyptus, pine, acacia plantations for wood or paper pulp or for cellulose production (often exported).[35] There is a clear link between export flows of biomass and the growth of such conflicts (e.g. the conflict on the Spanish ENCE cellulose plants in Uruguay in 2005).

5. Mangroves vs. shrimp. The movement to preserve mangroves for livelihood against the shrimp export industry, in Thailand, Honduras, Ecuador, Brazil, India, Philippines, Bangladesh, Sri Lanka, Indonesia.[36]

6. National / local fishing rights. Other forms of use of biomass give rise to other conflicts. Conflicts over fishing are both national and local. National conflicts lead to attempts to stop open access depredation by imposing exclusive fishing areas, as in Peru, Ecuador and Chile since the 1940s. The language here is public international law. Struggles also occur to defend (or establish) local communitarian fishing rights against industrial fishing (as in coastal India, or the lower Amazon).

Conflicts over transport, waste and pollution:

7. Complaints over oil spills from tankers or pipelines, over new motorways, harbours and airports, over electricity lines, or over 'hidrovías' (in Paraguay-Paraná); e.g., the Sethusamundram Ship Canal Project between Tamil Nadu and Sri Lanka that will shorten navigation time between the east and west coasts of India, but constitutes a threat to the local fisheries because of dredging. Physical indicators for transport (tons/km) grow faster than GDP, and faster than the material and energy throughput in the economy. Another case in point is the protest in Val di Susa in late 2005 against a new train line from Turin to Lyon (part of a wider European network) that would destroy a mountain landscape.

8. Toxic struggles. A name given in the US to struggles against risks from heavy metals or dioxins.[37] It describes also older cases in other countries, such as the Minamata mercury poisoning in Kumamoto Prefecture in Japan, caused by the chemical manufacturer Chisso Corporation in the 1950s and 1960s; complaints are still being made today.

9. Waste dumping. The ship-breaking yards at Alang (Gujarat) have a devastating environmental impact, a situation highlighted by the debate about a toxic Danish ship sent there in 2005, and again in February 2006 when Greenpeace won a court case in Paris forcing the aircraft carrier Clemenceau to come back to Europe for dismantling. Greenpeace had coined the term 'Toxic Imperialism' in 1988 to refer to waste dumping in poorer countries, the 'thousands of tonnes of electronic and electrical waste (e-waste)…being illegally exported every year…to developing Asian countries, including India, Pakistan, and China', a trade described by the New Delhi organization Toxic Links as 'absolutely illegal and against the spirit of the Basel Convention'.[38]

10. Transboundary pollution. This was a term applied in the 1970s and 1980s mainly to sulphur dioxide crossing borders in Europe, and producing acid rain; likewise from areas in central USA to New England, and from China to Japan.

11. Consumers' and citizens' safety. Struggles over the definition and the burden of unknown risks from new technologies (nuclear, GMO, etc.), which also affect producers (e.g. agro-toxics). Some conflicts are new (BSE, or 'mad cow disease'), others are old. Conflicts have arisen when regulatory authorities have failed to apply what is now called the 'precautionary principle'.[39] In China and India, the debate on nuclear safety will perhaps grow, given the growth of nuclear power.[40] Ulrich Beck focused on surprises (Chernobyl) more than on older technological conflicts (asbestos, DDT, CFC) or on well-known trends of metabolic flows (e.g. increased carbon dioxide emissions).[41]

12. Corporate accountability. When transnational corporations are involved, demands for 'corporate accountability' arise, e.g. claims under the Alien Tort Claims Act (ATCA) for compensation for damage caused in poor countries by Chevron-Texaco, Freeport-McMoRan Copper & Gold Inc., Southern Peru Copper Corporation, Dow Chemical and other companies. Another instance: the Indonesian authorities laid criminal charges against the world's biggest gold producer, the Newmont Mining Corporation, for disposing poisonous material into Buyat Bay in Sulawesi, damaging the inhabitants' health.[42] A similar case was settled out of court in 2004, when Unocal agreed to pay compensation in another ATCA case in California brought by Myanmar (Burma) villagers and Earth Rights International, concerning the Yadana gas pipeline to Thailand. Lack of corporate accountability is also at issue in the Bhopal case from 1984 to today.

13. Equal rights to carbon sinks. This refers to the proposal that there should be equal per capita use of the oceans, new vegetation, soils and atmosphere as sinks or temporary reservoirs for carbon dioxide.[43] Unequal emissions of carbon dioxide have given rise to a 'carbon debt', as Andrew Simms calls it.[44]

OTHER VOCABULARIES FOR ECOLOGICAL CONFLICTS

Claims for repayment of the 'ecological debt' owed by the North to the South bring together the 'carbon debt', i.e. damage done by rich countries through past and present excessive per capita emissions of carbon dioxide, and claims arising from biopiracy and ecologically unequal exchange. A contrast is also made between 'ecosystem peoples', who live off their own resources, and 'ecological trespassers' who live off the resources of other territories and peoples. This idea, proposed by Raymond Fredric Dasmann, was applied in India by M. Gadgil and R. Guha who identified three categories of people: 'omnivorous peoples', 'ecosystem peoples' and 'ecological refugees'.[45] 'Ecological footprint' is another term used in the context of international inequalities. The *'ecological footprint'* adds up the per capita use of food and other biomass, plus fossil fuels, plus the built environment, and translates it all into space. It has much merit as a communication device, and thrives politically, but it contains information that largely duplicates the energy (food, biomass and fossil fuels) statistics. Its success is due to its presentation of the issues in attractive spatial terms.[46]

Sometimes workers' struggles have had an ecological content, 'disguised' under different headings. For instance workers' actions for occupational health and safety are struggles (in the framework of collective bargaining or outside it) directly against capitalists to prevent damage in mines, plantations or factories (they are, so to speak, 'red' outside and 'green' inside). Something similar is true of urban activism for clean air, green spaces, sanitation, cyclists' and pedestrian rights. The actors (and the analysts) in such urban ecological conflicts have only recently learned an explicitly environmental vocabulary. Ecological conflicts also give rise to what Bina Agarwal called 'environmental feminism', meaning the environmental activism of women, motivated by their social situation.[47] The idiom of such struggles is not necessarily that of feminism and/or environmentalism. The 'environmentalism of the poor' describes social struggles with an ecological content, today and in history, of the poor against the relatively rich, mainly but not exclusively in rural contexts. Famous examples in the 1970s and 1980s were the Chipko movement in India, and Chico Mendes' struggle in Brazil.[48]

In resource extraction conflicts some actors deploy the language of 'indigenous environmentalism', that is, an appeal to territorial rights and ethnic resistance. In some cases Convention 169 of the ILO is cited, for example against gold mining in Sipacapa, Guatemala, in 2005. In India, similarly, the Constitution is appealed to for the protection of adivasi peoples through the courts.[49] The language of human rights is also used in environmental conflicts, since livelihoods and lives may be threatened. In the United States waste disposal has given rise to the notion of 'environmental racism', meaning the disproportionate environmental load in areas mainly inhabited by African Americans, Latinos, Native Americans. 'Environmental Justice' is used to describe the movement against 'environmental racism', in South Africa and Brazil (and also in Scotland where some relatively poor communities suffer from open-cast coal mining or waste dumps).[50] Uncertainties on the causes of illness have given rise to 'popular epidemiology'. 'Environmental blackmail' is a term applied to situations where 'locally unacceptable land use' (LULU) is finally accepted as the only alternative to the local population staying without jobs.

Table 1 classifies conflicts according to the stage of the commodity chains where they occur, and their geographical scale (local, national/regional, global). Local movements profit by adding the strengths of global environmentalism to their own local resistance, in turn reinforcing regional or global networks.

IDENTITY POLITICS OR STRUCTURAL CONFLICTS?

The defence of indigenous groups against oil extraction or mining, or against large dams, logging or biopiracy, and the 'environmental justice' movements insofar as they fight against 'environmental racism', may be seen as expressions of 'identity politics'. This is mistaken, however, because the conflicts arise from structural causes and because there are cross-cultural similarities between environmental resistance movements. Thus, in the fights around the world for biomass and against the private appropriation of common property lands, eucalyptus or other undesired plantation trees are pulled out, and other locally useful trees are put in. In another instance, in July 1998, I took part as a sympathetic observer in an action by Greenpeace together with Fundecol (a local grassroots group of about 300 people in Muisne, Ecuador), in destroying at sunrise the crop of shrimps in an illegal pond by opening a hole in one wall, letting the water flow out, and replanting mangrove seedlings.[51] The presence of the Rainbow Warrior's motley crew gave moral strength to the local group but both the destruction of that particular pond, and the replanting, were ideas proposed earlier by Fundecol. In December 2003 I travelled in Orissa and Tamil Nadu. In the conflict over shrimp farming in Chilika Lake, the traditional fishermen (200,000) were opposing a bill that would give rights to other groups practicing 'improved traditional' methods of fishing. Behind the words 'improved traditional' (taken from the

Table 1: A tentative classification of some ecological distribution conflicts

Geographical scope ---------------- Stage	Local	National and Regional	Global
Extraction	E.g. resource conflicts in tribal areas, such as bauxite mining in Kashipur, Orissa.	Mangrove uprooting. Tree planting for export. Collapses of fisheries.	Worldwide search for minerals and fossil fuels, and bio-piracy by TNCs. Regulation of 'corporate accountability'.
Transport and Trade	Complaints on urban motorways because of noise, pollution, landscape loss.	Inter-basin water transport. Oil/gas pipelines (e.g. Burma to Thailand).	Oil spills at sea. Also, 'ecologically unequal exchange' because of large South to North material flows.
Waste and pollution, post-consumption	Conflicts on incinerators (dioxins), or on tropospheric ozone in urban areas.	Acid rain from sulphur dioxide. Nuclear waste, Yucca Mountain, Nevada, USA.	CO_2, CFC as causes of climate change/ozone layer destruction. Persistent organic pollutants (POPs) even in remote pristine areas. Claims for a 'carbon debt'.

Supreme Court's decision of 11 December 1996), they feared commercial prawn culture was lurking. After 10,000 fishermen of the Chilika Matysajivi Mahasangh had camped for a few days in Bhubaneswar the Orissa government withdrew the bill for public consultation.[52] Further south, in Killai (Cuddalore District) in Tamil Nadu, where about 8,000 families made a living by fishing and agriculture, and where there were about 60 shrimp farms in 750 acres of cultivable *patta* and *poramboke* land, there was water pollution from the shrimp farms. As in Ecuador, so in Tamil Nadu, the proposal arose to break open the bunds of the shrimp farms. At midnight on 18 September, 2003 the shutters were opened. The following morning the police arrested

92 fishermen, including 32 women. The Campaign against the Shrimp Industries (CASI) declared that since 'all the arrested persons are victims of destructive shrimp industries, and the enforcement authorities [foreseen in the Supreme Court's decision of 1996] have failed to protect the resources of the people... it is the duty of the state to withdraw all the criminal proceedings'.[53]

On the Pacific coast of South America, movements in defence of mangroves insist on their role as coastline defenders against recurrent Niños, and against the risk of rising sea levels due to the greenhouse effect. The same claim to be protecting the coastline (but this time against cyclones) is often made in Bangladesh, Thailand, India and Sri Lanka, particularly since the 2004 Tsunami. Similarly Oilwatch, born out of local conflicts between oil companies and local populations, has learnt to use 'greenhouse' arguments against oil extraction. Local groups complain against the impact of oil extraction (in Ecuador and Peru, as much as in the Niger Delta), pointing out also that more oil extraction means more carbon dioxide emissions. Stopping oil production at some wells (as happens sometimes), and a moratorium on oil extraction in fragile areas, would make a global contribution against climate change, deserving 'carbon credits'. Other conflicts seem to be prompted initially by global influences: witness the use of the language of 'biopiracy' in conflicts over property rights in *ayahuasca, uña de gato, sangre de drago* and *quinua*, and also in basmati rice, neem and turmeric, in both Latin America and India. It is therefore not convincing to see ecological conflicts as a manifestation of identity politics. It is rather the other way around: identity politics is one idiom in which environmental conflicts are expressed.

TOWARDS ECO-SOCIALISM

What, then, is the 'class nature' of environmental conflicts? James O'Connor in his 1988 theory of the 'second contradiction' of capitalism put the variety of actors in such conflicts centre-stage. While the 'first contradiction' of capitalism is between capital and labour, the 'second contradiction' is more widespread and cannot be subsumed under the first. This variety of actors (and languages of valuation) baffles believers in the doctrine that history should progress from assorted 'primitive rebels' to working class unions and political parties. Nevertheless, alternatives to the present economic system are being born out of such socio-environmental movements of resistance, pointing the way towards what one might call 'eco-socialism'.[54]

NOTES

1   S. Funtowicz and J. Ravetz, 'The Worth of a Songbird: Ecological Economics as a Post-Normal Science', *Ecological Economics*, 10(3), 1994.

2   D. Pimentel, et al., 'Food Production and the Energy Crisis', *Science*, 182, 1973.

3   R.U. Ayres, 'Industrial Metabolism', in J. Ausubel, ed., *Technology and Environment*, Washington, DC: National Academy Press, 1989; M. Fischer-Kowalski, 'Society's Metabolism. The Intellectual History of Material Flow Analysis, Part I, 1860–1970', *Journal of Industrial Ecology*, 2(1), 1998; H. Haberl, 'The Energetic Metabolism of Societies, Part I: Accounting Concepts', and 'The Energetic Metabolism of Societies, Part II: Empirical Examples', in *Journal of Industrial Ecology*, 5(1) and 5(2), 2001.

4   K. Marx and F. Engels, *Lettres sur les sciences de la nature et les mathematiques*, Paris: Mercure de France, 1976.

5   Karl Marx, *Capital*, Volume I, London: Penguin, 1992, chapter 13.

6   Marx and Engels, *Lettres*. Liebig's name was associated by his own wish with a new sector of the economy, the fertilizer industry. He is also seen as a founder of ecology, before the name itself was invented. E.J. Kormondy, *Readings in Ecology*, Englewoods Cliffs, NJ: Prentice-Hall, 1965. He developed an argument against latifundist agriculture and agricultural exports because the plant nutrients would not return to the soil, favouring instead small scale agriculture and dispersed settlements. Marx shared Liebig's opinion. J.B. Foster, who rediscovered Marx's 'metabolism', analyzed in depth Marx's debt to Liebig and other authors, and wrongly dismissed Moleshott's influence, not quoting his books (1850-52) on the 'circle of life' and the physiology of metabolism in plants and animals. Foster, *Marx's Ecology. Materialism and Nature*, New York: Monthly Review Press, 2000.

7   L. Pfaundler, 'Die Weltwirtschaft im Lichte der Physik', *Deutsche Revue*, 22(April-June), 1902, pp. 29-38, 171-82; J. Cohen, *How Many People Can The Earth Support?*, New York: Norton, 1995.

8   L. Gordon, *Woman's Body, Woman's Right. A Social History of Birth Control in America*, New York: Grossman, 1976; F. Ronsin, *La grève des ventres. Propagande néo-malthusienne et baisse de la natalité en France, 19-20 siècles*, Paris: Aubier-Montagne, 1980; E. Masjuan, *La ecología humana y el anarquismo ibérico: el urbanismo 'orgánico' o ecológico, el neo-malthusianismo y el naturismo social*, Barcelona: Icaria, 2000.

9   J.R. Mayer, *Die organische Bewegung in ihrem Zusammenhang mit dem Stoffweschsel*, C. Drechsler: Heilbronn, 1845; Haberl, 'The Energetic Metabolism'.

10   21 March 1869, in Marx and Engels, *Lettres*.

11   Marx and Engels, *Lettres*. S.A. Podolinsky, 'Trud cheloveka i ego otnoshenie k raspredeleniiu energii', *Slovo*, 4/5, 1880, pp. 135-211. That is, human labour and its relations to the distribution of energy. (A Spanish translation was published in J. Martinez-Alier, ed., *Los principios de la Economía Ecológica*, Madrid: Argentaria-Visor, 1995). The German version with the title 'Menschliche Arbeit und Einheit der Kraft', appeared in *Die Neue Zeit*, Volume I, 1883, pp. 413-24, 449-57.

12   Author's translation of Podolinsky, 'Menschliche Arbeit und Einheit der Kraft',

p. 420.

13   Ibid., p. 453.

14   Podolinsky's work and life have a significance of their own, apart from his brief encounters with Marx and Engels. He is relevant for the history of ecological economics because he authored one of the first studies of the socio-metabolic flow of energy. Trained as a medical doctor and physiologist, he had a short life but left a strong trace in Ukrainian federalist politics (as a friend of Draho-manov) and also in the Narodnik movements against the Russian autocracy (as a young colleague of Piotr Lavrov though with close friends in the Narodnaya Volya group). His work on energy and the economy was praised by Vernadsky in *La Géochimie*, Paris: Alcan, 1924. Several authors (Felix Auerbach with his no-tion of *Ektropismus*, and John Joly) had explained life as a process which reversed or slowed down the dissipation of energy. Vernadsky then added a memorable phrase: Podolinsky had studied the energetics of life and tried to apply his find-ings to the study of the economy (pp. 334-5).

15   I. Susiluoto, *The Origins and Development of Systems Thinking in The Soviet Union. Political and Philosophical Controversies from Bogdanov and Bukharin to Present-Day Reevaluations*, Helsinki: Suomalainen Tiedeakatemia, 1982.

16   J. Martinez-Alier, with K. Schlüpmann, *Ecological Economics: Energy, Environ-ment and Society*, Oxford: Blackwell, 1987; J. O'Neill, *Ecology, Policy and Politics*, London: Routledge, 1993; J. Martinez-Alier, G. Munda and J. O'Neill, 'Weak Comparability of Values as a Foundation for Ecological Economics', *Ecological Economics*, 26, 1998; J. O'Neill, 'Socialist Calculation and Environmental Valua-tion: Money, Markets and Ecology', *Science and Society*, 66(1), 2002; J. O'Neill, 'Ecological Economics and the Politics of Knowledge: The Debate Between Hayek and Neurath', *Cambridge Journal of Economics*, 28, 2004; T.E. Uebel, 'In-commensurability, Ecology and Planning: Neurath in the Socialist Calculation Debate, 1919-1928', *History. of Political Economy*, 37(2), 2005.

17   John O'Neill, 'Socialist Calculation and Environmental Valuation: Money, Mar-kets and Ecology', *Science and Society*, 66(1), 2002, p. 137; F.A Hayek, *The Coun-ter-Revolution of Science: Studies on the Abuse of Reason*, Second Edition, Indiana-polis: Liberty Press, (1952) 1979.

18   F. Cottrell, *Energy and Society: The Relations between Energy, Social Change and Economic Development*, New York: McGraw Hill, 1955; R.P. Sieferle, *Der unterird-ische Wald. Energiekrise und industrielle Revolution*, Munich: Beck, 1982 (English trans., Cambridge: White Horse Press, 2001); J.C. Debeir, J.P. Deléage and D. Hémery, *Les servitudes de la puissance. Une histoire de l'energie*, Paris: Flammarion, 1986; C. Hall, C.J. Cleveland and R. Kaufman, *Energy and Resources Quality: The Ecology of the Economic Process*, New York: Wiley, 1986; C.J. Cleveland, 'Biophysi-cal Economics: Historical Perspectives and Current Recent Trends', *Ecological Modelling*, 38, 1987.

19   H.T. Odum, *Environment, Power and Society*, New York: Wiley, 1971.

20   S. Brigenzu and H. Schütz, 'Total Material Requirement of the European Un-ion' in European Environmental Agency, ed., Technical Report No. 55, Copen-hagen: EEA, 2001; EUROSTAT, 'Economy-wide Material Flow Accounts and Derived Indicators - A Methodological Guide', Luxembourg: Office for Of-

ficial Publications of the E.C., 2001; A. Adriaanse, et al., *Resource Flows. The Material Basis of Industrial Economies*. Washington, DC: World Resources Institute, 1997; E. Matthews, et al. *The Weight of Nations. Material Outflows from Industrial Economies*. Washington DC: World Resources Institute, 2000.

21   Material Flow Analysis consists in counting in tons all the inputs to the economic system, separated into Biomass, Fossil Fuels, Building Materials, Other Materials (metals), counting also which part accumulates as stock and which part becomes a throughput in the economy and reappears as output (waste), also counted in tons. The largest part of the output is carbon dioxide. Eurostat publishes such balances for European Union countries.

22   Accounting definitions:
Domestic Extraction: materials extracted in the national territory per year.
Direct Material Input (DMI): Domestic Extraction (DE) plus Direct Material Imports (I) (DMI=DE+I).
Domestic Material Consumption (DMC): DMI minus Direct Material Exports (E) (DMC=DMI-E=DE+I-E).
Water is excluded from MFA because its weight is of the order of one hundred times more than the material flows, and it would overshadow all trends. However, water use should be added to the metabolic profiles. The political ecology of water focuses on conflicts on dams such as in India the Narmada Bachao Andolan, also new conflicts in Pulichintala or in the North-East, and complaints against the 'interlinking of the rivers'. Also, conflicts on the use and pollution of aquifers (of which the Plachimada conflict in Kerala between farmers and the Coca-Cola company became world famous – there are many other such conflicts, often involving caste and gender inequalities). In Brazil there is an organized movement of *atingidos por barragens*. In 2005 a successful civic resistance movement led by a local bishop, stopped water transfer from the Sao Francisco river (see http://www.irn.org). The political ecology of water also studies the dumping of waste into water, or the energy and environmental impacts of new desalination projects, or the use and prices of water. There is also a new discussion on 'virtual water' (i.e. the water 'cost' of different products). Cf. A.Y. Hoekstra and P.Q. Hung, *Virtual Water Trade: A Quantification of Virtual Water Flows Between Nations in Relation to International Crop Trade*, Value of Water Research Report Series No. 11, Delft: UNESCO-IHE, 2002. See: http://www.waterfootprint.org.

23   S. Cañellas, et al., 'Material Flow Accounting of Spain', *International Journal of Global Environmental Issues*, 4(4), 2004.

24   S. Giljum and N. Eisenmenger, 'North-South Trade and the Distribution of Environmental Goods and Burdens', *Journal of Environment and Development*, 13(1), 2004.

25   G. Machado, R. Schaeffer and E. Worrell, 'Energy and Carbon Embodied in the International Trade of Brazil: An Input-Output Approach', *Ecological Economics.*, 39(3), 2001; R. Muradian, M. O'Connor and J. Martinez-Alier, 'Embodied Pollution in Trade: Estimating the "Environmental Load Displacement" of Industrialized Countries', *Ecological Economics*, 41(1), 2002.

26   Walter A. Pengue, 'Transgenic Crops in Argentina. The Ecological and Social

Debt', *Bulletin. of Science, Technology and Society*, 25(4), 2005.

27   M.A. Pérez-Rincón, 'Colombian International Trade from a Physical Perspective: Towards an Ecological "Prebisch Thesis"', *Ecological Economics*, in press, 2006.

28   R. Prebisch, El desarrollo económico de la América Latina y algunos de sus principales problemas, Santiago de Chile: ECLAC, E/CN, 12/89, 1949; H.W. Singer, 'The Distribution of the Gains between Investing and Borrowing Countries', *American Economic Review*, 40, 1950; A. Emmanuel, *Unequal Exchange: A Study of the Imperialism of Free Trade*, New York: Monthly Review Press, 1972.

29   The HANPP is not yet an official statistic. It is calculated in three steps. First, the potential net primary production (in the natural ecosystems of a given region or country), NPP, is calculated. Then we calculate the actual net primary production (normally, less than potential NPP, because of agricultural simplification, soil sealing), and then we calculate which part of actual NPP is used by humans and associate beings (cattle, etc.): this is the HANPP, meant to be an index of loss of biodiversity (because the higher the HANPP, the less biomass available for 'wild' species). This assumed relation is itself a topic for research. Results for Austria are presented in F. Krausmann et al., 'Land-Use Change and Socio-Economic Metabolism in Austria, Part I: Socio-Economic Driving Forces of Land-Use Change 1950-1995' and H. Haberl et al., 'Land-Use Change and Socio-Economic Metabolism in Austria, Part II: Land-Use Scenarios 1995-2020', both published in *Land Use Policy*, 20(1), 2003. Another research objective would be the modelling of the relations between MEFA and HANPP variables. For instance, intensive agriculture and use of fossil fuels has slightly decreased HANPP in Europe compared to the 1950s. An increase in the use of fossil fuels for cooking (kerosene or LPG) in India might lead to a slight decrease in HANPP, and therefore, to less pressure on wild biodiversity (so that kerosene and LPG would be good for the tigers). On the contrary, use of more fuel-biomass instead of fossil fuels, would reduce net emissions of carbon dioxide, but increase HANPP.

30   M. Giampietro, *Multiple-scale Integrated Assessment of Agroecosystems*, Boca Raton, FL: CRC Press, 2003.

31   *Down to Earth,* 15 April 2005, pp. 26-35.

32   *The Hindu*, 17 December 2004.

33   P. Blaikie and H. Brookfield, *Land Degradation and Society*, London: Methuen, 1987.

34   R. Carrere and L. Lohman, *Pulping the South: Industrial Tree Plantations and the World Paper Economy*, London: Zed, 1996.

35   http://www.wrm.org.uy.

36   See the reports of the Environmental Justice Foundations, London, http://www.ejfoundation.org.

37   L.M. Gibbs, *Love Canal: My Story*, Albany: SUNY Press, 1981; R. Hofrichter, ed., *Toxic Struggles: The Theory and Practice of Environmental Justice*, foreword by Lois Gibbs, Philadelphia: New Society Publishers, 1993.

38   See *Down to Earth*, 31 May 2005, pp. 16-17 and, for the source of the quotations, *The Hindu*, 18 December 2004.

39   See the report by the European Environment Agency, *Late Lessons from Early Warnings*, Environmental Issue Report No. 22, 2003 (available at reports.eea. eu.int). A new report with some more case studies is being prepared.

40   There is mistrust of breeder reactors both in Europe, where Creys-Malville was closed, and in Japan, where the Monju project in Fukui Prefecture was stopped by the courts. Meanwhile, the building start of the Kalpakkam breeder reactor near Pondicherry in 2005 was celebrated with such fanfare that it seems to be the main temple of modern India.

41   U. Beck, *Risk Society: Towards a new Modernity*, London: Sage, 1992.

42   *International Herald Tribune*, 3 December 2004.

43   A. Agarwal and S. Narain, *Global Warming: A Case of Environmental Colonialism*, Delhi: Centre for Science and Environment, 1991.

44   http://www.deudaecologica.org.

45   M. Gadgil and R. Guha, *Ecology and Equity: The Use and Abuse of Nature in Contemporary India*, London: Routledge, 1995.

46   M. Wackernagel and W. Rees, *Our Ecological Footprint*, Philadelphia: New Society Publishers, 1995.

47   B. Agarwal, 'The Gender and Environment Debate: Lessons from India', *Feninist Studies*, 18(1), 1992.

48   R. Guha, *The Unquiet Woods: Ecological Change and Peasant Resistance in the Himalaya*, Delhi: Oxford University Press, 1989.; R. Guha and J. Martinez-Alier, *Varieties of Environmentalism*, Delhi: Oxford University Press, 1997.

49   Samata, 'Surviving a Minefield. A Landmark Supreme Court Judgement Restoring the Rights of Tribals', Hyderabad, January 2003; V. Das, 'Democratic Governance in Tribal Regions - A Distant Dream', *Economic and Political Weekly*, 18 October 2003.

50   R. Bullard, *Confronting Environmental Racism: Voices from the Grassroots*, Boston: South End Press, 1993; P. Bond, *Unsustainable South Africa*, London: Merlin Press, 2002; K. Dunion, *Troublemakers: The Struggle for Environmental Justice in Scotland*, Edinburgh: Edinburgh University Press, 2003; H. Acselrad, S. Herculano and J.A. Padua, eds., *Justiça Ambiental e Cidadania,* Rio de Janeiro: Relume Dumará, 2004.

51   J. Martinez-Alier, *The Environmentalism of the Poor: A Study of Ecological Conflicts and Valuation*, Cheltenham: E. Elgar, 2002 (New Edition, Delhi: Oxford University Press, 2005).

52   Debrata Mohanty, 'Chilika Bill in Troubled Waters', *The Telegraph*, 22 December 2003.

53   CASI, 'Velippalayam, Nagapattinam, Tamil Nadu. Struggles against Shrimp Industries and the Role of the Campaign against Shrimp Industries. An Update', January 2004, pp. 41, 52-64.

54   At the *Socialist Register* conference in Oxford in February 2006, where this paper was presented, this perspective was still characterized by some participants as 'romantic'. Romanticism is not a bad word. The Romantics criticized the socio-ecological horrors of the Industrial Revolution; they had a good nose for pollution in dark smelly factories and for the dispossession of resources from communities.

ECO-SOCIALISM AND DEMOCRATIC PLANNING

MICHAEL LÖWY

> If capitalism can't be reformed to subordinate profit to human survival, what alternative is there but to move to some sort of nationally and globally planned economy? Problems like climate change require the 'visible hand' of direct planning. ...Our capitalist corporate leaders can't help themselves, *have no choice* but to systematically make wrong, irrational and ultimately – given the technology they command – globally suicidal decisions about the economy and the environment. So then, what other choice do we have than to consider a true ecosocialist alternative?
>
> Richard Smith[1]

Ecosocialism is an attempt to provide a radical civilizational alternative to what Marx called capitalism's 'destructive progress'.[2] It advances an economic policy founded on the non-monetary and extra-economic criteria of social needs and ecological equilibrium. Grounded on the basic arguments of the ecological movement, and of the Marxist critique of political economy, this dialectical synthesis – attempted by a broad spectrum of authors, from André Gorz (in his early writings) to Elmar Altvater, James O'Connor, Joel Kovel and John Bellamy Foster – is at the same time a critique of 'market ecology', which does not challenge the capitalist system, and of 'productivist socialism', which ignores the issue of natural limits.

According to O'Connor, the aim of ecological socialism is a new society based on ecological rationality, democratic control, social equality, and the predominance of use-value over exchange-value.[3] I would add that these aims require: (a) collective ownership of the means of production ('collective' here meaning public, cooperative or communitarian property); (b) democratic planning, which makes it possible for society to define the goals of investment and production, and (c) a new technological structure of the productive forces. In other words, a revolutionary social and economic transformation.[4]

For ecosocialists, the problem with the main currents of political ecology, represented by most Green parties, is that they do not seem to take into account the intrinsic contradiction between the capitalist dynamics of the unlimited expansion of capital and accumulation of profits, and the preservation of the environment. This leads to a critique of productivism, which is often relevant, but does not lead beyond an ecologically-reformed 'market economy'. The result has been that many Green parties have become the ecological alibi of center-left social-liberal governments.[5]

On the other hand, the problem with the dominant trends of the left during the 20th century – Social Democracy and the Soviet-inspired Communist movement – is their acceptance of the actually existing pattern of productive forces. While the former limited themselves to a reformed – at best Keynesian – version of the capitalist system, the latter developed an authoritarian collectivist – or state-capitalist – form of productivism. In both cases, environmental issues remained out of sight, or were at least marginalized.

Marx and Engels themselves were not unaware of the environmental-destructive consequences of the capitalist mode of production; there are several passages in *Capital* and other writings that point to this understanding.[6] Moreover, they believed that the aim of socialism is not to produce more and more commodities, but to give human beings free time to fully develop their potentialities. To this extent they have little in common with 'productivism', i.e. with the idea that the unlimited expansion of production is an aim in itself.

However, the passages in their writings to the effect that socialism will permit the development of productive forces beyond the limits imposed on them by the capitalist system imply that socialist transformation concerns only the capitalist relations of production, which have become an obstacle ('chains' is the term often used) to the free development of the existing productive forces. Socialism would mean above all the *social appropriation* of these productive capacities, putting them at the service of the workers. To quote a passage from *Anti-Dühring*, a canonical work for many generations of Marxists, under socialism 'society takes possession openly and without detours of the productive forces that have become too large' for the existing system.[7]

The experience of the Soviet Union illustrates the problems that result from such a collectivist appropriation of the capitalist productive apparatus. From the beginning, the thesis of the socialization of the existing productive forces predominated. It is true that during the first years after the October Revolution an ecological current was able to develop, and certain limited environmental protection measures were taken by the Soviet authorities. But with the process of Stalinist bureaucratization, productivist methods both in industry and agriculture were imposed by totalitarian means, while ecologists were marginalized or eliminated. The catastrophe of Chernobyl was the ultimate example of the disastrous consequences of this imitation of Western productive technologies. A change in the forms of property which is not followed by democratic management and a reorganization of the productive system can only lead to a dead end.

A critique of the productivist ideology of 'progress', and of the idea of a 'socialist' exploitation of nature, appeared already in the writings of some dissident Marxists of the 1930s, such as Walter Benjamin. But it is mainly during the last few decades, that *ecosocialism* has developed as a challenge to the thesis of the neutrality of productive forces which had continued to predominate in the main tendencies of the left during the twentieth century.

Ecosocialists should take their inspiration from Marx's remarks on the Paris Commune: workers cannot take possession of the capitalist state apparatus and put it to work at their service. They have to 'break it' and replace it by a radically different, democratic and non-statist form of political power. The same applies, *mutatis mutandis*, to the productive apparatus, which is not 'neutral', but carries in its structure the imprint of its development at the service of capital accumulation and the unlimited expansion of the market. This puts it in contradiction with the needs of environmental protection, and with the health of the population. One must therefore 'revolutionize' it, in a process of radical transformation.

Of course, many scientific and technological achievements of modernity are precious, but the whole productive system must be transformed, and this can be done only by ecosocialist methods, i.e. through a democratic planning of the economy which takes into account the preservation of the ecological equilibrium. This may mean, for certain branches of production, to discontinue them: for instance, nuclear plants, certain methods of mass/industrial fishing (which are responsible for the near-extermination of several species in the seas), the destructive logging of tropical forests, etc. – the list is very long. It first of all requires, however, a revolution in the energy-system, with the replacement of the present sources (essentially fossil) that are responsible for the pollution and poisoning of the environment by renewable sources of energy: water, wind, sun. The issue of energy is decisive because fossil energy (oil, coal) is responsible for much of the planet's pollution, as well as for the disastrous climate change. Nuclear energy is a false alternative, not only because of the danger of new Chernobyls, but also because nobody knows what to do with the thousands of tons of radioactive waste – toxic for hundreds, thousands and in some cases millions of years – and the gigantic masses of contaminated obsolete plants. Solar energy, which has never aroused much interest in capitalist societies (not being 'profitable' or 'competitive'), must become the object of intensive research and development, and play a key role in the building of an alternative energetic system.

All this must be accomplished under the necessary condition of full and equitable employment. This condition is essential, not only to meet the requirement of social justice, but in order to assure working-class support for the process of structural transformation of the productive forces. This process is impossible without public control over the means of production, and planning, i.e. public decisions on investment and technological change, which must be taken away from the banks and capitalist enterprises in order to serve society's common good.

But putting these decisions into the hands of workers is not enough. In Volume Three of *Capital* Marx defined socialism as a society where 'the associated producers rationally organize their exchange (*Stoffwechsel*) with nature'. But in Volume One of *Capital* there is a broader approach: socialism is conceived as 'an association of free human beings (*Menschen*) which works with common (*gemeinschaftlichen*) means of production'.[8] This is a much more appropriate conception: the rational organization of production and consumption has to be the work not only of the 'producers', but also of the consumers; in fact, of the whole society, with its productive and 'non-productive' population, which includes students, youth, housewives (and househusbands), pensioners, etc.

The whole society in this sense will be able to choose, democratically, which productive lines are to be privileged, and how much resources are to be invested in education, health or culture.[9] The prices of goods themselves would not be left to the laws of supply and demand but determined as far as possible according to social, political and ecological criteria. Initially, this might only involve taxes on certain products, and subsidized prices for others, but ideally, as the transition to socialism moves forward, more and more products and services would be distributed free of charge, according to the will of the citizens.

Far from being 'despotic' in itself, democratic planning is the exercise, by a whole society, of its freedom of decision. This is what is required for liberation from the alienating and reified 'economic laws' and 'iron cages' of capitalist and bureaucratic structures. Democratic planning combined with the reduction of labour time would be a decisive step of humanity towards what Marx called 'the kingdom of freedom'. This is because a significant increase of free time is in fact a condition for the participation of working people in the democratic discussion and management of the economy and the society.

Partisans of the free market point to the failure of Soviet planning as a reason to reject, out of hand, any idea of an organized economy. Without entering the discussion on the achievements and miseries of the Soviet experience, it was obviously a form of *dictatorship over needs* – to use the expression of György Markus and his friends in the Budapest School: a non-democratic and authoritarian system that gave a monopoly over all decisions to a small oligarchy of techno-bureaucrats. It was not planning itself which led to dictatorship, but the growing limitations to democracy in the Soviet state and, after Lenin's death, the establishment of a totalitarian bureaucratic power, which led to an increasingly undemocratic and authoritarian system of planning. If socialism is defined as the control by the workers and the population in general of the process of production, the Soviet Union under Stalin and his successors was a far cry from it.

The failure of the USSR illustrates the limits and contradictions of *bureaucratic* planning, which is inevitably inefficient and arbitrary: it cannot be used as an argument against *democratic* planning.[10] The socialist conception of planning is nothing other than the radical democratization of economy: if political decisions are not to be left for a small elite of rulers, why should not the same principle apply to economic ones? The issue of the specific balance to be struck between planning and market mechanisms is admittedly a difficult one: during the first stages of a new society, markets will certainly retain an important place, but as the transition to socialism advances, planning will become more and more predominant, as against the laws of exchange-value.[11]

Engels insisted that a socialist society 'will have to establish a plan of production taking into account the means of production, specially including the labour force. It will be, in last instance, the useful effects of various use-objects, compared between themselves and in relation to the quantity of labour necessary for their production, that will determine the plan'.[12] In capitalism use-value is only a means – often a trick – at the service of exchange-value and profit (which explains, by the way, why so many products in the present-day society are substantially useless). In a planned socialist economy the use-value is the only criterion for the production of goods and services, with far-reaching economic, social and ecological consequences. As Joel Kovel has observed: 'The enhancement of use-values and the corresponding restructuring of needs becomes now the social regulator of technology rather than, as under capital, the conversion of time into surplus value and money'.[13]

In the type of democratic planning system envisaged here, the plan concerns the main economic options, not the administration of local restaurants,

groceries and bakeries, small shops, artisan enterprises or services. It is important to emphasize, as well, that planning is not in contradiction with workers'
self-management of their productive units. While the decision, made through
the planning system, to transform, say, an auto-plant into one producing buses and trams would be taken by society as a whole, the internal organization
and functioning of the plant should be democratically managed by its own
workers. There has been much discussion on the 'centralized' or 'decentralized' character of planning, but it could be argued that the real issue is democratic control of the plan at all levels, local, regional, national, continental
– and, hopefully, international, since ecological issues such as global warming
are planetary and can be dealt with only on a global scale. One could call
this proposition *global democratic planning*. Even at this level, it would be quite
the opposite of what is usually described as 'central planning', since the economic and social decisions are not taken by any 'centre', but democratically
decided by the populations concerned.

Of course, there will inevitably be tensions and contradictions between
self-managed establishments or local democratic administrations, and broader
social groups. Mechanisms of negotiation can help to solve many such conflicts, but ultimately the broadest groups of those concerned, if they are the
majority, have the right to impose their views. To give an example: a self-ad-
ministered factory decides to evacuate its toxic waste in a river. The population of a whole region is in danger of being polluted: it can therefore, after a
democratic debate, decide that production in this unit must be discontinued,
until a satisfactory solution is found for the control of its waste. Hopefully,
in an ecosocialist society, the factory workers themselves will have enough
ecological consciousness to avoid taking decisions which are dangerous to
the environment and to the health of the local population. But instituting
means of ensuring that the broadest social interests have the decisive say, as
the above example suggests, does not mean that issues concerning internal
management are not to be vested at the level of the factory, or school, or
neighbourhood, or hospital, or town.

Socialist planning must be grounded on a democratic and pluralist debate,
at all the levels where decisions are to be taken. As organized in the form of
parties, platforms, or any other political movements, delegates to planning
bodies are elected, and different propositions are submitted to all the people
concerned with them. That is, representative democracy must be completed
– and corrected – by direct democracy, where people directly choose – at the
local, national and, later, global level – between major options. Should public
transportation be free? Should the owners of private cars pay special taxes to
subsidize public transportation? Should solar energy be subsidized, in order

to compete with fossil energy? Should the work week be reduced to 30 or 25 hours, or less, even if this means a reduction of production? The democratic nature of planning is not incompatible with the existence of experts: their role is not to decide, but to present their views – often different, if not opposite – to the democratic process of decision making. As Ernest Mandel put it: 'Governments, parties, planning boards, scientists, technocrats or whoever can make suggestions, put forward proposals, try to influence people… But under a multi-party system, such proposals will never be unanimous: people will have the choice between coherent alternatives. And the right and power to *decide* should be in the hands of the majority of producers/consumers/citizens, not of anybody else. What is paternalistic or despotic about that?'[14]

What guarantee is there that the people will make the right ecological choices, even at the price of giving up some of their habits of consumption? There is no such 'guarantee', other than the reasonable expectation that the rationality of democratic decisions will prevail, once the power of commodity fetishism is broken. Of course, errors will be committed by popular choices, but who believes that experts make no errors themselves? One cannot imagine the establishment of such a new society without the majority of the population having achieved, by their struggles, their self-education, and their social experience, a high level of socialist/ecological consciousness, and this makes it reasonable to suppose that serious errors – including decisions which are inconsistent with environmental needs – will be corrected.[15] In any case, are not the alternatives – the blind market, or an ecological dictatorship of 'experts' – much more dangerous than the democratic process, with all its limitations?

It is true that planning requires the existence of executive/technical bodies, in charge of putting into practice what has been decided, but they are not necessarily authoritarian if they are under permanent democratic control from below, and include workers self-management in a process of democratic administration. Of course, one cannot expect the majority of the people to spend all their free time in self-management or participatory meetings; as Ernest Mandel remarked, 'self-administration does not entail the disappearance of delegation, it combines decision-making by the citizens with stricter control of delegates by their respective electorate'.[16]

Michael Albert's 'participatory economy' (*parecon*), has been the object of some debate in the Global Justice movement. Although there are some serious shortcomings in his overall approach, which seems to ignore ecology, and counterposes 'parecon' to 'socialism' as understood in the bureaucratic/centralized Soviet model, nevertheless 'parecon' has some common features with the kind of ecosocialist planning proposed here: opposition to the capitalist market and to bureaucratic planning, a reliance on workers' self-organization, anti-authoritarianism. Albert's model of participatory planning is based on a complex institutional construction:

> The participants in participatory planning are the workers' councils and federations, the consumers' councils and federations, and various Iteration Facilitation Boards (IFBs). Conceptually, the planning procedure is quite simple. An IFB announces what we call 'indicative prices' for all goods, resources, categories of labour, and capital. Consumers' councils and federations respond with consumption proposals taking the indicative prices of final goods and services as estimates of the social cost of providing them. Workers councils and federations respond with production proposals listing the outputs they would make available and the inputs they would need to produce them, again, taking the indicative prices as estimates of the social benefits of outputs and true opportunity costs of inputs. An IFB then calculates the excess demand or supply for each good and adjusts the indicative price for the good up, or down, in light of the excess demand or supply, and in accord with socially agreed algorithms. Using the new indicative prices, consumers and workers councils and federations revise and resubmit their proposals... In place of rule over workers by capitalists or by coordinators, parecon is an economy in which workers and consumers together cooperatively determine their economic options and benefit from them in ways fostering equity, solidarity, diversity, and self-management.[17]

The main problem with this conception – which, by the way, is not 'quite simple' but extremely elaborate and sometimes quite obscure – is that it seems to reduce 'planning' to a sort of negotiation between producers and consumers on the issue of prices, inputs and outputs, supply and demand. For instance, the branch worker's council of the automobile industry would meet with the council of consumers to discuss prices and to adapt supply to demand. What this leaves out is precisely what constitutes the main issue in ecosocialist planning: a reorganization of the transport system, radically reducing the place of the private car. Since ecosocialism requires entire sectors of industry to disappear – nuclear plants, for instance – and massive investment in small or almost non-existent sectors (e.g. solar energy), how can this be dealt with by 'cooperative negotiations' between the existing units of production and consumer councils on 'inputs' and 'indicative prices'?

Albert's model mirrors the existing technological and productive structure, and is too 'economistic' to take into account global, socio-political and socio-ecological interests of the population – the interests of individuals, as citizens and as human beings, which cannot be reduced to their economic interests as producers and consumers. He leaves out not only the state as an institution – a respectable option – but also *politics* as the confrontation, of different economic, social, political, ecological, cultural and civilizational options, locally, nationally and globally.

This is very important because the passage from capitalist 'destructive progress' to socialism is an historical process, a permanent revolutionary transformation of society, culture and mentalities – and *politics* in the sense just defined cannot but be central to this process. It is important to emphasize that such a process cannot begin without a revolutionary transformation of social and political structures, and the active support, by the vast majority of the population, of an ecosocialist programme. The development of socialist consciousness and ecological awareness is a process, where the decisive factor is peoples own collective experience of struggle, moving from local and partial confrontations to the radical change of society.

This transition would lead not only to a new mode of production and an egalitarian and democratic society, but also to an alternative *mode of life*, a new ecosocialist *civilization*, beyond the reign of money, beyond consumption habits artificially produced by advertising, and beyond the unlimited production of commodities that are useless and/or harmful to the environment. Some ecologists believe that the only alternative to productivism is to *stop growth* altogether, or to replace it by negative growth – what the French call *décroissance* – and drastically reduce the excessively high level of consumption of the population by cutting by half the expenditure of energy, by renouncing individual family houses, central heating, washing machines, etc. Since these and similar measures of draconian austerity risk being quite unpopular, some of the advocates of *décroissance* play with the idea of a sort of 'ecological dictatorship'.[18] Against such pessimistic views, socialist optimists believe that technical progress and the use of renewable sources of energy will permit an unlimited growth and abundance, so that each can receive 'according to his needs'.

It seems to me that both these schools share a purely *quantitative* conception of 'growth' – positive or negative – and of the development of productive forces. There is a third position, however, which seems to me more appropriate: a *qualitative transformation* of development. This means putting an end to the monstrous waste of resources by capitalism, based on the production, in a large scale, of useless and/or harmful products: the armaments industry is a good example, but a great part of the 'goods' produced in capitalism – with their inbuilt obsolescence – have no other usefulness but to generate profit for big corporations. The issue is not 'excessive consumption' in the abstract, but the prevalent *type* of consumption, based as it is on conspicuous appropriation, massive waste, mercantile alienation, obsessive accumulation of goods, and the compulsive acquisition of pseudo-novelties imposed by 'fashion'. A new society would orient production towards the satisfaction of authentic needs, beginning with those which could be described as 'biblical' – water, food, clothing, housing – but including also the basic services: health, education, transport, culture.

Obviously, the countries of the South, where these needs are very far from being satisfied, will need a much higher level of 'development' – building railroads, hospitals, sewage systems, and other infrastructures – than the advanced industrial ones. But there is no reason why this cannot be accomplished with a productive system that is environment-friendly and based on renewable energies. These countries will need to produce large amounts of food to nourish their hungry populations, but this can be much better achieved – as the peasant movements organized world-wide in the *Via Campesina* network have been arguing for years – by peasant biological agriculture based on family units, cooperatives or collectivist farms, than by the destructive and anti-social methods of industrialized agro-business, based on the intensive use of pesticides, chemicals and GMOs. Instead of the present monstrous debt-system, and the imperialist exploitation of the resources of the South by the industrial/capitalist countries, there would be a flow of technical and economic help from the North to the South, without the need – as some puritan and ascetic ecologists seem to believe – for the population in Europe or North America to reduce their standard of living in absolute terms. Instead, they will only get rid of the obsessive consumption, induced by the capitalist system, of useless commodities that do not correspond to any real need, while redefining the meaning of standard of living to connote a way of life that is actually richer, while consuming less.

How to distinguish the authentic from the artificial, false and makeshift needs? The advertising industry – inducing needs by mental manipulation – has invaded all spheres of human life in modern capitalist societies: not only nourishment and clothing, but sports, culture, religion and politics are shaped according to its rules. It has invaded our streets, mail boxes, TV-screens, newspapers, landscapes, in a permanent, aggressive and insidious way, and it decisively contributes to habits of conspicuous and compulsive consumption. Moreover, it wastes an astronomic amount of oil, electricity, labour time, paper, chemicals, and other raw materials – all paid by the consumers – in a branch of 'production' which is not only useless, from a human view-point, but directly in contradiction with real social needs. While advertising is an indispensable dimension of capitalist market economy, it would have no place in a society in transition to socialism, where it would be replaced by information on goods and services provided by consumer associations. The criterion for distinguishing an authentic from an artificial need, would be its persistence after the suppression of advertising. Of course, for some time old habits of consumption would persist, and nobody has the right to tell the people what their needs are. Changing patterns of consumption is a histori-cal process, as well as an educational challenge.

Some commodities, such as the individual car, raise more complex prob-lems. Private cars are a public nuisance, killing and maiming hundreds of thousand people yearly on world scale, polluting the air in large cities – with dire consequences for the health of children and older people – and sig-nificantly contributing to climate change. However, they correspond to real needs, under present-day conditions of capitalism. Local experiments in some European towns with ecologically-minded administrations show that it is possible – and approved by the majority of the population – to progressively limit the role of the individual automobile in favour of buses and trams. In a process of transition to ecosocialism, where public transportation – above or under ground – would be vastly extended and free of charge, and where pedestrians and cyclists will have protected lanes, the private car will play a much smaller role than in bourgeois society, where it has become a fetish, promoted by insistent and aggressive advertisement, a prestige symbol, an identity sign (in the US, the drivers license is the recognized ID) and a focus of personal, social and erotic life.[19] It will be much easier, in the transition to a new society, to drastically reduce the transportation of goods by trucks – responsible for terrible accidents, and high levels of pollution – replacing it by rail transport, or by what the French call *ferroutage* (trucks transported in trains from one town to the other): only the absurd logic of capitalist 'com-petitivity' explains the dangerous growth of the truck-system.

Yes, the pessimists will answer, but individuals are moved by infinite as-pirations and desires, that have to be controlled, checked, contained and if necessary repressed, and this may call for some limitations on democracy. But ecosocialism is based on a reasonable expectation, which was already held by Marx: the predominance, in a society without classes and liberated of capitalist alienation, of 'being' over 'having', i.e. of *free time* for the personal accomplishment by cultural, sportive, playful, scientific, erotic, artistic and political *activities*, rather than the desire for an infinite possession of products. Compulsive acquisitiveness is induced by the commodity fetishism inherent in the capitalist system, by the dominant ideology and by advertising: nothing proves that it is part of an 'eternal human nature'. As Ernest Mandel empha-sized: 'The continual accumulation of more and more goods (with declining "marginal utility") is by no means a universal and even predominant feature of human behavior. The development of talents and inclinations for their own sake; the protection of health and life; care for children; the develop-ment of rich social relations...all these become major motivations once basic material needs have been satisfied'.[20]

As we have insisted, this does not mean that conflicts will not arise, par-ticularly during the transition process, between the requirements of environ-mental protection and social needs, between ecological imperatives and the necessity of developing basic infra-structures, particularly in poor countries, between popular consumer habits and the scarcity of resources. A classless society is not a society without contradictions and conflicts. These are inevi-table: it will be the task of democratic planning, in an ecosocialist perspective, liberated from the imperatives of capital and profit-making, to solve them, by a pluralist and open discussion, leading to decision-making by society itself. Such a grass-roots and participative democracy is the only way, not to avoid errors, but to permit the correction, by the social collectivity, of its own mistakes.

Is this Utopia? In its etymological sense – 'something that exists nowhere' – certainly. But are not utopias, i.e. visions of an alternative future, wish-im-ages of a different society, a necessary feature of any movement that wants to challenge the established order? As Daniel Singer explained in his liter-ary and political testament, *Whose Millenium?*, in a powerful chapter entitled 'Realistic Utopia',

> ...if the establishment now looks so solid, despite the circumstanc-es, and if the labor movement or the broader left are so crippled, so paralyzed, it is because of the failure to offer a radical alterna-tive...The basic principle of the game is that you question neither the fundamentals of the argument nor the foundations of society. Only a global alternative, breaking with these rules of resignation and surrender, can give the movement of emancipation genuine scope.[21]

The socialist and ecological utopia is only an objective possibility, not the inevitable result of the contradictions of capitalism, or of the 'iron laws of history'. One cannot predict the future, except in conditional terms: what is predictable is that in the absence of an ecosocialist transformation, of a radical change in the civilizational paradigm, the logic of capitalism will lead to dramatic ecological disasters, threatening the health and the lives of millions of human beings, and perhaps even the survival of our species.

To dream, and to struggle, for a green socialism, or, as some say a *solar communism*, does not mean that one does not fight for concrete and urgent reforms. Without any illusions about a 'clean capitalism' one must try to win time and to impose on the powers that be some elementary changes: the banning of the HCFCs that are destroying the ozone layer, a general moratorium on genetically modified organisms, a drastic reduction in the emission of greenhouse gases, strict regulation of the fishing industry, as well as of the use of pesticides and chemicals in agro-industrial production, the taxation of polluting cars, much greater development of public transport, the progressive replacement of trucks by trains. These, and similar issues, are at the heart of the agenda of the Global Justice movement, and the World Social Forums. This is an important new political development which has permitted, since Seattle in 1999, the convergence of social and environmental movements in a common struggle against the system.

These urgent eco-social demands can lead to a process of radicalization, if such demands are not adapted so as to fit in with the requirements of 'competitiveness'. According to the logic of what Marxists call 'a transitional programme' each small victory, each partial advance, leads immediately to a higher demand, to a more radical aim. Such struggles around concrete issues are important, not only because partial victories are welcome in themselves, but also because they contribute to raise ecological and socialist consciousness, and because they promote activity and self-organization from below: both would be necessary and indeed decisive pre-conditions for a radical, i.e. revolutionary, transformation of the world.

Local experiments such as car-free areas in several European towns, organic agricultural cooperatives launched by the Brazilian peasant movement (MST), or the participative budget in Porto Alegre and, for a few years, in the Brazilian state of Rio Grande do Sul (under PT Governor Olivio Dutra), are limited but interesting examples of social/ecological change. By permitting local assemblies to decide the priorities of the budget, Porto Alegre was – until the left lost the 2002 municipal election – perhaps the most attractive example of 'planning from below', in spite of its limitations.[22] It must be admitted, however, that even if there have also been a few progressive measures taken by some national governments, on the whole the experience of Left-Center or 'Left/Green' coalitions in Europe or Latin America has been rather disappointing, remaining firmly inside the limits of a social-liberal policy of adaptation to capitalist globalization.

There will be no radical transformation unless the forces committed to a radical socialist and ecological programme become hegemonic, in the Gramscian sense of the word. In one sense, time is on our side, as we work for change, because the global situation of the environment is becoming worse and worse, and the threats are coming closer and closer. But on the other hand time is running out, because in some years – no one can say how much – the damage may be irreversible. There is no reason for optimism: the entrenched ruling elites of the system are incredibly powerful, and the forces of radical opposition are still small. But they are the only hope that capitalism's 'destructive progress' will be halted. Walter Benjamin defined revolutions as being not the locomotives of history, but humanity reaching for the train's emergency brakes, before it falls into the abyss....[23]

NOTES

1   Richard Smith, 'The Engine of Eco Collapse', *Capitalism, Nature and Socialism*, 16(4), 2005, p. 35.
2   K. Marx, *Das Kapital*, Volume 1, Berlin: Dietz Verlag, 1960, pp. 529-30. For a remarkable analysis of the destructive logic of capital, see Joel Kovel, *The Enemy of Nature. The End of Capitalism or the End of the World?*, New York: Zed Books, 2002.
3   James O'Connor, *Natural Causes. Essays in Ecological Marxism*, New York: The Guilford Press, 1998, pp. 278, 331.
4   John Bellamy Foster uses the concept of 'ecological revolution', but he argues that 'a global ecological revolution worthy of the name can only occur as part of a larger social – and I would insist, socialist – revolution. Such a revolution... would demand, as Marx insisted, that the associated producers rationally regulate the human metabolic relation with nature... It must take its inspiration from William Morris, one of the most original and ecological followers of Karl Marx, from Gandhi, and from other radical, revolutionary and materialist figures, including Marx himself, stretching as far back as Epicurus'. Foster, 'Organizing Ecological Revolution', *Monthly Review*, 57(5), 2005, pp. 9-10.
5   For an ecosocialist critique of 'actually existing ecopolitics' – Green Economics, Deep Ecology, Bioregionalism, etc. – see Kovel, *Enemy of Nature*, chapter 7.
6   See John Bellamy Foster, *Marx's Ecology. Materialism and Nature*, New York: Monthly Review Press, 2000.
7   F. Engels, *Anti-Dühring*, Paris: Ed. Sociales, 1950, p. 318.
8   K. Marx, *Das Kapital*, Volume 3, Berlin: Dietz Verlag, 1968, p. 828 and Volume 1, p. 92. One can find similar problems in contemporary Marxism; for instance, Ernest Mandel argued for a 'democratically-centralist planning under a national congress of worker's councils made up in its large majority of real workers' (Mandel, 'Economics of Transition Period', in E. Mandel, ed., *50 Years of World Revolution*, New York: Pathfinder Press, 1971, p. 286). In later writings, he refers rather to 'producers/consumers'. We are often going to quote from the writings of Ernest Mandel, because he is the most articulate socialist theoretician of

democratic planning. But it should be said that until the late 1980s he did not include the ecological issue as a central aspect of his economic arguments.

9   Ernest Mandel defined planning in the following terms:'An economy governed by a plan implies… that society's relatively scarce resources are not apportioned blindly ("behind the backs of the producer-consumer") by the play of the law of value but that they are consciously allocated according to previously established priorities. In a transitional economy where socialist democracy prevails, the mass of the working people democratically determine this choice of priorities'. Mandel, 'Economics of Transition Period', p. 282.

10   'From the point of view of the mass of workers, sacrifices imposed by bureaucratic arbitrariness are neither more nor less "acceptable" than sacrifices imposed by the blind mechanisms of the market. These represent only two different forms of the same alienation'. Ibid., p. 285.

11   In his remarkable recent book on socialism the Argentinian Marxist economist Claudio Katz emphasized that democratic planning, supervised from below by the majority of the population, 'is not identical with absolute centralisation, total statisation, war communism or command economy. The transition requires the primacy of planning over the market, but not the suppression of the market variables. The combination between both instances should be adapted to each situation and each country'. However, 'the aim of the socialist process is not to keep an unchanged equilibrium between the plan and the market, but to promote a progressive loss of the market positions'. C. Katz, *El porvenir del Socialismo*, Buenos Aires: Herramienta/Imago Mundi, 2004, pp. 47-8.

12   *Anti-Dühring*, p. 349.

13   Kovel, *Enemy of Nature*, p. 215.

14   Mandel, *Power and Money*, London:Verso, 1991, p. 209.

15   Mandel observed: 'We do not believe that the "majority is always right"… Everybody does make mistakes. This will certainly be true of the majority of citizens, of the majority of the producers, and of the majority of the consumers alike. But there will be one basic difference between them and their predecessors. In any system of unequal power… those who make the wrong decisions about the allocation of resources are rarely those who pay for the consequences of their mistakes… Provided there exists real political democracy, real cultural choice and information, it is hard to believe that the majority would prefer to see their woods die… or their hospitals understaffed, rather than rapidly to correct their mistaken allocations'. Mandel, 'In Defense of Socialist Planning', *New Left Review*, 1/159, 1986, p. 31.

16   Mandel, *Power and Money*, p. 204.

17   Michael Albert, *Participatory Economics. Life After Capitalism*, London:Verso, 2003, p. 154.

18   For a selection of 'negative growth' texts see Majid Rahnema (with Victoria Bawtree), eds., *The Post-Development Reader*, Atlantic Highlands, N.J.: Zed Books, 1997, and Michel Bernard et al., eds., *Objectif Décroissance: vers une société harmonieuse*, Lyon: Éditions Parangon, 2004. The main French theorist of 'décroissance' is Serge Latour, author of *La planète des naufragés, essai sur l'après-développement*, Paris: La Decouverte, 1991.

19   Ernest Mandel was sceptical of rapid changes in consumer habits, such as the private car: 'If, in spite of every environmental and other argument, they [the producers and consumers] wanted to maintain the dominance of the private motor car and to continue polluting their cities, that would be their right. Changes in long-standing consumer orientations are generally slow – there can be few who believe that workers in the United States would abandon their attachment to the automobile the day after a socialist revolution'. Mandel, 'In Defense of Socialist Planning', p. 30. While Mandel is right in insisting that changes in consumption patterns are not to be imposed, he seriously underestimates the impact that a system of extensive and free of charge public transports would have, as well as the assent of the majority of the citizens – already today, in several great European cities – for measures restricting automobile circulation.

20   Mandel, *Power and Money*, p. 206.

21   D. Singer, *Whose Millenium? Theirs or Ours?*, New York: Monthly Review Press, 1999, pp. 259-60.

22   See S. Baierle, 'The Porto Alegre Thermidor', in *Socialist Register 2003*.

23   Walter Benjamin, *Gesammelte Schriften*, Volume I/3, Frankfurt: Suhrkamp, 1980, p. 1232.

PARTY-BUILDING FOR ECO-SOCIALISTS: LESSONS FROM THE FAILED PROJECT OF THE GERMAN GREENS

FRIEDER OTTO WOLF

In the early 1980s an emblematic event took place in Hamburg, in the north of Germany: after decades of silence about the poisoning of workers and the environment by dioxins and furans, which had been on-going in a local chemical factory, some workers' wives, whose husbands were suffering from the early stage of chlorate acne, the 'Seveso illness', phoned the Hamburg office of the newly-founded 'Green Alternative List' (later to become the Hamburg branch of the German Green Party), to say that 'things could not go on like this: their husbands selling their health to the company, leaving them with the prospect of being housewives nursing the sick and, later on, early widowhood – the new party should do something about this!'.

All the elements were there which had constituted the hopes and dreams of the new political formation under construction: working class radicalism, a concern with the ecological destruction caused by capitalist big industry, a feminist dimension – and the possibility of party-building opening new terrains of struggle. This was clearly not the middle-class environmentalism of the well-to-do, with the leisure and leeway to be concerned about a romanticized nature. This seemed to be the germ of a renewed anti-capitalism coming out of everyday struggles, tapping the combined potential of working class, ecological and feminist movements to reach a higher level of radical politicization, culminating in the building of a new type of party – i.e. a new start for anti-systemic politics in the metropolis comparable only to the rise in the 1890s of the Second International out of the cinders of the First. And this was happening in Germany, where the ruin of the nation-state, the self-inflicted demise of German imperialism, and the historical failure of Stalinism, symbolized by the Berlin wall, seemed to have brought about a deep break with traditional politics, and where the student and youth rebellion of the 1960s, starting especially in West Berlin, had begun to 'revolutionize' a traditionally authoritarian culture.

A quarter of a century later, all this seems to have been a pipe-dream. From 2002 to 2005 the German Greens were a party of a government in a reunited Germany vying for international respectability by sharing a renewed 'white man's burden' by sending troops to Kosovo, to Afghanistan, and, soon, to the Congo, or by sending its navy to participate in the 'anti-terrorist' controls around the horn of Africa. The 'humanitarian interventionism' of NATO against Serbia was legitimized by a majority of former radical pacifists; and a debt guarantee has been given to the nuclear industry in Germany by former radical ecologists and anti-nuclear activists. German Green parliamentarians have been avidly implementing neo-liberal 'reforms', in coalition with a so-cial-democratic party in which a translated Blairism has won the day. After the federal election of fall 2005 was lost by their social-democratic partner, some leading Green parliamentary representatives began discussing joining a centre-right coalition government. Within the (very much weakened) social movements of contemporary Germany, the example of the Greens is cited in order to refute any idea of intervening in party politics at all. Their negative example is actually important in reinforcing prejudices against a new German left party which is in the process of being formalized, after an impressive first presence in the 2005 federal elections.

Can anything be learnt from the Greens' failure? Apart from the simple statement that there is no better way of learning strategically than from the analysis of past defeats and failures, there are some specific lessons to be drawn from this historical experience (which for this author is also quite personal[1]). And as we shall see, these lessons are of considerable relevance to contemporary international left debates on party-building.

THE ROOTS OF THE GERMAN GREENS

It was a surprise to many that in the wake of the worldwide youth rebellion of the 1960s wherever the spontaneous initiatives of the 'new wave' of radical opposition could not be crushed, party building came high on the agenda. It is useful to distinguish two reasons for this unexpected turn by people who had seemed mere 'hippies' or 'culture rebels' a few years before. In fact, they are profoundly different reasons, although customarily lumped together: one is the problem of organizing the practice of a multitude so that it can reach out beyond the urban middle-class bohemian milieu and challenge established power relations; the other problem is how to participate effectively in electoral politics, the central mechanism of the reproduction of these power relations. The traditional left had, in fact, developed two distinct ways of connecting the two. On the one hand, by creating a comprehensive and well-organized working-class counter-culture, linking everyday life to 'the party' by a sense of class loyalty; and, on the other hand, by linking 'legal front' organizations to the more cadre-type organizations of political professionals (first developed by the European left in the post-1848 repression, then culti-vated by the SPD against Bismarck's persecution in the early 1890s, and sys-tematized by Lenin in his ideas on a 'new type of party'). By the 1960s both these linkages had ceased to function: the first, because the mass culture of capitalist 'consumerism' had started to dissolve distinct working class cultures; the second, because universal suffrage and the liberal 'rule of law' had made open persecution almost impracticable, even though more indirect ways of discrimination and political exclusion continued to be commonplace.[2] The parties of the old left in Europe were all becoming mere electoral machines, with no more programmatic or organizational foundation than was indis-pensable for electoral survival. In the West German SPD, which by the 1960s was well on its way to transforming itself definitively into an electoral party, this meant that the local 'Ortsverein', the traditional organizational backbone of the party responsible for integrating all kinds of social democratic organi-zations, lost its importance as an arena of political debate and decisions.

But it was not the question of organization that necessarily led to party building. All kinds of local coordinating initiatives sprang up from the late 1960s onwards, using autonomous 'centres' for youth or for women, and net-working by repeated conferences on overarching issues like those of peace and ecology. This was soon reinforced, however, by the extension of the cul-tural rebellion of the 1960s to working-class youth, including apprentices and migrant workers, whose new militancy raised the practical problem of how to go beyond the capacity to organize wildcat strikes so as also to or-ganize opposition within the trade unions, as well as in local politics. In spite of some emphasis on Luxemburgian and 'council communist' spontaneism (at the beginning of the 1970s a small journal in West Berlin ran with the slogan of 'social emancipation is not a party affair'), the focus of the debate on organization rapidly switched from grassroots organizing to a theoretical (and practical) rehearsal of Lenin's, Stalin's, Trotsky's and Mao's contributions on the problems of the construction of a revolutionary mass party.

As was clear to everybody involved at the time, the initiative in the 1960s rebellion had not come from the working class, let alone from its political parties. Instead students and young workers created a number of competing organizations oriented to 'rebuilding' *the* working-class party (the old ones having been 'betrayed' by their social-democratic or Stalinist leaders). This turned out to be rather unproductive – leading neither to a significant presence in the working class, nor to really innovative forms of organization, but rather tending to reproduce old forms of organizing that had long been rendered obsolete by the development of the technologies of communication (copying machines, telefax, and the computer) and transport (the spread of private car ownership), which facilitated travelling long distances by hitch-hiking.

There was also of course the development of a grassroots activism using violent means (taken up by self-styled 'urban guerrilla' groups, most notoriously the *RAF* in Germany, modelled upon the national liberation struggles in the Third World, and similar to the *brigate rosse* in Italy or the *GRAPO* in Spain); much to the unease of grassroots activists and networks, which continued to predominate in actual everyday practice, even after having lost their hegemony in the field of political ideologies. The public defeat of such violent activism had become patent to all sectors of society by the fall of 1977, and after their political isolation all kinds of urban guerrilla groups were successfully repressed by a modernized police force. This defeat, however, did not coincide with a decrease of grassroots militancy as such: most parts of a broadly radicalized youth continued on more localized and programmatically 'non-violent' paths of resistance for almost another decade.[3] This deeply changed the focus of the 'organization debate' in Germany from the building of a more or less conspiratorial vanguard to a question of mass politics. And here, at first, and mainly locally, the electoral process and existing forms of institutionalized politics came into view.

THE GERMAN GREEN PARTY: AN OVERVIEW

Before developing more systematic lines of argument, some empirico-historical narrative is required to remind the reader of what we are concretely talking about.[4] From 1976 to the mid-1980s the Greens emerged as a parliamentary force in the Federal Republic of Germany, developing out of a series of local and regional electoral initiatives, calling themselves green, alternative, multicoloured or citizens' lists and trying to translate the everyday concerns of the new social movements into political representation.[5] This broad 'electoral movement' regrouped mostly activists from the 'Basisgruppen', the different regional variants of the short-lived Maoist organizations, both having emerged from the student movement, with tactically co-opted 'notables', some of whom had right-wing backgrounds. This was far more decisive for the emergence of the party than the more or less 'putschist' attempts to occupy its political space from above (as represented by Gruhl's Grüne Aktion Zukunft, or the initiative around Petra Kelly for a green list of candidates for the European elections of 1979). The founding party congress of 1980 achieved a precarious unity of 'green' and 'alternative' forces, with strong principles of grass roots democracy as a guarantee against anybody 'centralizing' power. The much publicized problem of a right wing presence within the Greens (sometimes presented as if the new party had rendered obsolete the left-right divide) turned out to be largely non-existent, as most of the activists who had not come directly from the overarching broadly left-wing peace and ecology movements of the period had gained their previous political experience in political grass-roots initiatives, which had included dissident young socialists or young liberals.

But after their entry into the Bundestag in 1983 the opposition between left and right, between 'red' and 'green' ceased to play any political role within the German Greens. Instead, the strategic debate within the party now opposed a minority of 'Realos' (realists), who advanced a strategy of full parliamentary participation with the aim of forming a coalition government with the social democrats, to a majority of so-called 'Fundis' (fundamentalists) who treated parliamentary strategy more in terms of provoking a crisis of government,[6] in which some of them saw a chance of using their parliamentary presence to drive bargains in return for supporting minority governments (this became known as the 'toleration strategy'). The entire process was accompanied by a high-profile debate within the broader German new left – from the Bahro conference in 1979 to the ensuing Socialist Conferences in 1980-81 – partly resulting in the attempt to establish a green-left monthly 'Moderne Zeiten' (1981-1984) which brought together a considerable number of future green leaders.

As the 'Fundis' were losing a clear strategic orientation from the mid-1980s to 1989, the participation of Joschka Fischer in the state government of Hesse (which included practical proof of being able to break an alliance, if needed) increased the credibility of the Realo strategy. This led to a realignment within the Green left. A Left Forum was formed by left municipal[7] and regional pragmatists (who had been ignored by the left leadership while it focused on the Realo-Fundi confrontation), by the adherents of the 'toleration strategy' within the 'Fundis', and by a group of ex-Trotskyites who had joined the party. The Left Forum concentrated on the content of the policy to be advocated by the greens instead of on the question of government participation as such. Meanwhile, the small 'Aufbruch' group, which emerged by pleading for an end to the Fundi-Realo stand-off within the party through pressure 'from below', in the end turned out to be one of the spearheads of the introduction of neo-liberal conceptions into the greens, in the guise of libertarianism. In this short phase, which lasted until the first elections in the newly unified Germany, the Left Forum's hopes for an anticipated coalition agreement with a left-leaning SPD under Oskar Lafontaine seemed to present a productive, although deeply reformist, way out of the crisis of fordism. This was advanced under the general slogan of a new, 'eco-social', social compact.

All this was ended by the surprising advent of German unity. From 1990 to 1994, during which time the Fundis left the Green party, the Left Forum, feeling obliged to save the Western party from the ruins of the 1990 elections, made a truce with the Realos, and sought to re-integrate a party 'family' now consisting of the West German Green party, the inheritors of the civic movements of the GDR, and the small Eastern green party. Without the presence of the left forces which had abandoned the party – under the leadership of Jutta Ditfurth, who tried in vain to build a competing electoral organization – or who embraced the promise seemingly offered by the 'westward extension' of the new PDS which had been formed out of the GDR's Socialist Unity Party – and with the strong disorientation concerning left alternatives gripping civil society this proved to have been no more than a protracted rearguard action, deferring the final hegemony of the Realo wing for some eight years.

The same must be said for the 'Babelsberg circle' and its radical network which managed to keep alive the Green left, reinforced by exponents of the ex-GDR greens until the defeat on the Kosovo question in 1998. It managed, for some time, to stem the tide of neoliberal economic and social policy conceptions within the greens, and it has been able to formulate a political pacifism capable of underlying a realistically radical green foreign policy, while keeping and developing the international contacts with other left green and alternative forces in Europe. Already, in the moment of forming of the first Red-Green government, in 1998, the influence of Joschka Fischer and his Realos turned out to be dominant – mostly within the parliamentary group, although they were forced to observe at least a semblance of parity with the green left. In the end, however, the green left has lost to the combination of Realo tactics and media propaganda supporting militarist 'humanitarian interventionism' (in the name of antifascism).

Since 1998 the Realo wing, together with a governmental left group led by ministers and federal or European parliamentarians, has been leading the German Greens to produce the results quoted in the beginning of this essay. They have no chance of replacing the Liberal Party as the lynchpin of the German party system. As they still represent a significant segment of the electorate – the social professionals, and the age cohort of the old new social movements – it is not to be expected that they will vanish. But they are being faced with a new parliamentary challenge – because in the emerging new German five-party system it will be largely their decision whether a right-wing alliance can have a parliamentary majority (comprising liberals, conservatives, and greens), or whether a left coalition is formed (left party, social-democrats, and greens), or whether a 'grand coalition' avoiding any such decisions will again be formed.

PROBLEMATIC EXPLANATIONS

I shall not review the ample literature on the integration of the German Greens into the dominant political constellation, most of which has nothing to do with any perspective of emancipatory transformation.[8] Instead, I shall try to discuss typical explanations and arguments running through this literature, or through public debates in Germany, that pertain to the historical failure of the West German Greens as a political force opening up an historical alternative to the existing constellation of capitalist domination, i.e. *its failure as a project for an emancipatory transformation.* There are two kinds of trouble with existing explanations in this sense. On the one hand, they tend to mis-describe the existing situation out of which an alternative path of historical change has been sought. Instead of analyzing it in terms of unresolved contradictions, the resolution of which is driven by historical struggles, they assume a totally determined state of affairs which does not admit any real alternatives – no bifurcations, just an onward march of history (or of the reproduction of the biosphere). On the other hand, they seem to oscillate between explaining too much, and explaining too little: they are either referring to very broad structural explanations – e.g. the statism implicit in the very form of the political party or the deformations involved in trying to participate in the government of a leading 'imperialist' country – which, if they were true, would imply the absolute impossibility of using the party form as an instrument of liberation; or they imply the impossibility of any gradualist transformation in such a country.[9]

The type of explanation most current within the Marxist Left combines the two errors in an almost inextricable way, seeing green activists (or the electorate or the party builders) as possessing the wrong kind of 'essence', in terms of class, gender, race or societal location. Just because of their being 'petty bourgeois', male-heterosexual, white or 'Northern' the rebellion and opposition of the greens will never be more than a show, leading, in the very end, to a reinforced dependency on the existing structures of domination. In so far as class essence is stressed in this explanation (which derives from political and intellectual sources that should not be underestimated),[10] it badly mis-describes the prevailing situation. This is because it unduly reduces the class of people exploited by capital to a certain historical type of industrial manual workers,[11] whereas many indicators show that the 'green pool' of activists, voters and party builders represent the more modern segments of the working class exploited by capital, supplemented by public workers employed by the state. If it is considered in terms of gender and age composition this green pool may indeed seem more representative of the actually existing working class than the more traditional social-democratic or communist electorate.

There is, to be sure, the real problem of the expanding categories of 'precarious' and 'flexible' workers which poses a real challenge to all possible class politics. It would be an illusion, however, to think that these new types of workers are less accessible to green politics than the communist or social-democratic 'pools'; and the 'green pool', has at least the advantage of a more feminized gender composition and of less normalized types of employment. There are, of course, profound differences of perspective between those who enjoy real, self-controlled 'flexibility' at the upper reaches of employment hierarchies, and those exposed to the other-controlled 'precariousness' to which the low-level tiers of the hierarchy are exposed, as well as the emerging new 'under-classes'.

On the whole, the important issue of the changes in the 'class composition' of wage labourers exploited by capital is unduly side-stepped in such an approach, as well as the real problems of determining the relative weight of the processes of indirect exploitation of unpaid labour or the directly violent expropriation of workers in the dependent countries of global capitalism. But in any case, the assumption that the young and better-educated sections of the population in the metropolitan centres can be written off as having no motive or capacity for any serious opposition to the existing system – i.e., that only the most destitute segments are capable of this – would imply that the chances of success were very slim indeed. Without overthrowing 'the system' with one violent blow – which has never happened and should never be expected – any protracted oppositional struggle will tend to derive its strength more from its capacity to implicate those workers most urgently needed by capital than from just organizing the most destitute, and therefore most desperate segments of the working class.

The most current explanation of the German Greens' political failure within mainstream social science manages to combine both errors in a remarkably different way. The 'cycle' theory of social movements claims that there is a series of phases through which all oppositions must proceed, throughout human history: to begin with, a phase of blunt rebellion; followed by a phase of creative articulation; then a phase of routinization, ideologization and organization, required to constitute a mass basis for the new movements; then a phase of struggle to assert the place of the new movements in the arenas where power relations within society are determined; then a phase of institutionalization, when the new movement begins to 'take its seat' within the constituted 'places' of established power; and finally a phase of integration, when the former representatives of the movement are fully co-opted into the established constellation of domination, and the memory of the movement is turned into an ideological source of legitimacy of this new establishment. The empirical and historical bases for such a typology are indeed very broad. And the history of the German Greens may easily be told in a rather convincing way to give this omni-historical truth another striking illustration.

This explanation, in its popular vulgarization, is sometimes couched in terms of a comparison of the 'green movement' with Christianity – from the violent radicalism of Jesus and the early Christians via the establishment of churches, canons, and orthodoxies to the established churches linked to state power from Constantine onwards. The Green movement, it is then affirmed in this vein, managed to do in a decade what Christianity had taken half a millennium to realize: the transformation from a radical opposition movement to a part of the established institutions of domination. But this is a clear case of an empty argument: the green movement, although it touches – as any radical movement cannot avoid doing – on the question of the good life, and, in this context, on what is being conceived as spirituality by some, is certainly not a movement of faith, not a religious or millenarian movement.[12]

A less patently absurd popularization of the 'cycle' thesis, however, has been based on the analogy between the green movement and the labour movement – again stressing the relative velocity of development on the side of the greens, who took mere years to arrive at a betrayal of their original radicalism (i.e. 1980-89), whereas the labour movement had taken decades, (from the 1860s to World War I, in the case of the social democrats) or to the Stalinist betrayal of the Bolshevik revolution, in the case of the communists. The problem of this 'description' is twofold: on the one hand, it sees something as a 'betrayal', i.e. in terms of a subjective category involving individual and collective guilt, which is actually a complex objective historical process. On the other hand, paradoxically, it affirms the unavoidability of the outcome of being reintegrated into the established power structure. In order to be useful at all, such a comparison would have to be based on just the opposite premises: analyzing these processes in their objectivity – maybe even in their tragic 'entanglement' – as lived and suffered by its subjective actors, and at the same time looking for their objective indeterminacies, allowing for alternative outcomes and objective 'bifurcations'.

The central flaw in both arguments is, of course, inductive reasoning: as there has not so far been, in all history up to the present, any durably successful initiative for social emancipation and liberation, it is inferred that such an initiative is impossible. Impossibility cannot, however, be based on this kind of experiential inductivism. What has been defeated or simply failed in the past may work effectively in the future. The interesting question is not whether this type of cyclical development occurs, which cannot really be denied – but to find the explanations and reasons underlying it. Such a theoretical explanation, once found, would in turn make it possible to choose a different path, to avoid certain mechanisms of self-sabotage and to decline programmatic temptations leading to defeat, or to simply giving up the struggle. Such a closer look would also bring out more clearly the particularities and the distinct dynamics of each of the movements, which are systematically covered up by the analogical thinking involved in the 'cycle' theory of social movements. More especially, it would call into question the purity of the cyclical phases constructed – e.g. pointing to the ambivalences present within the labour movement since its very beginnings, torn between an Owenite reformism, a Proudhonian libertarianism, a Lassallean statism and the very specific kind of transformative revolutionarism advocated by Marx and Engels. Or, for example, it could highlight the presence of right-wing reactionary forces at the very beginnings of the green movement, and especially within the initiatives bringing it to a party form, well before any cycle of recuperation could possibly have drawn it to the side of the establishment; or the strong presence of municipal pragmatism within these same beginnings, which has always partly subverted the universalizing ideological stances structuring the Green's public political debates.

There are other more timid explanations which have a more myopic focus, and tend to explain far too little, concentrating as they do only on the immediate political processes within and without the Greens. The incapacity of many of the early left counterparts of the 'Realo' current led by Joschka Fischer to define and to implement a coherent strategy was certainly a major weakness. Even more so, as this incapacity was linked to a visceral dislike and refusal of 'theory'. This was somewhat understandable after the foreseeable failure of an 'instant revival' of Marxist theory from its protracted and repressed crisis, and after the elaborate counter-insurgency technologies which presented themselves as scientific theories; hardened intuition and historical experience seemed to offer better guides to action. Untheorized pragmatism, however, is a bad basis for strategic thought, 'bracketing off' as it does so many fundamental questions. It may, of course, support a stubborn but well-founded refusal to confuse elaborate arguments (presented, as a rule, from above) with more pertinent arguments (presented, again as a rule, from below). But it cannot lead to new thinking and structural insights informing a creative new strategy. This weakness of German Greens (which a handful of intellectuals were unable to cure) has not just been a matter of personal incapacities, but points to an unresolved strategic problem the Greens have shared and still do share with the left at large: how to find an adequate relation between practical experience and theoretical articulation.

The same kind of reasoning applies to even more anecdotal levels of explanation. Was it the failure of the 'fundamentalists' under the leadership of Jutta Ditfurth to anticipate the defeat at the Neumünster party congress in 1991 of the attempted take-over of the party by an alliance of the Realo wing with a new centre group and the majority of the East German citizens movement, and therefore the Fundis failure to support an alliance of the broad left wing of the party to get rid of this new right wing? Or was it the failure of the Left Forum group led by Ludger Volmer and others not to use that party congress to split or smash a party which was bound to be taken over by its Realo wing sooner or later? Or again, should the same kind of reasoning be applied to the party conference at Bielefeld in 1998, when the small majority in support of Fisher's 'bellicose' stance on Kosovo was facilitated by a few radical pacifists refusing to support an opposition motion less radical than they deemed indispensable? How to pose the right kind of questions here is the main difficulty, and even where it is possible to identify the questions that need to be examined, and even find out the right ways to answer them, the results will be so specific that they will remain unable to teach anything of significance to anyone who did not participate in the original events.

PLAUSIBLE EXPLANATIONS

There are, however, at least four other types of explanation for the failure of the German Greens which are interesting and may rightfully claim more attention. The first of these explanations pertains to the inability of the old and the new left to overcome their divisions, so that anti-capitalism became, on the one hand, frozen into obsolete 'reformist' or 'revolutionary' alternatives; whereas the new, autonomous social movements, on the other hand, tended to defend their autonomy by closing their eyes to the anti-capitalist consequences of their own demands. This has a specific force for explaining the early phases of the German green movement. Links to the labour movement have always been weak, partly caught up in older attempts to revive leftist forms of 'trade union opposition', partly hoping for a reconciliation with a trade union leadership which still was staunchly social-democratic. The self-isolation of the Communist and Maoist parties, as they went through their various crises, and were in any case still wary of accepting as relevant other struggles than that of the white, male, and national industrial worker, also limited the influx and the influence of even independent Marxist intellectuals. And the failure of a handful of eco-socialists, eco-feminists, and socialist feminists to impress the ecological or feminist movements at large further contributed to the Green party's losing access to all kinds of critical economic culture, not least the Marxist critique of political economy, which had just been reconstructed by leading figures in the 1960s student movements, in a tremendous effort. Their incapacity to join at least in a common debate was decisive for the discursive fragmentation of the alternative and multicoloured movements.

This actually made the green label more attractive for the new party, although a majority of its activists participated in the more socialist alternative part of the so-called 'electoral movement'. But the limitations of this were then seen in the consecutive failures to construct a space for theoretical debate in the party, where an eco-socialist current would not have to reduce itself to questions of day-to-day tactics and strategy. It may also have contributed to the fateful strategic decision of the greater part of the left green leadership in 1983 to stop playing a game of left vs. right wing, and instead begin to play the fundi-realo game – which they spectacularly lost in the end. The immediate consequence of the left's change of strategy had been the trashing of their own theoretical manifesto, originally conceived before this turn, and the loss to the Realo wing of the municipal pragmatists, mostly coming from far left organizations of the 1970s.

A second useful explanation is one which starts from the general crisis of the left, especially in the context of the downfall of the Soviet model of state socialism, which has, in fact, sapped the credibility of all kinds of radical emancipatory alternatives to the present constellation of global domination. This has a specific bearing for the alternative left in West Germany, and, therefore, for the West German Greens. At least since the Hungarian Revolution of 1956, if not since the workers' uprising in the GDR in 1953, German communism had lost its credibility with the masses as well as with most intellectuals. The building of the Berlin wall in 1961 had fortified the impression that an alternative left should be built only in West Germany and in West Berlin – one which would in no way rely upon the Eastern bloc and its political representatives. At the same time, it was expected that the co-existence of the Cold War blocs would continue indefinitely, or at least for the foreseeable future. As a consequence, the Soviet bloc was certainly not seen as an Alternative (this is why in the West Rudolf Bahro's spectacular publication was not a surprise in its substance).[13] Yet the Soviet bloc, while certainly not seen as an ally, was seen as a countervailing power capable putting of some pressure on the bloc one was living and struggling in – pressure which could at least be used to obtain political gains for one's own agenda. As such, however, Soviet-style communism was no longer considered really interesting by the alternative left in West Germany (it was only discussed by a tiny number of specialists), so they were deeply unprepared for the fall of the 'Berlin wall', and unable to build connections rapidly with the democratic left 'over there'. They were incapable of compensating for the ensuing loss of political leverage, and short of arguments against the propaganda wave proclaiming the 'end of socialism' along with the 'end of history'. This was repeated, although on a smaller scale, within the German Greens after the unification of Germany. A double party unification process led first to the absorption of the small green party of the GDR, which was integrated with the western Green party left to form the 'Babelsberg circle' as a new radical umbrella network; and then to the negotiated fusion with the 'Bündnis 90' group from East Germany's 'civic movements' – which had the effect of strongly reinforcing the party's right wing.

A third explanation that is worth paying attention to is based on the crisis of fordism. This is used to explain specifically the sudden ascendancy of central tenets of neo-liberal economics within the Realo wing after the late 1980s, starting from the notions of 'sustainable fiscal policy' and 'generational justice' discovered by municipal Realos in Frankfurt. This is also used to explain why the ideologies of the opposition against fordism seem to have lost most of their biting power, so that after the system had been deconstructed by neo-liberal interventions towards a 'market capitalism', it shed all kinds of politically imposed fetters that had been powerful under fordism. Green concerns about 'big business, big labour, and big government' reaching class compromises at the expense of environmental interests seemingly vanished into thin air; now the market place alone, without any extraneous power intervening, mediated interests of all kinds. This may seem intuitively quite acceptable to people without a solid left culture or direct personal experience of capitalist exploitation, who may assume that all pre-existing power relations would disappear in acts of market exchange, and who are attracted by the idea that the market puts some sort of real liberty into the hands of the consumer and the citizen to express their respective preferences. Both assumptions are, of course, faulty: capitalist markets are in fact constituted by power relations that are far deeper than those visible at the rather superficial levels of monopolization or cartelization; nor do these relations vanish under the light weight of a mere declaration of market equality, that is limited, anyway, to the postulate of one dollar, one unit of power, and not extended to any equality between people. But in the context of the crisis of fordism, such ideas had real appeal, and not only among the Greens.

A fourth explanation of some import relates to the effects on the Greens of the apparent abolition of the German nation state having been brought to a sudden end by the unification of 1989/1990.[14] The appeal of a post-national 'moment', which had been strong in West Germany's young generation before German unity, rapidly became a tangible possibility, and then a reality, has been lost after German unification. This unexpected turn of history immediately prevented a red-green constellation under Oskar Lafontaine from winning the elections against Chancellor Helmut Kohl, whose defeat had until then seemed certain. Both the red and the green side of the alliance lamented losing an election they had been certain to win, but it happened partly because the two sides were at loggerheads over the re-emerging 'national question'. Oskar Lafontaine antagonized the majority of the East Germans by calling into question the monetary integration which was the main engine of Kohl's unification strategy; and the Greens proved their non-German focus by campaigning blatantly with the central slogan of 'Everyone talks about Germany, we talk about the weather!' In the elections following Kohl's historic success, the West German Greens failed to pass the 5 per cent barrier, losing their representation in the federal parliament, while the East German alliance of civic movements and greens just scraped enough votes together to get into parliament.

There is a fifth explanation that demands consideration, and this pertains to a more general crisis of politics in an age of the spectacle where the media tend to over-determine everything else. But this is often the starting-point of many contributions to party-building discussions on the left today, and we will consider it below, placing the experience of the German Greens in the context of those debates, and trying to discern some lessons that may be relevant to them.

LESSONS FOR PARTY-BUILDING TODAY

The first lesson may sound trivial, indeed, but it should not be underestimated: it is simply that any initiative from below which does not succeed in displacing the existing constellation of domination by a revolutionary transformation will be used by this constellation as an impetus towards a 'passive revolution', granting a new lease of life to itself. This should, of course, not be invoked to stop revolutionary initiatives 'from below' simply in order to avoid 'recuperation' from above. But it is certainly true, and verified by the now historical experience of the West German Greens, that 'only a freely

evolving praxis of participation can mobilize the imagination and bring together the innumerable points at which anti-capitalist struggle originates' as
Joel Kovel has vividly argued in his blueprint for 'the eco-socialist party and
its victory'.[15] As, however, this was more or less exactly the idea underlying
the 'multicoloured' and 'alternative' line within the West German Greens,
the question has to be asked why it has shown so little resistance to being
drawn into a process of 'parliamentarization' which led to the Greens 'defining themselves as a progressive populism within the framework of bourgeois
democracy' and therefore 'solidifying as a kind of intermediate formation
that stops considerably short of what is needed for transformation'.[16]

Kovel rightly stresses the importance of party-building: '…only a "party-
like" formation that postulates a goal common to all struggles without con-
straining them from above can organize this into "solidarity solidified" and
press towards power'.[17] Relying upon a mere fluid network, such as that
recently postulated by John Holloway,[18] would underestimate the role of the
state in controlling the reproduction processes of society, and lead to some
variant of 'the social-democratic gap' experienced by radical social movements in West Germany before the advent of alternative and green electoral
lists.[19] In order to have their demands translated into institutionalized politics
and implemented by legislation and government, they had to address them
to more or less sympathetic social-democratic politicians who in fact acted
as gate-keepers to the 'real' political process. There are good grounds, therefore, for 'pressing towards power'. The question must be asked, however, if
and how such a 'party-like formation' can escape the vicissitudes of the party
form (which even in its revolutionary variants has been analyzed as an Ideological State Apparatus[20]). And the experience of the West German Greens
seems to indicate that the measures proposed by Kovel to cope with the
potentially sinister dialectic of the party form are structurally insufficient, i.e.
they are either realistically inapplicable or insufficient for reaching the goal
of the required transformation of the party-form itself as a condition of the
eco-socialist transformation of society.

The first principle of organization Kovel postulates[21] is that the party be
'grounded in communities of resistance', with 'delegation from such communities' supplying 'the cadre of party activists as such'. Such a principle had
been accepted in the early formative phase of the West German Greens, too,
but turned out to be impracticable from the moment the party organization
was also 'open to individuals', as Kovel himself acknowledges. And, in fact,
building a party on collective membership alone would create an innumerable series of problems of accountability and participation (in a real world
structured by the individualistic ideology of law) and would specifically need

a guarantee of the internal democracy of each and every one of the participating units.[22]

Kovel's second principle of organization may seem self-evident to his
American readers: 'The party is to be internally funded through contributions by members, structured in such a way that no alienating force can take
financial control'. In contrast to 'sponsors' buying politicians by their 'voluntary contributions' to electoral funds requiring many millions of US dollars
this is, in fact, self-evident. But what about constitutional state funding of
parties, which is a recent tradition in continental Europe, modelled on the
state funding of churches? The state does not, in these frameworks, intervene
as an 'alienating force', with funding based on general rules open to control
by the judiciary. Neither extreme left nor extreme right wing parties, in so
far they are legal, are excluded from state funding. In the German system of
party funding, even the 'establishment effect' of these rules is rather mitigated:
any party or electoral list getting more than 1.5 per cent of the votes cast is
entitled to its share of state money. Refusing to take this money would be
damaging in relation to competing political parties who all take it. Taking
it would certainly tend to reinforce the electoralist tendencies within the
party, by making its functionaries dependent on electoral success. If, however,
electoral success is any yardstick at all for the success of a party, judged for
example by the number of parliamentary seats won, this tendency towards
electoralism would seem inherent in the party form as such, and not the effect of a system of state finance for parties.[23]

Third, Kovel advocates a flexible variant of the 'imperative mandate':[24] all
'delegates and administrative bodies' should be subject to a system of regular
rotation and recall. This principle of grass-roots democracy[25] has been re-
elaborated and amply implemented in the early history of the West German
Greens. Are there lessons to be learned from its embattled abandonment
– stretching from the middle of the 1980s to the early 1990s? There are,
basically, two such lessons. First, these rules should be clearly distinguished
from the liberal principle of non-professionalism in politics,[26] which in reality serves to make politics a reserved area for professionals, civil servants and
teachers who possess or are granted enough disposable time to engage in
politics. This implies that there should be a real possibility of 'living from politics', and not only 'for politics' (as Max Weber put it) during the considerable
stretch of a life-time that is needed to build not only individual competence
with regard to specific areas of politics, but also the kind of media presence
and grass-roots trust needed to make one's voice heard. This could be made
possible by accepting rotation between different types of posts within one
area of politics, including NGO or social movement organizations, or – in a

maybe more radical vein – by a system of funding political activism by concerned 'communities of struggle'. Second, this principle should not be per-
verted by coercion, as in the case of 'democratic centralism', nor deflected to
serve as a means of hindering party initiatives and actions by a mechanism of
'checks and balances', as in the liberal tradition. It should be flexibly followed
with the aim of creating a higher kind of party unity in action, bringing different perspectives and sensibilities together within a common perspective of
radical transformation.

Fourth, Kovel postulates the need for openness and transparency in all
party deliberations 'except [on] certain tactical questions (for example, the
details of a direct action)'. This is unquestionable. And yet he seems totally
unaware of the 'other side' this principle has in a modern mass party, which
the experience of the German Greens has amply exemplified, and which
brings us to the perhaps most important explanation of their failure, as mentioned at the end of the previous section of this essay. Openness and transparency in fact operate in two directions, with the media serving as a hugely
important filter and agency – and are likely to result in published opinions
controlled by media tycoons, overlaying and dominating the internal debates of the party. In the case of the German Greens this has probably been
the single most important factor weighing in favour of the 'Realo' wing of
the party, which was consistently supported by the entire spectrum of published opinion, and secured the defeat of the party's left wing, which was far
more deeply anchored among the first generation of party activists, but was
framed by the media as being 'fundamentalist'. This went so far as to even
help change the very composition of party activists, giving the Realo wing,
reinforced by those parts of the left which preferred to stay in government,
a real majority at a party conference for the first time in 1998. Developing a
strong alternative media culture within the party and in its supporting areas
is certainly a must from this perspective, but also certainly not sufficient. The
left needs to take up the battle for media reform as a high priority; in the
meantime some degree of party control over general media access to internal
party debates, and some disciplinary rules for party members in using their
media access (e.g. excluding the use of certain tabloids and TV chains for
interviews) will also be needed.

Even if Kovel's principles had been fully applied, and handled with the
real 'artfulness and subtlety' that he calls for, it is doubtful whether such a
development as that of the German Greens (and more generally of the European continental Greens who have to some degree, although often less
markedly, travelled the same path towards a renewed political establishment)
could have been avoided, because these principles do not really address the

underlying paradox of the very form of the emancipatory political party, i.e. how to 'press toward power' with the aim of overcoming all structures of domination, and how to enter into the existing ideological system of electoral politics with the aim of achieving a liberating transformation of the society so as to abolish its structural relations of domination and dominance. A 'prefigurative vision surpassing the given society', as postulated by Kovel, would be very helpful indeed in handling this elementary paradox. But without clear ideas about the 'contradictions' and tendencies entailed in operating within existing society (all the more complex a question when we take the global situation into account), prefigurative visions may tend to sink into an increasingly infertile utopianism. There is an urgent need, therefore, to inform social movements by scientific inquiries into the nature of the societies they are rebelling against. Anti-capitalist, anti-patriarchal, anti-colonial, anti-sexist, anti-racist theorizing are needed to supply social movements and any emancipatory party with sufficiently clear and sharp ideas of what needs to be transformed in their societies. Marxist, feminist, and cultural analyses will have to be re-read and synthesized with a view to providing the leading ideas for such a new kind of emancipatory party. This is urgently needed, though not because the movement activists were somehow structurally unable to address the underlying causes of their predicament – as Kautsky and Lenin led generations of Marxists to believe about the working class, supposed to be bound in its 'spontaneous consciousness' to reformist 'trade unionism'. Rather, theoretical work is needed because the very articulation of the experiences underlying these social movements, which is required to be able to communicate them to other social movements with other experiences, or over time to ensuing generations – is simply impossible without adequate concepts. This can only be acquired by a critique of existing conceptualizations, which is the core work of critical theory.

While Joel Kovel has gone some way in pointing to more effective party-building by combining his four principles of organization with a call for an informed and emancipatory 'anti-capitalism as a point of reference'[27] (which he sees as especially important for guarding against petty bourgeois parochialism and localism), he leaves us feeling we still are a considerable distance away from the 'kind of self-generative and non-linear dialectic' he anticipates, 'that can rapidly accelerate the motion toward eco-socialism'.[28] And this raises the question of whether there are any lessons to be learnt from the experience of the German Greens on how to strive in an effective way to get from here to there. Some such lessons are indeed brought to mind on reading Stanley Aronowitz's most recent arguments for a radical party, which raise the more immediate questions of party building (although very specifically addressing the situation in the USA).[29]

Aronowitz's starting point is the diagnosis of another kind of parochialism which certainly has also been present within the German Greens – the 'parochialism of late Critical Theory'.[30] There were many ways in which the late critical theory of the Frankfurt School helped to shape the fundamental political outlook of green party activists (who were even less intellectually coherent than Anglo-Saxon greens).[31] The kind of parochialism Aronowitz describes does not need this kind of influence, as it may also be seen as being part of the 'common sense' of most people engaging in politics in Germany since the 1960s: 'only Western Europe and North America were worthy of concern' and 'only white men were capable of entering history'.[32] Therefore, Aronowitz argues cogently, they 'could not see ...the profound implications of the emerging global vision of the ecology, feminist and labor movements for the creation of a new opposition to transnational capitalism'.[33] So far Aronowitz's argument coincides with Kovel's;[34] but then he takes a slightly different turn by specifying the present situation: 'The Seattle demonstrations of December 1999, the subsequent mass demonstrations at Quebec, Genoa and Spain against the key institutions of global capital, and the development of the World Social Forum, whose location in Brazil's Porto Alegre was symbolic of a global shift, as both an attempt to create a new civil society and as a post-9/11 continuation of the protests, present new possibilities'.[35] This is relevant to one of the most salient lessons of the experience of the German Greens, which seems to be that the decisive element in the building and in the development of a party is never to be found within the party itself, but in the broader trends and tensions of the 'conjuncture' within which it lives as a social, ideological and political entity – in the 'occasions' and in the 'impossibilities' which it has to confront in order to survive as a meaningful political project.

These 'new possibilities' are identified by Aronowitz as a historical occasion for building a 'radical party' as a new type of 'third party' in the USA. His 'meditation on left political organization'[36] is not primarily referring to 'American exceptionalism'.[37] He expressly addresses the 'rise of the New Left in all western nations' after the bankruptcy of the 'main political parties of the Left' had become patent, with the end of the post-war period and the emergence of 'a series of "new" social movements which consciously spurn the concept of "party" itself'.[38] Aronowitz's moderate ironizing of the 'newness' of these social movements seems linked to the short diagnosis he offers of the 'exception, the global phenomenon of Green parties', seeing them 'in the framework of the revolt of the ecology movement against the social-democratic mainstream rather than as an attempt to form a new radical party'.[39] Aronowitz is indubitably right in putting into question the amnesiac illusions of newness that were widespread in the emancipatory movements of the 1960s. However, he seems to underestimate the importance of the demand for 'autonomy' which was a defining element in a whole set of radicalizing 'second generation' movements – from the *autonomia operaria* in Italy, which had counterparts in most other leading capitalist countries, and the autonomous women's liberation movement, which emerged trans-nationally from its very beginnings, to a new generation of anti-colonial, anti-racist, and ecological movements. It is also true, and in retrospect irrefutable, that all of these movements were historically marked very specifically by their opposition to the fordist constellation of capitalist domination, and vulnerable, therefore, to the lure of neo-liberal anti-fordism, seemingly promising to put an end to big capital as well as big unions and big government. This apparently leads Aronowitz into thinking that the ambition of green party building did not go beyond changing social democracy – which is in fact what has been mainly achieved by it, and what the Realo wing of the party has for some time claimed as a strategic objective (before aiming at displacing the Liberal party as the linchpin of the German party system, which they have failed to achieve).

But in actual fact, the building of a new party of systemic opposition, capable of bundling together all the radical opposition movements, from the new ecological movements, through the new women's movement, to the new peace movement, has been the explicit aim of the leading exponents of the green left in Germany. Their failure cannot simply be explained by assuming that they did not try. Nor did the difference between the Realo wing and the green left in the 1990s simply relate to the question of parliamentary vs. extra-parliamentary perspectives, as Aronowitz suggests.[40] It was about the strategy of parliamentary politics, the necessity of which itself had been accepted by all wings of the party:[41] was it to prepare for participating in governments by operating as a 'constructive' opposition or partner in government, or was it to develop political contradictions to a point where deeper changes would become possible – accepting the necessity of longer phases of opposition, insofar as participation in government could not be had under a radical political programme? And with the rising wave of the neo-liberal counter-revolution sapping the continental welfare-states, the key question of strategy became more and more whether the greens should support neo-liberal 'reforms' destroying fordist power structures (as the centre and right wing of the party affirmed), or whether they should support the resistance against them, with a view to turning them away from fordist nostalgia to a new kind of affirmation of democratic politics and a new kind of globalized anti-capitalism (as the green left in fact affirmed, but with far less media attention). The lesson to be learned here, with a view to realistically initiating the building of a radical party in any advanced country dominated by the capitalist mode of production, is rather how urgent and how difficult it is to disengage some key parts of today's opposition movements, like the trade unions, the women involved in gender-mainstreaming initiatives, or the environmental movements, from their entanglement in the vestiges of fordism – be it in the form of resentment or of nostalgia.

In spite of these criticisms the general conclusion Aronowitz arrives at seems to be convincing: before seriously engaging in party building in the sense of creating an organized agency for radical, transformative, and system-transcending politics[42] – which would effectively embody in a specific historical situation what Kovel postulates for his Eco-Socialist party[43] – 'one might propose to form an organization that would attempt to mediate between theory and practice, humans and history'.[44] Here again, I am afraid, the West German experience of creating – as it were – a new left out of the burnt and forgotten remnants of the old, practically without left father figures to rebel against, or without elder brothers capable of lending a helping hand, may offer a warning lesson: a series of – mostly Maoist – competing party building organizations were created to bring about the conditions for the re-building of the German Communist Party, before such a task could be seriously addressed. If I am not mistaken, all of them, after some time of frustrating attempts to create these conditions, which they never even came close to, have now declared themselves *to be* the reconstructed CP of Germany (and later on dissolved themselves, admitting their utter failure, some of them moving directly to the Green Party).

The tasks Aronowitz assigns to this party-building organization do not exclude such a turn in its development:[45] 'bring[ing] together those who are already discontented with the current state of things' (although this particular formulation would be unduly open to right-wing discontent which in part extends to right-wing 'anti-capitalism' and, more frequently even, to right wing 'anti-globalism', which an internationally active radical party must fight without any ambiguity) and 'the development of a public presence' is certainly as much a task of the emerging radical party as of the party-building organization preparing its emergence. 'To initiate a broad discussion of the central problems of social and political theory, situated in the actuality of global as well as of national situations', certainly is an important task in preparing the ground for the kind of radical party Aronowitz is advocating; but, once emerging or having formed, it will also certainly have to carry on with this task, or gradually lose touch with contemporary reality. The same holds true, I think, for the task of 'revisiting the history of the left' and of 'developing an adequate theory of our own situation'. It may be a better idea rather to think about the kind of party-building organization needed in terms of a broad alliance for education and self-education – like the People's Global Alliance, initiated by the 'Zapatistas', or the international network of ATTAC initiatives, initiated by the French ATTAC! Organization. Or even better to embed its creation in the process of the World Social Forum, and its Continental, National or Local/Regional levels of self-organized arenas of debate.[46]

CONCLUSION

Donald Sassoon has summarized the development we have tried to analyze in this way: 'The political challenge of the greens was never sufficiently strong to cause a real crisis in West European Socialism'.[47] Stanley Aronowitz, in a rather opposed perspective, insists that the greens was limited to 'the revolt of the ecology movement against the social-democratic mainstream'.[48] The most important lesson that the failed project of the German Greens has to teach may be simply that this is not the right kind of question: from our perspective, the experience of the German greens is not interesting or important because it tried to dislodge the established left, communist, labour, or social-democratic. It rather is interesting and important because it has lessons, especially from its formative phases, for those who are trying to build forms of explicitly political struggles giving voice and power to an emancipatory anti-capitalism in a positive way, addressing the unsolved conundrums from the history of the established left. Even this will still need adaptation to concrete conjunctures and conditions; yet it will also not be had without more general radical social and political theory. But, above all, it requires paying the most careful attention to what type of party-building organization can make eco-socialist popular education – and self-education – really effective.

NOTES

I would like to thank Matthias Oberg for commenting on an early draft of this paper.

1   This essay is an attempt at an analysis 'from inside'; therefore, implicitly, at self-criticism. Since the end of the 1970s I have actively participated in small activist groups looking for a way out of the crisis of the left by making good use of the impulses of the new social movements, especially in the field of renewed electoral politics. In Germany, this has led me, from time of the Socialist Conferences (1980-81), to participate in and often to co-ordinate, as it were, three

generations of leading left-green circles. This also involved participating in the preparation of strategic documents like the founding platform of the *Initiative für Sozialistische Politik*, the founding of the left-green monthly 'Moderne Zeiten' in 1982, and the publication of Thomas Ebermann's and Rainer Trampert's pamphlet on the Future of the Greens (*Die Zukunft der Grünen*, Hamburg: Konkret, 1983). I then participated in the organization of the left within the emerging Greens right up until the strategic defeat of the Green Left in Germany, with its opposition to NATO's war on Yugoslavia. Especially since the first tactical defeats of the Ebermann-Trampert line in the mid-80s, I have also put considerable emphasis on participating in strategic debates in Europe, using the possibilities of my international contacts from the 1970s (mainly with Althusserians, dissident Trotskyites, and various brands of communist renovators). This was subsequently reinforced by my position as a Green Member of the European Parliament, with an explicit responsibility for strategically liaising with the emerging green-alternative left in France (co-founding the 'Rainbow Movement'), in Great Britain (actively participating in various red-green conferences), and on the Iberian peninsula. This led to my co-authorship of the 'eco-socialist manifesto' initiated by Pierre Juquin (A.V., *Europe's Green Alternative,* Montréal: Black Rose, 1992). Looking back on these two decades from 1979 to 1999, I must say I have always worked beyond my real capacities, unable to control the outcome – as is, it seems, always the case in serious political and philosophical practice. This essay, however, does not undertake a personal self-criticism. It attempts to lay bare some strategic shortcomings underlying the first successes and the ensuing series of defeats of the German green-alternative left – so that a new generation of radical political initiatives may have the possibility of learning from this historical experience, taking up the thread of reflection already underlying my 'Warum fällt es uns in den Grünen so schwer, über unsere Perspektiven zu diskutieren?', in Erwin Jurtschitsch, Alexander Rudnick and Frieder Otto Wolf, eds., *Grüne Perspektiven (Grün-Alternatives Jahrbuch 1988)*, Köln: Kölner Volksblatt, 1988, pp. 88-117; and more recently, albeit much more briefly, in 'What Happened to the West German Greens', *Red Pepper*, 110(August), 2003, pp. 8-9.

2   The example of the FRG is telling here, because it made so explicit that this openness of the political sphere had its limits – by prohibiting an already marginalized CP in 1956. But these limits were also demonstrated, of course, by McCarthyism in the US, and even by the exclusion of the PCI from Italian government coalitions.

3   In Germany, there never was an exemplary police repression against the protest movement like that in France with the 'battle of Malville' in 1977, where non-violent protesters were relentlessly beaten and some killed by militarized police forces, breaking the neck, as it were, of the French protest movement. In Germany, by contrast, the 'battle of Brokdorf' in 1981, where 200,000 protesters participated in an 'illegal' demonstration against a planned nuclear site, could not be won by a huge police force going to the limits of legal police actions, against well-organized resistance. Cf. Simples Citoyens, *Memento Malville. Une*

histoire des années soixante-dix, Grenoble, 14 June 2005, available at http://www.piecesetmaindoeuvre.com.

4   I formulate it from memory – having practically lived through these developments since the end of the 1970s. There are a number of significant studies of the development of the Greens. To get a general background, I still recommend Werner Hülsberg's *The German Greens. A Social and Political Profile*, translated by Gus Fagan, London: Verso, 1988. The most relevant study from the perspective of our discussion has been Jorge Riechmann's very thorough and theoretically acute analysis of *Los Verdes Alemanes. Historia y análisis de un experimento ecopacifista a finales del siglo XX*, Granada: Comares, 1994. Of course, the great studies by Joachim Raschke, *Die Grünen: wie sie wurden, was sie sind*, Köln: Bund, 1993, and, *Die Zukunft der Grünen*, Frankfurt: Campus Sachbuch, 2001, are unbeatable in empirical detail and intelligent comment. But he tends to see things politically in a not very illuminating mainstream perspective, whereas Riechmann is defending a radical political perspective – without illusions, yet also without resignation.

5   The Anglo-Saxon literature on the German Greens, epitomized by the way the British ecologist Sara Parkin shudders at the leftism she found in most of the German Greens (see her *Green Parties: An International Guide*, London: Heretic, 1989), and the similar projections in Donald Sassoon's 'the New Left of the 1960s in green clothes' (in his *One Hundred Years of Socialism: The West European Left in the Twentieth Century*, London: Fontana, 1996, p. 678) misses the whole point. This is exactly what the German Greens – on the 'Fundi' as well as on the 'Realo' side – were about: to translate the dreams and wishes of the 1960s into effective politics.

6   This had not been the case from the very beginning (as Sassoon, *One Hundred Years of Socialism*, p. 677 believes), but was the result of a strategic realignment initiated by Thomas Ebermann from the left seeking a strategic alliance with Rudolf Bahro and Jutta Ditfurth in the summer of 1983 – leaving the pragmatic municipal activists of the green left 'out in the cold'.

7   The decisive role of local politics in the building and functioning of the German Greens has been analyzed by Bodo Zeuner and Jörg Wischermann, in their *Rot-Grün in den Kommunen*, Opladen: Leske & Budrich, 1994.

8   Useful overviews can be found in Margit Mayer and John Ely, eds., *The German Greens: Paradox between Movement and Party*, translated by Michael Schatzschneider, Philadelphia: Temple University Press, 1998, as well as in John Ely's review of pertinent books (by Markovits, Scharf, Frankland/Schoonmaker, Hülsberg): 'Green Politics and the Transformation of the Left in Germany', in *New German Critique*, 72(Autumn), 1997.

9   To those who will say that from a truly revolutionary perspective this is true, I would simply reply that this would mean deferring revolutions, at least in the 'imperialist metropolitan countries', indefinitely, or at least for a very long time.

10   On the one hand, the interest of the functionaries of the traditional (communist or social-democratic) labour movement in combining revolutionary principles with an acceptance of their own day-to-day practice of trying to gain 'improve-

ments' for the organized working class which could not even be conceived of as 'reformist' (in the strong sense of constituting steps on a path leading beyond capitalism); and, on the other hand, the interest of radicalized intellectuals who, given their difficulties in gaining access to the labour movement and having their ideas heard in it, tended to be receptive to an ideology that comforted them by explaining the utter impossibility of even trying. Paradoxically, both the Stalinist ideology of subservience to the party line (as beautifully 'theorized' e.g. by György Lukács in his *Lenin: Studie über den Zusammenhang seiner Gedanken*, Wien: Arbeiterbuch, 1924) and the 'absurdist' theory of the total impossibility of a praxis non-corrupted by the 'false totality' of the existing constellation of domination, as it has been popularly read into Adorno's and Horkheimer's later writings, are capable of satisfying this need – their relatively changing 'evidence' being mainly constituted by the relative fate of the political organizations of the labour movement outside of intellectual debates.

11   Classical examples of this are Eric Hobsbawm's mistaking the historical construct of 'the working class' in Great Britain for the 'working class' in the sense of Marxist class analysis and considering everything else as 'middle class' (cf. e.g. his 'Labour's Lost Millions', *Marxism Today*, October, 1983); and Donald Sassoon's persistent talk (in *One Hundred Years of Socialism*, pp. 697, 699 and 712) about the 'middle class', when referring to new strata of wage earners. At the same time, there is another version of such class analyses that in trying to explain why petty bourgeois, peasant or feminist rebellions will never lead to a real process of societal emancipation, perversely end up sustaining the position that, at the end of the day, such an emancipation will simply never take place. Since according to this argument the proletarian movements expected to bring it about will only materialize where and when all scope for non-proletarian politics has been thoroughly exhausted, this is tantamount to deferring emancipation to a never-never day, when all potential allies of proletarian anti-capitalism will have exhausted their own political resources – and when, therefore, the chances that the proletariat itself will challenge capitalist domination through its own class struggle will be very dim indeed.

12   To think otherwise has been the fatal error of Rudolf Bahro and his followers in the later 1980s (cf. the retrospective collection of Rudolf Bahro's essays in his *Apokalypse oder Geist einer neuen Zeit*, Berlin: Edition Ost, 1995) who paid for it by losing any measurable influence on the further development of the greens as a real social and political movement.

13   Rudolf Bahro, *Die Alternative: Zur Kritik des real existierenden Sozialismus*, Köln: EVA, 1977. What was surprising about it was the fact of being written by an author from the GDR, and that this author maintained a specific kind of 'communist' perspective.

14   Talking about 're-unification' is somewhat misleading: the territories effectively unified had never formed a German nation state, and considerable parts of the territories staying outside had been part of a German empire, which had colonized other nations, especially Poles – not to mention the Austrian traditions of empire, which had always been part and parcel of the German political

tradition, until the turn towards a 'smaller Germany' initiated by Bismarck in the 1860s.

15   Joel Kovel, *The Enemy of Nature: The End of Capitalism or the End of the World?*, New York: Zed, 2003, pp. 232-8.

16   Ibid., 233.

17   Ibid.

18   John Holloway, *Change the World Without Taking Power: The Meaning of Revolution Today*, London: Pluto, 2002.

19   Donald Sassoon has touched upon this problem as a 'fraught division of labour between new social movements and parties of the Left' (*One Hundred Years of Socialism*, p. 673). He does not, however, understand that Green party building in Germany has been an attempt to do something about this kind of problem, by creating a 'parliamentary arm' for the social movements (cf. p. 674).

20   Althusser's well-known general thesis was later concretized by him in a vivid plea for 'the liberty of a communist', as well as in a specific description of 'what cannot go on like this in the French Communist Party' (cf. his *Ce qui ne peut plus durer dans le parti communiste*, Paris: Maspéro, 1978).

21   The following quotes are all from Kovel, *The Enemy of Nature*, p. 233.

22   At this point, further reflection could take Althusser's radicalization and subversion of the concept of the communist 'party cell' as a starting point.

23   From this perspective, it is significant that since the late 1990s German Greens have started trying to add sponsor money to the party funds.

24   For a more detailed discussion of this instrument of democratic control in the left tradition cf. my contribution 'imperatives Mandat', in W.F. Haug, ed., *Historisch-Kritisches Wörterbuch des Marxismus*, Bd. 6.1, Hamburg: Argument, 2004, pp. 837-47.

25   This translation of 'Basisdemokratie' is very approximate. It specially does not give an adequate sense of the ambivalent 'metaphysics' linked to a 'base' which was at the same time the object of a passively plebiscitarian mobilization by informal leaders, like Joschka Fischer or Jutta Ditfurth, against the institutions of democratic procedure within the party – reminiscent of Robert Michels' or Alfredo Pareto's 'law' of 'oligarchical rule'. Cf. the very thorough and critical retrospective treatment of the real functioning of green 'grass roots democracy' by Paul Tiefenbach: 'Wie hat die grüne Basisdemokratie funktioniert?', in Tiefenbach, *Die Grünen: Verstaatlichung einer Partei*, Köln: PapyRossa, 1998.

26   Failing to make this distinction is the main flaw of Tiefenbach's treatment.

27   Tiefenbach, 'Wie hat die grüne Basisdemokratie funktioniert?', p. 234. Especially in Germany, it is impossible to forget about the existence of right-wing anti-capitalism, which is anti-semitic in its very essence. Kovel is more concerned with how such an anti-capitalism can overcome the 'petty bourgeois' side of green politics. This has, however, taken the form of the 'social advancement' syndrome in the case of the West German Greens, not so much as a reflection of localism and parochialism, as Kovel seems to think, as of making the political representation of migrants who 'made good' one of the strong points of green politics in Germany up to the present.

28   Ibid., p. 236.

29   I refer to 'The Retreat to Postmodern Politics', in *Situations: Project of the Radical Imagination*, 1(1), 2005 and 'Is It Time for a Radical Party?' in *Situations: Project of the Radical Imagination*, 1(2), 2006.

30   Aronowitz, 'The Retreat', p. 42.

31   And it certainly has been no accident that the Realo-Fundi opposition – overlaying so much of the internal struggles of the German Greens – has originated in the Frankfurt of the 'Frankfurt School'.

32   Aronowitz, 'The Retreat', p. 42.

33   Ibid., pp. 42f.

34   cf. especially Kovel, *The Enemy of Nature*, pp. 234ff.

35   Aronowitz, 'The Retreat', p. 43.

36   Aronowitz, 'Is It Time', p. 117.

37   Ibid., pp. 124ff.

38   Ibid., p. 140.

39   Ibid.

40   Ibid., p. 140.

41   The argument of the intelligent fundamentalists had been, from the very beginning, that the party would get a better deal from occasional agreements in critical situations – within parliament – than in coalition agreements stretching over an entire legislature (or even more).

42   It should be noted here that the current attempt to create a common parliamentary party out of the PDS (combining already, unequally, the remaining organizational heritage of the East German 'socialist unity party' and the remnants of the West German alternative left (after leaving the Greens again, or staying outside of them) and the WASG (combining trade union activists with some SPD dissidents and a considerable number of new radical activists, some of them of Trotskyite orientation) may, in so far it succeeds, constitute an important step in changing the parliamentary balance inside Germany, but certainly is not yet a process of 'party formation' in Aronowitz's sense ('Is It Time', p. 156). The new party still lacks a sizeable mass basis – although it has a real presence among trade-union rank and file – and is vulnerable to facile but sectarian 'solutions' to the unresolved strategic problems of the radical left which have also beset the German green left in earlier decades; it also still has to rely heavily on the organizational and ideological heritage of the PDS, which is far from having completed the self-critical process of overcoming the traditions of theoretical and practical Stalinism.

43   Kovel, *Enemy of Nature*, pp. 232ff.

44   Aronowitz, 'Is It Time', p. 156.

45   All the following quotations are from ibid., pp. 156-7.

46   On the other hand, given the complexity and foreseeable long-windedness of at least some of the necessary debates, the whole thing will not effectively be able to function without maintaining or even gaining some strongholds within the institutionalized social sciences, i.e. without a continued presence within academia.

47   Sassoon, *One Hundred Years of Socialism*, p. 679.

48   Aronowitz, 'Is It Time', p. 140.

THE LIMITS OF ECO-LOCALISM: SCALE, STRATEGY, SOCIALISM

GREGORY ALBO

The shadow cast by neoliberalism over the prospects of the Left in the current period has been unrelenting. A few rays of hope have broken through with signs of a resurgence of the Latin American Left, the defeat of the Nepalese monarchy, and a number of specific campaigns, both local and global, in opposition to the privatization of basic services. But scepticism about universal projects and collective struggles for societal transformation – a scepticism reinforced by theoretical antagonisms toward integrative paradigms – remains entrenched even on a broadly defined Left, where the embrace of more socially limited and spatially local projects has replaced revolutionary ambitions.

This embrace of the local has a wide variety of sources – and supports. The World Bank, for instance, is representative of the neoliberal case for localism in contending that 'the political objectives to increase political responsiveness and participation at the local level can coincide with the economic objectives of better decisions about the use of public resources and increased willingness to pay for local services'.[1] It also has a significant place in social democratic 'third way' thinking, epitomized in Richard Florida's best-selling policy manual for the knowledge economy, and its rejection of theses of urban decline. The urban 'turnaround', Florida claims, 'is driven in large measure by the attitudes and location choices of the Creative Class' which makes cities competitive. This class can be attracted by governments that furnish it with a supportive infrastructure – a suitable lifestyle environment, urban revitalization, educational institutions. 'Urban centers have long been crucibles for innovation and creativity. Now they are coming back'.[2]

The attraction of the local has also been marked on the radical Left, reinforced by the demise of the 'national projects' of social democracy and authoritarian communism, and revolutionary disappointments in third world states. Local resistance and community alternatives to the competitive imperatives of the world market have figured prominently in the demands of the anti-globalization movement, notably in the call of the International Forum on Globalization for 'discriminating actively in favour of the local in all policies'.[3] Robin Hahnel's important canvas of participatory economics concludes with 'living experiments in equitable cooperation' that are found in local exchange and trading systems (LETS), locally networked cooperatives, and local participatory budgeting.[4] And Mike Davis ends his provocative assessment of twenty-first century global urbanization sceptical of the claims that a new politics of 'multitudes' is ascendant at the global level. Instead, he argues, historical agency is now decidedly local: '[i]ndeed, the future of human solidarity depends upon the militant refusal of the new urban poor to accept their terminal marginality within global capitalism'.[5]

The case for political action focusing on the territorial scale of the local (and sometimes at the scale of 'the body') has been especially characteristic of the ecology movement. The political slogans that the 'greens' have contributed to the Left – 'think globally, act locally', 'reduce, reuse, recycle', 'walk gently on the earth' – are especially representative of the localist emphasis of their socio-ecological practice.[6] The American Green Party in 2000, with Ralph Nader running for President, put forward the following position:

> Centralization of wealth and power contributes to social and economic injustice, environmental destruction, and militarization. Therefore, we support a restructuring of social, political and economic institutions away from a system that is controlled by and mostly benefits the powerful few, to a democratic, less bureaucratic system. Decision-making should, as much as possible, remain at the individual and local level, while assuring that civil rights are protected for all citizens.[7]

And in a recent manifesto emerging from the British Green Party, localization is invoked as a panacea to virtually all societal ills:

> Economic localisation provides a political and economic framework for people, local government and businesses to diversify their own economies. It does not mean a return to overpowering state control – merely that governments provide the policy framework to promote rediversification. Crucially, this will increase community cohesion, reduce poverty and inequality, improve livelihoods, promote social provision and environmental protection and provide an all-important sense of security.[8]

The case for the 'local' as the scale appropriate for launching projects of socio-ecological transformation would appear, from such a broad consensus, self-evident. And the case for it would certainly seem to be reinforced as contemporary capitalism continues to foster an urbanization process of world historical proportions. Half the world's population is now urbanized, with mega-cities the size of Mexico City, New York, Tokyo, Mumbai and Cairo now forming in all corners of the globe. There is every reason to expect that the current rate of growth of urbanization (twice the rate of growth of the world's population) will continue. Few cities anywhere are not facing ecological challenges, such as waste and water management, transportation gridlock, and public health concerns over old and new viral epidemics, on an unprecedented scale.

These problems pale beside the emergent urban ecological scourge of a global slum population now estimated at 1 billion people (the UN projects a growth to 1.4 billion by 2020). These slums – clusters of ramshackle dwellings sprouting on toxic waste sites, mountain slopes and flood plains – are haunted by basic ecological problems such as open sanitation, inadequate or no water supplies, and much else. Some 3 million people are estimated to die annually from urban air pollution, primarily generated from the burning of fossil fuels that are also contributing to greenhouse gases; another 1 million die from indoor air pollution from the gases released by the burning of biomass fuels.[9]

There is every reason to conclude that neoliberal globalization will continue to bequeath such gifts to city life. As neoliberalism has come to dominate the global market and regulatory framework its institutionalization and logic has fuelled developments in agriculture that drive rural people into these slums, while at the same time fostering inter-local competition to reduce wages and environmental regulation. This also means, however, especially when we remember that most urban life on the planet bears no resemblance whatever to Richard Florida's image of yuppified city centres for the 'creative class', that the burden that 'the local' carries in strategies for a pro-sustainability, anti-neoliberal (and even an anti-capitalist) agenda is enormous. If 'place' and 'local space' are where the 'tangible solidarities' necessary to build an alternate way of life, and an anti-neoliberal politics, must form, then we cannot avoid confronting the systematic obstacles that have to be overcome in realizing such a project. Claims that sustainable local ecologies can serve as the foundation for political action and social alternatives at least require careful scrutiny.

THE VARIETIES OF ECO-LOCALISM

The ecology movement has always entertained a broad range of visions that offer more eco-friendly economies than industrial capitalism: from green capitalism and the eco-modernization of reforming markets, to deep ecology and eco-feminist images of small-scale and spiritual reconstructions, to the projects of anarchist social ecology and eco-socialism dependent upon new systems of property. If there is one element in such diverse ecological thought that emerges foremost, it is the primacy of localism as the central strategic focus.

The early texts of the modern environmental movement, from Rachel Carson's *Silent Spring* (1962) to Garret Hardin's 'Tragedy of the Commons' (1968), the Club of Rome's *The Limits to Growth* (1972) and *The Ecologist's* 'A Blueprint for Survival' (1972), are filled with references to limits, small-scale production and self-sufficiency.[10] Although none of these founding contributions laid out an explicit strategy for localism, it was the logical corollary of their central concerns about the earth's 'carrying capacity' in face of the forces of industrialism driving resource usage and population endlessly upwards. Few early theorists were as important, however, as E.F. Schumacher's *Small is Beautiful* (1973) in making localism both a virtue and a socio-ecological strategy. From the 1950s on, Schumacher began to question, along democratic, egalitarian and ecological lines, the kind of development that was taking place, and the technologies being applied, according to the singular 'logic of industrialism' that pervaded both capitalist and Soviet economies. These were inappropriate, he argued, for growth, ecology and community. Whereas a critic of this singular logic like J.K. Galbraith proposed constructing countervailing institutions to the industrial society's 'technostructure', but at the same highly centralized level, Schumacher argued for smaller, people-centred, ecologically sustainable ways of living, with growth and size displaced from the centre of socio-economic life. As he famously put it:

> From the point of view of Buddhist economics, therefore, production from local resources for local needs is the most rational way of economic life, while dependence on imports from afar and the consequent need to produce for export to unknown and distant peoples is highly uneconomic and justifiable only in exceptional cases and on a small scale. Just as the modern economist would admit that a high rate of consumption of transport services between a man's home and his place of work signifies a misfortune and not a high standard of life, so the Buddhist would hold that to satisfy

human wants from faraway sources rather than from sources nearby signifies failure rather than success.[11]

While Schumacher's promotion of 'Buddhist economics' did not travel well, the conceptions he advanced of appropriate technology and localist development were widely taken up, and soon multiplied into a whole host of alternative projects and ideas for community, cooperative and neo-artisanal development that have since become integral to green political economy (and, indeed, green lifestyles). Two signal interventions by Barry Commoner and Herman Daly reinforced this development, and shifted the question from scale in general to an issue of sustainability from a *material* point of view.[12] Commoner rejected the barbarism of the 'lifeboat ethic' involved in accepting the limits of the earth's carrying capacity in relation to population. His concern was with the type of science and technology that was supporting economic growth based on toxics and synthetics rather than natural products, and he issued a political challenge to the elites who controlled these technologies and disproportionately benefited from this growth, and who stood in the way of a change in techniques to eliminate pollution. For Daly, the answer lay in a 'steady-state economy' with low or no growth, so as to directly reduce 'material throughputs', particularly of matter and energy; this would address at its source the disorder produced by high-entropic emissions.

These varied warnings on the limits to growth generated a series of reformist attempts to show that capitalist growth and sustainable ecology could be made compatible, given an appropriate policy and market context. The Brundtland Report (1987) was an important – if ambiguous – marker in green thinking, and represented – and to a degree still represents – a synthesis of ecological reforms consistent with capitalist development. It defined sustainable development as 'meet[ing] the needs of the present without compromising the ability of future generations to meet their own needs'. In thus raising the issues of both needs and limits in its search for the kind of economic growth that would also sustain resources and communities, the Report made a range of development proposals in which greater decentralization, self-help and self-reliance figured centrally, pleading for greater focus on small-scale development projects within sustainable ecologies, and calling for 'city governments [to] become key agents of development'.[13]

But the consolidation of neoliberalism in political and policy frameworks at virtually all scales of governance by the early 1990s meant the Brundtland Report found no easy passage from discursive agenda to actionable policy. Any minimal 'green consensus' it could have said to have captured disappeared, although some of the sustainability programme became absorbed into the neoliberal market consensus forming in the international economic institutions through the 1990s (as was visible in the Kyoto Accord).[14]

The current spectrum of ecological thinking is heavily influenced by the emergence of 'green commerce' and the embrace of market solutions across wide swaths of the ecology movement, in both thought and action. Several positions especially merit attention for their localist programmes – and level of support. The most pervasive neoliberal strand of social thinking today is what can be termed *market ecology*. From Friedrich Hayek through Milton Friedman, neoliberalism had little concern with ecology, at any scale of activity, except to argue that markets are better allocators of resources than states, and that prices will effectively signal natural scarcities, drawing in new supplies and conserving existing ones, to restore a natural and social equilibrium.[15] But 'market ecology' has emerged as a powerful strain of thinking, whose influence has spread from ecological sceptics to virtually all the leading environmental NGOs, from Friends of the Earth, to Greenpeace to the Sierra Club, including market ecology measures in their policy campaigns. Faith in capitalist markets, it would seem, has become all pervasive.

Markets are foundationally decentralized and place-based regulators of human activity in that the behaviour of sellers and buyers is regulated by prices they individually accept. To some degree, markets are the ideal 'think globally, act locally' solution in that prices are transmitted across space to equilibrate all markets, information flowing from local markets to aggregate markets and back again. In the words of Earthscan's 1989 agenda-setting *Blueprint for a Green Economy*, such pricing would allow for 'the potential complementarity of growth and environment'. In policy terms, this is the need to 'create markets in previously free services', such as air or water, or access to parks and beaches, and to 'modify markets by centrally deciding the value of environmental services and ensuring those values are incorporated into the prices of goods and services'.[16] With all commodities marketized and all costs of production including externalities factored in, market prices would compel individuals and firms to adjust ecologically irresponsible behaviour and regulate scarcity. By decentralizing environmental regulation to the markets where prices are set, it becomes feasible (as neoliberalism has sought to do) to abolish extensive enforcement authorities such as state regulators and planning agencies.

Market ecology has also typically advocated discrimination in favour of smaller, locally-based capitals (and in this sense offers an alternative to the neoliberalism of big corporations and governments). David Korten, for example, argues that in the case of local business 'the social and environmental costs associated with an investment are more likely to be visible to and to some extent shared by investors and their neighbours'.[17] Paul Hawken and Jonathan Porritt make similar cases for greasing the wheels of commerce through locally-embedded micro-enterprises.[18] It is contended that the local enterprises are more likely to conserve and utilize local resources sparsely, thereby preserving ecological diversity while maintaining more sustainable economies. This is part of a more general tendency of ecologists to treat the environment as a kind of 'natural capital' that has been accumulated, and that should, therefore, be commodified, priced, traded and taxed to yield its greatest value (i.e. its preservation).

Another contemporary project, which can be termed *ecological modernization*, adopts many of the instruments of market ecology, such as green taxes and incentives, to transform firm behaviour in making a transition to a more sustainable economy. But it also urges wider technological and organizational transformations.[19] The substitution of resource-using and pollution-generating techniques by resource-saving and pollution-reducing ones is proposed as part of a lengthy green agenda that includes 'retro-fitting' the built environment, the reduction of automobile usage, 'soft energy' and local organic agriculture, to name just a few items. Ecological modernization encompasses both the transformation of the ecological structures of large firms and economic policy alternatives for developing community-based green industry. These are conceived so as to move beyond 'internalizing externalities' and advance toward an 'eco-efficient' transformation of the whole built environment. This leads directly to 'green city' projects for extending public transit, 'green-belting' urban sprawl, simultaneously increasing both urban density and urban green-space, and so forth.[20] This strategy is supported by environmental governance measures such as industrial conversion subsidies, research and development support and corporatist sustainability partnerships.

Ecological modernization often also embraces a contentious thesis: that the 'information society' is potentially 'dematerializing' the organizational logic of industrialism, as eco-responsible technologies are adapted and production and work are reorganized. Lester Brown, in his *Plan B 2.0*, argues that the economic imperative meshes today with ecological ones to 'de-materialize the economy'. This requires 'the creation of an honest market, one that tells the ecological truth' – which is, above all, that the new ecological industries provide 'the greatest investment opportunity in history'.[21] Dematerialization will also, it is claimed, allow the reconfiguration of cities, as new energy options and tele-work recast the possibilities and meaning of the local. In ecological modernization thinking, this eco-transition involves no necessary transformation of social relations, apart from an adaptation to soft-energy paths and a reduction in the scale of the technique and the exchanges associated with the new environmental and informational technologies, while output continues to grow.

Of course, many thinkers and activists reject the reformism of ecological modernization, as well as market ecology, for failing to register the inconsistency between capitalist imperatives for growth and ecological sustainability. Perhaps the foremost project that envisages a different sort of localism today is that of *social ecology*, which has strong roots in the traditional anarchist (or liberal) invocation of direct democracy (or community), in the form of extensively (even if never completely) self-reliant communities. Social ecology is often associated narrowly with the eco-anarchist thought of Murray Bookchin. But it really encompasses a host of approaches that are thoroughly localist in their views and rest on some mix of community and cooperative economics, semi-autarchic trade, local currency systems, and direct democracy in enterprises and local government. In this sense, social ecology also encompasses key anarchist tendencies in the anti-globalization movement like those of Naomi Klein and Jose Bove, but also of bio-regionalists like Vandana Shiva and Kirkpatrick Sale. In this vision, ecological balance is restored within decentralized communities by the need to find local solutions, eliminating at once both negative externalities and resource over-usage, as well as the disastrous effects of mass-production industrialism (whatever the property system underpinning it). In a decentralized 'relatively self-sufficient community', Bookchin asserts, 'there would doubtless be many duplications of small industrial facilities from community to community, [but] the familiarity of each group with its local environment and its ecological roots would make for a more intelligent and more loving use of its environment'.[22]

In the era of neoliberal globalization, the social-ecology vision of down-scaling and bio-regional self-sufficiency/integrity has spread widely. Community development projects of all kinds propose alternative systems of production and exchange, some of which are born out of a desperate need for basic provisions, while others grow out of support networks for using local resources to counter the internationalization of commodities and capital. This vision has intertwined with anti-free trade strategies. The former Greenpeace campaigner Colin Hines's *Localization: A Global Manifesto* promotes the reduction of scale in market exchanges, with the optimal size of economic communities depending upon their ability to balance economic self-organization, sustainability and the provision of goods.[23] The shrinking of long-distance trade and supply chains would also constrict mass production and compel production diversity. Recognizing that if localization is really to work as a process of eco-transition its mechanisms need to be specified, Hines advances a programme for a range of controls over transnational capital (but not its socialization), alternative investment codes and Tobin taxes, preferential tax structures, aid policies for self-reliance, and community regeneration.

This approach differs from that of other social ecologists whose goals – local self-governance, self-sufficiency, bio-regionalism – are more immediate, as are their political means – direct action aimed at establishing artisanal and other appropriate technologies, alternate markets, the redefinition of needs, the preservation of peasant economies, seed diversity, local currency systems, 'getting off the grid', and so on.[24] Implicitly or explicitly accepting that markets may be necessary for organizing socio-economic life, the social ecology approach assumes that locally eco-responsible community markets can displace eco-irresponsible global ones – even in the era of neoliberalism.

THE LIMITS OF ECO-LOCALISM

The green case for localism, then, rests on a critique of the existing resource-intensive and pollution-extensive system of industrialization. That system is seen, for the most part, as existing independently of the specific market system and social-property relations of capitalism, and thus as being amenable to transformation within that system to more ecologically-sustainable development trajectories.[25] This is the case even for social ecologists of an anarchist tendency who, just as Marx accused Proudhon of doing, tend to separate the system of production from the property system and, in turn, from the social relations particular to capitalism. The foundational green critique of modern capitalism and the bedrock of the eco-localist case is the abuse of scale. The industrial drive for scale without limits – whether in terms of capital equipment, consumption, trade or corporate and political governance – is seen as an assault on the limits of nature. This is why all green movements, from market ecologists all the way to social ecologists, have been more or less comfortable with trends toward decentralization that have accompanied neoliberalism. It is also why they have, for the most part, embraced the 'post-industrial' thesis of the 'information society' as containing the technological potential to reduce the scale of economic activity and hence the ecological footprint of industry. In this sense, the alternative varieties of eco-localism and market ecology are not really as antagonistic to one another as they are often said to be. They are all representative of the 'neither left, nor right, but green' political orientation which has characterized ecological politics, but which also accommodates the acceptance of (local) capitalist markets as the necessary regulators of socio-economic activity.

The following critique of eco-localism and its conceptualization of a transition to a sustainable economy encompasses five dimensions: (a) the effectiveness of prices for transmitting ecologically sustainable decisions for place-based regulation; (b) the limits of technical and organizational change – apart from issues of distribution and social relations – as a solution to ecological problems; (c) the coordinative and ecological failures of bioregional and community-based economic alternatives; (d) the issue of whether all supra-local scales are ecologically perverse; and (e) the scale and role of democracy in any ecological transition that is socially just.

(a) The magic of the market

The use of market measures to address ecological problems constitutes a voluntary environmentalism. Market actors are free to respond to market incentives or ignore them and go on polluting and consuming, depending on profit conditions and income constraints. The market ecology strategies of eco-transition literally depend on the 'magic of the market'. They are viable only insofar as prices are adequate to cover costs and thus able to valorize existing capitals or new 'eco-capitals' as part of market processes, and only insofar as income distribution is such as to allow consumers to adjust to more eco-friendly alternatives while still meeting their needs. Within these parameters of economic modelling, and with clearly defined private property rights and perfect information and foresight, the ecological behaviour of agents is supposed to change 'at site'; that is, they will adjust ecological inputs and control outputs where production occurs, and where consumers purchase and consume. But *caveat emptor*: such a 'place-based regulation' of the environment without reference to external extra-local enforcement authorities might work if, and only if, all the enormously hypothetical assumptions behind it were to hold.

There is an obvious initial limit to even such an idealized 'green capitalism' as applied to eco-localism: each location is necessarily subordinate to the logic of capitalism as a whole, and can do nothing to alter the anti-ecological drive toward increased accumulation of value and money. Since the market alone is to regulate behaviour, this raises a host of problems.[26] Capitalists in a competitive marketplace will only accept such costs willingly to the extent that other localities are imposing similar market conditions. If they are not, market imperatives will compel capitalists to shed these costs, possibly through technological advance, possibly by lowering costs by shedding or bypassing ecological restraints, and possibly by free-riding on others' 'good' ecological behaviour. With more liquid ownership structures (as with the kind of finance capital that has evolved under neoliberalism) capitalists are less tied to 'place' and more likely to use regulatory arbitrage to avoid any imposed environmental cost. And in key sectors with the greatest impact on the environment, capitalists have an incentive to increase mobility to pursue surplus profits gained from natural resource rents. As long as there are countries or regions that are not subject to ecological taxes any eco-localist strategy will be continually undermined by the inter-local competitive pressures internal to capitalism, in the absence of extra-local enforcement capacities and controls over capital mobility. And to the extent that each jurisdiction does not have common information, understanding of future impacts, common enforcement mechanisms and a unique ecology, the possibilities for 'regulatory arbitrage' increase.

The environmental problems of 'common property resources' and 'externalities' raise an additional concern, given the collective aspect of the resource used and/or the environmental impact of production. Market ecology proposes to address these issues through constructing prices and markets to compel firms and consumers to adjust their behaviour. Yet the very collective dimension of these 'goods' makes it impossible for market agents to 'price in' all impacts and regulate usage exclusively at site. Similarly, since the future is always unknown, there is simply no way to account for inter-generational allocation of resource uses by market means alone (any imputed discount rates and time horizons to incorporate the future require non-market agents to make estimates). Without appropriate prices, there is no way for the market to equilibrate. As Martinez-Alier has put it: '[t]he market economy cannot provide a guide for a rational intertemporal allocation of scarce resources and of waste'.[27]

These are far more general limitations on market ecology, and particular eco-local possibilities, than is generally recognized. As Elmar Altvater has argued, the general conditions of capitalist production are not produced in a capitalist way: nature and public infrastructures especially are used by capitalists as if they are 'free' goods.[28] Even when attempts are made to price these 'commodities' this does not mean that the market can fulfill its allocative and preservative tasks; indeed since 'public goods' tend to be 'inadequately' provided by the market, state provision and/or regulation has proved inevitable. Indeed, all socio-ecological processes depend on conditions of production which are inherently produced outside markets. As market imperatives compel the continual accumulation of a greater mass of value (and a greater technical composition of capital), the ecological footprint of any local space of production will increase. Eco-localist place regulation via the adjustment of prices and incentives to account for ecological impacts can never compensate for the structural dynamics internal to capitalist markets; nor can they encompass the unique characteristics of local ecologies.

(b) The illusion of 'dematerialization'

The limits of market prices often lead to equally misplaced eco-localist hopes in technique. Seldom has there been a more illusory social proposition than that of 'dematerialization' within a new 'weightless' information economy.[29] The 'information economy' requires its own massive infrastructure of cables, transmitters and so forth; energy usage continues to increase from the power needs of consumers and industry; the computer generates its own major re-cycling and emissions problems. This is a longer-term dynamic of capitalist economies. The long-run tendency of capitalism to reduce material through-puts per unit of commodity output is outstripped by the counterforce of the expansion in the overall circulation of commodities. Thus aggregate waste flows (even ignoring the quality and types of good being produced) continue to increase. Studies attempting to assess material throughputs in the current economy (or wider measures of the metabolic processes and ecological foot-prints of human activity) tend to show that considerable economic weight is still being gained.[30]

Further, whatever its level of eco-efficiency, the existing fixed capital stock creates significant barriers to any eco-rationalization of technique, even if market actions are embedded in supportive state policies. As James O'Connor has demonstrated, 'capitals will minimize waste, recycle by-products, use en-ergy efficiently …and so on, when it pays, otherwise not'.[31] The choice of technique that capitalists adopt, therefore, cannot be separated from the social and distributional conditions which determine the extraction of value from workers. Whether or not these are ecologically sound techniques is a subor-dinate question. Class relations figure more broadly than just in the labour process. To take the grossest example, the income structures of the 'North' allow a massive over-supply of eco-efficient housing for the wealthy, while the slums of the 'South' are built out of recycled materials. The 'market' is signalling two economically appropriate techniques, neither of which can be called ecologically or socially-just. Finally, massive fixed capital complexes, shaped by market choices, are major path-dependent obstacles to a switch in technologies: it is easier to develop fuel-efficient cars, so long as existing investments in urban sprawl help supply consumer demand, than to switch to public mass transit, which requires new tax revenue. A socially-just ecological modernization of local space would require not merely extra-market capaci-ties, but in fact anti-market and extra-local political conditions.

(c) The spatial division of labour

The deepening of the spatial division of labour that attends the process of capital accumulation is a fundamental tendency of capitalism. This leads to a differentiation of socio-ecological spaces, with a tendency for differentiation to increase as the complexity of production systems, built environments, mass urbanization and the appropriation of nature all grow through time. This has been integral to the dynamics of neoliberalism as local spaces respond to the imperatives of value formation in the world market. There are two quite distinct problems for the localist project that emerge in relation to economic co-ordination. In the existing neoliberal context, the various forms of 'alternative economic spaces' – artisanal community sectors, LETS money systems, the social economy, popular planning boards, city corporations – have added significant dimensions to eco-localist practice, but they have remained quite marginal in terms of total activity and subordinate to the larger valorization processes of the 'formal economy' affecting the city as a whole.[32] These sectors, moreover, remain quite dependent, in both positive and negative ways, on wider urban planning measures, including coordination and support from governments at other scales (in Europe, for example, often including the EU institutions).

The political incoherence of the eco-localist project is compounded when the exchange and coordination relations among localizing communities is considered. Here the question of the scale of democracy internal to each socio-ecological community is largely avoided, although it is a more and more pressing issue now that there are some five hundred cities with populations of over one million. The division of labour, the production and exchange of use-values, the uses of the surplus and the planning of infrastructures are urgent questions within existing cities.[33]

The question of economic coordination is also compounded when different cities are considered, each having differentiated specializations and social and ecological capacities. Even if the idealism of the most utopian social ecology perspective – such as is entailed in imagining semi-autarchic cities – were to be granted, the coordination of exchanges, distribution and regulatory relations between such cities (via the market, or via planning?) would still require considerable attention and deliberation. Confronting the contradictions of economic coordination produced by capitalism within and between territorial scales, concentrated as they are at the level of local socio-ecologies, is fundamental to the success of any strategy against neoliberalism. Equally complex questions of democratic negotiation in transitional strategies must also be faced.

(d) The lack of strategic vision

Besides the above problems with the market-oriented privileging of the local in socio-ecological alternatives, there are also serious objections to the eco-localist vision for a less complex, less mediated, less inter-linked, de-scaled eco-community, as it is advanced by its neo-anarchist proponents. First of all, how the transition from actually existing capitalism to more or less self-reliant bio-regional communities is to be achieved is left quite unspecified. This is astonishing, given that it radically reverses a dominant tendency in capitalism and ignores the complexity of modern economies. There is a lack of a strategic vision of how the obstacles of capitalist and state power will be surmounted, and large numbers of questions of coordination, determination of output, means of governance – many of the basic issues that all social projects, in practice and theory, of market socialization and planning have confronted – are simply left unanswered. The eco-localist vision for shifting the structure of production and output, reducing work-hours, and suppressing material throughputs and emissions (which are more widely shared objectives) is mainly a set of preferences, unsupported by any case for its advocates' concentration on political organization at the local level.[34]

Second, it is evident that informational technologies have not led to a reduction in scale in major economic sectors. The scale of factories and the capitalization levels of firms have both increased. Only a minority have been able to opt out and work in smaller production units by choice, as opposed to being pressured to do so by the growth of informal and contingent work. Nor is it clear, moreover, that smaller units of production are by definition more ecologically responsible. Large production units come into being partly because market imperatives compel resource-saving on inputs, but larger firms also have greater capacity to take on leading-edge 'environmental technologies'. Smaller units of production may involve duplication of inputs, inadequate financial leverage to incorporate leading technologies, and even relatively greater use of energy resources. The matter of the scale of production cannot be assessed apart from some means also to assess the needs being met. Endorsing small scale in production as foundational principle, as eco-localists do in general, and social ecology proponents do in particular, is empty romanticism. In capitalism the scale of production is determined in the market and settled by the processes of valorization. But if social needs are to be assessed against the scale of production and ecological costs some democratic and coordinative planning capacities will be required, as prices alone will not incorporate all these relations.[35]

Finally, there is nothing inherent in the deepening of local level governance that would ensure that it did not produce considerable economic damage. Even if it is granted that local participation in resource management in all forms is, indeed, a fundamental aspect of democratization, what the ecological consequences of this participation will be is a contingent question. Inter-local competition, between capitalist firms (even if they are internalizing all costs) or between bio-regional communities dependent on a degree of external exchange, can still induce ecological arbitrage as long as unsupervised markets exist. This is more likely to the extent that any local stewardship benefits can be offset by powerful local interests seeking personal or market advantages.

It is not at all clear how eco-localism – even in the most radical writings of social ecology, where private property rights are being socialized or limited – proposes to suppress powerful local interests. The mediation of these material political disputes, which are inescapable as long as class stratification and bureaucracy remain, cannot occur without encompassing democratic institutions and capacities for political mobilization.[36] These are some of the most important conceptual and political issues that have to be addressed in proposals for societal transformation, particularly in taking on the additional necessary burden of environmental justice, but they are met with major silences in the case made for an eco-localist project of 'descaling' socio-ecological life. The case for this too often dissolves into calls for 'ethically superior' individual consumption and production decisions, and alternative communal households – both of which can be endorsed, but they do not amount to a socio-ecological project of societal transformation.

(e) Taking democracy seriously

Eco-localist projects tend to treat the local as an authentic space of democracy, and other scales of democratic representation and struggle as mediated and false, because they impose external political-economic projects that violate local democracy and the appropriate scale of ecology. This conception involves a number of confusions, foremost among them thinking that the building of socio-ecological alternatives can be insulated from the non-local events and processes that constitute their context. Democratic processes and state institutions at other levels of governance raise central questions of power and distribution that cannot be ignored. The state, at whatever level of its apparatuses and functions, is the material institutionalization of power relations, and this includes struggles over resource extraction, usage and regulation, and distribution between places and persons. Local capitalist power relations are embedded in these wider relations and internalize these extra-local relations in the local power structures. There is, quite literally, no way to withdraw (even if it was judged desirable to do so) from these relations and remain in a capitalist market economy. It is a false dilemma to counterpose a more active local democracy of citizens building an alternative ecology to decaying forms of representative democracy supporting unsustainable ecological policies and class relations. The challenge, and it has been at the heart of the crisis of liberal democracy and the impasse of socialist alternatives, is quite different: a transformation toward a different kind of state and democratic administration that allows the development of new political freedoms, capacities and socio-ecological alternatives within *central* forms of representative democracy, while fostering new institutional forms of direct democracy and differentiated socio-ecological processes in local places.

David Harvey has put the issue in a slightly different way: localism, he points out, often allows the command of particular places, but this does not mean having the capacity to control or command the processes of producing either space or nature.[37] The capitalist class can shift capital, play one locality off against another, or undermine local strategies by the exercise of political power at national or global scales of governance. Thus 'liberated' ecological and political spaces can only be defended to the extent that the scale and scope of capitalist market activities are reduced and the scale and scope of democracy is extended. Attempting to reduce the scale of production and ecological processes along community development and bioregional lines (apart from the scale of market exchanges), and to reduce the scale of democracy in support of mutualism (discounting systems of representation, delegation, participation, accountability at other scales of political life), as eco-localism suggests, is to completely misrepresent capitalist power structures and the necessary challenges of democratization.

A LOCAL ECO-SOCIALISM?

Local spaces always exist in a contradictory relationship with other spatial levels of capitalist development. This can be seen in Marx's theory of capital accumulation. The opening section of *Capital* captures the quandary: the commodity as a use-value is always particular, worked up from specific resources by the concrete labours of workers embedded in particular communities and their local social relations; but the commodity as an exchange-value is driven to transgress all spatial boundaries as particular labours and ecologies are transformed into the homogeneous space of value in general. 'The production of commodities and their circulation in its developed form, namely trade, form the historic presuppositions under which capital arises'.[38] The particular and the universal, the local and the global, urban nature and global biosphere, are not opposites, but different dimensions of the scalar matrix of the world market.

The dynamics of capital accumulation pose these abstract determinations in a more complex form. The accumulation of capital, as Marx observed, tends toward an intensification of the forces of production as the mass of fixed capital put in motion by any individual worker increases in its organic mass, technical complexity and value. The competitive imperatives that emerge from the constant revolution in the means of production also produce the tendency of concentration and centralization of the productive capacities and ownership patterns of capital. The deepening of the organizational complexity of capital has, paradoxically, a corresponding tendency of 'statification': the long-term reproduction of capital and labour becomes increasingly intricate, requiring progressively more government support in infrastructure, research and development, technical training, financing and regulatory intervention.

The accumulation of capital is, then, also an uneven process of localization (Marx's 'antagonism between the city and the country'). It is in this sense that David Harvey has insisted that the accumulation of capital is always a production of space as a built environment that is being continually accumulated, transformed and discarded: 'it is through urbanization that the surpluses are mobilized, produced, absorbed, and appropriated and... it is through urban decay and social degradation that the surpluses are devalued and destroyed'.[39] As capitalism intensifies socio-economic activities at every scale – local, regional, national and global – so does it intensify, in the same process, the ecological-metabolic ones.

The unevenness of capitalist development concentrates productive capacities, populations and power in local urban spaces.[40] On the one hand, this devalues rural and regional social relations and spaces while valorizing urban centres linked to the circulation of capital in the world market; on the other hand, this increasingly transforms and makes dependent the metabolic relations of the 'rural' on the ecological relations and 'urban nature' of the city. This has always posed strategic dilemmas for the Left about how to 'even out' development, between centres and peripheries, urban and rural, and 'society' and 'nature' (though both are quite clearly 'produced' by both natural and socio-economic processes).

These features of capitalist development have led to distinct but related strategies constantly emerging within the socialist movement: proposals for decentralization to reduce the over-concentration of productive capacities, resources and power; and strategies of localism to build up organizational and political capacities and 'liberated spaces' and neighbourhoods within cities. These strategies have a long history, and have often been the defining element of various socialist tendencies, as in the cooperative movement, guild socialism and municipal socialism. The Marxian tradition's focus on the Paris Commune, workers' councils and building 'red zones' in the struggle over state power has also advocated local bases of power and administration, as well as the reorganization of economic activity. No one has said it better than Henri Lefebvre: '[a] revolution that does not produce a new space has not realized its full potential; indeed it has failed in that has not changed life itself, but has merely changed ideological superstructures, institutions or political apparatuses'.[41]

Calls for rethinking the place of the local in socialist strategy have hardly let up, and several of the most important contributions in recent years – from participatory budgeting to theorizations of 'negotiated coordination'[42] – have made this a central feature. Socialists have generally favoured the decentralization of power to local and regional authorities on the basis of extending democracy, arguing that this, rather than a mere defence of the centralized state is the best response to neo-liberalism's ideological appeal. It is extended democratic forms rather than extended markets that should be the central regulators of socio-economic life and management of enterprises and institutions.[43] In contrast to most green thinking, however, the devolution of power has not been treated as being, by definition, more democratic and sustainable. National and international parliaments (leaving aside debates about their composition and mode of representation) have been seen as fundamental to securing the diversity of developmental paths and strategies, allowing for a more even distribution of resources, ensuring that basic rights and needs are met, blocking intolerable forms of inter-local competition, and encouraging 'decentralized cooperation'. This perspective shifts the strategic issue of socio-ecological priorities away from an *a priori* prioritization of the eco-local to the centrality of democratization itself. The point has been well-made by Raymond Williams, in rejecting both centralized command economies and the limitations of experiments in small-scale enterprises and communities:

> ...the problem of scale is more complex than the customary contrast of small and large.... [T]he socialist intervention will introduce the distinctive principle of maximum self-management, paired only with considerations of economic viability and reasonable equity between communities, and decisively breaking with the... dominant criterion of administrative convenience to the centralized state.... [A]ny foreseeable socialist society must have fully adequate general powers, and... at the same time such powers must depend on deeply organized and directly participating popular forces.[44]

The particularities of this formulation might be disputed, but the guiding idea of connecting scales of political struggle with democratization of the state is clear enough. Its presupposition would be an evolving system of ecologically responsible cooperative production. It is, indeed, possible to imagine political interventions in the local context that carve out a space for an eco-socialism. A first one might be to demand that fundamental ecological rights also meet basic needs in reconstructing built environments. Establishing rights to clean water and air, housing and public green space, basic energy supply and public transportation links directly to campaigns for 'lifeline supplies' of water, redistributional pricing mechanisms in energy consumption, and the decommodification of basic services,[45] and will begin to recast local ecological struggles in terms of needs and social provision.

A second political theme is that all ecological transformations are also struggles over environmental justice. Ecological impacts are never neutral with respect to class, gender and race, or in terms of the relations between regions and states. Campaigns for producer responsibility for emissions and waste, for instance, raise immediate questions about the implications for social class, for the impact on neighbourhoods and relations between states, and for the unequal exchanges involved in the international trade in waste.[46]

The complex interdependencies between these social and environmental issues are such that very diverse political interests and agendas would obviously be involved in the distributional, metabolic and technological changes that would be required to deal with them. Existing liberal democratic forms can be seen as painfully inadequate in this light, and it is no less clear that the development of new democratic capacities cannot be limited to the local level alone. Hence a third aspect of ecological campaigns is the need to explore popular planning mechanisms involving workers, ecologists and consumers, and the fundamental democratization of social relations and state institutions necessary for a transition to a system of ecologically responsible production and exchange.[47]

LOCALISM, ECOLOGY AND THE LEFT

The drawing up of even a tentative eco-socialist agenda raises a central point of political contention between 'red' and 'green' politics over the scale of political action and the building of alternatives to neoliberalism. This is a division, of course, which also figures in the anti-globalization movement and its foremost symbol, the World Social Forum, where the fair of alternatives on offer blends together what is left programmatically un-reconciled.[48]

Historically, the territorial nation-state has been the central point of formation, legitimation, regulation and contestation of capitalist power relations.

It has also framed progressive politics. For distinct political reasons, social democratic and authoritarian communist movements focused on building productive capacities and redistributional social systems at the national scale via centralized bureaucratic capacities. During the postwar period, this fitted both with the strategies of metropolitan states bent on reconstructing national economies and the world trading system, after the turmoil of depression and war, and the strategies of liberated states embarking on new development paths after either decolonization struggles or revolution. Since the 1980s the internationalization of capital has intensified the global and local scales of accumulation as firms increase their asset base, scale of production and dependence on the world market. Nation-states, in turn, have re-ordered their administrative capacities to mediate global-local flows of capital, while giving up nationally-based development projects and redistribution policies. Neoliberalism has played no small part in reforging the matrix of governance: it has 'constitutionalized' a rules-based world market system and expanded the role of market imperatives in regulating local communities via competition over jobs and environmental standards.[49]

The strategic reaction to this unevenness in the scale of development by social democratic and trade-union forces has been twofold. For some, it has been imperative to re-establish 'territorial integrity' at the national scale via new frameworks of global governance over trade and capital flows and of corporate governance over firms. This, it is argued, would provide the institutional conditions at the international level for renewing traditional social democratic distributional bargains at the level of the nation state. This option has had little political traction, given the drastic shift of political forces it would require. For others, neoliberal globalization is now the terrain within which 'realistic' political options need to be formed. Their focus is on developing extra-market institutions to facilitate conditions for 'progressive competitiveness' at the scale of the firm and local community, particularly in the new 'knowledge economy'. Such a policy has been the project of 'third way' social democracy, as was noted in the introduction, and it has had considerable success in politically realigning its partisan adherents.

Green parties and many environmental NGOs have quite often been active allies in such social democratic rethinking, especially in those places in Europe and North America where these forces have significant electoral strength or mobilizational capacity. They see the knowledge economy as reshaping socio-ecological conditions – 'thinking smarter means thinking greener' – and they often share, as has been shown here, a faith in markets and technology. This political alliance has held less political attraction for social ecologists, whose project is one of territorial integrity connected to bioregionalism and local democracy. Specific tactical alliances, however, have often been built over social democratic support for self-administration, co-operatives, pro-Kyoto measures for local energy alternatives, and alternative local markets, effectively absorbing many social ecologists and environmental NGOs into the reformist bloc. This alliance amounts to a 'third way from below', in which civil society forces reinforce the political realignment that social democratic leaders have carried out 'from above'. It needs stressing that this alliance has had a measure of electoral attraction and durability; however, it has not offered an alternate ecological or economic project to neoliberalism, and has been incorporated as a subordinate policy regime within it.[50] It is plausible to characterize the present neoliberal period as the hegemony of a 'blue-green-pink' historic bloc.

The construction of an eco-socialist alliance and project will have to be a quite different undertaking, for none of the above offers an alternative to neoliberalism. This cannot be conceived apart from the necessary wider processes of renewal of both the socialist and ecological projects. The basis for such an alliance needs to be developed at a number of levels. The first is a recognition that the many forms of eco-localism reproduce an 'ontological dualism' between nature and society which has pertinent political effects: the call for a reduction in our 'internal' social scale simultaneously entails a call for an expansion in the scale of an 'external' nature existing in some natural state apart from human societies. But humans live in society and in nature. Local environments cannot be understood without reference to the mediations of social labour, and the continual metabolism of nature that produces both nature and society.[51] Environments are always produced in a combination of natural and social transformations, and local socio-ecological processes are always implicated in wider socio-economic and natural processes. Theoretical and political priority can never simply reside in a particular pre-given geographic scale: theoretical and political priority must always be located and defined in terms of the socio-ecological processes which constitute scale.[52]

This can be put another way. The market imperative to intensify productive capacities to produce value, and to transform transportation and communication capacities for realizing new value-added, means that within capitalism local class struggles can never be conducted, or local ecologies formed, within permanent bordered territories.[53] The construction of political projects against neoliberalism, which is continually redrawing the borders of markets and governance in order to break out of local barriers to accumulation, needs to take this into account.

This poses the most immediate and daunting challenge for renewing eco-socialist alliances and political organization. Political organization is always, in an initial and practical sense, necessarily local. Branches, cells, political clubs, educational meetings, planning for demonstrations, alliance-building, leafleting, debating, all have to be based in – and build from – where we work and live. Class and ecological struggles against capitalism depend upon campaigns won in families, workplaces, neighbourhoods and communities, all of which are located within particular environments. Political organization and capacity are, in the first instance, about reproducing these struggles across time in particular places in face of capitalist forces that are unrelenting in their efforts to undermine, incorporate and isolate oppositional political alliances and to commodify any ecologies and resources withdrawn from the accumulation process.[54]

In making the case for socialist 'parties of a different kind', Hilary Wainwright gave this warning a decade ago: '[w]ithout a process of constantly envisaging and stretching towards such an alternative, there is a danger that the activities and organizations inspired by recent left movements *would* collapse back, if not into the traditional party system, then into becoming part of an under-resourced, over-exploited voluntary and marginal sector'.[55] It can be debated whether in fact this is what has already occurred, and whether the politics of eco-localism, and the brittleness of 'red-green' political alliances, have been especially representative of such a 'collapse back'. But Wainwright's point also contains a contemporary message. Global social justice movements and world social forums mean little if we cannot challenge local accumulation and sustain campaigns and control in our most immediate political spaces – and thereby ensure that everyday acts of resistance in daily life connect with one another through time, so that they can become the building blocks in the process of collectively helping to envisage and build an organizational alternative. This is most basic element of socialist and ecological renewal.

Political organization also makes more widely accessible – both in knowledge and active solidarity – the class struggles of one place with those of other places, thereby accomplishing in practice what conceptual abstraction allows in theory. But it does so in a structured way, so that political mobilization, reflection, debate and learning can move fluidly across scales. Political organization allows a depth to strategic thinking and action in a way that international justice fairs, although they can be remarkably open spaces for cross-sectoral dialogue, cannot. The internet can generate fantastical amounts of global e-mail information and outrage but this can rarely be backed up, however much it is used to project an organic spontaneity onto the multitude, with social mobilization. A developing political capacity is necessary to translate local militancy into wider demands and socio-ecological programmes at other territorial scales of democracy and ecological sustainability. Politics then becomes transformative, dialectically moving between the scales of practical experience and the formation of a more encompassing social force. As Gramsci put it: '[o]ne may say that no real movement becomes aware of its global character all at once, but only gradually through experience'.[56] The eco-socialist political challenge is to connect particular local struggles, generalize them, and link them to a universal project of socio-ecological transformation, against the universalization of neoliberalism and capitalist markets as the regulators of nature and society.

The politics of eco-localism have been, in a sense, quite the opposite of the agenda just sketched here. Eco-localism projects the local as an ideal scale and conceives communitarian eco-utopias in a politics that is individualizing and particularizing. Under neoliberalism, eco-localism has evolved into a practical attempt to alter individual market behaviours, and to disconnect and internalize local ecologies and communities from wider struggles and political ambitions. But there is no reason to support, and every reason to oppose, any suggestion that the national and the global are on a scale that is any less human and practical than the local.[57] This is not to deny the importance of the local in anti-neoliberal politics; nor the importance of the question of appropriate scale for post-capitalist societies. It is to insist, however, that local socio-ecological struggles cannot be delinked from – and are indeed always potentially representative of – universal projects of transcending capitalism on a world scale. This is the meaning that Marx gave to the Paris Commune: at once a local embryonic society being born behind barricades and yet also 'emphatically international' in its ambitions and implications, so that this is what the Commune symbolized to the capitalist system:

> ...if united co-operative societies are to regulate national production upon a common plan, thus taking it under their own control, and putting an end to the constant anarchy and periodical convulsions, which are the fatality of capitalist production – what else, gentlemen, would it be but Communism, 'possible' Communism?[58]

Or, one could add, in this context, 'possible' eco-localism?

NOTES

1   This is from the document 'What, Why and Where' posted on the World Bank's resource site for decentralization and subnational regional economics, accessible at http://www.worldbank.org.

2   Richard Flordia, *The Rise of the Creative Class*, New York: Basic Books, 2002, pp. 285-6.

3   John Cavanagh et al., *Alternatives to Economic Globalization*, San Francisco: Berrett-Koehler, 2002, p. 109. See also: Walden Bello, *Deglobalization: Ideas for a New World Economy*, London: Zed, 2002; Martin Khor, *Rethinking Globalization: Critical Issues and Policy Choices*, London: Zed, 2001.

4   Robin Hahnel, *Economic Justice and Democracy: From Competition to Cooperation*, New York: Routledge, 2005, p. 341.

5   Mike Davis, *Planet of Slums*, London: Verso, 2006, pp. 201-2.

6   This is not to say that local ecologies are not posited as linked to the biosphere or 'gaia', the terms introduced respectively by *Scientific American* and James Lovelock in the 1970s, but that the scale of political action, and in particular the construction of economic solutions, tends to be resolutely local. See, for example, on this political duality: Wolfgang Sachs, *Planet Dialectics: Explorations in Environment and Development*, London: Zed, 1999, pp. 105-7, 197-212.

7   Green Party USA, *Ten Key Values*, at http://www.greenpartyus.org/tenkey.html.

8   Michael Woodin and Caroline Lucas, *Green Alternatives to Globalisation: A Manifesto*, London: Pluto, 2004, p. 70.

9   UN-Habitat, *State of the World's Cities, 2006-07*, at http://www.unhabitat.org.

10 Rachel Carson, *Silent Spring*, Boston: Houghton-Mifflin, 1962; Garrett Harden, 'The Tragedy of the Commons', *Science*, 162, 1968; D. Meadows et al., *The Limits to Growth: A Report for the Club of Rome's Project on the Predicament of Mankind*, Boston: Universe Books, 1972; The Ecologist, 'A Blueprint for Survival', *The Ecologist*, 2(1), 1972.

11 E.F. Schumacher, *Small is Beautiful: Economics as if People Mattered*, London: Abacus, 1973, p. 49. For a continuance of Schumacher's themes see: Paul Ekins, ed., *The Living Economy*, London: Routledge, 1986.

12 These themes were developed across a range of important books, but see their original source: Barry Commoner, *The Closing Circle*, New York: Knopf, 1971; Herman Daly, ed., *Toward a Steady-State Economy*, San Francisco: W.H. Freeman, 1973.

13 World Commission on Environment and Development, *Our Common Future*, Oxford: Oxford University Press, 1987, pp. 43, 249. This was followed by the Rio Earth Summit and its *Agenda 21*, New York: United Nations, 1992, and a host of international agency sustainability initiatives, each giving more emphasis to the local and market ecology. See: Peter Brand and Michael Thomas, *Urban Environmentalism*, London: Routledge, 2005, chapter 2.

14 See the essay by Achim Brunnengräber in this volume.

15 I once had a well-known neoclassical economics professor explain to me, when reviewing the debate that waged into the 1980s on growth models and *The Limits to Growth*, that prices were such efficient regulatory mechanisms that

natural limits of any kind were an impossibility with capitalist growth, as the right price would simply induce entrepreneurs to supply resources from surrounding planets in the solar system. Such parables, of course, continue.

16   David Pearce et al., *Blueprint for a Green Economy*, London: Earthscan, 1989, pp. 21, 155.

17   David Korten, 'The Mythic Victory of Market Capitalism', in Jerry Mander and Edward Goldsmith, eds., *The Case Against the Global Economy*, San Francisco: Sierra Club Books, 1996. p. 187.

18   Paul Hawken, *The Ecology of Commerce*, New York: Harper, 1993; Jonathan Porritt, *Capitalism as if the World Matters*, London: Earthscan, 2005.

19   Joseph Huber, 'Towards Industrial Ecology: Sustainable Development as a Concept of Ecological Modernization', *Journal of Environment Policy and Planning*, 2(4), 2000; Wolfgang Sachs et al., *Greening the North: A Post-Industrial Blueprint for Ecology and Equity*, London: Zed, 1998.

20   The urban planning literature on sustainable cities is filled with such schemes, most for the good, if limited in their social horizons. See: Nicholas Low et al., *The Green City*, London: Routledge, 2005; Mark Roseland, ed., *Eco-City Dimensions*, Gabriola: New Society, 1997.

21   Lester Brown, *Plan B 2.0*, New York: Norton, 2006, pp. 227, 247.

22   Murray Bookchin, *Post-Scarcity Anarchism*, Montreal: Black Rose Books, 1971, p. 80.

23   Colin Hines, *Localization: A Global Manifesto*, London: Earthscan, 2000.

24   Fred Curtis, 'Eco-localism and Sustainability', *Ecological Economics*, 46(1), 2003; Woodin and Lucas, *Green Alternatives to Globalization*.

25   The writings of Rudolph Bahro are paradigmatic here, but the anti-industrialism thesis is also more general. See: *From Red to Green*, London: Blackwell, 1986; Andrew Dobson, *Green Political Thought*, London: Routledge, 1995, chapter 3.

26   See John Bellamy Foster, *Ecology Against Capitalism*, New York: Monthly Review Press, 2002, chapters 1-3; Hahnel, *Economic Justice*, pp. 67-71. These critiques could be extended to the self-help and informal economy entrepreneurialism that has been part of the project of sustainable development, which also suffers from the problem of market competition generating over-exploitation.

27   Juan Martinez-Alier, 'Ecological Economics and Ecosocialism', in Martin O'Connor, ed., *Is Capitalism Sustainable?*, New York: Guilford, 1994, p. 26.

28   Elmar Altvater, *The Future of the Market*, London: Verso, 1993, pp. 219-22.

29   See Ursula Huws, 'Material World: The Myth of the Weightless Economy', in *Socialist Register 1999*.

30   See: Martinez-Alier in this volume; R. York and E. Rosa, 'Key Challenges to Ecological Modernization Theory', *Organization and Environment*, 16(3), 2003; World Resources Institute, *The Weight of Nations: Material Outflows from Industrial Economies*, Washington: WRI, 2000.

31   James O'Connor, *Natural Causes: Essays in Ecological Marxism*, New York: Guilford, 1998, p. 204.

32   Michael Pacione, *Urban Geography*, New York: Routledge, 2005, chapter 16; Andrew Leyshorn, Roger Lee and Colin Williams, eds., *Alternative Economic Spaces*, London: Sage, 2003. The prolific writings of Jamie Gough have been

the most inventive and sober on these issues. For example: 'Changing Scale as Changing Class Relations: Variety and Contradiction in the Politics of Scale', *Political Geography*, 23(2), 2004.

33   For some of these conceptual debates see: John Friedmann, *Planning in the Public Domain*, Princeton: Princeton University Press, 1987, chapters 9-10; David Schweickart, *Against Capitalism*, Boulder: Westview, 1996, pp. 286-7.

34   Hahnel, *Economic Justice*, p. 182.

35   Joseph Berliner, *The Economics of the Good Society*, Oxford: Blackwell, 1999, pp. 228-9; Joel Kovel, *The Enemy of Nature*, London: Zed, 2002, pp. 166-75.

36   Laurie Adkin, 'Democracy, Ecology, Political Economy', in Fred Gale and Michael M'Gonigle, eds., *Nature, Production, Power: Towards an Ecological Political Economy*, Cheltnham: Edward Elgar, 2000; Josée Johnston et al., eds., *Nature's Revenge*, Peterborough: Broadview, 2006.

37   David Harvey, *Justice, Nature and the Geography of Difference*, Oxford: Blackwell, 1996, pp. 320-4.

38   Karl Marx, *Capital*, Volume 1, London: Penguin, 1976, p. 247.

39   David Harvey, *The Urban Experience*, Baltimore: John Hopkins University Press, 1989, p. 54.

40   Neil Smith, *Uneven Development: Nature, Capital and the Production of Space*, Oxford: Blackwell, 1990, pp. 136-9.

41   Henri Lefebvre, *The Production of Space*, Oxford: Blackwell, 1991, p. 54.

42   Pat Devine, *Democracy and Economic Planning*, Boulder: Westview, 1988, chapter 9.

43   Ralph Miliband, *Socialism for a Sceptical Age*, London: Verso, 1994, p. 80.

44   Raymond Williams, *Resources of Hope*, London: Verso, 1989, pp. 273-5.

45   These themes are explored by Patrick Bond in his *Unsustainable South Africa*, London: Merlin Press, 2002.

46   The distributional relations of ecology are developed in Enrique Leff, *Green Production*, New York: Guilford, 1995, and Andre Gorz, *Ecology as Politics*, Montreal: Black Rose, 1980.

47   O'Connor, *Natural Causes*, chapter 15; and Michael Jacobs, *The Green Economy*, London: Pluto, 1991.

48   For accessible canvases of opinion see: William Fisher and Thomas Ponniah, eds., *Another World is Possible: Popular Alternatives to Globalization at the World Social Forum*, London: Zed, 2003; Jose Correa Leite, *The World Social Forum: Strategies of Resistance*, Chicago: Haymarket, 2005.

49   Neil Brenner, *New State Spaces*, Oxford: Oxford University Press, 2004; Andrew Herod and Melissa Wright, eds., *Geographies of Power*, Oxford: Blackwell, 2002.

50   Gerassimos Moshonas, *In the Name of Social Democracy*, London: Verso, 2002; Greg Albo, 'Contesting the "New Capitalism"' in D. Coates, ed., *Varieties of Capitalism, Varieties of Approaches*, London: Palgrave, 2005; Ash Amin, 'Local Community on Trial', *Economy and Society*, 34(4), 2005.

51   Paul Burkett, *Marx's Nature*, New York: St. Martin's Press, 1999; Roger Keil, 'Urban Political Ecology', *Urban Geography*, 24(8), 2003; Noel Castree, 'Commodifying What Nature?', *Progress in Human Geography*, 27(3), 2003;

Maria Kaika, *City of Flows: Modernity, Nature and the City*, London: Routledge, 2005.

52   Erik Swyngedouw and Nikolas Heynen, 'Urban Political Ecology, Justice and the Politics of Scale', *Antipode*, 35(5), 2003, p. 912; Nik Heynen, Maria Kaika and Erik Swyngedouw, eds., *In the Nature of Cities*, London: Routledge, 2006.

53   David Harvey refers to this as the 'non-neutrality of spatial organization in the dynamics of class struggle'. See: *Spaces of Capital*, New York: Routledge, 2001, p. 381.

54   This includes the active role of the state in 'political disorganization' of workers to reproduce the 'isolation effect' of the relations of production, as discussed by Nicos Poulantzas, and it also includes 'accumulation by dispossession' as discussed by David Harvey. See respectively: *Political Power and Social Classes*, London: Verso, 1973, p. 287; *The New Imperialism*, Oxford: Oxford University Press, 2003.

55   Hilary Wainwright, *Arguments for a New Left*, Oxford: Blackwell, 1994, p. 264.

56   Antonio Gramsci, *Selections from the Prison Notebooks*, New York: International Publishers, 1971, p. 158.

57   The foremost advocate of this position is the American bioregionalist Kirkpatrick Sale, *Human Scale*, New York: Coward, McCann & Geoghegan, 1980.

58   Karl Marx, *The Civil War in France*, Moscow: Progress Publishers, 1972, pp. 61, 58.

Socialist Register – Published Annually Since 1964

Leo Panitch and Colin Leys – Editors
2006: TELLING THE TRUTH

How does power shape ideas and ideologies today? Who controls the information on which public discussion rests? How is power used to exclude critical thought in politics, the media, universities, state policy-making? Has neo-liberal globalisation introduced a new era of state duplicity, corporate manipulation of truth and intellectual conformity? Are we entering a new age of unreason?

Contents: Colin Leys: The cynical state; Atilio Boron: The truth about capitalist democracy; Doug Henwood: The 'business community'; Frances Fox Piven & Barbara Ehrenreich: The truth about welfare reform; Loic Wacquant: The 'scholarly myths' of the new law and order doxa; Robert W. McChesney: Telling the truth at a moment of truth: US news media and the invasion and occupation of Iraq; David Miller: Propaganda-managed democracy: the UK and the lessons of Iraq; Ben Fine & Elisa van Waeyenberge: Correcting Stiglitz - From information to power in the world of development; Sanjay Reddy: Counting the poor: the truth about world poverty statistics; Michael Kustow: Playing with the Truth: the politics of theatre; John Sambonmatsu: Postmodernism and the corruption of the academic intelligentsia; G.M. Tamás: Telling the truth about the working class; Terry Eagleton: Telling the truth.

304 pp. 234 x 156 mm.

0850365597 hbk £35.00   **0850365600 pbk £14.95**
Canada: Fernwood Publishing; USA: Monthly Review Press; UK and Rest of World: Merlin Press

Leo Panitch and Colin Leys – Editors
2005: THE EMPIRE RELOADED

How does the new American empire work? Who runs it? How stable is it?
What is the new American Empire's impact throughout the world?
What is its influence on gender relations? On the media? On popular culture?

Contents: Stephen Gill: The Contradictions of American Supremacy; Varda Burstyn: The New Imperial Order Foretold; Leo Panitch & Sam Gindin: Finance and American Empire; Chris Rude: The Role of Financial Discipline in Imperial Strategy; Scott Forsyth: Hollywood Reloaded: The Film as Imperial Commodity; Harriet Friedman: Feeding the Empire: Agriculture, Livelihood and the Crisis of the Global Food Regime; Vivek Chibber: Reviving the Developmental State? The Myth of the 'National Bourgeoisie'; Gerard Greenfield: Bandung redux: Imperialism and Anti-Globalization Nationalisms in Southeast Asia; Yuezhi Zhao: China and Global Capitalism: the Cultural Dimension; Patrick Bond: US Empire and South African Subimperialism; Doug Stokes: US Counterinsurgency in Colombia; Paul Cammack: 'Signs of the Times': Capitalism, Competitiveness, and the New Faces of Empire in Latin America; Boris Kagarlitsky: The Russian State in the Age of American Empire; John Grahl: The European Union and American Power; Dorothee Bohle: The EU and Eastern Europe: Failing the Test as a Better World Power; Frank Deppe: Habermas' Manifesto for a European Renaissance: A Critique; Tony Benn & Colin Leys: Bush and Blair: Iraq and the American Viceroy

343 pp. 234 x 156 mm.

0850365465 hbk £35.00   **0850365473 pbk £14.95**

Canada: Fernwood Publishing; USA: Monthly Review Press; UK and Rest of World: Merlin Press

Leo Panitch and Colin Leys – Editors
2004: THE NEW IMPERIAL CHALLENGE

"As Rosa Luxemburg observed, it is 'often hard to determine, within the tangle of violence and contests for power, the stern laws of economic process.' This is what Panitch, Gindin, Harvey, Gowan, and their colleagues on the Marxist left are trying to do …. For this, whatevever our other differences, the rest of us owe them much gratitude" George Scialabba, *Dissent*, Spring 2004

What does imperialism mean in the new century?
Do we need new concepts to understand it?
Who benefits, who suffers? Where? Why?

Contents: Leo Panitch & Sam Gindin: Global Capitalism and American Empire; Aijaz Ahmad: Imperialism of Our Time; David Harvey: The 'New' Imperialism - Accumulation by Dispossession; Greg Albo: The Old and New Economics of Imperialism; Noam Chomsky: Truths and Myths about the Invasion of Iraq; Amy Bartholomew & Jennifer Breakspear: Human Rights as Swords of Empire; Paul Rogers: The US Military Posture - 'A Uniquely Benign Imperialism'?; Michael T. Klare: Blood for Oil - The Bush-Cheney Energy Strategy; John Bellamy Foster & Brett Clark: Ecological Imperialism - The Curse of Capitalism; Tina Wallace: NGO Dilemmas - Trojan Horses for Global Neoliberalism?; John Saul: Globalization, Imperialism, Development - False Binaries and Radical Resolutions; Emad Aysha: The Limits and Contradictions of 'Americanization'; Bob Sutcliffe: Crossing Borders in the New Imperialism.

290 pp. 234 x 156 mm.

0850365341 hbk £30.00   **085036535X pbk £14.95**

Canada: Fernwood Publishing; USA: Monthly Review Press; UK and Rest of World: Merlin Press

All Merlin Press titles can be ordered via our web site:
www.merlinpress.co.uk

In case of difficulty obtaining Merlin Press titles outside the UK, please contact the following:

Australia:
Merlin Press Agent and stockholder:
Eleanor Brash: PO Box 586, Artamon: NSW 2064 Email: ebe@enternet.com.au

Canada:
Co-Publisher and stockholder:
Fernwood Books, 8422 St. Margaret's Bay Rd, Site 2a, Box 5, Black Point, Nova Scotia, B0J 1B0
Tel: +1 902 857 1388: Fax: +1 902 422 3179 Email: errol@fernwoodbooks.ca

South Africa:
Merlin Press Agent:
Blue Weaver Marketing
PO Box 30370, Tokai, Cape Town 7966, South Africa
Tel. and Fax: +27 21 701 7302 Email: blueweav@mweb.co.za

USA:
Merlin Press Agent and stockholder: Independent Publishers Group, 814 North Franklin Street, Chicago, IL 60610.
Tel: +1 312 337 0747   Fax: +1 312 337 5985 frontdesk@ipgbook.com

Publisher: Monthly Review Press:
Monthly Review Press, 122 West 27th Street, New York, NY 10001
Tel: +1 212 691 2555 promo@monthlyreview.org